The Daily Round

Meditation Prayer and Praise

The Daily Round
Meditation Prayer and Praise

ISBN/EAN: 9783744677639

Printed in Europe, USA, Canada, Australia, Japan

Cover: Foto ©Lupo / pixelio.de

More available books at www.hansebooks.com

THE DAILY ROUND

Meditation, Prayer, and Praise

ADAPTED TO

THE COURSE OF THE CHRISTIAN YEAR.

"A FEW CALM WORDS OF FAITH AND PRAYER."

LONDON:
WHITAKER, 12 WARWICK LANE,
PATERNOSTER ROW.
MDCCCLXXX.

EDINBURGH:
PRINTED BY M'FARLANE AND ERSKINE,
ST JAMES SQUARE.

PREFACE.

A RIGHT faith gives motives for a right life. In means of grace we come for the power of God in order to do His will, and grow worthy of Him. Truth is made known, and grace is given that men may live soberly, righteously, and godly in this present world, looking for the blessed hope laid up for them in heaven. God did not send His Son, Christ did not die, the Holy Spirit did not come that heaven might be filled with pardoned felons, but that earth might be filled with children of God, led by the Holy Spirit towards their Father's home. No one now thinks to save himself; there is no risk of any one vainly trusting to his own works instead of Christ. Crowds are content to "trust in the Lord," while they do not "good," but evil, or nothing. They seem to think it matters not what they believe, or how they live, or what they are, so that they are only "saved" at last. It is as if man had no work to do here, no need of God's favour, day by day. It is as if God's laws need not, or could not, be kept, and the life lived here had nothing to do with forming the character, or fixing the state for man's hereafter. It is as if Christ lived and died to make sin safe, not to save from sin; to relieve man from the need of holiness, not to enable him to be holy.

Religion is not for the end of life, or for stray hours in life. It is for the whole life, and for every hour of life. It is vain so far as it fails to influence a man in his common work and pleasures, as well as to inspire his worship. It should make him "pitiful and courteous," true and kindly, as well as devout. It should guide him to make this world brighter for others, as well as to reach heaven himself.

Religion needs thought and care, if it is to be learned and practised well. The Bible is not one verse, but a large volume. To neglect any of God's words is to trifle with Him. To make light of any means of grace or help God offers is to show self-trust, and want of faith in God. To be unwatchful or idle in daily duty is to forget the seriousness of life, and to grieve God, Who worketh in man to will and do of His good pleasure.

The aim of "THE DAILY ROUND" is to help, day by day, in few, plain words, those who wish to know God's truth, to gain God's grace, and to do God's will. The course of the Church's year, and the order of the Church's services, are followed. Thus the deep things of God, the mysterious workings of grace, and the laws that claim to rule man's life, are dealt with as they come.

PREFACE.

Each page has five parts: 1. Some words of Holy Scripture. 2. A short statement of what those words mean and teach. 3. Some thoughts and reflections intended to bring home the general lesson, so as to make it of personal, practical use. 4. A prayer, in which what has been brought before mind and heart is laid before God. 5. A verse of a hymn.

Those who use the book can add to, or change, any part, as their own case needs. Thoughts, and feelings, and prayers of others may help to think, and feel, and pray; but the mind and heart of each must act for themselves: a living soul will always have its own words to say to its God.

"If thou desire to profit, read with humility, simplicity, and faithfulness."

The First Sunday in Advent.

"Blessed is He that cometh in the name of the Lord; Hosanna!"—MATT. xxi. 9.

WHEN man fell from God, he had no help in himself. His hope was in One greater than he coming to raise him. In manifold ways, God drew near. At length God was manifest in the flesh. Men saw Him—Emmanuel, God with us. Now, though the world sees Him not, He cometh ever. Those who meet Him in faith and love hail Him as "Blessed." Their heart's glad song of praise is "Hosanna," or, "Save now." They look for that coming when the King shall claim His kingdom, and make His people safe for ever in the holy land.

I am fallen, and without strength of my own. There is no hope for me but in Him who cometh from above. In one way He has come, and the work for me is finished. He cometh now, to be in me a living presence, a power of grace, that the fruit of His first coming may be mine, and that I may make ready for the coming yet to be. Do I prize what He has done? Do I rejoice in His nearness now, and thankfully seek Him where His presence is made known? Do I open my heart to the love that stoops down to bless me? Do I call Him Blessed, and enthrone Him king over all I am? Is "Hosanna," while I follow Him, the voice of my soul's hope? Do I prepare to welcome His appearing, and share His triumph?

Lord Jesus, I bless Thee for Thy love in coming to the help of helpless man. I believe that Thou shalt come to be my Judge. Come near, with that Divine power which alone can make me fit to stand before Thee. Be my King; claim my heart's homage; rule my life. Give me ever new cause to bless Thee, and more will to use Thy gifts. Draw nigh unto my soul, and save it always. So may I hail Thee at the last day, as my Saviour come to crown in me Thy work of love.

> Redeemer, come; I open wide
> My heart to Thee; here, Lord, abide.
> Let me Thy inner presence feel;
> Thy grace and love in me reveal;
> Thy Holy Spirit guide me on,
> Until my glorious goal is won.

Monday after the First Sunday in Advent.

"Now it is high time to awake out of sleep."—Rom. xiii. 11.

THE soul sleeps in the darkness of unbelief and sin, It is as if dead, with its God-given powers idle. The world to which its true interests belong is forgotten. It dreams of shadows, that please for a while, and then pass away. Life's true work is left undone. Armour is laid aside. Foes can do what they will. If the soul sleep long, death comes, which knows no waking. God's call warns that now is not a time for sleep. Light has dawned from heaven, and the perfect day is near.

Is my state sleep? Has my life as yet been spent in dreams? Alas! how dull my faith in those real things that are unseen! How cold my interest in them! How many clear calls are unheard, and solemn warnings unfelt! Where is my work for which the years have been given? What have I done with the strength and armour made mine for use? Have I slept at my post? Have I lain down in drowsy sloth, and forgotten the true aim and purpose of my life? I cannot bring back time gone. Now, at least, I will be aroused. I will show myself alert in mind to listen and to learn. I will be alive to each claim on my heart's feeling. All my powers shall be braced, and ready to act promptly and with full power; so, with God's help, I will watch and work as long as life lasts, and shall see in hope my salvation drawing nearer.

O Lord, Whose watchful eye is ever over me for good, pardon me for time lost and grace unused. Rouse me from the sleep of sin and unbelief. Let me not lie down in forgetfulness, or rest in false peace. Make me feel how short my life, how great my work, how hard my fight and pilgrimage. Give me Thy light and grace. Keep me watchful and earnest till the day of full salvation comes.

> Is this a time for slumber, or for sleep?
> Is this a time for sloth's enticements bland,—
> Now, when thou'rt called unceasing watch to keep,
> And wait the onset, standing sword in hand?

TUESDAY AFTER THE FIRST SUNDAY IN ADVENT.

"Let us therefore cast off the works of darkness, and let us put on the armour of light."—ROM. xiii. 12.

SINS are works of darkness. They are done by those who lose sight of God and their true good, and fall under the power of the prince of darkness. They bring grief, shame, fear. They cloud the conscience, sadden the heart, darken hope. In outer darkness the wages of them are paid. We are called to shake free from this bondage. God offers knowledge and grace, and all we need, that we may be secure, and win triumph as true soldiers of the light. All works of darkness must be cast off in will and deed. All the armour must be put on, not for ornament but use.

What are the thoughts, and feelings, and words, and deeds that make up my life? Are they such as I would hide, were I able, from myself and God? Am I going on in darkness, led or driven I know not whither, as temptations come? Does eternity look dark before me when I think? Is the prince of darkness my master, or is the God of light my leader? God claims me, and in mercy gives me a claim on His promises; He holds out to me the armour of righteousness, clothed in which I may shine as a light in the world, and lead others to serve God. I will, with the help He gives, cast off every work of darkness. I will receive from God that which will shield me from harm, and with which I may win a crown fit to shine in heaven. I will take care, lest the armour rust unused, or the doing of any work of darkness stain it.

Almighty God, give me Thy light and grace, that, forsaking all evil in my heart, I may be armed to resist and overcome it in my life, through Jesus Christ my Saviour

> Soldiers of Christ, arise!
> And put your armour on,
> Strong in the strength which God supplies
> Through His eternal Son.
> From strength to strength go on,
> Wrestle, and fight, and pray,
> Tread all the powers of darkness down,
> And win the well-fought day.

Wednesday after the First Sunday in Advent.

"The world passeth away."—1 John ii. 17.

NOTHING that is of this world can be kept long. All passes away. What is most fresh and bright fades and grows dim. What is strongest breaks down. What we love we love with trembling, for the hour of parting must come, and is ever drawing nearer. Wealth, health, friends, all good things here are only for a while. Sooner or later life becomes weary. The power of enjoyment fails. One day the world is no more passing, but has passed, to be ours no more.

In a shifting, fading world I find myself. I cannot change what is ; I must not forget what is. Let me not fasten myself to what sinks, or build my house on a quicksand. All is passing, but yet all has good in it for me. Let me use the world wisely, as an immortal being ought, and I shall find it so. God gives me work, and lends me help and comfort to occupy and cheer me on my way. Through all these things that pass, and through their passing, God would train me, and lead my heart to Himself and lasting things. Let me fall in with the Divine plan, and do God's will. So when all here has passed away, I shall live on, where all is good, and nothing fades, for ever.

O everlasting God, my help while here, my hope for eternity ; let not failing treasures hold my heart, or cares of time take up my thoughts. Show me how to value and to use the things that pass away. Make me thankful for the joys I have, while Thou dost leave them with me, and patient when they go away. Draw my love more to Thee and to eternal things.

> Well for him who, all forsaking,
>   Walketh not in shadows' train,
> But the path of peace is taking
>   Through this vale of tears and pain.
> Oh ! that we our hearts might sever
>   From earth's tempting vanities,
> Turning them on Him for ever,
>   In Whom all our fulness lies.

THURSDAY AFTER THE FIRST SUNDAY IN ADVENT.

"*Ashamed before Him at His coming.*"—1 JOHN ii. 28.

WHEN Christ comes in glory, His foes shall be ashamed. The veil shall be stripped off, and their evil laid bare. They shall see Him Who died for them, and pleaded with them. They shall be cast out of His kingdom, and go away disgraced. They shall long to hide, but their shame shall go with them. They shall know what they have been—blind to truth, hard against kindness, triflers with patience, careless of their own true good, false to promises, afraid of the world, daring God. Here is shame. There need be no accuser but their own heart.

I must one day see my God and Saviour face to face. But He sees me as plainly now as He shall see me then. I ought to feel deep shame, if my conscience tells me that He knows of what is shameful in my heart and life. He has opened a cleansing fountain; am I still unwashed? He has told me of holiness that may be mine; do I slight it, and remain unholy? He offers knowledge; do I choose darkness? Am I, in spite of all He has done and is doing, forgetful, cold, hard, unloving, unclean—a coward, ready to part with Him rather than with the sins that dishonour me? Well is it to feel shame now, and come to Him, lest at His coming I have to go away in shame.

O Lord, Thou art ever near me, Who didst die for me, and dost plead for me, and shalt come to judge me. Help me to live as if I saw Thee. Give me shame for all that is shameful. Make me careful to be true, and brave, and pure. Let there be no hidden evil in me, which the light of Thy coming shall lay bare. Fit me to stand before Thee and not be ashamed.

>Great Judge, to Thee our prayers we pour,
> In deep abasement bending;
>Oh! shield us through that last dread hour,
> Thy wondrous love extending.
>May we in this our trial day
>With faithful hearts Thy love obey,
>And thus prepare to meet Thee.

FRIDAY AFTER THE FIRST SUNDAY IN ADVENT.

"*It is appointed unto men once to die.*"—HEB. ix. 27.

MAN—every man—is born to die. Each day of life leads on towards the day of death. Once for all man must pass out through the dark valley. How and when each is to go, none but God can tell. Man is sure of one thing, that he shall die. He knows no more. Body and soul shall part. The world, with all its sorrows and its joys, shall be left behind. Worlds now unseen shall burst upon the soul's view. The endless stretch of eternity, with its unthought-of good or evil, shall have begun.

Others must indeed die; but is death appointed unto me? Shall the sounds of earth grow faint, while strange voices reach me from another world? Shall my spirit leave this body helpless, still, dead? Shall friends think of me as gone, and my place here know me no more for ever? Yes, I must die, and go away. An end is coming to my life here, but not an end of me, not an end of what I do. I shall go on living and acting in a new state which shall not end. What shall I be—where—with whom? How and when shall I go to take my place among those who have died? All this is mystery. I only know that "once" I must die, and that on what I am found in that hour will depend what comes after. Let me die to sin, and die in heart to all that harms my soul. Let Christ be my life now, and in the hour of death I shall fear no evil.

Almighty and Eternal God, in Whom I live and move and have my being, to Thy holy keeping I entrust my soul. Teach me to live as one who must die. Kill in me all that would kill my soul. May my life on earth prepare me for life with Thee, that when Thy call comes, I may be ready to depart in peace, through Jesus Christ.

> Oh! quickly come, true Life of all,
>   For death is mighty all around;
> On every home his shadows fall,
>   On every heart his mark is found;
> Oh! quickly come, for grief and pain
> Can never cloud Thy glorious reign.

SATURDAY AFTER THE FIRST SUNDAY IN ADVENT.
"*My words shall not pass away.*"—MATT. xxiv. 35.

GOD is true. God is Almighty. He does not speak vain words in haste, or mislead His creatures. None can hinder His love, resist His will, or baffle His plans. His wisdom foresees and overrules all to work His own ends. The overthrow of heaven and earth shall leave His purpose unmoved. His laws are firm and meant to be obeyed. What He promises we may be calmly sure He will fulfil. What He threatens shall fall. All He says He does, for His words reveal the mind and will of infinite wisdom and power.

God's words are spoken to me. They tell me of Him Who knows all things, and in Whose hand all things are. What high and solemn privilege to hear words from God! How mad to be heedless, or unbelieving, or disobedient! But, alas! how slow I am to weigh their meaning and value, and treat them as words of a living God, Who speaks in earnest! How I dash myself against laws which He has fixed firmly! How hard those warnings find me! What small cheer I draw from those promises so full of joy and peace, as if they were unreal, and a mockery of my needs! How coldly I hear what God tells me of His great love, and might, and care for my good! My want of faith or dulness cannot make God's word fail. His truth will stand and triumph, whether I obey His laws, escape His judgment, and win His blessings, or not.

Almighty God, give me grace to hear Thy words with lowly thankfulness and awe. Enable me so to understand, to believe, and obey, that I may go forward, guided by Thy voice, until I hear Thy word of welcome, for Jesus Christ's sake.

Lord, Thy Word abideth
And my footsteps guideth;
Who its truth believeth
Light and joy receiveth.
Oh! that we, discerning
Its most holy learning,
Lord, may love and fear Thee,
Evermore be near Thee.

The Second Sunday in Advent.

"*All Scripture is given by inspiration of God, and is profitable for doctrine, for reproof, for correction, for instruction in righteousness.*"—2 Tim. iii. 16.

THE Bible is more than a work of wise, and learned, and holy men. God raised up and prepared those who wrote it. He guided them in recording what they knew. He revealed what they could only learn from Him, and only partly understood themselves. He taught them what to write in the best way. They wrote as men, but as men whom God used for His ends. The same God showed the Church what books were to be heard as His message. Holy Scripture has in it manifold "profit." Its great end is to teach God's people, so that they may grow perfect in all good works to God's glory.

Through Holy Scripture God's wisdom, and love, and will, are made known to me. It is the text-book of "doctrine." In it I learn of God and of His ways of dealing with man. I find "reproof." The mirror is held up to show me my sin and shame, what I ought to be and may be, but am not. I find "correction," to warn back my straying feet into safe paths. I find "instruction" how to rule myself and copy Christ. I learn where and how to gain skill and force for the full doing of all good works. God would have me without fault. Do I value the Book He gives to help me to that end? Do I use it with a right aim and in the right way, as God wills? The same God Who inspired it can alone enable me to understand and profit by it.

Almighty God, give me grace to be not only a hearer, but a doer of Thy Holy Word; not only to admire, but obey Thy doctrine; not only to profess, but practise Thy religion; not only to love, but live Thy Gospel. So grant that what I learn of Thy truth I may receive in my heart, and show forth in my life to Thy glory.

> The childlike spirit, Lord, impart,
>   That with a simple faith receives
> The living Word, and in the heart
>   Keeps safely that which it believes,
> There, Lord, to work Thy holy will,
> And all Thy plan of love fulfil.

MONDAY AFTER THE SECOND SUNDAY IN ADVENT.

"That we through patience and comfort of the Scriptures might have hope."—ROM. xv. 4.

LIFE is dark, if we have only what our senses show us now. Holy Scripture throws light upon our path, and opens to faith a new spiritual world with which we have to do. It reveals to hope a better life to come. It brings wisdom from above. It unfolds the meaning of all that makes patience hard. It bears the message of Divine consolation. It assures of God's sympathy and care and loving purpose. It warns of danger, and marks the way of life. It tells of holiness and peace for ever, and of grace to make earthly trial a means towards larger joy.

What would life be, wanting what I owe to the Scriptures? What could I guess, or learn from those like me, of man's beginning and his end, and of the meaning of his life? What cheer could uphold me in hours of pain and parting? In what strength could I go on firmly through crowding cares, and hardship, and perplexity? What could light up the dark passage of death, and tell of hope beyond? Now I am told what sin and sorrow are, and how I may rise above them. I learn of God's good-will, and of His work for me in Christ, of the home prepared, and of grace to fit me for it. I am taught to find good in sorrow, and grow strong by trial. The example of Christ and of those who followed Him beckons me on. I hear the call to come, and the words that promise rest eternal. But it is vain to have God's Book, unless I read; vain to read, unless I learn; vain to learn, unless in devout meditation I receive its power into my being, and make its saving truths my own.

Blessed Lord, give me grace so to love and profit by Thy Holy Scriptures, that I may enjoy the patience and comfort they bring, and may have a well-grounded hope of life through Jesus Christ.

Read not this Book in any case but with a single eye;
Read not, but first desire God's grace to understand thereby.
Pray still in faith, with this respect to fructify therein,
That knowledge may have this effect, to mortify thy sin.

TUESDAY AFTER THE SECOND SUNDAY IN ADVENT.
"If ye know these things, happy are ye if ye do them."
—JOHN xiii. 17.

KNOWLEDGE of religion makes men happy, if it makes them godly. Those who gather it and let it lie idle are like miserly hoarders of money, who starve themselves. To know the nature of food will not nourish. To understand drugs will not cure sickness. To know how to use arms will not drive off foes. To know the way will not bring the journey's end nearer. So, he who would be happier by knowledge of God and His truth must do as well as know.

God has taught me much, and plainly. Perhaps I feel that I have learned what is hidden from others, that my faith is more full and true, and that I see more clearly the meaning of God's law, and the value of the means of grace. I ought to be thankful. But why? Surely because I can do more, and more perfectly, with more help, with greater calmness and courage, and surer hope. I know more, that I may feel more, and be roused to do more. I ought to rejoice with trembling, and to be earnest, lest I fail to use my knowledge, so as to be of those whom Christ calls happy. Better to know little and have few gifts, and in heart and life be faithful, than to receive great light and grace in vain. Each new privilege gives me more to do and to account for. It is mine to enable me to grow in holiness, and serve God better.

O Lord, I bless Thee for Thy gifts of knowledge and of grace. Help me to learn more diligently, and to seek grace more humbly. May my path of duty be plainer; may I have a readier will and a firmer strength to walk in it. As I know more may I love more, and as I love more may I do more, for Jesus Christ's sake.

> Give me faith to see more clearly
>   What Thou art, what love is Thine;
> Earnestness to press more nearly,
>   To enjoy Thy love Divine.
> Keep me patient, keep me lowly,
>   Ever looking unto Thee;
> Make me day by day more holy,
>   Till Thine unveiled face I see.

WEDNESDAY AFTER THE SECOND SUNDAY IN ADVENT.

"To-day if ye will hear His voice, harden not your heart."
—Ps. xcv. 7, 8.

GOD calls by His Word and His Church, in man's conscience and through nature. Men can hear if they will. Some shut their ears, or let other voices drown God's. Some hear but heed not. They do not choose to have their lives changed. They put God off. They will not yield yet. Day by day the call sounds less clearly, and they grow deafer to it. They become stiffer in sin, and less likely ever to soften. Days are lost, in which they might have God for their joy, and grow fit for glory. Any day the word may go forth, "They shall not enter into My rest."

Do God's calls find me too busy or too heedless to attend? Are the Spirit's gentle pleadings and solemn warnings vain? Do I make my heart hard, lest I should be moved to part with what I love, or to do what I shrink from? Does my life say that I fear not God's wrath, and care not for His love? Do I seem to take for granted that grace will always be at hand, and that Divine patience will not weary? Too many days have been lost already. Thank God if I am not yet quite hard, and can still hear His voice. To delay is to trifle with God, and to risk the loss of all. It is to give sin time to gain firm hold. It is to make repentance more sad and painful, and less likely. It is to waste the times of sowing, and thus to have less harvest of glory. Let me not harden my heart even a little against God, lest His love be turned away, and His voice be heard no more.

O Lord, forgive me that I have not loved Thy voice and obeyed it. Help me to adore Thee for Thy patience, and so to hear the calls of each day, that I may be prepared for Thy rest, through Jesus Christ.

Oh! let me hear Thee speaking in accents clear and still,
Above the storms of passion, the murmurs of self-will.
Oh! speak to reassure me, to hasten, or control,
Oh! speak to make me listen, Thou Guardian of my soul.

THURSDAY AFTER THE SECOND SUNDAY IN ADVENT.

*"Be ye also ready: for in such an hour as ye think not the Son of man cometh."—*MATT. xxiv. 44.

CHRIST surely cometh. No man knows when. He will take the world by surprise. He will come as a thief, unannounced; as a snare which a man sees not till he is taken; as the lightning flashing before all eyes in a moment. He will break in upon an unthinking world, as in the days of Noah and Lot. Of no day or hour can we say that in it He will not come. "Be ready each day and hour," is the warning. "Wait, watch, grow fit to meet Him, whenever He cometh; work, to make the world ready."

I may forget Christ now. A day comes when I shall only think of Him, and of what He thinks of me. He shall appear to wind up all things on earth; or I shall be stopped in my life's course, and know that I must die, and that my time of free choice has passed. God mercifully hides the day and hour. Did I know the end near, I could not calmly do life's work. Did I know it far off, I might be careless. Now I can go on in my way of duty, perhaps to last for years. Now I must be earnest, for any hour the books may be shut, and my account taken. Shall Christ find me at rest or work, in joy or grief, in worship or mirth? I know not, but I can be sure that He finds me ready. I will watch for Him, and watch myself. I will look for His comings in the power of grace, and for ways of doing His work. I will be ready for His use, and fit to share His glory. I will have my work ready for Him to examine and approve. The readiness of to-day will not do for to-morrow.

O Lord, enable me so to watch in faith, and hope, and work, and prayer, that I may be ready to welcome Thee as my Saviour at Thy coming.

Little skills it when or how,
If death cometh then or now,
With a smooth or angry brow;
Come it must, and we must die—
Jesus, Saviour, stand Thou by,
When that last sleep seals our eye.

Friday after the Second Sunday in Advent.

"Every one of us shall give account of himself to God."
—Rom. xiv. 12.

THROUGH death we pass to judgment. Our lives are not forgotten as time goes by. In the books of heaven the story of each life is plainly, fully written. Every day leaves on us its mark of good or evil. Before his Creator each one shall stand, as if he were the only one to be judged. Conscience, however blind or dull before, shall know and speak truth then. God, from Whom no thought can hide, and Whose hand none can stay, shall judge the life and state of each.

I am not free to go my own way, and do my own will. God made me. He will one day ask how I have used the time, and powers, and grace I have from Him. He will not judge me by what the world thinks right, or I may wish, but by His own just law. He gave me a mission in life, and He claims that I fulfil it. I am not passed over in the crowd, or in my littleness. God knows the true meaning and worth of each thought, word, and deed. He can do what He will. Even now He watches and judges my life and me. Hour by hour my sentence hangs over me. There comes a day when it shall fall. Am I living like one, the record of whose life God keeps, and will close, I know not how soon? As I wish to be found at last, so should I aim to be always. As God sees me, so should I try to see myself. In all my life I should judge myself, and look to the end.

Almighty God, make me always to remember that Thine eyes are over me, and so in all my life to look forward to the judgment, that I may at last give account to Thee with humble joy, through Jesus Christ, my Mediator and Advocate.

> Soon shall I hear with rapture or despairing
> The Judge's voice my final doom declaring—
> The doom for which my life is now preparing.
> Soon shall I reach the land where I am going,
> Soon shall I reap the harvest I am sowing,
> Soon shall I be in full what I am growing.

SATURDAY AFTER THE SECOND SUNDAY IN ADVENT.

"The voice of one crying in the wilderness, Prepare ye the way of the Lord, make His paths straight."—MATT. iii. 3.

IN the desert of Judæa St. John spoke as God's voice. He went before Christ the King, to warn of His coming, and rouse men to make ready for Him. Christ could not come as a Saviour to those who did not feel their need, or who clung to the pride and unbelief and sin that barred His way. Christ still is ever coming with all His power to save. His voice warns us how to wait for Him. Only to those who in heart forsake sin does He come bringing salvation. Those who obey the call to repent shall hear Him say, Believe the Gospel.

Christ draws near to claim me as His, to set up His throne in my heart, and rule in all my being. If I choose to hold fast to sin, and will not yield in faith, Christ is kept without. He longs to be my Saviour, and bless me with all of which He brings glad news. But He can only come as a judge, while I am content that mountains of pride block His path, that low earthly desires meet Him, that the way of my life is rough and wilful, that my thoughts and words are not straightforward, but false and crooked. He does not ask me to prepare for Him unhelped. He offers the grace He tells me to put forth. He is ready to take away all I am willing to part with, and free me from all that offends Him. If I will welcome Him as the Deliverer from sin, He will make my nature His realm, and glorify me for Himself.

Come, Lord Jesus, to my soul, and reign there. Let me not refuse or delay to hear the call that warns me to prepare. Help me to bring low my pride, and all that lifts itself against Thee; to raise my devotion towards Thee; to make firm my will; to loose my heart from all that might offend Thee. So may I hail Thy coming, and receive the blessings of Thy full salvation.

> Prepare thyself, the crooked highways straighten,
> Break the hard rocks that in thy bosom rest,
> Receive thy Lord Who ever cometh crowned
>   With footsteps blest.

The Third Sunday in Advent.

"Ministers of Christ, and stewards of the mysteries of God."
—1 Cor. iv. 1.

CHRIST was among men as one that served. He sends men now, to be for His sake servants of His people. The people are not their masters: Christ is the one Master, to Whom they must give account. Christ came, the mystery under Whose lowly form were hidden all the treasures of Divine truth and grace. Now He makes men His stewards. With their lips He speaks to mind and heart. With their hands He gives food and refreshment to souls. They have nothing of their own; all is from Him Who sends them. He will judge those through whom, and those on whom He bestows His gifts.

How solemn a charge—to bear to men God's messages and bounties! Those who serve in holy things are sent to be Christ's voice, making known the truth and will of God, and calling men to faith and holiness. They are sent to give the means of grace, by which God's unseen blessings pass to souls prepared for them. Those who have so high and solemn a trust claim my honour, as they need my prayers. I must esteem them for their work's sake, and their Master's sake. I must ask how best I can profit by what God sends, rather than blame or praise the manner in which the servant brings it. I have a responsibility as well as they. Before the same Master we both shall stand or fall, in the day when all things shall be known. Am I trying prayerfully, thankfully, and earnestly to use well the helps I have? Do I search for the inner meaning of the truth I know, and learn what it says to me? Do I strive to know in myself all the power of the means of grace within my reach?

O Lord Jesu Christ, grant Thy ministers and stewards faithfully to dispense Thy word and sacraments, and Thy people earnestly to hear and profit, that they may rejoice together in Thy presence.

> Then fearless walk we forth,
> Yet full of trembling, messengers of God;
> Our warrant sure, yet doubting of our worth,
> By our own shame alike and glory awed.

Monday after the Third Sunday in Advent.

"We have this treasure in earthen vessels, that the excellency of the power may be of God, and not of us."—2 Cor. iv. 7.

GOD never parts with His power. He commonly puts it forth by means. He often uses the heart, the voice, the hands of men to do what His love and wisdom plan. He wraps up His gifts and veils His work in what seems to tell of nothing divine. So, with care He keeps the glory of all to Himself. No one can mistake, and honour the bearer of the good news or gift instead of his Master. No one can confuse the inward grace with the outward sign that tells of it, or the form under which it is given.

Did glorious angels bear me the good news of God, and warn and guide me, might I not fail to look past them? Would there not be risk of their hiding God, and taking the honour which is His alone? Had the sacraments any outward look of greatness, might not their inner value be forgotten? God has guarded me by using men like myself and common earthly things. I think not of the weak messenger, but of the power of the Word he brings. I rest not on the poor worthless sign and means, but on the divine reality hidden, which God gives through them, and assures me of by them. I look beyond what I see; I rejoice in what faith grasps. The men and things before my eyes can do nothing. The power of God can do all, as He wills. To Him I give the glory.

Almighty God, Who canst do what Thou wilt as it seems good to Thee, give me faith in Thy promises, and glad desire for Thy grace. May I never doubt Thee because of the poorness of the means Thou dost employ, nor forget, while receiving Thy gifts, that the power and the glory are Thine alone.

> O Guardian of the Church divine,
> The sevenfold gifts of grace are Thine;
> Thy priests with wisdom, Lord, endue,
> Their hearts with love and zeal renew;
> Turn all our weakness into might,
> O Thou, the source of life and light.

TUESDAY AFTER THE THIRD SUNDAY IN ADVENT.

"I stand at the door, and knock."—REV. iii. 20.

IF Christ is to be a Saviour, He must be more than a guide and teacher. He must get within man's being, and, by changing that, change the life that shows it. Man is, by nature, closed against Him. Christ does not force His way. He stands without, and asks to be let in. He waits on, trying to win a welcome. When man's will opens for Him, He enters as a friend. He and the soul rejoice together. To shut out Christ is to shut in evil. To admit Christ is to be strong to drive and keep out all that harms the soul.

Does Christ care for me? Has He died to save and bless me? Does He seek the close union with me meant in the words, "I will enter in and sup with him, and he with Me?" And am I shut against Him? Do I let Him wait without, while I lie down in carelessness, deaf to His summons, now loud, now gentle, always loving? Well might He leave me to myself and sin, but His loving patience tires not. He waits on, while there is hope. Have I not heard His knock in careless days, or when sin had shut Christ out, and strange warnings sounded in my heart? Can I not hear it now, telling of Christ's goodness and my shame; pleading with me to rise to meet and welcome the Divine Guest, and open my whole being to receive Him?

O patient, loving Saviour, make me to long for Thy presence as Thou dost long to dwell in me. May I ever watch for Thy calls, and meet Thee with a thankful heart and a ready will. May I yield all I am to Thee alone, and so find my joy in communion with Thee.

> Behold the Saviour at thy door!
> He gently knocks, has knocked before,
> Has waited long, is waiting still;
> You treat no other friend so ill.
> O gracious attitude! He stands
> With melting heart and laden hands;
> O matchless kindness! lo, He shows
> This matchless kindness to His foes.

WEDNESDAY AFTER THE THIRD SUNDAY IN ADVENT.

"Make not My Father's house an house of merchandise."
—JOHN ii. 16.

CHRIST drove traders from the temple twice. He claimed even the outer courts for God alone. God may be found everywhere: yet now, as of old, there are times and places which speak of a Presence over and above. There are means and ways of drawing closer. When sinners meet before the mercy-seat, everything should remind of God. The soul when it worships should be free from all that might distract. No wandering or worldly thought should mar the purity of praise and prayer. No low aim should drag the heart towards earth.

I would not be like the Jews who profaned the temple, but like Christ, who was jealous for His Father's house. Our houses of prayer have a glory greater than that which the Presence in the Holy of Holies gave. They claim at least as careful reverence. Where Christ makes known His sacramental nearness, and gives Himself to be my soul's food, is to me holy ground. When I enter where God meets His praying people, worldly things must be left behind, all that might divide thought must be put out of sight. I may sin as did the Jews, and provoke Christ. I may worship for the eye of man, or for worldly ends. I may place myself before God and ask Him to watch and hear me, while my heart is far away, and my desires are set on gain. What if memories and schemes of pleasure, or vanity, or ambition, mingle with my worship? What if I thus make the house of prayer a house of merchandise, and my prayer sin?

Almighty Father, grant that love and fear of Thee may make me jealous for Thine honour, and carefully reverent in all that has to do with Thy service; so may I worship Thee to my own soul's profit and Thy glory, through Jesus Christ my Saviour.

> Let vain or busy thoughts have there no part,
>   Bring not thy plough, thy plots, thy pleasures thither;
> Christ purged His temple, so must thou thy heart.
>   All worldly thoughts are but thieves met together
> To cozen thee. Look to thy actions well,
> For churches either are as heaven or hell.

Thursday after the Third Sunday in Advent.

"Saying, Peace; and there was no peace."—Ezek. xiii. 10.

MEN are uneasy in their sin. Often they seek to remove unrest instead of its cause. They ask to be told smooth things. They close their eyes to danger, as if it were made by being seen. A wall built only for comfort, or to look well, will fail in storm or war. The wise are careful not to seem or feel, but *be* at peace. Better for them than for the foe to find out a weak point. Better to labour to make it strong at all cost, than to leave a breach for the foe to pass. Better to throw down what is untrustworthy, that what is firm and will last may take its place.

I would not be lulled into a false security, or be happy in dreams of peace, while ruin draws on. I want a peace built strongly on firm ground, which no power of earth or hell can shake. Am I drowning the alarms of conscience, that I may go on easily in sin? This peace must soon be awfully broken up. Do I still forebodings that disturb a life of covetousness or trifling, by the thought that I am no worse than others, and do no harm? Am I trusting vaguely in God's mercy, and counting upon a miracle to save me from the end towards which I go? Do I quiet misgivings by forsaking some sins among many, or using some means of grace, while others are neglected? Do I think to make a bargain with God thus, while my heart is not right with Him? There is no true peace to the wicked. The only peace is the peace of God, which "keeps the heart and mind" of those who are "in Christ Jesus," and "love God's law."

Almighty God, grant me the peace which those enjoy whose hearts and wills are Thine, who walk in wisdom's ways, guided by Thy law, and cheered by Thy promises, and who abide in Christ by the power of the Holy Spirit.

> Search me, O Lord, and try my ways,
> And prove the motives of my heart;
> Be Thou my guide through all my days,
> Till I am holy as Thou art.

FRIDAY AFTER THE THIRD SUNDAY IN ADVENT.

*"Depart from Me, ye cursed, into everlasting fire, prepared for the devil and his angels."—*MATT. xxv. 41.

THE Saviour, Who died to give life, dooms to death. The voice that long has said in vain, "Come unto Me," says, "Depart." Those after whom blessing has been borne, go away cursed—not by God, but by their own deed. Shut out from heaven, they go to the gloom where no light from God comes. Unfit to dwell with saints in their Father's home, their lot is in the place prepared for evil angels.

Christ warns of hell, lest I lose heaven. What a thought, that this unknown doom may be mine! How can I rest while this is possibly before me? What despair to feel—"I am lost, and by my own fault. Time is spent and gone, grace and hope have left me. I am without a Saviour, in sin's power. I must sink deeper into that pit of evil which has no bottom, growing ever more like those whose lot I share!" I will come while God's voice calls, and seek His grace, while it may be mine. I will make sure now that death shall not find me unfit to meet God. I will fear to leave my Saviour now, lest He bid me go from Him, and holiness, and hope at last.

Lord make me to fear hell, lest it be my end. Let me not work the works of Satan, lest death be my wages. Let me not learn evil ways, lest they become habits for ever. Let me not fall into the power of sin, lest I be bound by its chains. Let me not make sin my pleasure, lest it be my torment hereafter. Let me not make sinners my friends, lest I have no other after death. Let me not go from Thee now, lest I be driven from Thee at last.

From the black, the dull despair
Ruined men and angels share,
From the dread companions there,
From the lusts that never tame,
From the fierce mysterious flame,
From the everlasting shame,
 Save me, holy Jesus.

SATURDAY AFTER THE THIRD SUNDAY IN ADVENT.

"What manner of persons ought ye to be in all holy conversation and godliness, looking for and hasting unto the coming of the day of God?"—2 PET. iii. 11, 12.

THE day of God draws near. The world that now is shall ere long be no more. We profess to look forward to that new world which God prepares, wherein dwelleth righteousness. What ought our whole life with men, our careful holiness and devotion before God, to say? How plainly should we be marked as those to whom the day of God will bring the crown of their toil and the fulfilment of their hopes.

Only the holy may find a place where righteousness dwelleth and is parted from evil. Nothing that stains or is untrue can enter that good world. Am I like one who looks to go to it from here? Do I try to live more truly as all live in the holy land? Am I seeking to know God, and by faith to see Him, and to live before Him as one who longs to be pure, so as to see Him face to face? The day of God shall make known the truth. It shall bring me to the end of my life's long climb or fall, and shall make me in full what I grow towards now. It will come, whether I prepare for it or not. But how can I forget it or what comes after it? I must, with mind, and heart, and will, do what God requires. I will live, so that as far as in me lies I and the world may be ready. I will shorten the time of delay by work and prayer. I will show in all I am and do that I look for and desire the day of God.

Almighty Judge and Saviour, give me grace to look for Thy coming, and to live as one who longs for it, that I may hereafter have a godlike nature, and be perfected in holiness, through Thy mercy, Who art, with the Father and the Holy Ghost, one God.

> So should we live that every hour
> May die, as dies the natural flower,
> A self-reviving thing of power;
> That every thought and every deed
> May hold within itself the seed
> Of future good and future meed.

The Fourth Sunday in Advent.

"The Lord is at hand."—PHIL. iv. 5.

HE Whose loving care never fails His own is near. He holds all things in His power. He is at hand, watchful and ready to guide, to cheer, to help, to guard, to avenge. The time draws nigh when He shall make all know how close He has always been to every one, and shall set all wrongs right.

Glad thought, that I am not alone, weak, helpless, and without hope. In work, in conflict, in temptation, in sorrow, the Lord is at hand. He sees, and hears, and understands all, and cares for me. I may rejoice always. How brave and calm, steadfast and earnest, I must be! for, beside me, though unseen, the Lord is. How calmly I may go on! What peace may be mine, even in the midst of storm! for He knows the end, and guides all surely, holding the helm with firm power. Let me do my work, however hard; and bear my lot, however trying. He is at hand and knows my least need, and listens to my heart's faintest call. He will never fail me nor forsake me. Ere long my eyes shall see Him. He is at hand to finish the work He has begun, and end my faith's trial. The signs of His coming grow plainer. The time of waiting shall soon be passed. Then shall I know what I believe now, and shall rejoice in peace. He is patient and calm, for He knows and rules all things. Sure of this, I may calmly do His will, and be patient till He shows the triumph of His work.

Almighty Saviour, grant that in all my cares and sorrows I may be able to believe and hope in Thee. Be Thou nigh at hand always, giving calmness and joy, and preparing me to rejoice in Thy glory, Who art, with the Father and the Holy Spirit, one God.

> Jesus, still lead on
> Till our rest be won;
> And although the way be cheerless,
> We will follow, calm and fearless.
> Guide us by Thy hand
> To our Fatherland.

Monday after the Fourth Sunday in Advent.

"Seek ye the Lord while He may be found, call ye upon Him while He is near."—Isa. lv. 6.

SIN parts us from God, and hides His face from us. We cannot see Him because of unbelief. But He can be found. He is not far off, and He is glad to hear our call. The invitation to seek and call upon Him makes this sure. He even seeks us that we may seek Him. But the words warn that there comes a time when He shall be sought in vain, and no call shall reach Him.

Is there no God Whom I have found, and on Whom I call? Or have I felt His nearness? Yet, all life is a time for pressing nearer. How am I to seek and call on God? In the means of grace, in the pleading of Christ's work, in believing prayer, in faithful following of Him Who shows God. When am I to seek and call? While the light of truth shines, while my conscience lives and feels, ere I have strayed out of hearing of Christ's voice. What joy to find God more fully day by day, and to know by the answer to my call that He draws nearer, till at last I see Him! What woe to seek Him where He is not, to call out in the lonely valley, and learn from the silence that the time when God was near has passed! God wills not my woe; He seeks and calls to me. He holds out grace to help me to seek Him so as to find Him, and to call upon Him so as to gain all I need for my soul's full eternal joy.

Seek me, O Lord, that I may seek and find Thee. Call me, that my heart may answer and call upon Thee. Come Thou ever nearer, and be more precious while I am on earth. Bring me where I may be with Thee and have Thee as my everlasting good: for His sake, through Whom alone I can draw nigh and pray.

> To-morrow I will seek the Lord,
>   The foolish heart will say;
> To-morrow may no life afford,
>   So seek the Lord to-day.
> Seek Him, and Him you soon shall find,
>   And own how blest are they
> Who cast the morrow from the mind,
>   To seek the Lord to-day.

Tuesday after the Fourth Sunday in Advent.

"There the wicked cease from troubling; and there the weary be at rest."—Job iii. 17.

HEAVEN is the abode of everlasting peace. No evil breaks the happy calm of holy souls. The evil one is far away. All around are only the pure. There is no evil self, for body and soul are purified. The toil, the care, the fight, the doubts, the partings of life are all passed. Quiet from fear of evil, ever active but never tired, ever glad with joy that does not lose its freshness, the saved are in heaven with God.

Heaven is the home to which my Father calls me. Heaven is the rest which Christ won for me, and now makes ready. Heaven is the end towards which the Holy Spirit leads, and for which He seeks to fit me. Thither I may go, leaving all sin behind, and be for ever out of reach of evil. There I may end whatever wearies, and lay down all my burden of care and grief. There I may regain friends, and enjoy for evermore pleasures that do not pall. No sin, no shame, no want, no fear, no passing away or parting there. Knowledge and love shall ever grow. All desires shall be pure and shall be satisfied. But does what is wicked trouble me? Am I weary of the way of sin? Do I long for the rest of holiness?

Lord, I thank Thee for the hope of glory and for Thy help to bring me to it. May I long more for heaven, and be more earnest in living for it. May no temptation lead me out of the upward path. May no love of earth hold my heart down. May no enemy of my soul make me despair. Fit me for that which Thou dost prepare for me, and bring me to Thy rest and glory, for my Saviour's sake.

> There is a land where all is peace,
>   Where pilgrims watch and toil no more;
>   The sounds of storm and tempest cease
>   When they have gained that tranquil shore.
> They rest, for now the race is run,
>   Beyond the goal they lay them down;
> They triumph, for the fight is won,
>   And all receive the victor's crown.

St. Thomas the Apostle.

"Blessed are they that have not seen, and yet have believed."
—John xx. 29.

THOMAS failed in hope, not in love. The words, "Let us also go, that we may die with Him," had shown where he was weak, and where strong. Now he loves more than he did, and finds it harder to hope. Absent when Christ first came, he will not believe that others have seen more than he. But he stays with the Church and waits for proof—doubting, but candid and earnest. Christ comes and offers what he asked. But Thomas needs not this now. He hails Him, "Lord and God."

Am I tried by doubts and hard questions? Whence are they? Do they spring from want of love, or from the timid love that trembles for its all? Are they born of self-trust, or want of trust in God? Do I call for proofs, while I fail to see and weigh those before me; or am I an honest seeker after truth? Do I wilfully look at the dark side of things; or do my wishes make me dare to pretend unbelief? I may be faithless, though the living Lord bid me touch Him: I may be blessed with the gift of calm belief, though I have not seen. Only the unloving and proud are rejected. Christ feels for a true heart in its doubts as in its other cares. He is tender with the weak and sad. He comes to those who long for Him, though sometimes not till after many days.

O Lord Jesus Christ, save me from the sins of pride and self-trust. Make me always lowly and honest in my search for truth, and ready to obey it in the love of it. Give me now the peace and hope that a sure faith bestows, and so prepare me for the joy of seeing Thee hereafter.

> For all thy rambling doubts so sore,
>   Love thou thy Saviour still,
> Him for thy Lord and God adore,
>   And ever do His will.
> Though vexing thoughts may seem to last,
> Let not thy love be quite o'ercast;
> Soon will He show thee all His wounds, and say,
> "Long have I known thy name—know thou My face alway."

December 22nd.

"Grace and truth came by Jesus Christ."—John i. 17.

THE law given by Moses taught men in type, and shadow, and prophecy. It told men their duty, held out rewards, and warned of punishment. Christ came as the end of prophecy, the reality that types foretold. He was "full of grace and truth." He showed God, and made His will known. He gave power, and said to men, not "Thou shalt," but "Thou canst. I show in Myself what man should be; I give through Myself the will and power."

Jesus Christ is the answer to the questions of man's mind, and the longings of man's heart. His life and words make plain the love and will of God. In Christ I look on God, and know Him. In His work I see those realities to which the figures of the old time pointed. He is also the bringer of grace. In Him is stored the power of the love of God, which I need to enable me to act on my knowledge. Sacraments are means of grace, because in them I gain and strengthen oneness with Him, Who is one with the Father. I need grace, that my knowledge of the truth may not be unfruitful. I need knowledge that I may use grace wisely. I find both in Christ. In His life and words I have truth. He teaches me how to draw near, and to abide in Him, that from His person I may be filled with grace.

O Lord Jesus Christ, give me Thy grace, and write Thy truth in my heart. Teach me Thy will, and show forth Thy power in me. Grant me the will and power to become what Thou wouldst have me be; to Thy honour and glory, Who livest and reignest with the Father and the Holy Spirit, one God.

> God has come, to man revealing
> All the treasures of His grace,
> Bringing hope, and strength, and healing
> To our lost and guilty race.
> All that prophets wrote, foreshowing
> Of the Father's wondrous plan,
> Jesus came, Himself bestowing
> On unworthy, sinful man.

DECEMBER 23RD.

"Emmanuel, which being interpreted is, God with us.
—MATT. i. 23.

GOD might have sent help to man, and blessed him while still far away. He might have shown care and kindness, while hidden Himself. But this was not enough for the love of God to do. He sought union with our fallen nature. The Eternal Word, who was with God and was God, was seen by men in the likeness of their sinful flesh. God came to be one with us in all but sin, and to share our greatest weakness and sorest woe. He took our nature in its feeblest form, that in it He might rise, and might lift us up.

It were great mercy that God should spare me; great bounty that God should bless me and give me a good hope. Herein is love, that God reaches down to draw me to Himself. As the Son of Man, the Son of God comes. God with God is man with man. God is on earth with man, that man may be in heaven with God. God takes a nature in which He can suffer and die, that man may triumph over suffering, and have eternal life. A ladder stands between earth and heaven by which the powers of God pass. New life comes into the nature to which sin struck a death-blow. The Almighty does not stand afar off commanding. He comes near to help. He makes Himself one with the fallen whom He would raise. He is not only on my side; He makes my cause His own. He loves me as what He has made one with Himself. How can I know aright what this great truth means! How can I feel and act as I ought, in presence of its glory, and in the power of which it tells!

Almighty Father, Who hast sent Thy Son to join me to Thyself, grant that, being made partaker of the Divine nature, I may daily be renewed by the Holy Spirit, and grow into the likeness of the same Jesus Christ.

> Thou art the Incarnate,
> God with man made one,
> Giving man once more the place of son.
> Through Thy holy manhood
> Flows the life divine
> To our dying natures, joined to Thine.

Christmas Eve.

"There was no room for them in the inn."—LUKE ii. 7.

SO Christ was crowded out. He was turned from the inn door. Those who had no room to give Him might have entertained the Lord of Angels. But they knew not what they did or what they lost. The poor tired strangers from Nazareth met no welcome. The house was full of those who came on business or on pleasure. No place could be given to Christ. So Christ was not born there. The glory and the blessing passed on till they rested in the lowly stable.

It is the eve of the day on which I hail my Saviour's birth. Is my heart prepared? Am I with lowly, loving zeal asking how I can best give Him welcome? Am I ready, if need be, to part with all, that I may have room to receive the one Guest? He comes not among careless merry makers or eager worldlings. What if I let these take up all my thought and time? What if I can spare no word for Him, and leave no room for Him in mind or heart, so that He must pass by? What if Christmas bring me no new gift of Jesus' presence? I am unworthy that He should come under my roof. But He is lowly. If I will long for Him, and open the door of my heart, cold and hard though it be, He will glorify me, as He glorified the stable and the manger.

O Lord Jesus, Who in Thy lowliness dost ask to dwell and rest in my heart, make me humbly glad to give Thee welcome. Let not my heart be as an inn so full of care and worldliness that there is no room for Thee. I am unworthy to receive Thee aright, but Thou canst make me worthy by Thy presence in me. Come, Lord Jesus, I offer Thee all I am. Enter in, and make me all Thine own. Glorify me with all Thou art.

> Ah, dearest Jesus, holy Child,
> Make Thee a bed soft, undefiled,
> Within my heart, that it may be
> A quiet chamber kept for Thee.

Christmas Day.

"The Word was made flesh."—JOHN i. 14.

WHERE do the love and thoughts of Christians meet on Christmas Day? In a cave outside a village, a poor woman tends her new-born child. Rough clothes cover Him, He lies in a manger on the straw. Cattle share His shelter. An old man, meanly clad, waits on the mother and her Child. No one else seems to know or care for them. But all heaven is stirred. The mightiest angels adore. This Child is God manifest in the flesh. The Almighty is thus feeble and dependent. The Maker of all things is thus mysteriously in His world, to be the beginning of a new creation.

Let me, with the Church on earth and the hosts of heaven, adore the new-born King. Let me learn the lessons He teaches from His manger-throne. Here faith is called on for its first great effort. If it can see God, and worship now, all after-efforts will be easy. It will be strong to welcome God, in whatever lowly form He veils His presence, however mean the covering that wraps up His gifts. Here hope is made sure. If God thus begins, He will do all unto the end. If Christ thus comes to His world, He will not scorn me, if I will open my being to give Him room. Though I am but a babe in Christ, and His life in me scarce seems feebly to breathe, yet I may hope to grow like what He is in His glory. Here love is won. How lowlily and gently God draws near! as if to disarm all distrust, and win by the pleading of His feeble, almost friendless infancy, the love of those whom He would save.

O Lord Jesus Christ, grant me sure faith in Thee, and hope in Thine unchanging goodness. Bind my heart to Thee, that I may have the fruits of Thine incarnation, and that Thou mayest be my great joy now and for ever.

> God in human form is shown,
> God His yearning love makes known;
> He has left the throne on high,
> And to fallen man draws nigh;
> He has come to seek and save,
> Conquer sin, and spoil the grave.

St. Stephen's Day.

"*Henceforth there is laid up for me a crown of righteousness.*"
—2 Tim. iv. 8.

STEPHEN was the first to die for Christ. He first received the martyr's crown from the Lord's hand. Like his Master, he was obedient unto death, going straight on, where God's will led. He was faithful unto death, a witness firm and brave for truth. Like Christ, he prayed for those who slew him. He fell in the front of the fight close after his Leader. The glorified Christ watched His true soldier, and cheered him with a vision of the glory awaiting him.

From adoring with the shepherds, I turn to-day and look up with Stephen. I look from Bethlehem to the opened heaven, from the manger to the right hand of God, from the swaddled Son of Mary to the Christ in glory. One helps me to understand the other. Let me gaze on both. Christ is the same. At Bethlehem He begins to "suffer many things." As Stephen sees Him, He has "entered into His glory." Let the meekness of the holy Child teach me to be holy and harmless. Let the glory Stephen saw cheer me on. I must be like Him now, if I would go to Him and see one day what met the dying eyes of Stephen. What harm can those who hate me do, if I suffer for Christ and truth? At worst they can but bring me faster whither I go after Christ.

Grant, O Lord, that in all our sufferings here upon earth, for the testimony of Thy name, we may steadfastly look up to heaven, and by faith behold the glory that shall be revealed; and being filled with the Holy Ghost, may learn to love and bless our persecutors by the example of Thy first martyr St. Stephen, who prayed for his murderers to Thee, O blessed Jesus, Who standest at the right hand of God to succour all those that suffer for Thee, our only Mediator and Advocate.

> For the crown that fadeth never
> Bear the torture's brief endeavour;
> Victory waits to end the strife:
> Death shall be thy life's beginning,
> And life's losing be the winning
> Of the true and better life.

St. John the Evangelist's Day.

"*The disciple whom Jesus loved.*"—JOHN xxi. 20.

JESUS loved St. John with a love over and above that which, as God and man, He felt for all. St. John was formed to be the friend His man's heart needed. Jesus gave him of His own love. The disciple drank in his Master's spirit as he leaned on His breast. Christ made the man most like Himself the son and guardian of His mother. He left him to bear his cross on, long after all the rest were crowned. The love of Jesus nerved St. John for his great calling, and enabled him, while on earth, to know and to make known the mysteries of heaven.

Great to be an apostle and evangelist, greater to be the disciple whom Jesus loved. What must he have been who bore this title! I may not be blessed as he was, but I may be a disciple whom Jesus loves, if I long to love Him and prize His love. I may draw near and lean on Him, and, speaking to Him all that is in my heart, receive the love of His heart. In the Sacrament of His love, I may know His nearness and His tenderness. How can I test my place in His heart, and His place in mine? Do I love, for His sake, those whom He loves? Does His love in me care for them? Does love make my faith more clear-sighted? Am I ready to bear much and long, and to love on still?

O Lord Jesus Christ, bring me near to Thee, and give me of Thy Spirit, that I may become such a disciple as Thou lovest. Teach me the wondrous things of Thy law, and the mysteries of grace. Help me to love Thy loved ones for Thy sake, and to be ready to bear and do all things for love of Thee.

> Upon the Saviour's loving breast
>   Invited to recline,
> 'Twas thence he drew, in moments blest,
>   Rich stores of truth divine.
> There, too, with that angelic love,
>   Did he his bosom fill;
> Which, once enkindled from above,
>   Breathes in his pages still.

The Innocents' Day.

"*Except ye be converted, and become as little children, ye shall not enter into the kingdom of heaven.*"—MATT. xviii. 3.

THE holy Innocents bore what was aimed at Christ. He came into the world, welcomed by few, and He stayed for a life of woe. They passed to that world of joy from which Christ came, and angels caught them in loving arms. They were taken from the evil to come, ere they had felt the world's power, or known its care and sin. In Rama there was a voice of weeping heard. There was gladness in their new home.

Blessed are those who have forsaken sin and grown pure. Blessed, in another way, those who have never learned sin's ways, or tasted the world's bad joys, but have followed the Lamb from the first. Blessed are those who bear and do great things, counting the cost. Blessed, also, those who have left themselves so simply in God's hands, that they need no new effort of will to give up all. Dear to God were those guileless ones, slain in Christ's stead; and dear to Him are all who aim to have a lowly, childlike spirit. I will seek to be in malice a child. I will receive the kingdom of heaven with the lowly, unselfish spirit of a child. I will aim to be pure and patient, like the holy Child Jesus; and like those who, fresh from God's hand, and unspotted by the world, fell asleep here, to awake among the angels.

Almighty Father, Who didst call infants to be the first to die for Christ, give me such childlike faith that I may be ready at all times to yield to Thy holy will; and make me harmless and pure, and ever fit to pass into Thy presence, for Jesus Christ's sake.

> Glory to Thee for all
>   The ransomed infant band,
> Who since that hour have heard Thy call
>   And reached the quiet land.
> Oh! that our hearts within,
>   Like theirs, were pure and bright;
> Oh! that as free from deeds of sin,
>   We shrank not from Thy sight.

DECEMBER 29TH.

"God . . . hath in these last days spoken unto us by His Son."—HEB. i. 1, 2.

GOD'S voice spoke to man from the first, and all through the ages. In changing forms, and part by part, His teachings came. One after another, heralds brought and left their message. Works of love, and wisdom, and judgment spoke to man's heart and intellect, and hopes and fears. Law, and prophecy, and type told of God and His will. Now as love's last effort, God has spoken by His Son. In Him man sees what God is, and God's voice speaks in a more plain and moving way.

Now in the last days God has come most near, and makes His last appeal. Not by a man like myself does He speak, but by His Son, Who, though true Man, is very God. His words are the words of the Truth. His works are those of the Almighty and All-wise. He is Himself a manifestation of what God is. His words and acts are God's own, meant to teach and warn and win me. All that I read in the Gospels, and the Spirit tells me of Christ, makes known God. What love and care does God show! Of what bliss have I here the promise! What shame and loss if, when God speaks to me thus, I fail to profit! He by Whom God made the world can make me very good for God's delight. He Who died to purge my sins wills not that I should be impure. He, Who from the right hand of the Majesty on high speaks to me, may not be mocked.

O Lord, Who dost ever watch over me for good, may I ever watch for what Thy love and wisdom have spoken. May I never miss the meaning of what Thou, in Thy works of nature and of providence, dost teach. May I always prize and fully profit by what is made known of Thee in the person and work of Thy Son, my Saviour, Jesus Christ.

    Jesu, we hail Thee, Saviour of the sinning,
        Dear Lamb of God, that can our guilt atone,
    Man from his enmity and sorrow winning,
        God in His truth and mercy making known.

DECEMBER 30TH.

"The adoption of sons."—GAL. iv. 5.

GOD sent forth His Son to make us sons. He loved us when we loved Him not. He found a way to save us from sin and death, and make us His own, in whom He could delight. He did more than give us the name of sons. He made us what He called us. The Son of God became man; joined to Him, made one with Him, Who is one with God, we receive of God's life, and can call God Father. We are all children of God by faith in Christ Jesus; for "as many as have been baptized into Christ have put on Christ."

Union with God is the great gift of Christmas. I claimed my part in Christ when I was "baptized into Christ." The gift of sonship has in it a promise of all else. I am sure of a Father's care. He wills His children's good, and can do all things. He is love, and He is almighty now, as when He sent His Son, and when He took me into His family. He seeks to train me after Christ's likeness, that I may be able to enjoy the inheritance prepared. He gives the spirit of adoption, that I may feel and live as His child. But also He claims the trust and honour which are a father's due. He warns me to keep in mind my name and calling. The Son of God was born of woman, and lived as man on earth. I am born of God; let me aim to live a God-like life, mindful always of my Father and my home in heaven.

O Lord, Who hast given me the name and place of son, give me also the spirit of one born of Thee. May the divine life grow and strengthen in me, while evil weakens and dies. May I never forget that Thou art my Father, or bring dishonour on Thy name, or fall short of my high calling; for Jesus Christ's sake, our Mediator and Redeemer.

    God's child in Christ adopted—Christ my all—
      What that earth boasts were not lost cheaply, rather
    Than forfeit that blest name, by which I call
      The Holy One, the Almighty God, my Father!

December 31st.

"And a book of remembrance was written before Him for them that feared the Lord, and that thought upon His name." —Mal. iii. 16.

GOD heard, when His people blamed their lives before Him. He remembered for help and blessing those who roused themselves to live in His fear. He is the same God still, knowing those who obey His warning. As years pass, life should grow earnest. Each year comes but once. Its light and grace, its joys and griefs, leave their mark; but it goes away for ever. Its work, if undone, must remain undone. The shortened future only is left. Well if it be sobered and made earnest by a sense of past shortcomings, and a loving reverence for God.

Another year is dying; one less is before me. So much time to grow more pure and strong, to live and work for God, is mine no more. If wasted, it is lost for ever. Yet, let me look back, and with God's help find what may rouse to more careful use of time remaining. What has the year done for me? What have I done in it? For how many hours can I account? In how many have I tried to make the world or myself better, and bring God glory? What warnings have I heard; what calls obeyed? What truth have I gathered; what wisdom gained? What means of grace have I learned to prize more, and use better? What virtues have grown, and faults died? Do I hunger more for righteousness, and feel more distaste for sin? Am I nearer God and heaven, as I am nearer death? God has spared me, though sorely tried. Oh! that I might know and own my failings, and find pardon, ere the year goes! Oh! to begin a new life with the new year, reckoned among God's faithful!

O everlasting God, Who hast spared and blessed me through another year, show me my sins and Thy goodness; forgive me, and renew Thy mercies; make me to live henceforth in Thy fear and favour, and to prepare for the unending life; through Jesus Christ.

> Grant me, dear Lord, from evil ways,
> True absolution and release,
> And bless me more than in past days,
> With purity and inward peace.

The Circumcision of Christ.

"His name was called Jesus."—LUKE ii. 21.

THE eternal Son of God was made man. The All Holy was on earth in likeness of sinful flesh. Born under the law, He bore its burdens. As Abraham's Son, He was circumcised. His name marked Him the Son of God. He began His work as Jesus, Jehovah, Saviour, to be the head of a new people, to lift away from them sin's curse, to make them sharers in His own life, to save them from their sins by the shedding of His blood, and the power of His holiness.

Who can guide, and help, and save me in the work and trial of the year I begin to day? My spirit may rejoice in God, my Saviour. One has come from heaven, Whose name has in it all promise. Heaven proclaims Him God, born to save. He can take away the guilt and stain of old sins, and make me safe in all danger and temptation. The name Jesus assures me that He can and will do all this. But am I of His people, who own Him Saviour? Am I one with Him in His longing that I should be free from sin? He took the name of Jesus at His circumcision. I have no part in His work unless I will to separate sin from my heart. He does not offer to save me in my sin, but from my sin. He is Jesus, not to give pardon only, but to give holiness; not to make me safe as a sinner, but safe as one freed from sin.

O Lord Jesus, be my Saviour, and help me to yield to Thy saving power. Let not my heart hold to anything from which Thou wouldst save me. Draw me to Thee, that I may be set free from the guilt and power of sins past, and may be guided safely on towards the enjoyment of the full salvation which Thou dost prepare for Thy people.

> Jesus is the name exalted
>   Over every other name;
> In this name, whene'er assaulted,
>   We can put our foes to shame;
> Strength to them who else had halted,
>   Eyes to blind, and feet to lame.

January 2nd.

"I have sworn, and I will perform it, that I will keep Thy righteous judgments."—Ps. cxix. 106.

GOD'S judgments are right. They fence off the way of righteousness that leads to peace. He justly claims the obedience of His creatures. His goodness commands only what is for our good. He does not force obedience. He points out duty, and offers grace with which to do it. All who use His least gifts own Him as their Lord, by Whose laws they are bound. He asks us to be of one will with Him Who knows what is our good and wills it. He asks us with firm purpose to lay hold of and use the light and grace He gives.

I am bound to learn and do the will of Him Who made and owns me. I must be true to Him Whose work gained me the place of son. In each prayer I have acknowledged duty. When I have asked grace, I undertook to use it. When I have claimed the name of Christian, I have owned my baptismal vows. In confirmation I pledged my word before God and the Church. At each communion I devoted myself, my soul and body, anew to God. How have my vows been kept? Let my past dishonour warn me of my weakness, and send me humbly to the one source of strength. I am resolved no more to trust self, but, with God's help, to try more earnestly henceforth. I will learn God's truth and laws. I will neglect no means of grace. I will omit no duty. I will give place to no temptation. I will guard against sins, one by one. I will aim at growth in each virtue. I will seek to have Christ with me always, to be my guide, and strength, and holiness.

O Lord, grant me grace to feel the shame of my past unfaithfulness. Give me an honest heart and a firm will to set forward and go on in the straight path of duty after Him through Whom alone I can please Thee, Jesus Christ.

> Thou, O Lord, hast made and saved me,
> Thou alone my Lord shalt be;
> Take me then to love and serve Thee,
> Now and in eternity.

January 3rd.

"Mary kept all these things, and pondered them in her heart."
—Luke ii. 19.

MARY did not understand all. She had to bow in lowly, patient faith. She knew that all had to do with her joy, the world's good, and God's glory. So her heart kept all safely with loving care. Nothing was set aside as small or unmeaning. In devout thought, alone with God, she put each part of the great mystery before her, and looked at it in the light of the rest. Love helped her meditation; the more she thought, the more she loved. So her mind gained clearer knowledge, and her heart found fuller joy.

Am I like the mother of my Lord, watchful, lowly, patient, earnest? Or do the truths of God fail to fix my thoughts? Am I dull and heedless, or at best only roused to idle wonder? Am I apt to pass by what seems hard, or of less worth, or without bearing on my present needs? Am I impatient when the meaning and aim of parts of revelation are kept back from me? What time and toil do I spend in trying to make the Gospel truths so real to my mind as to move my heart and life? Devout thought can alone, by God's grace, make them to me a living power; for they are deep, and God shows their blessedness to those who seek in patient study and in longing prayer. What I know not now must be "kept." "Pondering" in faith brings a blessing of its own. What seems darkest and most baffling may prove in some hour of need the one best light. What seems little may have in it that on which joy and peace, nay, even my soul's life, may depend.

O Lord, grant me with lowly meekness to receive, and with earnest devotion to meditate upon Thy truth, for my own growth in holiness and joy, and for Thy glory, through Jesus Christ.

> Oh may we keep and ponder in our mind,
> God's wondrous love in saving lost mankind;
> Trace we the Babe Who has redeemed our loss
> From His poor manger to His bitter cross;
> Tread in His steps, assisted by His grace,
> Till, changed like Him, we see Him face to face.

January 4th.

"Glory to God in the highest, and on earth peace, good-will toward men."—LUKE ii. 14.

THIS is the angels' song of love to God and man. They call on men to share their gladness and their praise. The birth of Christ was a manifestation of God to the powers of heaven, as well as to man. They saw the glory of Him Who is Love shine forth in a new way. Christ came as man's peace, bringing pardon and grace, overcoming man's distrust of God, winning him back to the Creator, drawing men together in a divine bond of love. He was a sure pledge of God's boundless goodwill. He brought grace to enable men to have goodwill towards God.

Can I be cold, while angels sing what God does for me? It is my God as well as theirs Who is glorified. Unto me this Child is born, this Son is given, Who makes known God's love. He is my Peacemaker, bringing me pardon, and power to overcome what needs pardon; calming the disquiet of my fallen nature. He comes to win away my slavish fear, and be in me a Divine Presence, enabling me to love God, and my brethren for God's sake. In Him is made over to me all that the All Good wills for me His creature, that I may will and do what leads to God and joy. Shall I not thankfully make known what fills heaven with rapture, and in the power of Christ born in me, live for God's glory? Shall I not strive with the unbelief and sin which hinder my enjoyment of God's peace? Shall I not seek God's glory by leading others to be reconciled to Him, and at peace among themselves? Shall I not pray and work that men may have goodwill to welcome the great love that is so lavish, and seeks its glory in their joy?

Glory be to Thee, O Lord, in my pardon and holiness, and in the enjoyment by all men of the peace which Thy goodwill gives when welcomed through Jesus Christ.

> Hasten, mortals, to adore Him,
>   Learn His name, and taste His joy,
> Till in heaven ye sing before Him,
>   Glory be to God most high.

The Second Sunday after Christmas.

"*And the shepherds returned, glorifying and praising God.*"
—LUKE ii. 20.

THE shepherds left their flocks to go to Bethlehem. An angel sent by God had told them the good news; but they did not rest till they made the truth their own. They saw the sign which marked the newborn Saviour, and worshipped Him. Then they went back to their work with hearts full of thankful gladness, and made known abroad the great things they had seen and heard. In their after-lives they gave praise to God. They kept their flocks as new men—as those who felt that God had come to save.

Messengers from God have told me of Christ the Lord, born to save. But He is no Saviour to the heedless or unbelieving, or those who will not turn from earth's cares to seek Him. To know the truths of Christmas, as the shepherds did before they went to Bethlehem, will not help me. Have I only heard of Christ, and known that He made others glad? Or have I sought to see Him with my own soul's eye, and know Him for myself, and worship in His presence? Now, let me go away from all else, and be alone with Him where He is, till the great truth lays hold of mind and heart and will. Ere I go back to the world's work, let me seek to be filled with that truth's power. So shall I be able to make known the good news to others, for I shall in a true way know it myself. So shall my life as well as lips show forth God's praise, and bring Him glory.

O Lord, Who hast made known to me the good news of the Incarnation of my Saviour, may I seek earnestly that Saviour's presence in all the ways which Thou dost tell me of, that, feeling the blessedness of the strength and peace and hope He gives, I may live to Thy praise and glory, through my Saviour, Jesus Christ.

    Come, then, let us hasten yonder
      Here let all, great and small,
    Kneel in awe and wonder.
      Love Him, Who with love is yearning;
    Hail the star that from far
      Bright with hope is burning.

The Epiphany.

"When they saw the star, they rejoiced with exceeding great joy."—MATT. ii. 10.

GOD made known to the wise men the glad news of joy which all people were to share. He gave them the will to seek the presence of the King of the Jews. He sent a light to guide them. Where that light led they followed, leaving home and friends, daring all perils of the way, heeding not what others thought or did. They asked those who knew to help them in their search. When God's light shone, they rejoiced. They followed it, till they came with joy where the King was, and saw Him.

So God teaches the willing, and leads them on. Christ is not now in lowly form in a lowly home on earth, but enthroned on high. Thither I must press on to see His face. Much must be left behind. The way is long. There are dangers to be met, and hindrances to be overcome. Through a lonely desert I must often go. Few, or perhaps none, around, will care for what I seek, or give me help and cheer. But God bids me travel on, and each day's course is plain. I may learn from even those who do not use their own knowledge. And the light God sends me by the way will not fail me while I need it. When other helpers fail, that will shine. It will guide to where He is Whom I seek. That which tells me of Him cheers the way. What comfort in each sign that God still leads me onward! All trial and hardship shall be forgotten when I behold the King in His glory.

O Lord Jesus Christ, help me to hail with joy whatever tells of Thy presence, and guides me towards it. Grant that I may go forward in earnest faith and hope, till I see Thee where Thou art in Thy glory with the Father and the Holy Spirit.

> Holy Jesus, every day
> Keep us in the narrow way;
> And when earthly things are past,
> Bring our ransomed souls at last
> Where they need no star to guide,
> Where no clouds Thy glory hide.

January 7th.

"They saw the young Child with Mary His mother, and fell down, and worshipped Him: and when they had opened their treasures, they presented unto Him gifts; gold, and frankincense, and myrrh."—MATT. ii. 11.

THE wise kings did not doubt when they saw the lowly Child. Faith, which had led them on, did not fail them in the end. They fell down, doing homage to the King, offering themselves to His service. Then they spread before Him the best their land gave. Gold was tribute to a king. Incense was the right of God. Myrrh told of one who was to die, and yet not to see corruption. In another way, the gifts meant the offering of their wealth, their worship, and the service of a self-denying life.

All my life I must aim to do as the wise men did. Christ calls me to His presence to bow before Him as my King and God, and one Who feels for me as a brother man. As yet I can only see Him by faith. One day I may look on His glory. He asks me first to give myself —to seek Him in all my life, and to bow before Him. He asks me to bring the best of all I have and can, with a will and heart made His. My alms-deeds and works of love shall be as if laid at His own feet. My prayers and praise shall be to Him sweet incense. He will bless the bitter but wholesome discipline of a self-denying life, to make evil in me die, and to save me from its corruption. Let me gather up all these gifts now, and make them a ceaseless offering. So, when I gain His presence on high, I shall find them laid up for me—a treasure in heaven made mine through His mercy.

O Divine Saviour, give me grace to honour Thee in Thy twofold nature, and first giving myself to Thee, to serve Thee faithfully with all the powers and means with which I am entrusted by Thy mercy.

> When to the manger came the three,
> They fell in worship on the knee,
> Then to the Child their gifts unfold,
> The myrrh, the frankincense, the gold.
> God, take our gifts in Jesus' name,
> Heart, body, soul, wealth, blood, and fame.

January 8th.

"For this purpose the Son of God was manifested, that He might destroy the works of the devil."—1 John iii. 8.

THE works of the devil are seen in all that makes the world not good as God made it. The sins men do wilfully or through inborn weakness are his works. That unsteady, strengthless will which shows man's fall, and every woe man feels, tell of the same foe's work. Man is a victim to be pitied, as well as a wrongdoer to be blamed. The Son of God appeared as Son of Man to be man's champion. His mission was to break down the power of the prince of this world, to loose man from the hold of evil, to re-build the ruins of the nature which God made in His own likeness.

I find around me and in me the works of the devil. They are not God's works, nor wholly mine. My past life—how full of sin! My nature—how slow to good, how ready to fall, how held by evil habits! My temptations—how strong, and sudden, and manifold! My cares —how great and varied! My future—how mysterious, with only death sure! But the work of God goes on with the power of almighty love. God does not forsake what He has made. The Son of God has come forth to undo the whole work of Satan's hate, and make all I am very good. He wills to pardon my past sin, and blot out its least stain. He wills to cleanse my inmost being, and make me quick to do right. He wills to make my trials steps to triumph and means of growth, and to change my sorrows to blessings. He wills to brighten my future with the light that sure faith and hope give, and to make death a way to life. Do I work with Christ in this work for me and all men?

O Lord, grant that the power of sin may be destroyed, and all Thou hast made may be created anew, to be very good, through the might of Jesus Christ our Saviour.

O wisest love, that flesh and blood which did in Adam fail
Should strive afresh against the foe, should strive and should
    prevail;
And that a higher gift than grace should flesh and blood refine,
God's presence, and His very self, and essence all divine.

January 9th.

"Now are we the sons of God; and it doth not yet appear what we shall be: but we know that, when He shall appear, we shall be like Him; for we shall see Him as He is."—1 John iii. 2.

GOD made us sons when He called us to the life of faith in His Church on earth. We shall look like His sons when He calls us to the life of glory in the Church on high. We cannot see God now, or imagine the heavenly image we are to bear. Enough that we are God's sons, whom God means to grow to be as our Father. We are changed, as we learn to know, and love, and copy God. What faith does slowly, light will perfect. When we see Him as He is, all that makes us unlike Him shall pass away.

Am I indeed a son of the Most High—a prince of heaven, a partaker of God's nature? God says so. The hope built on this truth is, that I may one day look on God, and know that He sees in me His own likeness. As the glorified manhood of Christ so may I be, if I will. The duty I am called to is to live as a son of God, aiming in all things to become like my Father, as Christ shows Him. The world, the flesh, the devil, ought to have no power to tempt one with such a name and hope as mine. Man's scorn need not move me, while I know myself God's son, and live under my Father's eye. Toil, loss, pain, are in God's hand: they can only serve His sons. If I am true to the grace that called me, that grace will not fail till all that is ungodlike passes away before the vision of God. I ask not where I shall be, or what I shall have. If I am like God, where I am shall be heaven, and all joy shall be mine.

O Lord, Who hast made me Thy son, and given the hope of being like Thee, help me so to live that I may be daily purified, till I am glorified in Thy presence.

> Lead us, heavenly Father, lead us
>   O'er the world's tempestuous sea;
> Guide us, guard us, keep us, feed us,
>   For we have no help but Thee;
> Yet possessing every blessing
>   If our God our Father be.

January 10th.

"And every man that hath this hope in him purifieth himself, even as He is pure."—1 John iii. 3.

WE hope to see God and be made pure as He is. Our hope is in God, Who has made us His sons, and alone can give us what we hope for. Purity is from God, but those who will be pure must purify themselves. Grace enables for work, does not excuse from it. Those who have this hope unite with grace in putting off what makes them unlike God, and in copying Christ in heart and life. They try to grow pure while God sees them now, that they may be pure when they see God.

What do I hope for beyond the dark way out of life? Have I any clear end before me, any good which I look forward to on right grounds? Perhaps I trust idly in God's mercy, or dream of finding quiet, away from life's care and toil, somewhere, somehow. The one hope set before me is of being perfected in purity, and made like Christ. The one sign of this hope being true is a longing to be pure, shown in earnest willing effort. Does this hope inspire my life and lead me on? Am I seeking to grow towards what I hope to be? Is my "hope in Him" Who only can help and crown my work? Do I use the grace given, and mark Christ's character as the standard I must aim to reach? If so, I may be humbly sure that my hope shall not perish, that I do long for Christ's likeness, and may look forward to wearing it. God will make me, in His own time, what in His strength I wish and try to be. I shall have all things then.

Almighty Father, Who hast given me the hope of being pure as Thou art pure, grant that, by the power of the Holy Spirit, I may purify myself from all evil, and be formed after the image of Thy Son, Jesus Christ my Saviour.

> Make me pure, that I may be
> Able to be one with Thee,
> And reveal Thyself, for Thou
> Art the King I long for now;
> When the veil at last is riven,
> To behold Thee will be heaven.

January 11th.

"Let no man deceive you: he that doeth righteousness is righteous."—1 John iii. 7.

GOD calls us to be righteous. He tells us we can be righteous, and gives us a test by which we can know whether we are or not. Leave the opinions of men and our own thoughts or wishes. Let our Judge be our Guide. If we do righteousness we are righteous, not otherwise. God asks not only for thoughts and feelings, but for works that come from right belief and love. These prove what a man is, to himself and others. They show the working of the indwelling righteous spirit. They form habits and change the character of the man, making him more righteous as God is.

God warns me against deceivers. My own heart may mislead, and there are many vain talkers. Some tell me I only need be called righteous as a forgiven sinner. But God calls no one what he is not. With pardon He gives grace to live righteously. Some bid me "trust in Christ." But can I not trust in Him as One to save me from sin by imparting righteousness? Some warn against "works." What I do cannot save me, but it can show how far Jesus is my Saviour, dwelling in me a power of righteousness. Some ask about my feelings of joy and devotion. I want to know how things are with me, not how I feel about them. Feelings do not prove what I am, or my life is. Deeds show what God is doing in and with me. I want to forsake evil and do good. I want to be righteous so as to please God, not to be called righteous so as to be safe. I want to be called what God enables me to be.

Almighty God, grant that living in Thy faith and fear and in union with Christ, Who is the righteousness of Thy people, I may do righteousness, and daily grow more righteous, through the same Jesus Christ, my Saviour.

Faith must obey her Father's will, as well as trust His grace,
A pardoning God is jealous still for His own holiness;
When from the curse He sets us free, He makes our natures clean,
Nor would He send His Son to be the minister of sin.

The First Sunday after the Epiphany.

"Jesus also being baptized, and praying, the heaven was opened, and the Holy Ghost descended in a bodily shape like a dove upon Him; and a voice came from heaven, which said, Thou art My beloved Son; in Thee I am well pleased."—LUKE iii. 21, 22.

THE sinless Son of Man came to the baptism of repentance. He set an example of careful use of God's ordinances. Representing sinners, He fulfilled all righteousness. The water told of no cleansing of His spotless soul. He sanctified it to be a sign and means of His baptism of the Spirit. As He prayed, the Holy Ghost came from the opened heaven, and the Father's voice declared Him His beloved Son. So He was anointed for His work as the Christ, and through Him came the assurance to man of love, and grace, and welcome.

Thus I learn how the three Divine Persons are one in carrying out the work of my salvation. I am helped to think of what takes place when Christ's baptism of water and the Spirit is duly received. Faith can know of that which was seen and heard when Jesus was baptized, and be thankfully sure of the coming of the Holy Ghost, and the blessing of a Father. Christ is still on earth, in those who are baptized into Him. God is unchanged, still heaven is opened; and when God is sought in any of His appointed ways with prayer, the word of a Father's love is spoken, the Divine Spirit lights on those who are one with the Beloved, and in Him are accepted. Be it my care to fulfil all righteousness in lowly obedience and faith, praying in Christ's name, and trusting in His mediation, looking up to Him Who is my Father, because He is His, trusting ever for new gifts of the Spirit to enable me to please Him more perfectly.

Almighty Father, give me faith to seek Thy blessing in the devout use of Thy appointed means, and in careful fulfilment of all righteousness, after the example of Christ, that I may receive more of Thy Holy Spirit's power to love and please Thee.

Glory to Thee, O Lord, Whose grace, to our baptizing given,
Hath washed our souls, and poured on us the Holy Ghost from heaven;
Glory to Thee, in Whose dear Son our sonship we may claim,
And as Thy new-born children call upon our Father's name.

Monday after the First Sunday after Epiphany.

"I beseech you therefore, brethren, by the mercies of God, that ye present your bodies a living sacrifice, holy, acceptable unto God, which is your reasonable service."—Rom. xii. 1.

ST. PAUL points to the mercies of Him Who has made and spared, and upheld and redeemed us, and Who gives us the place and the hope of sons. In God's name he prays us by those mercies, and the love of which they tell, to bring all we are, and devote it all to God. In the burnt-offering the victim was laid on the altar, part by part, and all consumed. So are we asked to give our whole selves, with each power, to God. God will accept the devotion of a pure life, given to Him by a will which faith enlightens, reason guides, and love makes earnest.

To mercy I owe all I am or have, or hope for, that is good. God "upbraideth not," but beseeches me by His mercies. What can I refuse to render unto the Lord, Who comes with such a claim? He, as it were, lets me be my own, that I may give myself to Him. Chiefly through my body evil comes to my soul, and shows itself. In my outward life I can serve God, and let the light of knowledge and love shine to His glory. God asks for my body, that its senses may be closed against the coming in of evil, and that each of its powers may be used only for what is good. Shall I not with willing heart yield it to be all His? The ceaseless binding down of my sinful self, the glad, thoughtful, loving, active life for God, will be precious in His sight. As my nature becomes holy, I shall be more and more a "cheerful giver." I shall feel sacrifice cost less effort, and it will bring down larger blessing.

Most merciful Father, grant that all the mercies I have and hope for may rouse me to live for Thee, devoting every power to Thy service, so that I may be accepted through Thy mercy in Jesus Christ.

> Every day that passeth, every hour that flies,
> Tells of love unfeignèd, love that never dies;
> All we have we offer, all we hope to be,
> Body, soul, and spirit, all we yield to Thee.

TUESDAY AFTER THE FIRST SUNDAY AFTER EPIPHANY.

"Be not conformed to this world; but be transformed by the renewing of your mind."—ROM. xii. 2.

THE world is God's great rival. Its power is felt all around us. The changing fashions of the age, the stern rules and maxims of worldliness, claim submission. If these are allowed to guide the life, worldly habits are formed, the whole character takes, in time, a worldly shape; God is as if He did not exist, or need not be regarded. The world must be resisted. The "mind," the conscience, and will must be put into God's hands. When the inner man is renewed by His Spirit, the whole being becomes transformed, and the direction of the life is changed. The man grows strongly into the form which his Creator wills.

To which do I yield myself—to God or to the world, to the eternal or the passing? Which do I love? Which do I fear to offend, and try to please? Does my rule of life change with the shifting opinions and fashions of the time, or the habits of those with whom I live? Does my conscience lose its firmness, and my will give way when the world presses? Am I in the world's hands to become what the world makes me? Or does the Spirit of God within me guide my thoughts, and aims, and ways? Have I, as God's gift, a mind and will of my own, made wise, and pure, and strong by the Divine indwelling? Does God's will, approved by my renewed conscience, fix my rule of life and the standard I aim to reach? Am I thus being transformed in life and character by the power of God within me, and under His shaping hand?

O Lord, Who hast placed me here to form me for a purer life, help me to resist the strong evil of the world around, and grant that Thy Holy Spirit may so renew my affections and my will, that in life and character I may please Thee, through Jesus Christ.

May we ne'er, by guilt depressed, lose the way to endless rest;
Nor with idle thoughts and vain bind our souls to earth again.
Rather may we heavenward rise, where eternal treasure lies,
Purified by grace within, hating every deed of sin.

WEDNESDAY AFTER THE FIRST SUNDAY AFTER EPIPHANY.
"*Wist ye not that I must be about My Father's business?*"
—LUKE ii. 49.

THESE are the first written words that Jesus spake. They give the key-note of His life. He came to do His Father's will, not His own man's will. He must be always in the place and at the work which God wills. Of this He gently reminds His mother, preparing her for the days when His divine work shall withdraw Him almost wholly from her. In the temple He set an example for all in all time. He waited on God, learned from those who taught God's Word, gained knowledge and strength for His man's mind. So He prepared the outfit for His after-life's work.

I have a Father on high. He has given me "business" of His to do. I am bound to be always and earnestly "about it." My common studies, my every-day duties, may be all done for my Father, and be a most real part of my religion. But this is not enough. Religion must be brought into everything; but there are times when all else must give way to religion. My Father calls me to His house, and where His special presence is, that I may learn and worship. He gives me work to do which is all of heaven. I must visit His temple, and love to linger there. I must give my mind work in laying up store of divine truth, and seek grace where God promises that it shall flow. If Christ could not but do this, how shall I without loss neglect? No earthly work, no human friendship, or kindred must stand in the way. I must be in my Father's house, about His business. Only so can I prepare to make my whole life acceptable to Him and blessed to myself.

Almighty Father, make me to love Thy house, and desire to grow in wisdom and grace, that I may be able to spread the knowledge of Thee, and prove myself Thy child in all my life, after the example of my Saviour.

> Work shall be prayer, if all be wrought
> As Thou wouldst have it done;
> And prayer by Thee inspired and taught
> Itself with prayer be one.

THURSDAY AFTER THE FIRST SUNDAY AFTER EPIPHANY.

"And He went down with them, and came to Nazareth, and was subject to them."—LUKE ii. 51.

FOR eighteen years Christ lived a hidden, silent life. He did His mother's bidding, and obeyed the rules of the household. He learned to use the builder's tools, and became known as "the carpenter, the Son of Joseph." In that obscure village, few marked the peasant boy, who seemed nothing more. Jesus all the while was hallowing our common tasks and homely cares. He was training His manhood. He was working our salvation as truly as by His miracles, preaching, and death.

Do I seem held back and kept down? Let the long silent years of the subject life of Jesus teach me to wait. He never called aimlessly, nor need I. Time spent in being schooled for work is not wasted. That is part of my Father's business, no less than active work. Does what I have to do seem of no profit to the world or me? If it be what God sets me to do, it is what He wants done by me, and is best for me and for His glory. He knows how it fits into the rest of His plan. Patience and obedience to God are learned and shown by submission to those under whom He places me here. The common drudgery of life is changed, since Jesus worked in the joiner's shop with wood and nails. No honest lot can degrade me. I can make the lowliest honourable. I can do it in Christ's Spirit and for Him. It is not lost, though it seems to lead to nothing. If I am true, God will give it a place in His scheme for me. It will help to fit me, perhaps, for higher work here, surely for higher trust hereafter.

Almighty Father, grant that no pride or self-will may tempt me to cast off the burden Thy wisdom calls me to bear; but that in patient lowliness I may ever wait for and obey Thy leadings, after the example of my Saviour, Jesus Christ.

> The task Thy wisdom hath assigned
> Oh! let us cheerfully fulfil,
> In all our works Thy presence find,
> And prove Thy good and perfect will.

Friday after the First Sunday after Epiphany.

"And Jesus increased in wisdom and stature, and in favour with God and man."—Luke ii. 52.

JESUS began His human life as an infant. He willed to grow in mind and body, as we do, by degrees, and by the diligent use of means. He heard, and asked questions, and so gathered knowledge. He gained wisdom by thought. He grew in "stature," or in maturity, like others. He became more ripe—less a child, more a man. He gained power, without losing purity. God saw His human nature developing towards perfection, and found new cause for "favour." Men watched, with growing respect and love, the winning goodness of the child ripen into the strong virtues of the man.

So Jesus Who, as God, had all within His reach, made Himself one with those who toil to know and to be wise. He goes side by side with all who learn in the hard school of experience, and grow mature under the ripening heat of life's trials. He assures of His sympathy and help, while men train to the character which God and the right conscience of mankind approve. If the Son of God was thus one with me, let me be one with Him. If He willed to inform His mind, and bring out its powers by thought and study and close effort, let me welcome, not only the end laboured for, but the labour, as good and useful. Let me aim at the full-grown maturity that He, as man, by the use and improvement of man's powers, reached, and to which His example beckons me. Let me seek, each day, to gain more favour with God by some new grace gained, or gift turned to good account. Let man's favour be deserved, whether it be won or not, by a life and character growing day by day more like His.

All wise and perfect God, give me grace so to grow as my Saviour did, that I may more and more deserve the favour of men and win Thy favour, through the same Jesus Christ, my Saviour.

> Still in duty's lowly round,
> Be our patient footsteps found;
> With Thy counsel guide us here
> Till in glory we appear.

SATURDAY AFTER THE FIRST SUNDAY AFTER EPIPHANY.

"Let your light so shine before men, that they may see your good works, and glorify your Father Which is in heaven."— MATT. v. 16.

FROM God alone comes the soul's true light. Men are in darkness till Christ gives them light. Made one with Him, they are "light in the Lord." He imparts to His members His own wisdom and holiness. Through them He shows His light. They must not hide it; but let the world see, by their life and work, what God's light can make men able to be and do. They must not use God's light for their own glory. Self-forgetting lowliness is among the good works by which the world is to be won to glorify God.

The light I have is only darkness, if it be not from God. God's light does not help me, unless it is in me. Knowledge and grace are mine, not for selfish use, but that they may be light to others. The more they shine abroad, the more blessing I have. If they shine not on others, my own way is dark. They must *so* shine that they may be known as God's light in me, showing forth His praise. Have I been enlightened by Him, through Whom the truth and grace of heaven come to souls? Is my light hidden, so as to be no help or cheer even to myself? Is it gloom, not brightness; repelling, not attracting? Is it used for display, held up to draw to myself glory that belongs to God? Or, do I aim to let God's clear light shine in me, and make the world less dark with sin and sorrow? Do I aim to lead others to choose a path bright with my example? Do I seek to glorify my Father by living as His child, and winning others to give Him the honour due from sons?

O Lord, the source of light, shine upon my darkness, enlighten my understanding and my will, that living in union with my Saviour, I may show myself Thy child, and win men to give Thee glory.

In thy life and actions try
God to praise and glorify;
Do Thy work in Jesus' name;
So His help and blessing claim.

The Second Sunday after the Epiphany.

"What have I to do with thee? Mine hour is not yet come."
—John ii. 4.

SO Christ put away the interference of her who was nearest to Him on earth. The words are gentle, yet firm. As man He was subject to the blessed mother, from whom He took flesh, that His Divine Person might live in servant form. As God He did His Father's business. He had His own way and time fixed by that Father's will. He did not forget; He cared for all things. None might dictate, or hurry, or question. The safe and right course was to see that "whatsoever He said was done," and leave all in his hands.

Christ encourages me to spread my great and my least cares before Him. I must always doubt myself, not Him. When I am anxious for others, I may not speak as if He were less thoughtful, or less kind than I. He knows when and how best to make known His goodness. It is always my "hour" to do whatsoever He saith. Do I delay Him by failing to do my duty? Am I wondering and questioning, when I ought to obey? Perhaps He waits, in order to show me that what He does He does alone, and not "with me." Perhaps He would make His work plainer by doing it when my need is plainer. The mother of my Lord sets me an example. She was sure of His power and goodness. She provided for the prompt doing of His will, and thus made ready for a miracle. When human resources are drained, and I have learned that all help must come from God alone, the Saviour's hour is come. He proves that His way and time are best.

O Lord, Who workest all things by Thine own will and power, save me from hindering Thee by impatience or unbelief. Grant that I may always fully and promptly obey Thy Word, leaving my cares in lowly quiet faith to Thee, Who art, with the Father and the Holy Spirit, one God.

> In every work and every prayer
>   I do my best;
> And in His hands, without a care,
>   I leave the rest.

Monday after the Second Sunday after Epiphany.

"Every man at the beginning doth set forth good wine; and when men have well drunk, then that which is worse: but thou hast kept the good wine until now."—John ii. 10.

THE world gives its best first. The joys it sets before men do not satisfy, and soon fail to please. As the taste lowers, coarser pleasures are given, which only make more painful the nature's craving. Then comes want, which only God can relieve; or despair, which turns even from Him. Christ begins by making want felt. He humbles and calls for obedience and trust. He bids bring in what seems to promise nothing. Then is found a brimming source of cheer. The power to relish the good joy grows ever more pure and strong. The supply never fails.

In the beginning the world may seem to promise more joy and ask less sacrifice than Christ. The world's good soon fails. Christ's blessings are renewed and deepen for ever. The best earthly delights cannot quench my soul's desires. If I have only all the pleasant things the world provides, I am still in want. These may, for a while, drown thought, but God has made me for what is higher. Well for me if I can lay my need before Christ, Who alone can find me what satisfies and lasts. He may seem at first to put me off. I may think He mocks me with strange and hard commands, that try faith and patience sorely. Yet I may be sure, if I only will obey and wait. New and richer pleasures shall be mine, with truer power to enjoy them. In heaven, with a nature changed by Him, so as to care only for what is holy, I shall be able to say, "Thou hast kept the good, the purely perfect, until now."

O Lord Jesus Christ, be with me at all times, making holy by Thy presence all life's harmless joys. Grant me to long for those best things which Thou alone dost give, and to enjoy now a foretaste of the endless cheer that is laid up for Thine own in heaven.

  Such is Thy banquet, dearest Lord;
   Oh! give us grace to cast
  Our lot with Thine, to trust Thy word,
   And keep our best till last.

TUESDAY AFTER THE SECOND SUNDAY AFTER EPIPHANY.
"Rejoice with them that do rejoice, and weep with them that weep."—ROM. xii. 15.

WE are members one of another. As Christians we cannot live alone, or for ourselves. We are bound to feel with others in their joys and griefs, to be sorry for what makes them sad, and—a harder thing—to be happy in their welfare. This feeling must be no idle one. It must rouse us to do all to make the joys of others more, and their griefs less. So shall we gain new cheer and consolation for ourselves, and have the blessing of Him Who sends us as the bearers of His sympathy.

When I fare well, I am tempted to turn from those whose sadness might cloud my joy. In my adversity I am tempted to envy those who enjoy what I am denied. But it is good to go to the house of mourning. I may be taught what it costs the mourners dear to learn. And it will help my own joy to bear some of their burden. When I am tried, I should be thankful that all are not alike in pain and sorrow. The merry heart of the glad may do me good like a medicine. The Man of Sorrows helped the joy of the wedding feast. He also wept with those who mourned the dead. He feels with our least griefs, and in our bright times there is no guiltless joy for which He has not sympathy. Like Him let me be. Rather, let His love be in me, and show itself through me. There is perhaps more weeping on earth. In heaven there will be only rejoicing. Now is the time to train my heart to sympathy.

O Lord Jesus Christ, Who didst move among men, showing the loving-kindness of God; give me of Thine own sympathy, and use me to help the joy of the glad, and soothe the sorrows of the mourners, to Thy glory, Who livest and reignest with the Father and the Comforter, one God.

> I ask Thee for a thoughtful love,
>   Through constant watching, wise,
> To meet the glad with joyful smiles,
>   And wipe the weeping eyes;
> And a heart at leisure from itself,
>   To soothe and sympathise.

WEDNESDAY AFTER THE SECOND SUNDAY AFTER EPIPHANY.

"Abhor that which is evil; cleave to that which is good."
—Rom. xii. 9.

TO abhor is to shrink from with heart-felt horror and dislike. To cleave to is to embrace with firm and lasting devotion. God calls to loathe evil as evil, and put it away as loathsome; to love what is good for its goodness, and hold it fast because we love it. To forsake evil is not enough; it must be forsaken in heart, and hated. To hate evil is not all. At the root of that hatred must be jealous love for what is good. As the nature grows pure and God is more loved, the heart will shrink from evil and cling earnestly to good.

How far I fall short of this high aim! I am asked to live, guided by a feeling about good and evil like God's. Do I shun sin from fear of wrath, or lest I lose heaven, for worldly ends, or for the sake of my peace of mind? This is not to abhor evil. I may still love it, and wish that the pleasures of sin might be enjoyed along with the blessings of purity. Do I work and worship with zeal? I may yet have no true love for God and goodness, but be only selfish and mechanical. While I am in the body, my blind lower nature will crave for things evil; but I, my true self, must learn to hate them, tempting though they be. I may well hate evil. It has degraded and ruined me; it parts me from God, God hates it, and, to my bitter shame, I find my weak earthly heart long for it. I may well cleave to what is good; for good is of God, and only by fastening my love to it can I escape from the deadly attraction of evil. What I grow to love and shrink from, tells what I am, and may hope to be.

O Lord, give me grace to love what pleases Thee, and to hate what grieves Thee. So may I, with my whole heart, abhor evil, however tempting, and cleave to good, at whatever cost, through Jesus Christ, my Saviour.

> Sin is my sorrow, passion is my pain,
> To Thee their vileness, and in me their stain.
> Christ is my joy, and out of all distress
> He doth deliver with His righteousness.

Thursday after the Second Sunday after Epiphany.

"Not slothful in business; fervent in spirit; serving the Lord."—Rom. xii. 11.

HE who toils for heaven may not be slothful in his everyday duties. In all things he must show the active, earnest zeal of one whose joy it ever is to serve the Lord. True religion gives new meaning and a higher motive to man's whole life of labour. He who feels that he does all under God's eye, and for God, and who is sure of God's help, will show a faithful hearty spirit in the least things. In what bears directly on the good of his own or his neighbour's soul, and God's glory, he will be ready to do his best with fervour. But he will also keep in mind that Christ, his example in all things, was no second-rate or careless carpenter.

How are my daily duties done? Do I work wearily, going through settled tasks with half-braced will and force, as if nothing given me to do were worth while doing well? Do I feel "above my business," and mistake carelessness about the common work of life for heavenly-mindedness? Is the zeal I think I have a slothful thing that the Holy Spirit fails to kindle into fervour? I am bound and able to serve the Lord in the business of every-day life. A habit of coldness in this will follow me in my worship and religious work. Hearty zeal in common tasks need not prove me worldly. It may show that I feel how serious is all by which God trains me to earnestness, and fits me for the better life. If in this spirit I do small things, fervour will not be wanting in the greater. God accepts all service done honestly for Him.

O Lord, Who dost use me to work Thine ends of love, and dost train me by toil for rest, grant me by Thy Holy Spirit zeal to serve Thee in all things, and strength for the diligent and faithful doing of the work set before me, for Jesus Christ's sake.

Lord, it belongs not to my care, whether I die or live;
To love and serve Thee is my share, and this Thy grace must give.
Come, Lord, when grace hath made me meet Thy blessèd face to see;
For if Thy work on earth be sweet, what must Thy glory be!

FRIDAY AFTER THE SECOND SUNDAY AFTER EPIPHANY.

"*Ye are not your own, for ye are bought with a price: therefore glorify God in your body, and in your spirit, which are God's.*"—1 COR. vi. 19, 20.

GOD made us to be His own. He redeemed us with the price of all Christ did and bore. His love spared not this great sacrifice. We were always in His power; but His love prized us, and sought to win our trust and love, that He might make us willingly His own. He claims all we are. We have no right to use wilfully any of our powers. God comes to dwell in body and in spirit. In the whole man, and in each part, He asks to be glorified. God's glory is in man's good, for God is love.

God has twofold rights over me. I owe Him all for which a Creator and a Saviour has claim. It is a glory to be the creature of God, the adopted child of a Divine Father, saved for Him at the cost of the work of Christ. I am His: He is mine. I may be sure of His love always; I have the use of His power for my good. What shame if I forget or deny what I am, or fail to live accordingly! Does God indeed dwell in my body and spirit? It is to glorify me. My part is to glorify God. I cannot add to His glory, but I can make it known. I will seek to show in my life and in myself the character God's Spirit forms. I will seek to grow like my Saviour, and act as He would in my place. All my powers shall be put to their right use, ruled by God's holy will. My body shall show forth my inward devotion; my spirit shall give life to the outward work and worship, by which I own myself God's. He Whom I am called to glorify is my Father. His glory is in my true good and joy.

O Lord, my Creator and Redeemer and Sanctifier, teach me to remember always Thy rights over me, and to trust Thy will for my good. Grant that in all I am and do I may seek to glorify Thee, and show the work of Thy love and power.

> Cast down thyself, and only strive to raise
>   The glory of Thy Maker's sacred name;
> Use all thy powers that blessèd Power to praise,
>   Which gives thee power to be, and use the same.

SATURDAY AFTER THE SECOND SUNDAY AFTER EPIPHANY.

"Whosoever shall confess Me before men, him shall the Son of Man also confess before the angels of God."—LUKE xii. 8.

FAITH sees Christ's divine glory, however the world scorns Him. Love is faithful, come what may. All wish to be acknowledged by Christ when He comes in power. What shame to be untrue when faithfulness costs anything! What is man that he should be ashamed of God? It is glory to bear shame for Christ before an evil world. Christ calls the true His own even now, and will acknowledge them at last before His Father and the angels. When He comes in glory, He will disown those who in word or life deny Him now.

Christ was made man, and died for me. He is not ashamed to number me among "His brethren." What the world thinks of Him or His cause makes Him no less my Lord and Saviour, as glorious as angels see Him, and men shall own Him in the end. All my hope rests on His acknowledging me. I am glad of all I gain from Him. Shall I be base enough to grudge what He asks me to do and bear for Him? His eye is always on me, and He notes all it costs me to be true. If I fail through weakness, He will still own me His care, as He did St. Peter. Only if I go on working iniquity will He say, "I never knew you." What a reward for not being unfaithful, that Christ should proclaim me His before His Father and heaven's glorious ones! The hope of this may well brace me for all things. The fear of His disowning me may well overcome all other fear. Is my life thorough? Are my works consistent? Am I taking Christ's side, as I want Him to take mine?

O Lord Jesus Christ, grant me faith and love, that I may always in word and life be true to Thee, and that Thou mayest own me as Thine when Thou appearest in the glory which Thou hast with the Father and the Holy Spirit.

Oh! what, if we are Christ's, is earthly shame or loss?
Bright shall the crown of glory be, when we have borne the
   cross.
Enough if Thou, at last, the word of blessing give,
And let us rest beneath Thy feet, where saints and angels live.

The Third Sunday after the Epiphany.

"Lord, if Thou wilt, Thou canst make me clean."—LUKE V. 12.

DISEASED, an outcast, loathsome to himself, the leper was past man's help. He was a type of the sinner; only God could heal him. He heard of Christ. He sought Him, listened and believed. He fell on his face, and in the words, "Lord, if Thou wilt, Thou canst," owned Christ's power divine. This act of faith was a prayer. He showed no doubt of Christ's goodness by saying, "If Thou wilt." He proved the lowly submission of his prayer. He left it with the Almighty and Wise and Loving to grant it or not, as seemed well.

Christ can heal all this life's woes. He does not always will, but He is always kind. I may ask help, but must not in my prayer show doubt of His wisdom or goodness, and press my will against His. He knows what is for my true good; I do not. He always wills to cleanse the soul; my unwillingness alone keeps me unclean. Sin is like leprosy. Beginning with little that alarms, it lays hold on one power after another, till the whole spiritual being is tainted and as if dead. It cuts off from communion with God and those who are His. No man can find a cure: God is the one healer and restorer. Christ stooped, in His Incarnation, to bring purity from Himself to sick humanity. He cleansed me once when I was baptized unto Him, and His spotless nature touched me. Alas, how I have again and again become unclean! Ever do I need to come anew for the touch of the Almighty Saviour, and to abide where His cleansing hand of mercy is stretched out. But my prayer must be, Lord, Thou canst and Thou art willing; make me willing, make me clean.

Lord, I trust my earthly griefs with Thee, in faith. I would long for a pure soul. Stretch forth Thy healing hand, and let Thy purity pass to me and be mine for ever.

> Oh! wash our hearts; restore the contrite soul;
> Stretch forth Thy healing hand, and make us whole;
> Oh! bend our stubborn knees to kneel to Thee;
> Speak but the word, and we, once more, are free.

Monday after the Third Sunday after Epiphany.

"Lord, I am not worthy that Thou shouldest come under my roof; but speak the word only."—Matt. viii. 8.

THE centurion was sure of Christ's power. He himself obeyed the orders of those set over him. His own word to soldier or servant met prompt obedience. He believed that the powers which blessed or afflicted men were under Christ's control. As he realised this, he felt how unfit he was to receive One so great. He did not even presume to go into His presence. He sent others to bear a message of apology, and ask Him only to speak —to give the order which would heal his servant.

This half-taught Roman shames me by his knowledge. This proud soldier reproves my presumption by his lowliness. I know that Christ rules all things by His word; and yet how little do I seem as if I knew it! How slow is my faith to send me to Him in my need! He comes to me and tells me how sorely I want His help. He knocks at my heart's door, and asks to be let in with all His store of blessing. Perhaps I do not fear to keep Him waiting, or I question how far His power can aid me. Or I make bold claims on His goodness; I hasten Him with fretful impatience as if my rights were withheld. I demand that He shall do my bidding, in my way, at once. Alas, for my communions! Have I not, when I called my God to come and dwell in me, shown my lack of faith by my lack of lowly reverence? Have I not presumed to seek His visits with an unbowed heart, with little feeling of the awfulness of His lowly coming, and of the saving power with which He came?

O Lord Jesus, I am not worthy that Thou shouldest draw near to me. Speak the word, and take away the pride and unbelief that keep Thee from me. Come to my soul, unworthy though I am, and by Thy presence impart the worthiness that I have not in myself.

> Lord, we Thy presence seek;
> May ours this blessing be;
> Give me a pure and lowly heart,
> A temple meet for Thee.

TUESDAY AFTER THE THIRD SUNDAY AFTER EPIPHANY.

"If it be possible, as much as lieth in you, live peaceably with all men."—ROM. xii. 18.

PEACE is not always possible. Sometimes it can only be kept at the cost of what is even more precious. But such cases are rare. Seldom is all done that might be done to save peace. Strife breaks up the soul's calm, checks brotherly help, multiplies temptations, and brings reproach on religion. Few things repay for the evils of it. It is not enough to live peaceably with the peaceable. Some even fail in this. Among the "all men," with whom we must try to live peaceably, the most quarrelsome ones are included. When others will not be at peace, yet, on our side, all should tend towards peace.

God's work thrives in calm. Evil prospers where there is confusion. What makes for peace is always my duty. Though others "make them ready to battle," my duty is unchanged; I must still "speak to them of peace," and act peaceably. Perhaps I seek strife, or go to meet challenges. Perhaps I live quite peaceably with no one, or only with those who never try me. God knew how sorely many would provoke, when He taught me how to "live with all." The most quarrelsome test me. This rule of life applies not only to great matters but to the least, to home life as well as to the work of the world and the Church. I can gain most good ends better by peace than by strife. Strife opens the way for all sin and harm to my soul and the souls of others. If peace be broken, let me be sure that, on my part, no efforts have been spared, and that it was not "possible" to preserve it. Let me still labour on, "as far as in me lieth," to live peaceably, and to win others to peace.

O God of peace, give me such a strong and loving spirit, that I may never cause or help strife, but, as far as in me lies, live peaceably with all men, to Thy glory, through Jesus Christ.

When we think how much our Father
  Has forgiven, and does forgive,
Brethren, we should learn, the rather
  Free from wrath and strife to live;
Far removing all that might offend or grieve.

WEDNESDAY AFTER THE THIRD SUNDAY AFTER EPIPHANY.

"Be not overcome of evil, but overcome evil with good."
—ROM. xii. 21.

HE is overcome of evil whose Christian firmness gives way under wrong, and who sins when he is sinned against. So the sufferer becomes a sinner also, and evil spreads and gains power. He overcomes evil who, by the force of goodwill and words and deeds, disarms malice, and wins foes to peace. He overcomes evil who guards his soul in faith and patience, who shows the calmness of one whose good is from God, and, gaining strength and purity in trial, turns into blessing what is meant to harm him.

Evil can only harm me if I yield to it as a temptation. My foes can make me suffer. They cannot make me sin without my consent. If I meet evil with evil, I sin, and I tempt those who wrong me to more sin. I lose God's favour and my own inward peace. I am proved weak, and in the power of what thus moves me. Christ calls me to be strong as He was, and in His strength; to give good words for curses, and kindness for wrongs. So may I show myself too firm to be shaken from my Christian place. What if I can soften the bitterness of my foes, and bring them in the way of God's blessing, willing captives of His love? I may not be able to do this; but I can, in the school of the cross, learn wisdom and grow like Christ. So those who think to harm me may do me more true lasting good than my best friend. While overcoming evil in Christ's way, I may draw down more good from God to overcome evil in myself.

Almighty God, make me strong in Thy grace, that no evil may overthrow my charity, but that I may always seek to win triumphs for Thy love, and overcome evil in myself, through Jesus Christ.

May we evil lusts subdue,
Long for what is good and true
And our duty always do.
May our lips our faith confess;
Teach us, when reviled, to bless,
Conquering by gentleness.

THURSDAY AFTER THE THIRD SUNDAY AFTER EPIPHANY.

"*Soberly, righteously, and godly.*"—TIT. ii. 12.

MAN is called and strengthened by God's grace for threefold duty—to himself, his neighbour, and his God. He is charged with the care of himself, and is bound to live soberly, restraining his desires, so that their blind indulgence may not harm him. He belongs to a community. His fellow-men have a claim on him, that he be righteous, true, trustworthy, giving to all their due, and asking no more than his right. He is, besides, the creature of a God to Whom he owes all he is and has— Whom he is bound to honour by a godly life.

Do I live soberly, careful to keep my whole nature firmly under rule? So far well. But I am not by myself on earth; I have duties to others. Do I love my neighbour as myself, and deal righteously with him? Can he charge me with no wrong, or point to no rights of his withheld by me? This might be enough, were there no God. There is a God, and from that fact new duties arise. God's claim upon me gives a fresh motive for living soberly and righteously. The three divisions of duty make up together the will of a right life. No one part can in truth be fulfilled by itself. Each helps the other. My temperate, regular life will not be a set-off for unfairness with my neighbour, or neglect of God. Harming none, and acting straightforwardly in business, will not make up for destroying myself and wronging God. Religion is a mere form and mockery, when it is a cloak for private sin and want of uprightness between man and man.

Almighty God, give me grace to order my own life soberly, and to be upright in my dealings with others, and so to live godly in this evil world, that in all I am and do I may show forth Thy glory, through Jesus Christ.

Love well thy Father, in all men thy Father's children see,
In works of love and holiness be follower of me.
Seek from the Word of Life to learn thy heavenly Father's will,
Seek, in the means of grace, the power thy duty to fulfil.

FRIDAY AFTER THE THIRD SUNDAY AFTER EPIPHANY.

"*To him that knoweth to do good, and doeth it not, to him it is sin.*"—JAMES iv. 17.

GOD makes known His will that it may be done. He offers grace that it may be used. Men are meant to grow in knowledge and power, so as day by day to do better and become better. It is sin to resist grace given for any end. It is sin to work evil, and it is sin not to work good. It is sin to fall; it is sin also not to rise. Doing no harm will not save; doing no good will condemn. God claims that men do all the good they know and can in all ways, at all times. The slothful servant is wicked. The unused talent is taken away.

God has made and redeemed me, not only to be harmless, but useful; not only to shun what is bad, but do what is good; not only not to grow worse, but to grow good. I am a son, a servant, a soldier, a workman. I am given great things to do for God in my nature and in the world. I have means of knowledge and of grace, for the rightful use of which God will ask an account. I sin if in any way I make vain the life from God in me. I sin so far as I let my sloth and want of heart be a drag on its activity. I sin if I fail to go where Christ calls and leads. I must obey God as well when He says, "Thou shalt," as when He says, "Thou shalt not." I can keep from evil only by doing good. Poison kills; so does starvation. If I would reach heaven, I must do more than avoid the wrong road. I must press on in the right.

O Lord, Who hast made and redeemed me, give me faith and love, that diligently learning Thy holy will, and readily obeying the leadings of Thy grace, I may do well my work for Thee, through Jesus Christ.

> I have not served Thee as I ought,
> Alas! the duties left undone—
> The work so coldly, feebly wrought—
> The battles lost, or scarcely won!
> Lord, give the zeal, and give the might,
> For Thee to toil, for Thee to fight.

SATURDAY AFTER THE THIRD SUNDAY AFTER EPIPHANY.
" Unto whomsoever much is given, of him shall be much required."—LUKE xii. 48.

ALL are not gifted alike now, and all shall not be judged alike at last. The just God will ask more from those who have enjoyed larger privileges. He knows the knowledge and the grace entrusted to every one, and how far sin and failure in each one are wilful. He knows how far light and grace, put within reach, have been neglected or wilfully refused. Those who are given power to do most for God can wrong God most. Those who are called to highest holiness can be the most hardened sinners, and can deserve the lowest doom.

What could God have done for me that He has not done? What is there of truth of which I need be ignorant? What is there of duty that I cannot learn? What grace is not within my reach? And God promises to make all things, even what seems most against me, work for my good. Surely my calling is a very high one. I can become great in holiness, and do great things for my God, and win a glorious crown if I will. But the ground of my hope is ground for lowly carefulness, lest it but make my condemnation heavier. All I have is mine, to be turned to profit. Moreover, I must answer for knowledge that I fail in through idleness, for grace that I neglect to use the means of gaining, for power that I might have did I seek it, for opportunities that I could find if I tried. Does my life meet in any true way what God has a right to demand? Let me take account with myself, and so prepare for God's day of reckoning.

O Lord, from Whom all good gifts come, arouse me to seek diligently and to use faithfully the light, and grace, and opportunities within my reach, that I may worthily set forth Thy praise in my life, and may be everlastingly rewarded through Thy mercy in Jesus Christ.

> O let my life be given,
>   My years for Thee be spent;
> World-fetters all be riven,
>   And joy, with suffering blent;
> Thou gavest Thyself for me,
> I give myself to Thee.

The Fourth Sunday after the Epiphany.

"*The ship was covered with the waves: but He was asleep.*"
—Matt. viii. 24.

THE storm swept over the boat. The skilled sailors strove in vain—all seemed lost. Christ, wearied with long work, slept. As man, He lay as if He neither knew, nor cared, nor could help. The untiring God was awake to all. The powers of nature were His creatures and servants. The disciples seemed left alone in despair till they called on Christ. He arose, and first stilled their alarm with His calming voice of power. Then He removed its cause. With Him they found trial; from Him they gained peace in it, and deliverance from it.

Where Christ is, trial is sure to come; ruin cannot come. Storms beat more fiercely against the Church, because He is in it. The waves of sin and unbelief and of the world's hate lift themselves against Him. Often Christ gives no sign, but He knows all. Nothing can harm Him, and He cares for the Church's safety. Perhaps He waits for more earnest prayer when the need of Him is most felt. While I watch and toil for the Church, I must not dare to think that her Saviour sleeps and cares not. She is more dear to Him than to me, and her boldest foes must yield to His "Be still." When the deep waters of sorrow and temptation pass over my soul, He waits to help and calm. He is careful lest my soul sink. If He seems to close His eyes to my peril, the fault is mine. He will hear me now, if I will call on Him. In the sleeping Man on the sea of Galilee I can see One Who can feel with the weak and tired. In the God rising up to quiet the storm, I see One able to give peace within me and around.

O Lord, Whose sleepless power and love guard Thy Church and each soul, help me in all trial to trust Thee calmly, and only doubt my faithfulness in work and prayer.

> Lord, when our life is clouded o'er,
> And storm-winds drift us from the shore,
> Say, lest we sink to rise no more,
>   Peace, be still

Monday after the Fourth Sunday after Epiphany.

"Why are ye fearful, O ye of little faith?"—Matt. viii. 26.

THE disciples were obeying Christ's word, and He was with them. So they had nothing to fear. They ought from the first to have done their best calmly, looking for His help and sure of it. But they toiled alone in their own skill and strength, and did not turn to Christ till these had proved vain. Their words were impatient, and spoke doubt of His care and power. Christ gently blamed them. "O ye of little faith" (St. Matt.); "How is it that ye have no faith?" (St. Mark); "Where is your faith?" (St. Luke). They had faith, but "little" for them. They had no faith to calm them. It was not ready when wanted.

When the storms of life threaten to overwhelm me, this need be my only care—am I in the path of duty; is Christ with me? If so, I need not fear. The tempest will but bear me faster on towards the safe shore. But my faith is little, and often fails me when I need it most. I am apt to trust to myself, and delay to call on God till the force against me proves my utter weakness. Then perhaps I cry to Him out of the depth of despair. I might have felt Him with me all along, and been strong and brave to meet my trials and do my work. I complain that help has not come, which I have not sought. I speak and feel as if Christ had forgotten me, while in truth I have forgotten Him. Faith's hold on Christ should be firm and constant. I should look to Him to be my power in all I do and suffer, not only to save me from the consequences of trying to do without Him.

O Lord Jesus Christ, be with me in the toil and danger of my tempted life. Give me now the peace of the obedient and believing. Bring me past life's storms to the quiet of rest with Thee.

Though life's billows rage and swell, they are waiting His command;
In the tempest all is well, if we know the Lord at hand.
Trial shall our souls prepare for a calm eternity,
In the holy haven where those who love their Lord would be.

TUESDAY AFTER THE FOURTH SUNDAY AFTER EPIPHANY.

"Render therefore to all their dues."—ROM. xiii. 7.

"THEREFORE," because God has given men claims on you, own those claims. To give tribute, custom, fear, honour, where due, is part of religion. All are bound to share the cost as they share the benefits of public safety and order. All are bound to strengthen the hands of rulers by prompt obedience, and by honouring them for their office's sake. Christ paid tribute, and kept the laws of the land and of the Church in which He had rights. God makes it sin to break man's laws, except when they plainly command to break His.

It is good for me to be under rule. God's hand controls me through those whom He allows to hold power. No human rule is faultless. The worst is better than none. If all may judge the laws and choose which shall bind them, laws are vain. Conscience rarely commands resistance. When it seems to do so, I must beware lest some low selfishness or vanity be taking the name and place of conscience. If, as St. Paul counsels, I yield to wrong and bow for conscience' sake to God's will, thus trying me by others' sin, God blesses the sacrifice. I would not rob one man, nor must I steal from the State by withholding tax or duty. I must not encourage others to treat lightly what God calls sin. I must not deny myself my due, by keeping any from his right. When for God's sake I honour in word and deed those set over me, I do my duty to myself and honour God. If I name the name of Christ, I must be blameless in common duties.

Almighty God, give me grace to be a faithful member of Thy Church, and a loyal citizen, rendering gladly to all their dues, for Thy sake, Who dost rule all things, and after the example of Jesus Christ my Lord.

> I give to every man his right,
> As in my heavenly Father's sight,
> With word and deed sincere:
> As one who bears a Christian name,
> I guard my honour free from blame,
> I keep my conscience clear.

WEDNESDAY AFTER THE FOURTH SUNDAY AFTER EPIPHANY.

"By faith Noah, being warned of God of things not seen as yet, . . . prepared an ark to the saving of his house."—HEB. xi. 7.

NOAH was "just, and walked with God." He heard the Divine warnings as the voice of love and truth, for he knew God. The things threatened were "not seen as yet;" but faith assured him they would come. He warned others. By his words he was a "preacher of righteousness," but more so by his work. He made ready against the evil day. Faith encouraged him to spend time and toil on what the world counted folly. All the while, by doing God's will, he was gaining the righteousness that comes to faith, and preparing an ark for the saving of his house at last.

Though I walk with God in righteousness, like Noah, I still need to listen to God's warnings, and prepare an ark as He directs. I may be tempted to feel secure, and as if all were done or would be done for me. The day of the world's doom seems so far off, that I may think I need not live and work with it always in view. The world around heeds not God's warning, and mocks those who earnestly attend to it. Only strong faith that brings God near in each step of life, and knows that He means in mercy all His warnings, can move my slow will. I must be a preacher of righteousness. My words may be feeble; I may seldom be able to speak to others. I can walk with God before men, and show my faith in Him by my doing simply and fully what He commands. So by my prayer and words and example, I must provide that the ark which saves me shall also be for the saving of my house, and of all who are within my influence.

Almighty God, give me grace to believe Thy Word, and walk with Thee in righteousness, and so to live and labour that I may be saved myself, and be the means of saving others, through Thy mercy in Jesus Christ.

Time only bears Thee to eternity,
Tread then the path thy great Exemplar trod;
Think on the day when this vast earth shall be
In bursting flames dissolved—yon skies so broad
Shrink like a shrivelled scroll—"Prepare to meet thy God."

Thursday after the Fourth Sunday after Epiphany.

"Choosing rather to suffer affliction with the people of God, than to enjoy the pleasures of sin for a season."—HEB. xi. 25.

THE luxuries of Pharaoh's court, and the society of Egypt's noblest and wisest, were part of Moses' life. His prospects were splendid, as "son of Pharaoh's daughter." It was hard to forsake all this, and turn his back on friends with what seemed ingratitude, and cast in his lot with an enslaved, down-trodden race. But faith showed him on one side pleasant things and sin for a while, on the other affliction with the people of a God Who could recompense in eternity. He went where God called, counting the cost, and sure of Him in Whom he believed.

Some pleasures are so bound up with sin that they cannot be had without it. Some honours are the price of the soul's truth and purity. Many good things can be only kept by neglecting duty, and leaving undone the work of life. I may be called, like Moses, to some heroic sacrifice, or my life may be made up of many smaller efforts. Faith, by which I see God and look forward through my eternity, will rouse me to seek grace for all trials. I cannot doubt or hesitate. When the "season" is over, when the "pleasures" are past, and only the sin remains, the worth of what tempts appears. I must choose to be with the people who obey God's Word and have His promises. I must forego and refuse all that keeps me from the work and grace God has for me. If affliction come, it is but for a season. There is a sure recompense, compared with which sin's richest joys are worthless. The thought of this can cheer me if I falter. True at all costs to God, He will be true to me.

Almighty God, give me faith to refuse all pleasures which are tainted with sin, and in the path of Thy will to meet affliction calmly looking for the reward of righteousness, which Thou dost promise in Thy mercy, through Jesus Christ.

> I leave the world, its wealth allures not me;
> With God alone will I contented be.
> The creature shall no longer fill my mind;
> In the Creator what I want I find.

FRIDAY AFTER THE FOURTH SUNDAY AFTER EPIPHANY.

*" Lot dwelt in the cities of the plain, and pitched his tent toward Sodom."—*GEN. xiii. 12.

LOT chose the land which promised most worldly good to him and his. Those among whom he went to live were "sinners before the Lord exceedingly." But he ran the risk. His righteous soul was vexed; but he was not warned away. God saved him, only by fire, and with the loss of all. His wealth was destroyed. All his children but two who lived for worse than death, died with those for whom they had left him and God. His wife perished with her heart towards evil. Angels almost forced him as he lingered. We last see him in the cave near Zoar, miserable, poor, and shamed.

Richer worldly prospects do not make up for added danger to the soul. It is often true wisdom, both for this world and the next, to choose a way of life in which work is harder and gain less easy. If ambition or covetousness lead me into the neighbourhood of sin, I am sure to lay up sorrow. Presumption forsakes grace. To neglect the Spirit's warnings against temptation is to forfeit His help in it. I may only mean to "pitch my tent towards Sodom." I know not how soon I may be at home there. I may be "vexed" by the ungodliness around. Soon, perhaps, custom will blunt my feeling about sin. What if, like Lot's children, I become one in thought, and love, and life, with the wicked! What if, like Lot's wife, when I try to go away, my heart clings and I die! What if, like Lot, I am saved by God stripping me of all for which I have risked losing Him, and bringing me out to shame and desolation! What if I only just escape by the forcing of the good angels God sends!

Almighty God, grant that I may never peril my soul for the sake of worldly gain or advancement, but always act with a view to my everlasting good and Thy glory, for Jesus Christ's sake.

Oh, wherefore do I live and breathe? and wherefore have I still
The mind to know, the sense to choose, the strength to do Thy will?
Is it for honour, wealth, or power, my heaven-born soul to sell?
Is it to grasp at pleasure's flowers upon the brink of hell?

SATURDAY AFTER THE FOURTH SUNDAY AFTER EPIPHANY.

"Abraham believed God, and it was accounted to him for righteousness."—GAL. iii. 6.

ABRAHAM'S faith was accounted to him for what it was, not instead of what it was not. Always tried, it was always victorious. He went out into a strange country among strangers, not knowing whither God led. He sojourned there, believing the promises, though he had no son, and no land. He looked for a better country, content that his seed and not he should possess Canaan. In will he offered up his son, of whom God had said, "In Isaac shall thy seed be called." He was sure that God would raise him from the dead, and make good the promise, he knew not how.

If I would be blessed with faithful Abraham, let my faith be like his. Faith manifests its life in childlike obedience. God's will leads, though it seem strange and hard. God's promises cheer, though their fulfilment seem far off, and to all but faith unlikely or impossible. God calls me often to "go out, not knowing whither." Enough for me that God knows, and in time I shall know. I may see no end gained by leaving and doing so much; faith tells of good to others, and of a heavenly country where the blessing of it all shall reach me. I may seem to sacrifice, at God's bidding, my whole earthly joy, and even that with which are bound up my best spiritual hopes. Faith is sure that God knows how to give back, with new preciousness, treasures laid on His altar; and to make the yielding of what is dearest to the devout soul a means to closer union with God, and larger blessing, God can raise from the dead what is sacrificed for His sake. He knows "whither" He calls me, and how to make all things help to bring me there.

Almighty God, may I faithfully obey Thee always, and be ready to sacrifice at Thy bidding what is dearest, believing in Thee, and seeking the better country, promised through Jesus Christ.

Thy way, not mine, O Lord, however dark it be;
Lead me by Thine own hand, choose out the path for me.
Not mine, not mine the choice, in things or great or small;
Be Thou my guide, my strength, my wisdom, and my all.

The Fifth Sunday after the Epiphany.

"Whatsoever ye do in word or deed, do all in the name of the Lord Jesus."—COL. iii. 17.

GRACE comes through Christ. Through Him the work of grace is offered to God. He sanctifies man's whole life. All words of prayer and praise, all works done for God have worth, if united to Christ's worthiness. All common tasks fulfilled, all daily trials well borne in the faith and love of Christ, are parts of a life laid before God to His praise. When those who worship and toil are one with Christ, what they bring is accepted as His. For His sake and through His mediation God is well pleased.

My prayers are cold and weak, my praise seems hardly more than sin. As I feel my need of prayer, and my sense of God's love deepens, my worship shames me more with its unworthiness. What I do for God is so little, and its motive is so mixed, that I scarce dare lay it before Him. But in union with Christ's merits all has a value not its own. Let me do my best, looking for Christ's help and in His name. For His sake God will accept the signs that I wish and try to love and serve Him. I may lay all my life upon God's altar. Each patient word and kindly act may be as if Christ said and did it. I may live as one guided in all things by Christ's example, doing all in His strength and for Him. So in all the parts of my life I may please God, in the power of Christ living in me, and trusting in Christ pleading for me.

Almighty and all holy God, grant me by Thy Spirit a living union with the Lord Jesus, that He may be the pride and strength of all I do. May my worship offered in His name be accepted for His sake. One with Him, may I live so as to please Thee on earth. One with Him, and for His merits, may I enjoy Thy presence in heaven.

    Lord! I am weak, and Thou art strength—sustain me.
    Thou art all goodness, Lord, and I all ill.
    Thou, Lord, art holy—I unclean before Thee.
    Lord! I am poor, and Thou art rich—maintain me.
    Lord! I am dead, and Thou art life—revive me.
    Justice condemns; let mercy, Lord, reprieve me.

Monday after the Fifth Sunday after Epiphany.

"Let both grow together until the harvest."—MATT. xiii. 30.

GOD sows good seed through His Son. It shows itself in the children of the kingdom. Where God is reclaiming, an enemy again sows evil. It springs up and is seen in the children of the wicked one. The time when the evil shall be taken from among the good is not yet. Man's judgment may err. His rash hand may harm the good while roughly rooting out the evil. His work is to gather in, not to cast out of God's field. The worthless may become good. The presence of evil may strengthen what is of God. Both must be left to grow. When they are ripened, God will part them.

Evil are mingled with good. I find evil where I least look for it. Let me lay my difficulty before God. He tells me enough—that evil is not from Him, and things shall not be always as they are. I am not judge. I have not skill to know the evil, or how and when to remove them. God bears their presence in His Church. I may do so. God spares, in mercy to the evil and to the good. The good may help to change the evil, and the evil are a discipline for the good. My part is to labour with God, that what is of Him may increase and strengthen. It is well to be tried, that I may be careful to grow and ripen as God wills. Am I sure that I know myself? Do I search for and root out all evil from my own nature? I am growing for the harvest. Am I growing fruitful, and repining to be parted from evil and made safe by God for ever?

Almighty and all holy God, Who dost make known Thy patient careful love, grant me so to be separate in heart and life from evil, that when the time of harvest comes I may be gathered into Thy safe keeping, through Jesus Christ my Saviour.

All this world is God's own field,
Fruit unto His praise to yield;
Wheat and tares therein are sown,
Unto joy or sorrow grown;
Ripening with a wondrous power
Till the final harvest hour.

Tuesday after the Fifth Sunday after Epiphany.

"I love them that love Me; and those that seek Me early shall find Me."—Prov. viii. 17.

SO speaks the second Person in the Godhead, Whom love led to seek and save man. God's love for man enables man to love God. He seeks the love of those to whom He gave being. He loves in a new way those whose hearts are drawn towards Him. Those who love God seek Him actively, and God makes Himself known as the soul's rest and satisfaction. To love early is to seek early Him Who longs to be found that He may bless. To put off God's seeking love is to give to other things the first and firmest hold on the heart, and to risk losing Him for ever.

Am I only loved by God with the love of compassion and forbearance? Have I shut off from my soul all other love of God? Or do I yield my cold heart to be quickened, that the love which blesses those who love Him may be mine? Does my love take form, and live, and move as a true seeking after God? So far as I have wasted life's early hours, I have grieved God, and lost blessing, and hardened my heart. It is not early now, but it is not too late while God's love still seeks me. I may still find Him if I will seek. My weakest desire to love is proof that God has first loved me, and is a pledge that all the wealth of Divine goodness is ready to be poured out upon me. As my love grows, God will give a larger claim on His. As I seek more earnestly, God will make Himself more known, and give me firmer assurance that I am His, and He is mine.

Almighty God, Who lovest all, grant that, loving Thee, I may not delay to seek Thee, so that I may find in Thee and in Thy love, fulness of satisfaction, through Jesus Christ.

> God only knows the love of God;
> Oh that it now were shed abroad
> In this poor stony heart.
> For love I sigh, for love I pine;
> This only portion, Lord, be mine,
> Be mine this better part.

WEDNESDAY AFTER THE FIFTH SUNDAY AFTER EPIPHANY.

"Fools make a mock at sin."—PROV. xiv. 9.

HE who sins breaks God's law, dares the Almighty, wrongs the All Good, insults the All Holy, persumes on the long-suffering of the All Merciful. He tramples on Christ's blood, outrages His love, makes His work vain. He resists the Holy Spirit's patient pleadings, and defiles His temple. Sin imperils man's all for ever. It stains the sinner; it spreads evil, and causes woe. Sin has ruined man, and it stands in the way of what God does to save him. What darker sign of the state of heart and mind of any one, than to laugh at sin and treat it lightly?

Only in wicked foolishness can I treat sin as a joke. What shame to laugh at another's pain of body! how heartless and thoughtless to sport with the signs of his soul's deadly sickness! I do not make a jest of what threatens my life or goods, or place in the world's esteem; what madness to make merry over what tells of my soul's danger, of my want of grace, of my dishonour before heaven's holy ones! I would not grieve a human friend, or act basely to an earthly benefactor; shall I be as those who jeered around the cross? shall I mock my Father in heaven, to Whom I owe all? shall I dare to be amused with what renews my Saviour's sorrows, and grieves the Holy Spirit? God only knows how sad and awful sin is. If I am in my senses, and not quite careless and hard, I can know enough to make me full of seriousness and dread at the thought and sight of it. Sin may be sport for devils. It is no sport for me, whom Christ died to save from it.

Almighty and all holy God, give me such a love for souls, and for holiness, and for Thee, that I may never make light of the least sin, but in thoughtful earnestness strive against sin, through Jesus Christ.

> Who laughs at sin laughs at his own disease,
> Welcomes approaching ruin with his smiles,
> Dares at his soul's expense his fancy plead,
> Affronts his God, himself of peace beguiles.

Thursday after the Fifth Sunday after Epiphany.
"He that walketh with wise men shall be wise."—Prov. xiii. 20.

THE company men keep shows what men are, and makes them what they are to be. It shows character, and forms it. Men are drawn to those whose tastes are like their own. They catch, without knowing it, the ways of thought and feeling of those with whom they live, or whose work or amusements they share. Through books the influence of the writers reaches heart and mind. What does not improve, harms; what does not lift, lowers. Man's life is short, and is a "walking"—a going on. Companions should be chosen whom it would be well to learn from and grow like.

I can learn much of my own character by knowing whom I choose as friends, and what reading gives me pleasure. The same test will show me whether I am seeking wisdom, and growing wise or not. Perhaps when I am alone with myself my thoughts are not those of one who seeks to rise towards better things. Mind and heart must be forced with God's help to put away whatever is not true and pure. I must not be one with those whose aim is low, and who would not rouse me to improve. Far less must I risk my soul in fellowship with those who are going down in sin and folly, and falling farther from salvation. Let my friends be the thoughtful, the high-minded, the earnest. Let me hold converse, through their writings, with the great thinkers, the men of purest feeling and loftiest virtue. Above all, let me walk with God, and seek close fellowship with Christ, that the Divine Spirit may ennoble me, and make me wise and great. Let me walk now with those whom I wish to rest with for ever.

Almighty God, grant me to be the companion of the wise, and of those who are taught by Thee, that I may become more worthy to serve Thee there, and may grow wise unto salvation, through Jesus Christ.

    Not with the light and vain,
        The man of idle feet and wanton eyes;
    Not with the world's gay, ever-smiling train;
        My lot be with the grave and wise.
    With them I'd walk each day,
        From them time's solemn lessons would I learn,
    That false from true, and true from false, I may
        Each hour more patiently discern.

FRIDAY AFTER THE FIFTH SUNDAY AFTER EPIPHANY.

"In the multitude of words there wanteth not sin; but he that refraineth his lips is wise."—PROV. x. 19.

IN much talking there is sure to be some sin. The heart's evil will make itself known and felt if the tongue be not reined. The talkative often do more harm than the wilfully false and malicious. They betray secrets, part friends, embitter foes, wound hearts, blight characters, hinder truth. They do all wrong often without meaning it, often to their own shame and grief. They forget the tongue's power, and the peril of its wild use. It is a fire, good for cheer and for the work of life when kept in bounds, bringing ruin when unrestrained.

Sinful words may be few and carefully chosen. This warning is against many words. To bridle the tongue is part of Christian duty; without it my religion is vain. There are more times to keep silence than to speak. To give words is not more blessed than to receive. The power of speech is mine to help, not to hinder myself and others in business and in pleasure. Much talking shows vanity, and want of thought and right feeling. I cannot learn unless I hear in silence. Why make known all that rises to my lips, which perhaps none cares to hear? Why say heedlessly what I may earnestly wish unsaid? I would not do wilful harm; but if I wilfully let my tongue run loose, it will surely wound my neighbour's peace or good name, and drag me into trouble and sin. "Idle words" lead to "corrupt communications." The tongue is a power for good or evil. I am bound, by my trust, to see that heaven-taught love and wisdom guide it, lest it be "set on fire of hell" to do the work of sin.

Set a watch, O Lord, before my mouth, and keep the door of my lips, that offending not in word I may be enabled to bridle the whole body, according to Thy holy will, for my perfection, through Jesus Christ.

God listens to the words you say,
Let love and wisdom guide them all;
Unbridled tongues that run away
Will surely be their owners' fall.

Saturday after the Fifth Sunday after Epiphany.

"Profane person, as Esau, who for one morsel of meat sold his birthright."—Heb. xii. 16.

ESAU, as Isaac's firstborn, was heir of the spiritual blessing given to Abraham. He did not prize it, or fit himself to hold, and hand it on. He lived an animal life, following his own will, enjoying things present, forgetting his great calling. When wearied and ready to die with hunger, he was offered food in exchange for the birthright. He doubted God's care of his life, and sold what to his unbelief was valueless, and already as if lost. The deed was done. He could not win back the blessing, though he sought it carefully with tears.

I have the birthright of a child of God, made one with Christ the promised Seed. How high a dignity to care for and use well! I profane it, if I live for earthly good, and waste my energies on pursuits that draw me away from God, and life's true aim. I am profane if I show in what I am and do that I despise or think lightly of my spiritual calling. The lower being grows strong if it is allowed its way; while the higher loses its force, and yields its place of rule. The blessings of eternity will fade from view, and seem of less worth, if my life be spent on what is passing. If I weaken my better will and my hold on God, I may be tempted so as to fall hopelessly. I may part with God's eternal blessing for the sake of one fleeting indulgence, and repent too late. I can spare all here. I can even die. I cannot do without my birthright. God Who gave it will preserve me to enjoy it, if I am true to Him and to myself.

Almighty Father, Who in Jesus Christ has given me a birthright as Thy child, grant me grace to prize and guard it, so that no fear of pain or death, no desire for earthly things, may tempt me to lose Thine everlasting blessing, through Jesus Christ.

O child of God—thy Father's name, and care, and gifts divine,
The promise of the heritage of joy in heaven, are thine;
Take heed, waste not thy hope, make not thy calling vain,
Live as one born of heaven, and strive thy heritage to gain.

Septuagesima Sunday.

"O Lord, how manifold are Thy works! in wisdom hast Thou made them all."—Ps. civ. 24.

THE book of nature reveals God. His wisdom, power, and love are written on it. The great worlds moving in far-off space, and the wings of a tiny insect, alike show His glory. There is endless variety. As in the Holy Scriptures, the simplest can gain wisdom, and delight, and help for his needs, while the strong trained mind has ever new interests to tempt research. And there are mysteries which we profit by but cannot explain. Difficulties come mainly from narrowness of knowledge. The more is known of God's works and the laws He has given them, the more His glory appears.

I am a work of God, and I live in the midst of what He has made and He upholds. He spreads His works before me, and gives me a mind to learn from them the mind and heart of their Creator. I dare not despise nature, as I dare not despise Scripture. Each revelation has its own place in teaching me of God and of His will, and of my duty. Both should be read together. Nature illustrates much of Scripture. Scripture throws light on many of nature's mysteries. Knowledge can only help truth if I be true. The more I know of God's works, the more intelligently I can praise Him. The more I know of the laws of nature, the better I can obey God's will thus proclaimed, and help the good of man. My feeling of the beauty of sea, and sky, and hill, and vale, may be a hymn of praise to the Almighty Architect and Painter. To scorn and neglect the tokens of wisdom, and power, and goodness round me, is no honour to God. Let me prize and study them. Let me with reverent thankfulness enjoy them, but as earnests of better things.

Almighty God, give me grace and wisdom that what I read in nature and in Scripture may help me to know, and praise, and serve Thee, and may lift my heart towards heaven.

> Thou Who hast given me eyes to see
> And love this sight so fair,
> Give me a heart to find out Thee,
> And read Thee everywhere.

MONDAY AFTER SEPTUAGESIMA SUNDAY.

"Why stand ye here all the day idle?"—MATT. xx. 6.

THEY stood idle because no man had hired them. They went at the first call. In God's vineyard each has his duty for his own soul, and the souls of others, with the promise of eternal life. He who is not a "labourer," doing earnestly this work, lives idly, however busy he may be in the world's schemes and tasks. Some do not go where God's calls are spoken. Some hear, but heed not, till they find that the call of the eleventh hour has sounded and is silent, and that night, in which none can work, has overtaken them.

God gives my nature to my care, that by my close toil, and through His blessing, evil may be rooted out, and fruit of holiness may ripen for His glory. Work in God's vineyard, the Church, is marked as mine; I am called to do it, and without me it is left undone. God calls me as a "labourer" to use for Him the strength He gives. He might drive me as a slave. He leaves me free, and offers "hire." There is great reward in a character trained in God's service, and a nature changed to be fruitful in pleasing God. Work done in the spirit of free love and obedience God remembers. Does the day go by, and call after call leave me still idle before God? Am I "standing idle," looking at my work without doing it, or doing it idly? Do I expect God to do for me what He has given me strength to do? Am I sure that a call to true work will come again? When the day has gone, can I plead that "no man hath hired me"?

Almighty God, Who dost give me work in Thy vineyard, and strength with which to do it; forgive my past idleness, and grant me to obey Thy call, and be an earnest labourer for Thy glory and my own eternal good, through Jesus Christ, my Saviour.

As labourers in Thy vineyard, still faithful may we be,
Content to bear the burden of weary days for Thee;
We ask no other wages, when Thou shalt call us home,
But to have shared the travail which makes Thy kingdom come.

TUESDAY AFTER SEPTUAGESIMA SUNDAY.

"Every man that striveth for the mastery is temperate in all things."—1 COR. ix. 25.

HE who hoped to conquer in the Grecian games went through long hard training. It was no use to do his best when the hour of trial came, if he was not ready beforehand. So he took all pains to be found fit to do well. He lived by stern rule. He was sparing in his use of life's good things. Rest and food were taken as means to help to the end before him. He denied his wishes for lesser things, and guided his whole life with firm will towards one great purpose.

I profess to seek an incorruptible crown. It must be fought for against all comers, if it is to be won. I know not when I may be called to face one or other of my soul's strong foes. My hope may depend on my fitness to meet well some sudden challenge. I am bound to be always ready, and getting more ready, more firm in will and purpose, more free from what might clog. I must use, not some things, but everything God gives to help me in my life's great aim. I must draw into me all strength from God, and take all care lest I lose it. I must check my desires for passing good, lest I lose what is unfading. I must rule myself now, lest I be mastered and enslaved. I need fear nothing if I am earnest, firm in will, true in heart, with all myself trained in faith and obedience. Temptation shall be overcome, evil shall yield. I shall be strong in the Lord, and my own weakness shall not keep me from the crown.

Almighty God, grant me grace so to rule my desires, and use the things of this life, that I may be able to strive well with all that is against my soul, and may at last receive the crown of righteousness which Thou dost promise, in Thy mercy, through Jesus Christ.

> By the love, O Jesu, of Thy cross,
> I will live, and counting all else but loss,
> For the love of Thee my cross will bear,
> And will follow Thee till the crown I wear.

WEDNESDAY AFTER SEPTUAGESIMA SUNDAY.

"I therefore so run, not as uncertainly."—1 COR. ix. 26.

GOD calls the Christian life a race, to teach us how we must act, so as not to fail. He who would win a race must know the course as marked out, and keep to it. He must learn the rules, and follow them. He must start promptly, and press on to the goal with no swerving aside, falling back, or stopping. If he has delayed or stumbled, he must put forth more strength, and make up his mind to a harder struggle. The Christian who so runs to the end, in God's strength, surely obtains.

Am I "running"—making a true effort to press on fast, or is my Christian life a lazy, easy-going lounge? Have I a plain goal towards which I strain, or am I content to trust I am moving or looking some whither? Do I take pains to know from God how to guide my steps, or do I take my own way, and go on as if the rules laid down by Him Who gives the prize need not be obeyed? Did I set forward from the first, or delay till others were far before me? Am I making up, as best I can, for wasted time, or am I still only half in earnest? Do I go on steadfastly in the fenced course, or is my religion a thing of fits and starts, with many halts and goings out of the way? I cannot "obtain" unless I "run"—press on fast. If I run aimlessly, carelessly, wilfully, or unsteadily, I run uncertainly; I have no sure hope that I am so living in union with Christ, as through Him to gain the crown.

Almighty and merciful God, pardon me for past sloth and wilfulness, for wasted time, and light, and grace. Make me so to learn Thy will, and put forth my strength, that I may run my Christian course in humble but sure hope of Thy reward, through the merits of my Saviour.

> Run the straight race through God's good grace,
> Lift up thine eyes and seek His face;
> Life with its way before thee lies,
> Christ is the path, and Christ the prize.

Thursday after Septuagesima Sunday.

"So fight I, not as one that beateth the air."—1 Cor. ix. 26

MEN beat the air who strike weakly with no straight clear aim, or who care little how the fight ends. Those who are front to front with a strong skilled foe, for glory or shame, life or death, waste no strength in wild efforts, which only weary. They put their whole force into each well-aimed blow, and try to make it tell towards victory. They follow up each advantage quickly, carefully, and stoutly, till the foe yields or dies.

I am face to face with strong evil. I know the greatness of what is at stake—even my all for ever. Am I a coward or a traitor to my own life? Am I fighting aimlessly, and as if there were little to be lost or gained? Do I only strike at evil when I feel its wounds smarting in my soul, or when its close assaults frighten, or when some disgraceful fall shames me? No one wins who thus wars with sin. I must watch and try to be beforehand with my foe, weakening him ere he can harm me. I must find out where I am open to danger, and so know how I most need to guard and to put forth strength. I must beware lest I spend my force on weak foes, while I leave the wily sins that most beset me unresisted. I must not let my hands hang down, or my ready watchfulness fail. As each form of evil rises against my soul, each must be promptly, firmly met. Blow must follow blow till all the powers of sin are, one by one, beaten back, and my soul is, through God's help, in peace.

O Lord, Who knowest how many and how strong my soul's foes are, give me grace so to watch and fight against each form of evil, that I may beat down all, and be free to serve Thee in peace; to Thy glory, through Jesus Christ, my Saviour.

> Dream not of calm repose away from strife,
> Watch well the cunning foes who seek your life;
> Fight for the home on high as soldiers true,
> Think of the Father's eye that watches you.

Friday after Septuagesima Sunday.

"The last shall be first, and the first last."—MATT. xx. 16.

THE last called may use a short time well, and win a foremost place. The first called may lose heart, grow cold, and fall away. The last in powers and opportunities may be first in lowly faithfulness. Self-trust may spoil the promise of the most rarely gifted. He whom man counts lowliest may bring the offering God counts best. He whose gifts seem most worthy may, before God, be a selfish idler. The last in his own eyes may be first in God's; the first in his own eyes may be last in God's.

Have I wasted long years, and been late to own God's claim? Let the thought of past neglect spur me to greater zeal. I may yet hear my Lord's "well done," as I have heard His call to repent. Are my gifts lowly; does the best I can do seem nothing? God needs not my work or offerings; He accepts the true heart and loving will. Did God's Spirit early awaken an answer in my spirit, and gladden me with divine consolations? The same Spirit warns me to take heed lest I be last. I may be lifted up, to fall through self-trust. Are my gifts of nature and grace large? Have I great opportunities? This is that I may do more and better work, not that my work may be easier and cost me less. Am I in the front as a toiler for God and the good of man? A low aim, a selfish motive, may make all worthless, and put me far behind those whose work seems common.

Almighty God, give me grace to be always watchful, and lowly, and earnest, and so diligently to use the talents entrusted to me, that in the end I may win the blessing of a good and faithful servant; through the merits of my Saviour Jesus Christ.

Oh may Thy Spirit seal our souls, and mould them to Thy will,
That our weak hearts no more may stray, but keep Thy precepts still;
That to perfection's sacred height we nearer still may rise,
And all we think, and all we do, be pleasing in Thine eyes.

SATURDAY AFTER SEPTUAGESIMA SUNDAY.

"Without a parable spake He not unto them: and when they were alone, He expounded all things to His disciples."—MARK iv. 34.

CHRIST, at first, taught plainly. When men would not receive His teaching, He veiled it under the form of parable. In judgment, He withdrew what they slighted. In mercy, He spared them the sin of persevering boldness in scorning clear light. Alone with His disciples—those who honestly wished to learn—He opened the deep meaning of His words. The parable, which veiled truth from those who sinned against it, helped to make it more plain and striking to the earnest and candid.

Such is Christ's way now. The heedless, the proud, the merely curious, find faith grow harder. The earnest souls that love His words, and wish to be led aright, see more clearly their deep meaning. Mysteries send them to seek His help and listen to His other words. Does Christ's teaching seem to me parable—words and little more—awakening no answer in my soul, leaving me doubting and uncheered? Was it always so? Is the cause, perhaps, my slowness to profit? Have I turned from the truth, and lost the power of seeing it? Is it made dim to spare me the sin of despising clear light? Is it withdrawn in judgment for my long neglect? Let me not blame Christ for what may be the punishment of my sin, or the proof of His mercy. Christ does not wish to hide His truth from any. He will make it known to me if I will be a true disciple. Not among the questioning worldly crowd can I gain the mind and heart needful. Alone with Christ, all things shall be made plain. I shall learn to see their beauty, and feel their power.

O Lord, save me from the doom of those from whom Thy light is withdrawn. Grant that, as a faithful disciple, I may be willing to learn and ready to obey, and so may ever grow in knowledge and in holiness, to Thy glory.

'Tis Thine to teach, 'tis ours to bow
With meek docility to Thee;
Our only rightful Master, Thou,
The children of Thy wisdom, we.

Sexagesima Sunday.

"A sower went out to sow his seed."—LUKE viii. 5.

CHRIST is the sower, and He is the good seed. He came into the world, bringing the truth and grace of God. By His Holy Spirit and by those whom He sends, He sows now. By Him the barren earth of man's nature is made able to be fruitful for God. Without that heavenly seed, and the Divine care and blessing, it can only bring forth thorns and briers. The good seed is plentifully sown over all God's field. The dew and rain and sunshine of God's grace are sent freely to make knowledge fruitful. Where there is failure, the fault is man's, not God's.

I am God's field. He looks to reap what He has sown. Where is the fruit of all the truths planted in my mind, the claims made on my heart and conscience that should have moved my will? Where is the fruit of all the grace given to change me? Have the light and dark days of my life helped on towards harvest? Do I show a promise of what the angel reapers may store for my eternity? Is Christ growing in me? Am I "earth that drinketh in" what falleth upon it, and so "receiveth blessing from God;" or am I earth that beareth thorns and briers, wasting my nature's strength on what will wither and be burned? Do I show the growth of what Christ sowed in my regeneration, or what the evil one planted at the fall? If God's care and toil for me are vain, He will withdraw the good seed, and leave me waste. As my fruit is good, and ripe, and abundant, so my blessings shall be great.

O Lord, Who hast sown in me the good seed of Thine own pure nature, and dost give me light and grace, grant that it be my care always to grow in holiness, and to ripen daily towards perfection, for thy glory, Who, with the Father and the Holy Spirit, livest and reignest one God.

Behold the heavenly Sower goes forth with better seed,
The Lord of sure salvation, with feet and hands that bleed;
Here in His Church 'tis scattered, our spirits are the soil,
Then let an ample fruitage repay His pain and toil.

MONDAY AFTER SEXAGESIMA SUNDAY.

"Some fell by the wayside; and it was trodden down, and the fowls of the air devoured it."—LUKE viii. 5.

THE wayside was trampled hard. The seed could not sink or strike root. It lay there for a while. The feet of passers-by crushed it. Birds bore it away. Soon the ground was as if no sower had cast seed on it. So is it with those who hear God's Word with a heedless mind and an unsoftened heart. It does not enter into them. Their memories carry it for a while; but worldly thoughts come and tread it down. The temptations that Satan has ready soon leave no trace of any sowing.

Even the sower's feet harden the ground if it be not cared for. So, each time I hear God's Word I am in danger of being made less ready to receive and hold it fast. Each sowing which is in vain leaves me harder. Teaching and holy influences may only dull my mind, and shut closer my heart. Does the seed of God's truth and living power lie on my soul unheeded and unloved, not made mine by meditation and prayer? Do I hear without "understanding" its meaning for me, without "believing" so as to "be saved"? Do I receive, but only to give Satan new ways of spoiling me? I must wait with softened heart for what God sows. I must pray for devotion to keep it safely, and cherish it deep within my heart. I must fence off vain and sinful thoughts, and hide it where no temptation can take it away, and no passing trifle can destroy it.

Almighty God, I mourn the dulness of my mind, the hardness of my heart, the slowness of my will. Soften me by Thy grace that I may receive readily the seed of knowledge and of power. Help me so to guard and cherish it, that no temptation or foe of my soul may take it away, but that it may be fruitful to Thy glory.

> Saviour, come, my heart prepare,
> Leave no barren hardness there;
> Keep me as a field of Thine,
> Plant the seed of truth divine
> Guard me, lest the watchful foe
> Steal away what Thou dost sow.

Tuesday after Sexagesima Sunday.

"They on the rock are they, which, when they hear, receive the Word with joy; and these have no root, which for a while believe, and in time of temptation fall away."—LUKE viii. 13.

THE seed fell where a thin layer of soil scarcely covered rock. Because there was no deepness of earth, it sprouted fast. But the root had no room to strike down, no hold on what could nourish its life. The sun and dry blast parched it. So withers the religion of those who make loud hasty professions without counting the cost. The heart's hardness remains unbroken, and the inner being is unchanged. All seems well till trial comes. Soon a dry form only is left. Soon that is gone, and the hard earthly nature is bare.

To bear fruit upward, God's Word must take root downward. The fruit, to be of value, must grow and ripen until harvest. I want a joy that is well grounded, and a growth that will go on to perfection. The secret life of the soul with God makes the outward life true. My religion must be a real power implanted by God in the whole man, rooted deeply in the heart and will; it must be fed where no eye of man sees, from the hidden sources of grace. Does the joy I have prove more than shallowness of feeling, and want of earnest thought? Or does it show that I have "sown in tears," and learned to know Him in Whom I believe? Do the leaves of profession tell of a deepening hold on God, and so promise fruit? Am I so making ready for the evil day, and watching in lowly prayer, that when the trial comes I may have store of grace to draw upon, and may be ripened, not burned?

Almighty God, grant that Thy Word may be rooted in the deep places of my being, and nourished by Thy grace. So may I be found true in all time of tribulation, in the hour of death, and in the day of judgment.

> Rain, and dew, and sunshine give,
> That the precious seed may live;
> Let its root lie deep below,
> Let it upward strongly grow,
> Still unharmed in trial's heat,
> Or when storms around it beat.

WEDNESDAY AFTER SEXAGESIMA SUNDAY.

"Some fell among thorns; and the thorns sprang up with it, and choked it."—LUKE viii. 7.

THE soil was not hard or shallow, but it was preoccupied. The corn sprang up and promised well. But the roots of thorns were left to grow among it. There was not room or strength for both. The corn failed. So it is when men give to the cares of the world, or the joys of life, a place in heart and thought where they can rival religion. Nothing must use the strength which religion needs, or come between the soul and heaven. Else is the Word unfruitful.

The mind may be open to receive truth, the heart may be softened and feel deeply, there may be earnest will and effort; and yet there may be no good progress towards perfection. The hidden roots of all evil remain in my nature, ready for rank growth, if my watchfulness fail. I may needlessly multiply cares, and let them occupy and distract my thoughts. I may make the care of my soul only an equal among other cares wholly of this world. I may allow life's good things, or the desire for them, to hold the firmest, best place in my heart. I may do this without knowing. Cares which make me careless about God and growth in holiness must be put away, where they cannot interfere with eternal interests. Pleasures and gains which hinder my prayers and spoil the work of grace, and lessen my relish for hearing truth, must be kept in check or abandoned. When harvest time comes I shall only value what God has sown in me and ripened for eternity.

O Lord, root out of my soul all worldly care and love of earthly things, which might hinder me from wholehearted devotion. May all my nature be so cleansed that it may be free to profit fully by the teaching of Thy Word, and the power of Thy grace, through Jesus Christ.

Let my heart be holy ground
Where no evil thing is found;
Let no thorn or noxious weed
Mingle with the heavenly seed;
Let no worldly joy or care
Spoil its growth or promise fair.

Thursday after Sexagesima Sunday.

"That on the good ground are they, which in an honest and good heart, having heard the Word, keep it, and bring forth fruit with patience."—LUKE viii. 15.

THE ground was ready. It received and held the good seed sown. The roots struck deeply. The stalk grew upward steadily, helped by the whole strength of the soil, and by the dew, and rain, and sunshine from above; so good fruit ripened in abundance to perfection. He who will profit by God's Word must receive it with fair mind and ready will, hold fast what he is given, and with whole-hearted earnestness yield all he is to God.

My nature is a fallen one—hard, rocky, weedgrown. Am I stiffened by long habits? Does the rock of a hard heart lie hidden under shallow feeling? Do earth's cares and joys take up nearly all my time, and thought, and love? This need not be. God can change all this. There is power in His Word, if I am willing to be changed. It is my fault if I lie waste and barren. God waits to give the honest and good heart instead of the heedless, wilful heart. He can give the power to understand, and feel, and obey. He can break up the hardened nature, and open it to receive holy influences that lead on to holiness. He can take away the rock of unbelief and impenitence, which hinders my religion from taking root downwards. He can free me from the power of the world, which checks its upward growth. I am God's; let me own His claim, and put myself wholly and patiently in His hands. He will make me indeed His own. He will reclaim and renew my nature. The ceaseless help and blessing from on high shall make fruitful.

Almighty God, give me an honest and good heart to receive Thy Word aright, enable me to prize and hold it fast, and to obey it in patience till Thou dost see in me the fruit of Thy work in me, through Jesus Christ.

> Lord, Thy Word and grace impart,
> Give a good and honest heart;
> Teach me heavenly truth to know,
> Help me in Thy grace to grow,
> And in patience persevere,
> Till the harvest morn appear.

Friday after Sexagesima Sunday.

"Ye shall not surely die."—Gen. iii. 4.

EVE listened to doubts of God's truth and goodness. She looked on what was forbidden. Her eyes told her of pleasures within reach of her senses and her mind. She longed to taste the joy, and have the knowledge God withheld. There seemed no reason for the command. She did not think the warning meant what it said. Why should she not enjoy what looked harmless and useful? Knowledge must be good. Why remain with eyes unopened on a fresh world of interest? How could death follow from so small an act? She took, she enjoyed, she knew, she was ashamed, she died.

I am tempted, as Eve was, to be unthankful for what God gives, and pine after what He withholds; or I long to be wise in what is evil. I do not mean to do it, but to know, to read, talk, think about it. I question the careful love that denies only what would harm me, and keeps back only knowledge that is unsafe. I put forth my hand, in spite of God's plain "Thou shalt not." So I choose my own way, and leave the path of obedience. Moreover, I put into my mind a growing power of evil, scarce to be wholly driven out. A new seed of death is planted in me, shaming me and making my struggle for life harder. Or, in another way, I doubt the love that offers help for my soul in means of grace. They seem as powerless for good as the forbidden fruit for harm. I ask how the want of them can make my soul's life weaken and fail. I listen to the temptation, "Thou shalt not surely die." I refuse to put forth my hand. I slight God's bounty, defy His law, risk my soul's shame and death.

O Lord, give me grace to use thankfully what Thou givest, and to desire nothing Thou withholdest. So may I enjoy Thy blessing now, and life for ever, through Jesus Christ.

> See here the fruit of wandering eyes,
> Of worldly longings to be wise,
> Of passion dwelling on forbidden sweets;
> Ye lawless glances freely rove;
> Ruin below and wrath above
> Are all that now the wildering fancy meets.

SATURDAY AFTER SEXAGESIMA SUNDAY.
"Where art thou?"—GEN. iii. 9.

ADAM thought to hide his shame from God and from himself. But God's eye followed him, and God's voice reached him. He was bare to his own conscience, which cried out against him. He had opened his eyes to a new world of evil, and let it into his being. He had lost the ruling grace of God. Helpless against evil, with the beginnings of death in body and spirit, with shame and the foreboding of all sorrow in his heart, he shrank from God. God asked, "Where art thou?" that He might tell him of hope.

"Where am I?" God asks, and I ought to know. Without God, I am as Adam was. For I am born with a dying body, and with the beginning of corruption in my soul. Alone, I can but suffer and perish. I cannot hide from God. No work of my own can fit me to appear before Him, or cover my shame. The evil is within, and the power to overcome it must begin there. I need to be clothed in that which God provides from sacrifice. I need that Divine gift of indwelling grace which shall shine out in holiness. Christ dying for me gives me hope in drawing near. Christ living in me restores what is fallen, renews what has lost its purity and brightness, is the hope and the beginning of glory. Where am I now? Am I hiding under the shadow of earthly things, deceived by vain attempts to cover the signs of sin, while my sin remains? Or am I trusting God for that in which I may approach Him, and growing brighter with the shining forth of Christ the second Adam in my nature and life?

Call me to Thee, O Lord, and show me my lost state without Thee. May Christ's sacrifice cover my sin. May my nature be restored by union with Him Who is one with Thee and the Holy Spirit.

> Nothing in my hand I bring,
> Simply to Thy cross I cling;
> Naked, come to Thee for dress;
> Helpless, look to Thee for grace;
> Foul, I to the fountain fly,
> Wash me, Saviour, or I die.

Quinquagesima Sunday.

"Now abideth faith, hope, charity, these three; but the greatest of these is charity."—1 Cor. xiii. 13.

FAITH is dead, except it work by love. Hope is vain, where love fails. Faith and hope receive; love gives, which is "more blessed." Faith and hope are gifts of God. Love is God's very presence in the soul. Faith and hope do not make men like God. Love forms His image in them. God does not believe or hope—God is Love. The saved shall be kept faithful by perfect Faith such as angels have. Undoubting Hope of ever fresh joy shall add zest to their blessedness. Love shall be in them that by which they see God, and are like Him, and enjoy Him.

I must know God by Faith, and be cheered on in His service by Hope. I am nothing without Love, which is God himself. Love is the test of my faith, whether it live and profit. Love is the warrant of my hope. I can only believe and hope aright in One Whom I love, and Whose love dwells and works in me. Love removes all doubt from Faith, and all cloud from Hope. If my life be a life of love, my faith is real and will grow clearer; my hope shall not fail in what it looks for; I am becoming like Him Who draws my heart, and guides and fashions my life by the power of His love. No unbelief shall disturb the faith with which in heaven I shall trust God; I shall lean on His wisdom, and do His will without a question. No misgiving shall mingle with the hope which in my pure joy shall ever tell of yet higher blessedness. Love shall give me what I have, Love shall make me what I am, and be my everlasting joy.

O God, the object of Faith, the Giver of Hope, Who art Love, enable me to believe and hope in Thee, but above all, to love Thee, that so Thou mayest dwell in me now, and I may see and enjoy Thee for ever.

Faith, and hope, and love we see,
Joining hand in hand, agree;
But the greatest of the three,
And the best, is love.

MONDAY AFTER QUINQUAGESIMA SUNDAY.

"And have not charity, I am nothing."—1 COR. xiii. 2.

MEN do not commonly covet the best gifts. They see not as God sees. The man who wins fame by great genius, or efforts in the Church's cause, or lavish works of mercy; the man even who earns the name of martyr, may in God's sight be nothing, and unprofited. All this may be where charity is not. The unknown and ungifted, whose lowly commonplace life is guided by charity, is before God great.

Few are called to use in God's work great gifts of mind, the influence of high place, or large wealth. Few are called to lay down life for God. That is within my reach which God counts more precious than all these, which alone I cannot do without. God is Love, and Love is Charity. God comes to abide wherever He is welcomed as a presence and a power of love. If I have rare gifts and opportunities, if I do or give up much, let me take heed, lest, after all, God is not with me, ruling what I am, and guiding what I do. Wanting charity, all is worthless. If my place among men be lowly, yet I may have a "more excellent gift" than those I am tempted to envy in others. God has it for me, and wills to give it more and more largely. He does not need man's greatest work or sacrifice. He values the cup of cold water given by charity. Love can ennoble the littleness of my unmarked life. It can prove what the gifts men prize most do not prove—that God dwelleth in me.

O Lord, Who hast taught me that all my doings without charity are nothing worth, send Thy Holy Spirit, and pour into my heart that most excellent gift of charity, the very bond of peace and of all virtues, without which whosoever liveth is counted dead before Thee: grant this for Thine only Son, Jesus Christ's sake.

  Faith that mountains could remove,
   Tongues of earth or heaven above,—
  Knowledge, all things, empty prove,
   Without heavenly love.

TUESDAY AFTER QUINQUAGESIMA SUNDAY.

"*Behold, we go up to Jerusalem, and all things that are written by the prophets concerning the Son of man shall be accomplished.*"—LUKE xviii. 31.

CHRIST came to die. He knew all He would suffer in the man's nature He made one with Himself. Who can tell how the dread prospect grew plain before the Man Christ Jesus? Day by day He saw more clearly the path of sorrow by which He went on to meet the cross. The shadow darkened ever more deeply over Him; but His will was fastened to the will of God. His love clung to those whom He had given Himself to save. Knowing all, He looked past all. Love led Him forward till love's work was done.

Each day brings me its own burden—as much as I can bear. I pass from trial to trial; I see not tomorrow's clouds. Hope tells of good in store, and when I am cast down, bids my heart cheer itself with looking forward. What mercy is this! How could I go on, were the veil lifted which hides the griefs and conflicts of days not yet come? How could I but sink, were the gathered load of all laid on my strength? I cannot know the strain upon the will and love of Him to Whom all was as if present, or the true steadfast devotion with which He bore, for my sake, through those sad years. I cannot tell the worth of souls for whom He thus gave His life from day to day. Not for a few hours, O my Saviour! didst Thou carry Thy cross, and feel the smart of my sins. All Thy life was one long dying—one sustained holding of Thyself upon the altar, that the love of God, even Thine own love, might win my soul. How can I love and serve Thee with right devotion?

O Lord Jesu Christ, give me grace in my life of trial to remember Thine, and to bear bravely any cross, if only I may follow Thee, and be at last where Thou art.

> He sees the gathering of His foes,
> The meaning of His death He knows,
>   His heart in anguish fails;
> Yet faithful to His mission still,
> Resolved to do His Father's will,
>   He struggles and prevails.

Ash Wednesday.

"Turn ye even to Me, saith the Lord, with all your heart."
—JOEL ii. 12.

SOME turn from God with all their heart; they only love the world and sin. Some are half-hearted; they long for God, while they forsake Him; or outwardly follow God, while their hearts go after evil. They will not give up sin; they dare not give up God. Few are steadfast; for few are whole-hearted. "Turn ye," saith the Lord, "ye—all ye are—mind, heart, will, life—from evil; turn towards Me, turn to come even to Me. I will draw you on, and make your heart all Mine. So shall ye have no heart for evil, and shall cleave to Me as your perfect good."

I have turned from God, and been led away. I am often tempted, and often yield. His voice calls to me from time to time, and in many tones. Now, on the first day of the Spring fast, let me listen to Him telling of danger and hope. The shadow of the cross reaches me, and shows the deadliness of sin, and the glory of God's tenderness. "Turn ye even to Me—away from this sin to this love." So speaks my Maker and my Saviour, "Bring to Me the whole heart that is now all the world's —bring to Me the part which has been kept back from Me." Shall I refuse? Shall I not renounce wholly what is against or rivals God? Shall I not yield my whole heart and will to the gentle power that would draw me ever closer to God? So, in growing union with Him, I may be far from what tempts to turn away, and find the joy and rest God only gives.

Almighty Father, Whose mercy has never turned from me, though I have gone so often and so far away in heart and life, give me grace to turn to Thee, keeping back no power of love or will, and pressing nearer to Thee, till, at last, I find rest in perfect union with Thee.

> Since, from Thy foot I dared to roam
> My soul has found no rest:
> Chastised and contrite, back I come,
> To seek it in Thy breast.

The Second Day in Lent.

"Search me, O God, and know my heart; try me, and know my thoughts."—Ps. cxxxix. 23.

TRADESMEN keep their books with care, and count up gains and losses. The sick watch symptoms that tell of rallying or failing. Travellers note landmarks, and judge if they have left the path or lost time. Sailors mark on the chart each rock and shoal where they have met risk or loss, that they may steer safely. Builders test their work, and compare it with the plan. Much more should men, who have eternal interests at stake, search their hearts, and try their lives.

I must, on some unknown day, stand at God's bar. I ought, every day, to judge myself, and seek to learn my state. Times of communion, and the Church's solemn seasons, call me to more close, stern self-searching. Sloth and pride will tempt me to be careless and irregular. Satan will tell me to go on, trusting blindly that all shall be well. But how can I do any Christian duty well, if I neglect this duty? How can I hope that I am in earnest, if I grudge the trouble of finding out how my spiritual life thrives, and wherein it fails? Only by learning my sins, can I know what to mourn and confess, and where to amend. Only by learning where I am weak, shall I know what grace to pray for. Testing my motives I shall be saved from pride. Seeing where I stray, I shall be warned to return ere I have gone too far. Marking God's loving forbearance, I shall be cheered to go forward, and be taught my need of lowly watchfulness, and trust in Him.

Almighty God, Who knowest the secrets of my heart and life, teach me to try myself by Thy law and Christ's example. Give me a tender and enlightened conscience, quick to know and mourn my sins, that I may bring them to Thee, and find pardon and grace to sin no more through Jesus Christ.

> Sum up, at night, what thou hast done by day;
> And, in the morning, what thou hast to do;
> Dress and undress thy soul. Mark the decay
> And growth of it. If, with thy watch, that too
> Be down, then wind up both. Since we shall be
> Most surely judged, make thy accounts agree.

THE THIRD DAY IN LENT.

"My sin is ever before me. Against Thee, Thee only, have I sinned."—Ps. li. 3, 4.

SIN shames and lowers man. It robs him of much present good. It spoils his joy and calm of mind. It dares God's might and justice. It will drag down past hope those who are not loosed from it. So man may well mourn that he has sinned, and is sinful. But more, sin pains God's love. It brought Christ to shame and death. It makes His work vain now. It grieves, and resists, and threatens to quench the Holy Spirit. Here is the true ground why men should look on their sin with sorrow, and turn from it with hate.

My sin has cost me many a sorrow. Through sin much of my past is shameful, and my nature is stained and weakened. I am brought under the doom which hangs over sinners, and which only the mercy I have sinned against stays from falling. It is good to feel this, and to bow before the Most High in lowly fear. But the true sorrow that leads to joy comes not from love of self, but love of God. It deepens as fear gives way to hope, and God's goodness purifies and cheers the soul. My sin has been against a Father, I have pained the All Good and Kind, and trifled with His patience. I have used God's gifts as new ways and means of sinning against Him. I have slighted the love which led the Saviour to the manger and the cross, and trodden under foot His cleansing blood. I have turned a deaf ear to the Spirit's pleadings, and profaned the presence of God in my soul, which alone saved me from sinking utterly to ruin.

O Lord, show me Thy goodness, and give me a heart to grieve for whatever in me grieves Thee, and makes me unlike Thee, and threatens to part me from Thee. Grant that as I learn my sin I may prize Thy love, and as I grow able to rejoice in Thy mercy, I may mourn my wrongs against it.

> I have sinned, O God, Thy power defied;
> I have grieved Thy love, and Thy patience tried;
> My ungrateful life I now deplore,
> And I firmly purpose to sin no more.

The Fourth Day in Lent.

"I said, I will confess my transgressions unto the Lord; and Thou forgavest the iniquity of my sin."—Ps. xxxii. 5.

GOD sees each heart, and knows all about each sin. He has seen good to make confession a condition of forgiveness. To confess our sins is far more than to own that we are sinners. We may do this, and yet remain blind to our true state, and quite unhumbled. God bids men confess their sins that they may know them, and have a clear aim in asking for pardon, and for grace to amend. He who would confess aright must try to see his sins, one by one, as God sees them, and tell out the whole sad tale, as if to one who did not know it.

The shame of sin is in doing, not in owning it. Angels grieve when I sin. They rejoice when I search my heart, and spread all before God, resolved to sin no more. A sin should be confessed as soon as it is known. Confession of all that is known should form part of every prayer. How blessed when God's Spirit warns, and I can unburden my heart to a Father! How fearful to bear my sin till told of it by my Judge. Now, there is a fountain opened ever flowing. The good Physician waits to heal, and to restore. I can bring each stain and wound to God, knowing that He feels for me with infinite compassion, and that the same love that sent a Saviour is ready now to save. If I doubt myself, and fail to find the peace I need, there are those whom God sends to hear me when I open my grief to Him. When they speak in God's name God's pardon, I may be sure that, according to my faith and the truth of my repentance, it is done unto me.

Most merciful Father, give me grace to lay my sins truly and fully before Thee, and with humbled heart and firm faith to look for the pardon and renewal which Thou dost promise, through Jesus Christ.

> Fear not, without reserve disclose
> The festering wounds of sin;
> Your case, the Lord, your Healer, knows;
> His blood can wash you clean.

The First Sunday in Lent.

"*I thought on my ways, and turned my feet unto Thy testimonies.*"—Ps. cxix. 59.

HE who owns sin and asks forgiveness, undertakes, with God's help, to try his best to sin no more, and to undo wrong done. Without this, confession is self-deceit, and prayer is a vain mockery. He who thinks to escape the punishment of sin, while he keeps the gain of it, or means to go back to it, trifles with himself and God. The worth of repentance may be judged by the zeal shown in restitution. A true man, honest with God and himself, will spare no cost to free his purse, his heart, and his life from the accursed thing.

I examine myself that I may be guided in seeking grace for the future, as well as pardon for the past. Sorrow for sin and confession must be joined with resolves and prayers as I look forward. Have I forgotten God, and denied Him His due of love? let me vow and try to keep Him more in mind, and give Him my heart more wholly. Have I in life wronged Him, and left my work undone? let me be more zealous for His glory, more eager to serve Him with my might. Have I gained by oppression or unfairly? let me restore in full. Have I hurt others' good name? let me as far as possible undo the wrong by words of kindness. I cannot keep the pleasure or profit of sin, and have the pardon of it too. If God and honour call me to part with money, to spend time and toil, to put my pride to pain, be it so. Thus I prove that in truth I hate sin, and mean what I profess to God.

Almighty God, make me ready to bear any loss or pain rather than Thy displeasure, and to part with all things rather than Thy grace. May the remembrance of past sins and shortcomings make me more zealous for Thy glory and my neighbour's good, for Jesus Christ's sake.

> To Thee, my God, though late, at last I turn;
> Not for my sufferings, but my sins I mourn.
> For all my crimes Thy mercy I implore;
> And to those mercies Thou hast shown before,
> Add, Lord, Thy grace, that I may sin no more.

MONDAY AFTER THE FIRST SUNDAY IN LENT.

"When ye fast, be not as the hypocrites."—MATT. vi. 16.

CHRIST does not bid us fast. He takes for granted that we do. He tells us how to fast, lest we make what is good and useful worthless. He who fasts to gain man's praise, has what he seeks, and nothing more. He who denies himself only in self-chosen ways or outward things is of course unprofited. God blesses true fasting as a means of grace, an aid to prayer, a help to purity. It is a way of showing shame for sin and love for Him Whom our sins slew. It holds the flesh down, and strengthens the Spirit's rule over the whole man.

Holy men of old fasted. So did Christ Who knew no sin. God's book and God's Church teach the duty, and guide how to make good use of the means of grace. I cannot disobey and neglect without loss. Let me thankfully and earnestly use this, as well as other aids for Christian life. It is vain to fast from food, unless I deny self in other ways, and carefully abstain from sin. I must not fast for pride, or be ashamed to fast. I must not fast for form's sake, or spare myself, through fear of being formal. Doing all before "my Father, which seeth in secret," as part of my strife with sin, He will guide and bless me. He will strengthen me, through fasting, to drive back the tempter, to tame the flesh, and wean the heart from earth. My soul shall be set more free to rise in prayer, my will shall be braced to meet temptation. I shall have larger alms for the poor, and be able to give myself with readier heart to God.

O Lord Jesu Christ, Who didst fast for my sake, and hast taught me how to fast, enable me so to subdue my flesh that my spirit may be free to obey the leadings of Thy Holy Spirit, Who art with the Father and the same Spirit, one God.

> O Lord, instruct us to improve our fast
> By starving sin, and taking such repast
>   As may our faults control;
> That every man may revel at his door,
> Not in his parlour—banqueting the poor,
>   And among those, his soul.

TUESDAY AFTER THE FIRST SUNDAY IN LENT.

"Then was Jesus led up of the Spirit into the wilderness to be tempted of the devil."—MATT. iv. 1.

THE Holy Spirit came down on Christ at His baptism, and the Father's voice declared Him His "beloved Son." Then He was "driven" into the wilderness to meet Satan's onset. This was the next part of His work. He went willingly to do His Father's will. He bore temptation as one of us. He overcame for us. He showed how to meet it, and assured of His sympathy. We know not in what form the tempter came. We know that we can have the same strength in which Christ triumphed, and can triumph as He did.

I must not think temptation strange or hard. To bear it is a needful part of my work for God, and my following of Christ. I am likely to be most beset when I have the surest tokens of God's favour, and the best gifts of the Spirit. When I am rich, Satan will try to spoil me. When I am strong, God asks greater efforts against His foes and mine. I dare not seek temptation; but when it comes, must meet it with calm faith and lowly firmness. Satan can put sin before me; he cannot force my will to choose it. He may bring me into the wilderness; but he cannot make me alone even there. Christ is with me in all trials borne for Him. The same strength in which He drove back Satan is offered to me. Each temptation may be a sign that God has great work for me to do. It may lead me more close to God for needful grace, and bring me on towards full victory over evil.

O Lord Jesus Christ, Who for my sake didst suffer being tempted, be with me always, that I may bear my temptations as a child of God, led by the Holy Spirit. May each trial find me ready in faith and steadfastness, and leave me more strong and brave, to Thy glory, Who art with the Father and the Holy Ghost, one God.

> Why should I fear the darkest hour,
> Or tremble at the tempter's power?
> Jesus vouchsafes to be my tower.
> Against me earth and hell combine;
> But on my side is power divine:
> Jesus is all, and He is mine.

Wednesday after the First Sunday in Lent.

"Man shall not live by bread alone, but by every word that proceedeth out of the mouth of God."—Matt. iv. 4.

AFTER long fast and conflict, Christ hungered. Satan tempted Him to prove Himself the Son of God by making stones into bread for His need. Christ would not leave His place of dependence as man, but wait God's way and time to end His trial. The Spirit brought Him out, and God would not forsake Him. God had fed Israel, and would care for His life. Bread is but a means used by God to carry that by which He upholds life. Man's spiritual being lives by the Bread of God, which God gives in what form He wills.

God gave, and alone upholds my life. I can trust it to His keeping. I may not forsake in unbelief the place of obedience and the path of duty to which He calls me. Satan will tempt in times of weariness and care. "I must live—I must get on. These inborn desires must have what they crave for; God will not judge me hardly for following the nature He has given." So I may be led to snatch at what is not meant for me, and to lose the good things with which angels are on the way. Have I never tried to make bread of what God plainly made stones for me? Have I never left the way of patience, or truth, or duty, or honesty, to grasp some worldly good or pleasure? Bread not given by God poisons my true life. My soul does live by bread—by Christ the living Bread. Commonly my spiritual being is renewed in life by the use of means which unite me to Him. But I am not dependent on these, however holy, or on the form in which they are given. I am bound to means; but God is not. He can do what He wills as He wills.

Almighty God, by Whose Word alone man lives in soul and body, teach me to look upon all means as veils of Thy power, and in patient faith and obedience to glorify Thee, through Jesus Christ.

  Israel, on the heavenly bread,
   Fed, and died, in days of yore;
  But the souls upon Thee fed
  Never thirst or hunger more.

Thursday after the First Sunday in Lent.

"Thou shalt not tempt the Lord thy God."—Matt. iv. 7.

CHRIST was sure of His Father's care. Satan tried to make Him presume upon it by leaving the "ways" in which God was pledged to keep Him safely. Christ had used God's Word as a defence. Satan used it as a snare, misquoting and misapplying it. Christ met the assault with another written word. God's promises are not to be read apart from His commandments. Their comfort and blessing are for those who humbly keep in the "ways" which God's will appoints for them.

Do I tempt God, counting on the use of His power and goodness, whatever I do or fail to do? Am I quicker to hear promises than laws, to take life's blessings for granted, than to seek them as God teaches me? Have I rebelled, because God did not bring me harmless through risks run wantonly, and save me from the plain fruit of my own sloth, wilfulness, or folly? Have I gone needlessly in the way of temptation, trusting to be brought through it unscathed? Have I delayed repentance, and withstood grace, as if sure that God's patience would not tire? Have I even cast myself down into sin, trusting that God would stop me from falling too far, or lift me up unharmed? Have I tempted God, by looking for holiness, while neglecting means of grace, by expecting health without the good Physician's medicine, strength without the soul's needful food, victory without war, life without living union with life's source? How far am I now going in self-chosen ways, trusting to find myself at last where God's way leads?

Almighty God, may I never forget Thy Majesty, while thinking of Thy tenderness, or Thy laws, while rejoicing in Thy promises. Make me earnestly to use Thine appointed means of grace, and to seek for Thy free salvation in the path of faithful lowly obedience.

> If aught should tempt thy soul to stray
> From heavenly wisdom's narrow way,
> To fly the good I would pursue,
> Or do the sin I would not do;
> Still He, Who felt temptation's power,
> Shall guard me in that dangerous hour.

Friday after the First Sunday in Lent.

"Thou shalt worship the Lord thy God, and Him only shalt thou serve."—Matt. iv. 10.

IN some unknown way, Satan brought before the mind of Christ the power and glory of the world. All his influence over these as "prince of this world" he offered to yield for one act of homage. The bribe was surely real and great. How far, had it been possible, it promised an easier way to triumph, we know not. It was impossible; worship was God's right; what was His could not be given to another. God's work must be done in God's way. "Get thee hence, Satan," drove off the temptation and the tempter.

To sin is to withdraw from God His rightful worship, and to serve the evil one. I am tempted, as Christ was, though with smaller bribes. Some gain, some place of power, some joy can be mine, if I will only do one act of sin, and turn for a moment from God. Or the snare is more wily and dangerous. I feel held back from becoming, or from doing good. It seems as if falling once from uprightness would open up the way to the vantage ground I long for. But can I be sure of rising from the first fall? Can I count on the help of Him Whom I forsake? Will Satan free me when I begin his service? Will God accept me when I wish to return? Moreover, God will not have His cause helped by sin. For no end, however fair its promise, dare I swerve from loyalty to God. The more subtle the temptation, the more prompt and firm must be my "Get thee hence." Each "No" to the tempter is an act of homage to God.

Almighty God, Who dost claim the worship of all my heart and life, let no promise of earth's good or snare of Satan tempt me to give Thine honour to another. May I be always true to Thee and to Thy cause, in faith and obedience, through Jesus Christ.

> How know I, if Thou shouldst me raise,
> That I should then raise Thee?
> Perhaps great places and Thy praise
> Do not so well agree.

SATURDAY AFTER THE FIRST SUNDAY IN LENT.

"He that hath My commandments, and keepeth them, he it is that loveth Me."—JOHN xiv. 21.

CHRIST teaches His disciples how to prove their love, or learn their want of love. True love is no idle or selfish feeling; it is active and self-forgetting. It does not ask, "What can I gain, what joy can I have?" but, "What can I do and give, to show devotion?" Christ's commandments make known how to please Him. True love prompts obedience. Acceptable obedience is that which is inspired by love. Warm feelings are no sure sign of love, such as Christ asks. Those who mourn their coldness most, often have and show the truest love.

Christ himself imparts the love He asks for. His commandments answer the question of true love, that longs to know how to do His will and bring Him glory. By faith I lay hold on His gift; in obedience I show that I have it. I shall be asked not what I have felt, but how I have lived and worked for Christ. His love is given that I may, in the power of it, try to become myself, and make the world, pleasing to Him. I cannot love aright, for my faith is weak, and sin hides God, and my heart is easily drawn away. It will do no good to mourn idly. Let me be thankful that I have love enough to feel my want of love. Let me cleave to God with what love I have, and look to Him with what faith I have, and using what grace I have, try to serve Him. The wish to love God, and the effort to please Him, show love, and are a drawing near for more. The warmest feelings are to be doubted while I go on in one way of wilful sin, or neglect one known duty, or refuse one offered means of grace.

O Lord Jesus Christ, give me grace to love Thee, and to prove my love in a life lived for Thee, that I may grow fit to enjoy Thy love, where Thy loved ones love and please Thee perfectly.

> All mine is Thine; say but the word,
> Whate'er Thou willest shall be done;
> I know Thy love, all-gracious Lord;
> I know it seeks my good alone.

The Second Sunday in Lent.

"Thou shalt have no other gods before Me."—EXOD. xx. 3.

GOD made us, and upholds our being. He saved us from the power of evil. From Him comes all that makes life good and glad, and gives hope in looking beyond death. Gratitude, love, trust, obedience, hope, worship are His right, which He claims. We sin when we seek our good apart from Him, or look to His gifts instead of Him, or withhold the love and service which His love asks and He deigns to value. Much more do we sin when we love what He hates, and seek our good in that from which at great cost He saved us.

I am in the power of my Creator. To Him I owe all the good I have, or hope for. His love is jealous. He warns me not to deny Him the honour that is His due, or lose the blessing of continually claiming Him as my God. I may bow down to the world, live for the flesh, serve Satan more than my Maker and Saviour. I may give some evil or some good thing the place God claims for Himself. Friends whom God gives to cheer me must not be rivals to dethrone Him. The work and aims of life must not make me a worshipper of mammon, or a slave of care. God's blessing alone can make me prosper, and His is the glory of all I do well. Earthly pleasures must not tempt me to forget heavenly, and to wrong Him from Whom all pure joy comes. God asks from me outward worship and the service of a holy life, expressing the inward homage of faith, and hope, and love, and thankfulness. He asks me to remember His presence always, and to own Him as the source, the guide, and the end of my being.

Almighty God, may I never give my heart and life to sin, or let Thy gifts be rivals to Thyself. May I love, and worship, and serve Thee always with all my powers.

> Whatever passes as a cloud between
> The mental eye of faith and things unseen,
> Causing that brighter world to disappear,
> Or seem less lovely, and its hope less dear;
> This is our world, our idol, though it bear
> Affection's impress or devotion's air.

Monday after the Second Sunday in Lent.

"Thou shalt not make unto thee any graven image."
—Exod. xx. 4.

GOD makes Himself known, and teaches us how to worship Him. Men fashion a god, not with their hands, but with their heads—such a one as themselves—after their own thoughts. They bow down in superstitious dread or bold presumption before this image, dishonouring to the true God. They are guided by their own opinions or wishes, rather than God's Word; they worship wilfully as they think well, not obediently as God teaches. They trust in or are awed by vain superstitions, which set aside Him Who alone rules the course of things. God is a jealous God, judging those who will not think worthily of Him, and worship Him aright.

I am not tempted to worship idols of wood or stone, yet I may be an idolater. I may form in my mind a false and degrading idea of God; I may set up this image so as to have it before me while I worship, and live in its presence; I may have unworthy thoughts of God, so that He is to me hard, unjust, partial, or unloving, without what wins trust and love, or claims reverence. So I may blaspheme God, and the unreal object of worship which my own heart has invented may bring a blight on my religion. I may, again, have a faith which I am ashamed to own, in dreams, or signs, or charms, or the idle superstitions of men who trust not in God's providence! Be it my earnest prayer and aim to know God as He reveals Himself, and to worship Him as He wills. Growing knowledge will purify worship; in truer devotion knowledge will become clearer.

Almighty God, grant me a true and intelligent faith, a loving reverence, a lowly but sure trust, that all my life and worship may please and glorify Thee.

> O Lord, fill Thou mine inmost heart
> With worthy thoughts of Thee,
> That I may fear, where'er Thou art,
> And lowly bow the knee.
> For what though idols now no more
> Are carved in wood and stone,
> If meaner things our hearts adore,
> Which should be all Thine own?

Tuesday after the Second Sunday in Lent.

"The Lord will not hold him guiltless that taketh His name in vain."—Exod. xx. 7.

STRANGE, that man should dare to use lightly the name of the awful God! Strange, that man should wantonly insult his Divine Father and Saviour! should ask the All True to witness to what is false, or call on Him to bring down doom on others! The Lord will not hold such as do so guiltless. Neither will He clear those who talk idly, and profanely, and jestingly of holy things, or who speak to Him in prayer words they do not mean, or who by their lives bring scorn on His name and on religion.

God forbid that I should appeal to God with falsehood on my lips; or, with a heart full of malice, bid Him curse those who provoke me. But I need to be on my guard against sins as real, though less startling, to which those are most tempted who have much to do with the things of God. What if I become so accustomed to tread on holy ground that I lose my reverence, and draw nigh without fear or preparation! What if my worship lose life and purpose, and become a dead form, a calling on God by name to hear what comes from neither mind nor heart! What if I become able to profess to God, in hymns and prayers, feelings which I have not, and do not wish or aim to have! What if, by light talking about holy things, and light use of holy names and words, I encourage others to sin! What if the name of the Most High be blasphemed through my inconsistent life! I would not trifle with God's majesty, or wound His love, could I see Him. Let me live feeling His presence, and as if I beheld His glory.

O all holy God, my Father in heaven, give me a holy fear of Thee and a loving jealousy for the honour of Thy name, that I may please Thee in all my words and life.

> I have not feared Thee as I ought,
>   Nor bowed beneath Thine awful eye,
> Nor guarded deed, and word, and thought,
>   Remembering that God was nigh.
> Lord, give me faith to know Thee near,
> And grant the grace of holy fear.

WEDNESDAY AFTER THE SECOND SUNDAY IN LENT.

"*Remember the Sabbath Day, to keep it holy.*"—EXOD. xx. 8.

ALL our days are God's. In each we are bound to serve and praise Him. In one out of seven He calls us from earth's work and care to refresh ourselves with holy rest and pleasures. So He prepares us for the calm of the blest. So He provides a breathing time in life's hurry, that tired mind and body may regain their tone. So He invites us to depart for a while, and be more alone with Christ, that we may gain new grace to meet temptation, and to do our Father's will.

My Maker knows my needs of soul, and mind, and body. To do this world's work well, I must, at times, relieve the strain of care and toil. My religion cannot thrive without quiet days for thought and prayer away from the world's rush. The law—"six days shalt thou labour"—binds me to do my part amongst honest workers. I break God's commandment by not working on six days, as really as by working on the seventh. One day out of seven is mine, that I may grow more holy while I hallow it, and be strengthened to live holily all my days. On the day of Christ's rising from the dead I am called to shake off the dust of earthly things, and rise to newness of life. On the day of the Holy Spirit's coming, I am called to use diligently the means of grace which He makes real, that I may grow into closer union with my Saviour. On all seven days I must remember God; on the Lord's Day I must forget the world.

Almighty God, Who givest me all my days for Thy service, enable me so to profit by those days which Thou dost set apart from worldly use, that my soul, and mind, and body may be refreshed and strengthened to work better for Thy glory, through Jesus Christ.

> Thou art a cooling fountain
> In life's dry dreary sand;
> From Thee, like Pisgah's mountain,
> We view our promised land;
> A day of sweet refection,
> A day of holy love,
> A day of resurrection
> From earth to things above.

Thursday after the Second Sunday in Lent.
"Honour thy father and thy mother."—Exod. xx. 12.

SO speaks the "first commandment with promise." The apostle bids us "honour all men" whom God has made in His likeness, and has redeemed. Those through whom God gave us being, and to whose care He committed us, have a special claim. So have those whom our parents trust to act for them. So have those who are set over us to guide our souls, or to rule us as citizens. A true, wise, grateful heart will give honour gladly, and seek to prove by deeds that it is no idle feeling. Those whose position claims honour are bound to prove themselves, in life and character, worthy of it.

First, among "neighbours," to whom I owe love and duty, are my father and mother. Nature and reason tell me what claims they have. God has shown in many ways how jealously He guards their rights. He requires me, as I would have His blessing, to love and obey them; to treat them with thoughtful respect in word, and manner, and deed; to help them; and, when they have departed, to honour their memories. Not for me to dwell on their failings, and so excuse mine, but to think of the place God gave them, and the duty He lays on me. Those who watch for my soul as those who must give account, those who rule me as a member of the state, have their authority from heaven. Let me beware of the pride and self-will of those who despise government and shake off control, grieving God and good men, and going in Satan's way to Satan's doom. If I am a parent or ruler, be it my care so to do my duty as to lead those under me to do theirs with glad will.

Almighty Father, give me grace for Thy sake to render due honour to all those under whose rule and care I am placed by Thy providence, that I may receive Thy promise of length of days for ever and ever.

> While subject to His mother, and while ruled
>   By human laws, Christ did His Father's will;
> Like Him may I on earth be trained and schooled,
>   A heavenly Father's purpose to fulfil.
> In those who rule me is God's power made known;
> In those who love me is God's kindness shown.

Friday after the Second Sunday in Lent.

"Thou shalt not kill."—Exod. xx. 13.

GOD'S laws reach farther than man sees. They check thought and feeling as well as act. We are bound to love all men. He who lets hatred take love's place is a murderer of his own soul; he hath not eternal life abiding in Him. He who in his heart cherishes malice is often more truly a murderer before God than he who in sudden anger takes life. To shorten one's own life, or that of others, through neglect or greed, is murder. To tempt souls by scoffs or by example, is to work for him who is a "murderer from the beginning."

Have I nursed anger against others, wished them evil, been glad when evil came? Have I harmed others in life or character through ill-will or neglect? God calls me a murderer. Have I allowed those dependent on me to lose health and shorten life through my greed or culpable want of thought? Their Father, Who careth for the sparrows, holds me answerable. Have I led souls to risk the loss of eternal life, and infected them with deadly sin? Who will free me from the guilt of blood? Who will undo what I have done, and bring these souls again into union with God's life, lest they cry to heaven against me? My own life is a trust. Have I disobeyed known laws of health, and wilfully cut short my years, and lessened their usefulness? Only I myself can kill my soul. If it die, I am the murderer, destroying that which owed its life to Christ's death. May God, Who is Love and is eternal Life, abide in me. So I shall live indeed, and, loving others, shall help their life of body and of soul.

Almighty, everliving God, in Whom all live, grant me to cherish Thy life in my soul, and to labour to make others blessed in union with Thy life, and in the enjoyment of Thy love, through Jesus Christ.

> Give the love to anger slow,
> Fearing seeds of strife to sow,
> Never helping strife to grow.
> Loving man and loving Thee,
> May we here Thy children be,
> And prepare Thy face to see.

SATURDAY AFTER THE SECOND SUNDAY IN LENT.

"Abstain from fleshly lusts, which war against the soul."
—1 PET. ii. 11.

OUR whole nature—body, soul, and spirit—is "for the Lord." The Holy Ghost dwells in us to make us worthy of God. We are "members of Christ," bound to live as He lived, by the power of Him "living in us." God seeks to draw our whole nature up towards high and holy things, till we become all pure in thought, and wish, and life. But we may let our lower nature have its way till the flesh drags the spirit down to its low level, till all taste for pure joys and holy work is gone, till the Holy Spirit is quenched, and we die from Christ.

The choice is continually before me, to rise or sink, to let my flesh rule, or to rule it. My body does not reason; it only has its blind desires. The higher part of me, which is akin to God, must rein and guide it, with God's help. Shall I indulge the greedy cravings of my body, till it masters and enslaves me? Shall I open my mind to what grieves the Holy Spirit, and allow thoughts of evil to dwell there under the eye of the all holy One? Shall I seek delights which stain and shame, while they dull the taste for those which refine and enlarge the mind, and ennoble the whole being? Shall I yield to sloth, or train myself to brave healthy work for God and man? Shall I leave my will to weaken in idleness, or brace it to be firm for myself and God? Shall I "defile the temple of God," or cherish the Divine hallowing Presence, so that only what is high and pure may find place in me?

Almighty and all holy God, give me grace to shrink from all that might grieve the Holy Spirit, and make me unfit to be His habitation. Enable me, with pure heart, and mind, and body, to serve and glorify Thee, through Jesus Christ.

> We will master the flesh, and its longings restrain,
> We will not be the bondslaves of sin;
> The pure Spirit of God in our nature shall reign,
> And our spirits their triumph shall win.

The Third Sunday in Lent.

"Be ye therefore followers of God, as dear children."—Eph. v. 1.

TO God's love we owe our place as His children, made after His likeness. We owe our place in His spiritual family, the Church, to the redeeming love which gave us the adoption of sons through Jesus Christ. We cannot imitate God in His wisdom, power, or glory. We can imitate Him in love. The pattern of Christ, Who shows us God, is before us, that we may copy it. We can show Christ, Who is God, living in us. He calls us to walk in His steps. He gives the power to live like Him, and become like Him.

I am dear to God as His child. God's love gave me this great glory. Countless proofs show His fatherly care. I am beloved still, in spite of all unworthiness. There is nothing in me of my own to make me dear to the great and holy God. All His love is free, forgiving, forbearing in its longing to do me good. "Therefore," because of this, I am commanded to "imitate" God. "Therefore" I am able to do so. God says, "Let us make this one in our own image." By the power of the blessed Trinity I can be as Christ was in the world. I can bring the love of God to those who, like myself, are His "dear children." I can prove myself alive to the truth that God indeed loves me, and grow more what one loved of a Divine Father ought to be. The harder the trial to my love, and the more unworthy those seem to whom I show it, the more does the power of God aid and possess me, and the more closely do I imitate the love with which God in Christ has loved me.

Almighty Father, to Whose love I owe all good now, and all hope for ever, give me grace to remember my great calling, and to be a follower of Him Who showed in His life and work the love of God to me.

> O Love, who formedst me to wear
>   The image of Thy Godhead here;
> Who soughtest me with tender care
>   Through all my wanderings wild and drear;
> O Lord, I give myself to Thee,
> Thine ever, only Thine to be.

MONDAY AFTER THE THIRD SUNDAY IN LENT.
"Thou shalt not steal."—EXOD. xx. 15.

GOD'S law shields man's goods. God will punish for wrong done. Man's law does not reach all thieves; God's law does. The worst thieves are not those whom the world finds out. The worst often blind themselves to their sin. He who holds what he knows he has gained unfairly or dishonestly, makes his life one long theft. The spoil of God or of the poor brings a sure curse. That gain for which a man dare not thank God, and in the use of which he dare not ask God's blessing, he ought to be afraid to keep.

I may not be tempted as some are; but am I quite clear from sin against this law? Have I never gained unfairly, or saved myself from losing, by what the world calls sharp practice? Do I keep nothing now that is not mine by right? Have I wasted or misused time that I was paid for, or done badly what I undertook to do well? Have I raised the price of what I sold, or lowered the price of what I bought, by false statements? Have I bought when I was not sure of being able to pay? Have I caused loss to others through carelessness or neglect? Have I taken unfair advantage of the needy, or those in my power? Have I become dependent and a burden on others, through my faults or idleness? Have I robbed God of His due by spending too much on self, or failed to provide for those dependent on me? Have I robbed the State by smuggling, or by withholding taxes? I must not judge myself in this matter by the world's standard. I cannot well err in ever jealous care to be honourable and honest in my own eyes and in God's.

Almighty God, Without whose blessing nothing profits, grant me to remember Thee always, and never to seek gain at the cost of my honour and Thy favour, for Jesus Christ's sake.

> Far better to lose all things than to win
> The wealth of empires at the cost of sin;
> I will not keep what tells of wrong and shame,
> Or gain by means that God and conscience blame.
> I cannot part from Christ, my heavenward Guide,
> Or risk the loss of treasures that abide.

TUESDAY AFTER THE THIRD SUNDAY IN LENT.

"A false witness that speaketh lies, and he that soweth discord among brethren."—PROV. vi. 19.

SUCH sinners, the Bible says, "God hates." How few are not more or less in the list! The word condemns him who, by a false oath, harms his neighbour; but much of the common talk of the world is mere false witness. What would be left of the conversation of many, were it cleared of slander, scandal, backbiting, charges made on hearsay or suspicion, unfair, groundless, needless imputation of low or bad motive? By this sin the speaker, the hearer, and the person spoken of are harmed. As the receiver is as bad as the thief, so the listener is as bad as the slanderer.

I would not falsely swear away my neighbour's life, or liberty, or goods. But have I never done any thing to rob him of good name, or friends, or peace of mind, or some other prized possession, by reckless or malicious talk? Have I never dealt with my neighbour's character as I would think it most base in him to deal with mine? Have I hinted evil, and laughed at or welcomed what told against him? Have I, after speaking hardly or unfairly, failed in the honour to try to make amends? I ought to be unwilling and sorry to know of others' sin. I ought to be glad to be able to think well of all. If an evil tale reach me, it may not be true. If it be not all false, it may not be all true, or may admit of explanation. If I repeat as true what I am not sure is true, I am a false witness. It is seldom my duty to repeat true tales against others. Before I speak, I ought to be quite sure that silence is failure in duty.

Almighty and most merciful God, Who hast warned me that the "false witness shall not go unpunished," grant that I may be always unready to hear or repeat evil of my neighbour, but may love him as myself.

> Truthful Spirit, dwell with me,
> I myself would truthful be;
> And with wisdom, kind and clear,
> Let Thy life in mine appear;
> And with actions brotherly
> Show forth Thy sincerity.

WEDNESDAY AFTER THE THIRD SUNDAY IN LENT.

"Thou shalt not covet."—EXOD. xx. 17.

GOD commands industry and thrift. He warns against love of money, which opens the way to manifold temptation and sorrow. Some men "will be rich," and make money-getting or money-keeping life's great aim. Some long for what others have, instead of working to win for themselves. Some repine idly, instead of doing their duty when they can, and so using the best means to rise to higher place. The rich are tempted to trust in their wealth, and to use it selfishly, neglecting the poor. The poor may sin as really by slothful discontent and envy, which are other forms of the same sin.

God knows what is best for me, and wills it. My part is to use well the powers and means I have, trusting in God's help. If I succeed, let me employ what I gain thankfully, not in sin or self-indulgence, but so as to help others, and make my treasure in heaven greater. If I cannot make my lot to my mind, let me make up my mind, through God's grace, to bear my lot. I can be rich in faith, and heir of wealth in heaven. My lowly place may be my own fault; let me be humble, and not fret under the heavier task I have laid on myself. It is sin and folly to grudge my neighbour his well-being. It spoils the joy I might have with even my lesser means of joy. It makes me poor towards God, and no richer among men. If I am covetous in heart, I shut out the "love of the Father." I lay myself open to be tempted to gain my desires sinfully, to part with my peace of conscience, to force myself against God's will among cares, and to sell heaven for what cannot make earth happy.

Almighty God, Who alone canst make me happy in my work in life, save me from discontent and avarice, give me diligence and faith, through Jesus·Christ, Who became poor to make me rich.

All earthly joy shall fail at last, all earthly love grow cold,
Save loves by that one love made fast to Jesus and His fold.
One aim there is of endless worth, one sole sufficient love,
To do Thy will, my God, on earth, and reign with Thee above.

Thursday after the Third Sunday in Lent.

"He that is not with Me is against Me; and he that gathereth not with Me scattereth."—Luke xi. 23.

THE war between good and evil is real. Christ calls every one to take His side openly, firmly, actively. He will have no idlers or cowards. He disowns those who will not own Him. None can be neutral: those who do not help, hinder. Those who do not work and fight with Christ to bring in souls and advance His cause are "scatterers," whom He ranks among the foes "against Him." The choice is plainly set before us. On one side is the Saviour; on the other side is the enemy from whose power He died to save us.

Dreadful to be against Christ—the Almighty and All Kind—my best Friend, my one hope! Dreadful to hinder and undo His work, to make His love and cross in vain! Dreadful to turn His very love for souls against me! Can this be possibly my state! If I am not "with Him," it is. He tell me how to judge whether I am truly on His side, or apart from and opposed to Him. Decency in outward life is not enough. I may not think to have the joys and profits of religion without wielding Christian armour, and bearing a cross. I cannot hope to use Christ's grace secretly and selfishly for my own private good, while I hold aloof from the toil and danger of His war in behalf of other souls. I must stand out apart from the evil of the world, and boldly take my stand for Christ. I must aid in His great work of gathering in the straying and the lost. I must do this "with Him," in His way, trusting in His help. If I do not, He looks on me as "against Him"—"scattering," undoing His work. What will the end be?

Almighty God, give me grace to be earnest and decided in my Saviour's cause, and with whole-hearted brave devotion, to labour with Him for the triumph of His love.

A charge to keep I have, a God to glorify,
A never-dying soul to save, and fit it for the sky.
To serve the present age, my calling to fulfil;
O may it all my powers engage to do my Master's will.

FRIDAY AFTER THE THIRD SUNDAY IN LENT.
"Empty, swept, and garnished."—MATT. xii. 44.

THE evil spirit was gone out. The man was freed from the bad force that tormented him. His life was swept from the gross sin that shamed it. It was garnished with deeds that won praise. But the house was "empty." No Divine Presence had been called in to rule the man. The heart, withdrawn from sin, was not given to God. The powers were not yielded to His service. So the evil spirit could still speak of him as "my house," to which he might at will return. He found him lulled into false peace and off his guard. He entered in with sevenfold power, and the man yielded in despair.

I am not free when one besetting sin is mastered. I am not pure because my outward life is changed. I am not strong because all seems well to me. I may be empty of that Presence which alone can strengthen me against my strong foes. The evil one may seem to leave me for a while, that he may get me more fully into his power. A false peace, while I am without God, lays me more open to the tempter. Then the shame and discouragement of falling make the after-struggle with sin harder; my state is worse than before. If I would be safe, my whole being must be surrendered to be possessed by God, so that no room be left for evil. The love, the will, all the powers must be devoted to God's service. His purity must sweep before it my uncleanness. His strength must guard me from sin, and uphold me lest I fall. My life must show the beauty of what His indwelling Presence inspires.

Almighty God, Who hast created and redeemed me for Thyself, come by Thy Holy Spirit and fill me with Thy Presence, that evil may be cast out and have no room to return, that my life may be garnished with works done in Thy strength, and that in my last state I may bear the image of my Saviour.

> O that the Comforter would come,
>   Nor visit as a transient guest,
> But find in me His constant home,
>   And keep possession of my breast;
> And make my soul His loved abode,
> The temple of indwelling God.

SATURDAY AFTER THE THIRD SUNDAY IN LENT.

"*Let us not be weary in well-doing: for in due season we shall reap, if we faint not.*"—GAL. vi. 9.

TO begin well, is easy. To go on to the good end tries faith, and courage, and patience, and strength of will. Men are tempted to tire when, day after day, they must go on in the same toil, and the season of rest and joy seems still far off. Doubts come that all is vain, and heart and will faint. God forewarns of this. He promises to bless the toil of those who persevere. Let man wait on God in well-doing. When the due season comes, God will show His work and give the harvest.

Well-thinking, well-feeling, and well-saying will not win a harvest for the husbandman, nor will they win a spiritual harvest for me. God calls me to well-doing; He gives strength for it, and promises that it shall not be fruitless. Now is the time to plough, and cleanse, and plant, and seek Heaven's blessing. God does not tell me the time of reaping, but He knows, and I may look forward in sure hope. Only let me not be weary, as if my faith in God's true word failed. Let me not faint as if I doubted the worth of God's reward, or the rightness of the way by which He leads me to it. Is my strife with sin hard? Is my growth in holiness slow? Do my prayers seem unheard? Still the effort I make in God's strength against discouragement is part of the well-doing to which I am called. It will help growth and ripening. When the due season comes, I shall see the fruit of all. The grace and power given to enable me to persevere shall be part of my harvest for ever. My trials shall train me for perfect well-doing, where none faint or weary.

O Lord, Who dost promise that they who sow in righteousness shall reap in mercy, grant me to be diligent in well-doing, never fainting or being weary, but looking forward to that good time when I may enjoy the fruit of Thy work in me and by me, through Jesus Christ, my Saviour.

I long for Thee, my God! I wait upon Thee now,
I tarry for Thy leisure; give me what I need—
A patient loving heart, quite true to Thee,
One that will never weary in its work for Thee;
So my soul longs for Thee.

The Fourth Sunday in Lent.

"*If any man will come after Me, let him deny himself, and take up his cross daily, and follow Me.*"—LUKE ix. 23.

WE may will to follow Christ, or not. All who follow must deny self, and bear a cross. The cross must not be self-chosen. The one given must be taken up, and borne for Christ's sake, and in order to follow Him. It must be lifted with an ever new willingness, by the higher better self, which is one with Christ, that the old self may be weakened, and at last die. Daily the temptation to leave it and Christ has to be denied; the call to grasp it tighter, and press on more firmly, has to be obeyed.

My old self is evil and ease-loving. It has no will to go where Christ leads. All through life I shall feel in me what needs to be forced down and held down as sinful. Need of self-denial proves my sinfulness. In much not in itself wrong, my wishes must be checked, that higher wishes may be free to bring me after Christ. This hard sore struggle with evil is part of my cross. Daily I must lift its weight and go forward. Well for me to feel temptation a sorrow, and know from my pain that I am bearing up against its pressure. In the common sorrows of life I can make my patient self-surrender a following of Christ. When I suffer for righteousness' sake, I can welcome the pain for Christ's sake, feeling that so my cross is made more like His. My cross is the best for me. I dare not please self in choosing my cross. God gives me strength to bear my own, not another. Daily grace will come for my daily effort. Christ bore His cross for me, and now bears mine with me. He will lift off my cross when it has done its work, and the old evil self which makes me unlike Him is dead.

O Lord Jesu Christ, draw me by Thy love that I may deny self, and, taking up my cross daily, may go after Thee, till I am like Thee, and with Thee where Thou art.

  Take up thy cross and follow Christ,
   Nor think till death to lay it down;
  For only he who bears the cross
   May hope to wear the glorious crown.

MONDAY AFTER THE FOURTH SUNDAY IN LENT.

"*As Moses lifted up the serpent in the wilderness, even so must the Son of man be lifted up.*"—JOHN iii. 14.

ISRAEL'S sin brought suffering. Suffering led to repentance. Repentance found mercy. By God's command, Moses set up a harmless image of that which slew the people. It was a witness to them of their sin, and of God's promise. The dying looked to it, and God healed them. Before a world which is the prey of the spiritual serpent the Son of man is lifted up, in the likeness of sinful flesh, but sinless. Perishing man is bidden to see in Him what condemns his sin, but assures of mercy. There is life for dying souls that in faith look to the Crucified.

The venom of sin is in my nature, but I am not left to perish. My fear may be calmed, my hurts healed, my life, though fast failing, may be made eternal in me. To the cross and Christ crucified I am pointed. As healing was for every Israelite that looked, so the power of the lifted-up Son of man is for whosoever believes. That death destroys death, that seeming triumph of sin is victory over it. The power of the Divine Saviour is there, ever going forth. Unbelief shuts it off. Faith opens a way for it to save me. Thus God wills to give me healing. I ask not how: enough for me that the work of death in me is stayed, and life and death are mine. I believe in Christ, resting my whole hope and trust on Him. As faith grows clearer, I see more what tells of my great need and sin, and of the love that found a remedy. I turn always to the cross; I live looking to it; for, alas, I am ever in danger of being wounded afresh, and I stand in need of ever new healing.

Almighty God, grant me to feel my sin and danger, and so to believe in Thy Son Jesus Christ, that through Him I may have eternal life.

> Sweet the moments, rich in blessing,
> Which before the cross I spend;
> Life, and health, and peace possessing
> From the sinner's dying Friend.

Tuesday after the Fourth Sunday in Lent.

"Lord, dost Thou wash my feet?"—John xiii. 6.

THE Master was as the lowest slave. He knelt to wash the feet of Judas and of the rest, whose hearts He knew. Thus He taught them how Divine love will stoop, and in what spirit they should act to one another. He showed, too, in a mystery, how He is always among His people as one that serveth, and how our least defilements cost our careful Saviour fresh humiliation. Only He can wash away the stains we gather in walking through life. Only His cleansing touch can restore the purity we are ever losing.

How lowly should I be, who owe all to my Lord's humiliation! Had He not taken servant form, and touched me with His own pure nature, I had lain helpless in the sin of my birth. Were He not at hand now with patient love, waiting to make me clean, evil would soon gather thickly over my soul. He washed me when I was "born of water and the Spirit." He washes away the defilement of my daily sins. My head may be lifted towards heaven, my will may be sincere, my love may be true, my hands may be kept clean and be active in holy work, yet I must walk on the earth even in going after Christ and working for Him. The lower nature will often need cleansing, even in the most faithful. With what lowly care should I walk through this staining world, lest I soil what He has cleansed, and need a new humbling of my Lord! What shame to ask Him to stoop, and remove the marks of carelessness and of wilful guilt! How readily should I bow my pride to keep others from sin, or help them to yield to the Saviour's hands! What sin, to stain those for whom He died, and undo His work in them.

O Lord, teach me in lowly love to serve my brethren, make me watchful lest I fall, wash away what stains me in passing through this evil world, and be my Saviour to the end.

> The while I fain would tread the heavenly way,
> Evil is less with me day by day;
> Yet on mine ears the gracious tidings fall—
> Repent, confess, thou shalt be loosed from all.

WEDNESDAY AFTER THE FOURTH SUNDAY IN LENT.
" And the Lord turned, and looked upon Peter. And Peter remembered the word of the Lord."—LUKE xxii. 61.

THE brave-hearted St. Peter proved a coward. He who had felt ready to die rather than in any way deny the Lord he loved, said with oaths that he did not know Him. Christ turned to the fallen disciple. That sad, searching, gentle look reminded St. Peter of his boasts, of the unheeded warnings, the threefold fall. Now shamed and crushed in his known weakness, he was stronger than when he thought no power could move him. Self trustful, he had courted danger, and been found wanting. His fall taught him in what strength alone he could stand firm.

I do not know or love my Lord as St. Peter did. I am not as brave as he. I have more need than he to doubt myself, and to hold fast humbly to the one help that can keep me true. I know not what new form or might of trial any day may bring against me. I know not my weakness or my strength till I am proved. Alas, how often have I belied before the world vows of faithfulness made secretly with Christ, or openly before the Church! How often have I seemed, and been content to seem, like one who knew not Christ, and cared not for His sorrows! How often have I in act, and almost in words, disowned my Lord, and feared or been ashamed to be numbered among His followers, and share His reproach! How often have warnings been unheeded, and His sad appealing eyes been turned on me in vain! Blessed be the love that does not cast me off! Oh, for grace to feel my baseness, and to mourn, like St. Peter, that like him I may be lifted up.

O Lord Jesus Christ, make me strong in the strength that comes through self-distrust and faith in Thee. Look on me always, and keep me true and brave. If I fall, look on me and restore me to live for Thee.

> Thrice was he put to shame,
> Thrice did the dauntless fall;
> But, oh, that look that came
> From out the judgment-hall.
> It pierced and broke the spell-bound heart,
> And foiled the tempter's sifting art.

THURSDAY AFTER THE FOURTH SUNDAY IN LENT.

"*Friend, wherefore art thou come?*"—MATT. xxvi. 50.

JUDAS drew near with the old words of greeting, and the sign of friendship. But thus he marked Christ to His foes. Did he indeed foresee Christ's death? Or did he mean to force the proof of the Lord's power, hoping to hide his sin, and keep his part in the kingdom? Or had greed grown so strong in him that he sought his mean ends at all risk? He shrank not before his Master's calm, searching eye. The gentle appeal, reminding of old friendship, spoke to a hardened heart.

A true disciple will wait his Master's time. My sin can never help Christ's cause; it can but insult Him, and part me from Him. What a dread power of wronging Christ the knowledge of Him gives! I can betray Him, as only a disciple can. What if I come where He is, bringing with me as my friends my sins, which are His foes! What if I seek Him with low unworthy aims! What if I am the hireling of bad lusts while I hail Him Master, and my selfish heart is the world's while I make show of love to Him! Did He meet me with the question, "Wherefore art thou come?" what would my honest answer often be? When I draw near to touch Him, and my soul seeks His sacramental presence, am I careful enough lest my sin give Him to the cross afresh? One sin harboured may render a long life with Christ worse than fruitless. Let me be warned by Judas, who fell from such a height to such a depth. Let me learn from the Lord's gentleness, even with him, what patient love my treason wrongs.

O Lord Jesus Christ, let no bribe of the world or the flesh, no temptation of pride or impatience make me false to Thee. Give me carefulness, lest I betray Thee or Thy cause, Who art my Saviour and my God.

  The traitor with his band draws near,
  Unshamed by love, unawed by fear,
   And with a kiss betrays.
  So false disciples now draw nigh
  And give their Lord again to die,
   While bringing prayer and praise.

FRIDAY AFTER THE FOURTH SUNDAY IN LENT.
"Let this mind be in you, which was also in Christ Jesus."
—PHIL. ii. 5.

THE mind of Christ was shown in humbling Himself to work God's will for others' good. One with God, God's acknowledged equal in power and glory, He took on Him our weak and lowly nature. He was made like man in all but sin, subject to the same conditions of life, bound to the same rule and toil. He obeyed the Divine will, the call of love, the "mind" that led Him down the path of humiliation, to serve men. The "mind" that brought the Son of God from heaven guided the Man Christ Jesus till human nature was in Him glorified as the "form of God" in heaven.

What higher glory than to be like-minded with Christ! To humble myself in His Spirit, and after His example, is to be exalted. I have not what Christ had to "empty" away. I cannot go from His height or reach His depth, or do all He did. But I can have His Spirit, and show an aim like His in my common daily life. I can learn from His words and example, and gain from Him the will and power to follow Him. Knowing what He was and did, how can I be proud, and hard, and grasping, jealous for my own dignity or rights, wrapped up in self? How can I even make my own soul's interest and joy my one selfish care? When I do violence to my love of self to serve others, my outward humiliation veils a nature growing Christ-like. When I generously seek the good of needing souls and God's glory, I help my own soul best. Christ's human nature rose towards its perfection, as the mind that was in Him led Him on the way of the cross. He wills to bring me by a like lowly path to the same glorious end.

Almighty God, grant that I may always show in me the mind that was in Christ Jesus, and, humbling myself to do Thy will and serve my brethren, after His example, may in Thy time be exalted, through His merits.

> I long to be like Jesus,
>   Meek, loving, lowly, mild;
> I long to be like Jesus,
>   The Father's holy child.

SATURDAY AFTER THE FOURTH SUNDAY IN LENT.

"*Weep not for Me, but weep for yourselves, and for your children.*"—LUKE xxiii. 28.

THE daughters of Jerusalem bewailed Christ as He went to His death. They had known Him as the healer of sick hearts and bodies; the friend of the poor, and of little children. Their tender womanly feeling was moved as they saw Him, faint with outrage, stagger on under His cross. He did not try to check their tears, but to show them why they ought to weep. He would have them mourn, not for, but with Him. He grieved not for Himself, but for the sin of the world, and the surely coming woe. He grieved for those who refused to know the things that belonged to their peace.

The sufferings of Christ appeal to the emotions. But my feelings may be stirred while my conscience sleeps, and I live on in sin. I dare not grieve for Christ as for a man in pain; He is far above my compassion. He goes to the cross as a conqueror, forcing His way through all to triumph. I do well to lament as I seek to realise His sorrows. But He asks me to feel with what is in His heart—to grieve for the world's sin and my own, and to dread the doom of that sin which He bears for me. While I follow with trembling heart the way of the cross, Christ teaches me of His compassion. He shows how He sees my sin, and dreads for me the woes that threaten to fall. Let His sorrow for me lead me to search and know myself; and let my sorrow for my sin lead me to learn His love, and lay hold on His salvation. Let me try to change His sorrow for others into joy, by leading them to learn from Christ the meaning of the cross.

Almighty God, grant that the sorrows of my Saviour may move me to mourn for my sin, to know its awfulness and danger, and to value the love of Him Who bore the cross to save me.

Thou didst not, loving as Thou art,
 Shrink from the cursèd tree;
Thy grief was for the loveless heart
 Of sinners such as me.

Passion Sunday.

"Father, forgive them; for they know not what they do."
—LUKE xxiii. 34.

CHRIST is being slain, a willing sacrifice for man's sin. He prays as man, forgiving and loving, and as the Son of God, one in will with the Father. He prays aloud for our consolation. He asks pardon for His murderers, as if they, not He, needed help. His prayer is, that they may know what they do, and in penitence and faith be forgiven. Not only the soldiers and the Jews, but all for whom He dies, cause His death, and share His intercession. There is hope in this prayer for all who are brought to see, in Christ's death, the work of their sin and His work for them.

My sins did their part in crucifying my Saviour. Alas, for my sins when I knew I sinned, and for my sins of willing ignorance! Alas, for sins which old habits of sin had made me unable to feel! Can I take hope from Christ's prayer? Yes; it looked back to man's first sin, and on to all that ever should be done. He knew what I would be—so dull of heart, so prone to sin, so heedless of His love and sorrow. Yet He died for me, and in this prayer pleaded that His death might win my pardon. Surely I know not what I do when I put such love to pain. Oh, that I might know what sin means, and be led to pray for my forgiveness, and plead the death upon the cross with earnestness like Christ's! Oh, to have more of the Spirit of Christ in loving those who wrong me, and in not sparing self to do them good! Oh, for a larger heart in judging others, and more hope and faith in praying and working for them!

O Lord Jesus Christ, Who didst pray for those who slew Thee, give me Thy Spirit, and grant that through Thy sacrifice and intercession my sins may be pardoned, and my nature changed.

> No pained reproaches gave He to them that shed His blood,
> But prayer and tenderest pity, large as the love of God.
> O depth of sweet compassion! O love divine and true!
> Save Thou the souls that slight Thee, and know not what
>   they do.

Monday in Passion Week.

"To-day shalt thou be with Me in Paradise."—Luke xxiii. 43.

THE virtue that went out of Christ softened and changed the dying robber's heart. He pleaded with his old comrade to "fear God." He owned that his death was but his sin's due, and that Christ had done no wrong. Then in humble faith and hope he turned to Christ. He called Him Lord, and spoke of the kingdom to which He should pass from the cross, "in" which He should come. He asked as his one lowly prayer to be only "remembered." Christ had watched his heart and led it on. He met him with more than he dreamed of.

Blessed is the cross that brings and holds me close to Christ. Only on a cross, perhaps, can I learn to know aright my sin and my Saviour. Well to be with Him in pain, if only thus I can be lifted above earth now, and pass to be with Him in the place of resting souls. Not for me to upbraid Him, and press Him to show His power in setting me free. Let me fear God, and own my worst sufferings to be what my deeds deserve. Christ is near, knowing the pain of my cross, having felt His own. Let me look to His cross from mine, and in lowly faith ask to be in His mind and heart always. He is the same as He ever was, ready to save all who will own their unworthiness, and cast themselves upon His mercy. He will make my sorrow seem light, and but for a moment. He will point me to Paradise where I may be without sin, without sorrow, and with Him.

O Lord Jesus Christ, be near me in my sorrows, and let the virtue of Thy cross and passion change and cheer me. Speak to my soul, and grant me, even while on my cross, a foretaste of the peace which Thou dost give in Paradise with Thee.

> Let but the cross on which I bleed
> Stand, Jesu, near to Thine;
> Then, in my sorest hour of need,
> Thy heart shall speak to mine.
> My cross shall keep me near to Thee,
> While evil in me dies;
> The cross at last shall set me free
> To pass to Paradise.

TUESDAY IN PASSION WEEK.

"Woman, behold thy son! . . . Behold thy mother!"
—JOHN xix. 26, 27.

THE Son of God comes close to us, when as Son of Man He speaks out of His man's heart to mother and friend. In His hour of great conflict He cares for those who love Him, and have been nearest to Him. He is to be no more with them in the old way. Till He calls them to His Father's house, He gives them into one another's keeping. Thus He teaches His people to help one another, and care for those who are His care. The household of faith is the family of Jesus. He has said, "He that doeth the will of My Father, the same is my brother, and sister, and mother."

The Lord Jesus is out of sight, and I am left in a world where He is little known. Faith and love can prize His legacy of blessing and of holy work, and can rejoice in His spiritual nearness. High on heaven's throne as He is, He cares for all that soothes my heart-wounds, and helps my joy. He hallows the common ties of kindred and affection. He wills to make each Christian home like that which, in obedience to Him, St. Mary and St. John shared. He wills to bind those who love Him in holy fellowship. He bids me be His voice and hand to make His love known and felt. I need not be lonely; I may be numbered among those whom Christ calls "brother, sister, mother." I need not feel my life aimless; I have holy work given me; I can do my part where God places me to lead others to do God's will, and so become the spiritual kindred of my Saviour. I can, in His name and for His sake, care for those who love Jesus and whom Jesus loves.

O Lord Jesus Christ, make me faithful even though Thy cause seem lost. Enable me to make known Thy love to others, and to care for Thy sorrowing ones for Thy sake. So may I do the will of Thy Father, and be a disciple such as Thou lovest.

> May we in Thy sorrows share, and for Thee all peril dare,
> And enjoy Thy tender care.
> May we all Thy loved ones be, all one holy family,
> Loving for the love of Thee.

WEDNESDAY IN PASSION WEEK.

"My God, My God, why hast Thou forsaken Me?"
—MATT. xxvii. 46.

AT mid-day darkness fell. For three hours the crosses were hidden. The crowd was hushed. At last, out of the deep of His soul's woe and darkness, Christ cried aloud to God. The Father's changeless love did not forsake, in His sorest need, the Son Who thus did His will unto death. Christ still held fast, saying, "My God." But the felt consolations of the Divine presence were withdrawn. Our sins, which He made His sorrows, came, like a thick cloud, between Him and heaven. In Christ mankind prayed for the light of God.

Wonderful, that Christ should live and die for me! More wonderful that He should bear for me the hiding of His Father's face. That cry shows how His heart is with me when the world is dark, and there seems to be no God near; when only sin seems all around, and no light from heaven breaks through upon my soul. He has gone down into the lonely depths. He teaches me what is indeed despair—to have so left God that He leaves me. But He tells of a God still my God, though my soul feels orphaned. While I cry to God and long for Him, I know that I am not forsaken. If the reason of my sorrow is that some sin hides God's face, and shuts me off from His consolations, let me in lowly earnestness search for and forsake it. If I am only being tried, let me hold fast with what faith I have, and learn in my sadness the value of that love which shines still, though clouds hide it. Let me wait and pray in patience till the shadows pass, sure that there is a "why" for all.

O my Saviour, make me to dread, above all, woe, the loss of God. May I never lose Him indeed by wilful sin. Be with me in my dark hours of trial; help me to be true, and to call on God in faith, waiting for the light.

> Lord, should fear and anguish roll
> Darkly o'er my sinful soul,
> Thou, Who once wast thus bereft,
> That Thine own might ne'er be left,
> Teach me by that bitter cry
> In the gloom to know Thee nigh.

THURSDAY IN PASSION WEEK.

"I thirst."—JOHN xix. 28.

THE darkness lifts away, and to Christ's soul God's light comes again. The great spiritual conflict is over. He can think now of His body's torture. He said, "I thirst." Parched with the burning fever of His wounds, He felt the thirst of the dying, the crucified. But what the soldiers gave did not quench His deepest want. His voice spoke for man's nature, gasping in its dryness for God, and for what God alone can give. It was the voice, moreover, of infinite Divine love, thirsting for the love of man and the bliss of souls.

Christ felt His thirst, and asked relief, that in all my griefs and pain I might know of His sympathy. But that dreadful dryness that parched His lips and throat was a figure of His deep-felt desire to win my love, and make my soul glad. To gain my pardon, and to make me His own, He bore this thirst of body, and all His other woes. From the hot furnace of His suffering He asks me to "give Him to drink." Shall I "let be," as if I cared not? and refuse the refreshment He pleads for? Shall I not bring Him all I have and am? I can comfort Him by thirsting for God and for His righteousness. That inward dryness which craves for what the springs of earth fail to give is His thirst in me. He longs to lead me to the living God, that even here, in this barren and dry land, I may have a well of water springing up unto everlasting life. He longs to refresh and cheer me with His grace, till I am satisfied in His presence, and "thirst no more" for ever.

O Lord Jesus, Who for my sake didst thirst upon the cross, thirst for me, and thirst in me, that I may always be athirst for God, and be refreshed by Thy grace, till I come before Thy presence, and wear Thy likeness.

> O Love, most patient, give me grace;
> Make all my soul athirst for Thee;
> That parched, dry lip, that fading face,
> That thirst, were all for me.

FRIDAY IN PASSION WEEK.

"It is finished."—JOHN xix. 30.

CALM, strong words of peace! The full cup is drained. The crowded woes of the hard, tempted life are left behind. All His Father's will is done. The work given Him to do is fulfilled. Each prophecy and type has found its end. Man's sorrows have been borne and learned. Man's sin is atoned for. The fount of grace is filled and opened. Christ Himself is "finished" —"made perfect," through His obedience unto death. He is the author of eternal salvation to all who will obey Him. It remains only to receive and to bestow the gifts which He has won.

Christ's own word gives me firm ground on which to rest my faith, and hope, and joy. All that my Saviour undertook to do on earth in servant form is finished. The way to God and holiness is open. All things are now ready. Christ is an example through life to death. In Him are stored exhaustless treasures of grace on which I need never fear to draw. There is a finished sacrifice to plead. I have an Advocate with the Father, Who is the propitiation for my sins. Christ is wisdom to guide my foolishness, righteousness to be a new nature in me, sanctification to raise my soul to a purer state, redemption to set me free at last from all that stains. Alas! how is it that I am so imperfect, and my work is so unfinished? Surely it is because I do not will to come, to take, to use. Be it my prayer and my life's aim to be made through His grace complete in all the will of God: so at life's end I may know that His work in me and my work for Him are "finished."

O Lord Jesus Christ, grant me so to profit by Thy work finished for me, perfecting holiness in the fear and love of God, that when I leave my cross Thy work may be finished in me, to Thy glory and my salvation.

It is finished—all the woe, care, and toil are past;
It is finished—every foe owns His power at last.
Christ our mortal frame has worn, Christ for man has bled;
By the sorrows He has borne, He is perfected.

SATURDAY IN PASSION WEEK.

"*Father, into Thy hands I commend My Spirit.*"
—LUKE xxiii. 46.

CHRIST has "finished" His work as a suffering Saviour. He has held Himself on the cross; now He need stay no longer. No man takes His life; He lays it down by His own free act. He goes to bear to waiting souls the tidings of His triumph. He goes to carry on His work for us in new ways, and to come again to be with us in a more blessed manner. He brings with Him, and gives to God's keeping, all who through Him can call God Father. He shows us how to die, and assures of a rest, when our work on earth is finished.

From Christ I learn how to be holy in life, and to be strong and peaceful in the hour of dying. If I am one with Him, and follow Him while bearing my cross, I need not fear to follow Him in death. His Father is my Father. He has opened the path to Paradise, and gone to prepare a place for me. His hand is ready to hold mine when I tremble as I pass into the dark valley. His voice tells me of a Father waiting to welcome me. It is enough: for in the unknown land, where my Father is, I shall find a home. All through this dying life of mine, be it my ceaseless care to be one with Christ in doing and bearing His Father's will: so shall I be able always to commend my spirit to my Father's keeping. So shall the trials and temptations of life be guided by Him for my good. So shall death but set me free from my cross, and lift away the burden of the flesh, that I may go to Christ's Father and to my Father, Whose care I have learned to trust.

Almighty God, enable me always to know and trust Thee as my Father in Christ, and to give myself to Thy holy keeping. So, when my work is finished here, may I commend my spirit to Thy hands in peace, through the merits and mediation of my Saviour, Jesus Christ.

> Freely Thy life Thou yieldest, meekly bending
>   E'en to the last beneath our sorrow's load;
> Yet strong in death, in perfect peace commending
>   Thy Spirit to Thy Father and Thy God.

Palm Sunday.

"And when He was come near, He beheld the city, and wept over it."—LUKE xix. 41.

FAIR and strong stood the city on its hills. Christ, as He drew near, was the centre of an enthusiastic multitude, whose hearts seemed all His. Why, then, that sad, yearning gaze, that outburst of grief? What made God weep thus with human eyes? He knew the past, and read the future, and saw under the bright outside. The love of God in Christ felt the bitterness of failure. He thought not of His own agony on the tree, but of those for whom it would be fruitless. God could not, because man would not. Christ knew what might have been, and what must be. He showed what is in God's heart, when man refuses to be blessed, and forces his way to ruin.

Each offer of grace, each claim of duty, each drawing of the Spirit, each quiet voice heard in my conscience is part of my "visitation." There is a day which is "my day," and there is a "night" when God has done all that can be done. My Saviour watches and knows all. There are times when He may be said to "behold" me, searching my inmost being more closely. His look is the look of Him Whose name is Love. Can it be that He gazes on me as sorrowfully as He did upon Jerusalem? What a thought that He should know that my sin had put away His grace and my last hope of peace! What a thought that this might be while all seemed well, and even while I greeted Him with signs of faithful love! Oh, for ears and heart to know and prize the comings of my patient God! So shall the things meant for my peace bring peace, and my Saviour shall rejoice over me.

O Lord Jesus Christ, grant me grace to watch for each time of my "visitation," and to know the things that belong unto my peace, that I may show the fruit of Thy patient love, and see Thy full salvation.

> Behold the Lamb of God!
> O Thou for sinners slain,
> Let it not be in vain that Thou hast died.
> Thee for my Saviour let me take,
> My only refuge let me make Thy wounded side.

MONDAY IN HOLY WEEK.
"Tarry ye here, and watch with Me."—MATT. xxvi. 38.

THE God-man was weighed down by all He felt, and knew was coming. The world's sin and woe, in some dreadful mysterious way, gathered over His soul. Man's enemy tried his worst temptations. The sorrows of death, understood in all their meaning, were around Him. None could know His heart's bitterness, or share His load. He must be the single-handed champion in that war. Yet, as man, He longed for the sympathy of those who loved Him. He asked them to be near, though they could not be with Him; to stay there in the solemn loneliness, and let their thoughts and hearts be towards Him. It comforted Him; it was good for them.

The words come to me with their sad appeal. For love of me, my Saviour meets my foes, to win my life and joy by His own sore pain and death. Shall I refuse to go out from the world for "one hour" to be alone in spirit under the olive-trees with Christ, Who left heaven to suffer thus for me? Shall I "sleep," not from "sorrow," but from my soul's sloth and my lack of feeling? Let me with wakeful devotion follow Him, and be in thought and love as close to Him as He permits. So shall I be within reach of the holy power of His agony, I shall learn His love and the sin which wounds it. I shall learn to mourn with Him and for myself. I shall be sure that as He asks me to watch with Him, so He is with me in my Gethsemane. I shall see how real is the conflict of which He warns, and be roused to watch with Him, lest my foes find me sleeping or alone.

O my Saviour and my God, enable me with devout mind and heart to meditate upon Thy sorrows. Show me Thy love and my need of watchful prayer. Watch over me in all my conflicts, and uphold me by Thy grace.

Go to dark Gethsemane,
  Ye that feel the tempter's power,
  Your Redeemer's conflict see;
    Watch with Him one bitter hour.
Turn not from His griefs away;
Learn from Him to watch and pray.

TUESDAY IN HOLY WEEK.

"And He went a little farther, and fell on His face, and prayed, saying, O My Father, if it be possible, let this cup pass from Me: nevertheless not as I will, but as Thou wilt."—
MATT. xxvi. 39.

NONE ever felt like Christ, or had so much to bear. To Him Who was the Life, death had strange awfulness. His pure, finely-strung nature was quick to feel pain. His tender heart took up all woe of all men. He felt, with holy loathing, the evil one close for a last fierce grapple. All was seen as sin's work. He laid His shrinking before God. His human will longed that God's will might take away the cup. His desire still was, that at all costs to Him that will might be done. The weakness of His flesh only proved more the wholehearted willingness of the Spirit.

My God lays bare to me His man's heart. He brings me within hearing of His cry of pain, and prayer of faith, and meek, firm "As Thou wilt." All is to warn, and help, and comfort me. Shall I think it hard that the path of God's will is painful to me, when my sin helped to make Christ's an agony. Shall I dare to rebel, when Christ thus bowed His will to God's? It is no sin or shame to feel nature's recoil from suffering, or pain, or death. It is no cowardliness to hate the onset of the evil one. Christ did so, strong, and brave, and holy as He was. All is well so long as my will is ready to make common cause with God's. I am safe while Christ is with me. He knows how weak I am, and how sore my trial. He will sweeten by His own sympathy the cup at which my lips tremble. He will enable me to hold my will down, and bind it fast to God's. Not an angel, but the Lord of angels shall "strengthen" me.

O Lord Jesus, teach me, after Thy example, to bring my griefs and fears to my Father, and while I meekly ask relief, to pray that His wise loving will be fully done.

    Oh, the wonders love has done!
    Oh, the prayer, the sweat of blood!
    Oh, the depths of woe, by none,
      Man or angel, understood!
    Who can Thy deep marvels see,
    Wonderful Gethsemane?

WEDNESDAY IN HOLY WEEK.
"The cup which My Father hath given Me, shall I not drink it?"—JOHN xviii. 11.

THE conflict is ended; the triumph begins. The human will of Christ struggles no longer in its sinless shrinking. His Father has given Him the cup, and with it strength to hold it to His own lips. Isaac goes with his father to the mount of sacrifice, and flinches not. There is now sublime majesty and power in each moment of the passion. Fallen on His face under the olive-trees, Christ showed how He shares our weakness. Standing firm before His foes, holding fast to the purpose of His love and the Divine will, He shows the strength we may share with Him.

There is mystery in all sorrow. Man and his God meet alone on that sacred ground. I can but stand afar off, reverently beholding. No sorrow ever was like Christ's; for He was like none else. His power and love enable Him to suffer more than other sons of men. He is God, and His man's heart is mightier to feel from its oneness with God. Each moment He bears the agony of all moments. Each pang of suffering needs an act of His will to yield Himself to it. He keeps the hearts beating that hate Him. He gives strength to the voices that mock, to the arms that smite. His power holds Him to the nails, and steadfastly keeps His soul in its agony till all is finished. And this is for me!—to gain my salvation, to win my heart! Oh, to be like Him in divinely-given faithfulness and strength when I am brought low, and all seems dark! Oh, for faith to hold fast to Him, that I may never put from me what my Father gives, and that my Saviour's triumph may be mine!

Almighty Father, give me with each trial more of the faithfulness and strength of Christ, that I may not sink in my own weakness, but may endure unto the end.

I dare not choose my lot; I would not if I might;
Choose Thou for me, my God, so shall I walk aright.
Take Thou my cup, and it with joy or sorrow fill
As best to Thee may seem; choose Thou my good and ill;
Choose Thou for me my friends, my sickness, or my health;
Choose Thou my cares for me, my poverty, or wealth.

Maundy Thursday.

"Behold the Man!"—JOHN xix. 5.

PILATE wished, though he feared, to let Christ go. He tried to move the Jews to pity or to scorn. He brought forth their victim that they might see Him as one too weak to be feared, too wretched to be hated. He was more marred than any man. Fasting, and sleeplessness, and long agony of soul had worn Him. His face was disfigured by dust and blood-stains, and the marks of blows and spitting. The crown of thorns tore his brow. The purple robe scarce hid the quivering form.

God's Word calls me to "behold the Man." I know Who He is—even the Son of man, who is the Son of God. He is my Saviour. These wounds are for my transgressions, these stripes are for my healing. He has met my foes; their malice falls on Him. His anguish of soul, His agony and shame, are the tokens of His love for me. They tell the worth of my salvation, and at how great a cost He redeems me. His meek look pleads with my heart by all He suffers. Can I behold and realise His sorrows in any weak way, and be unmoved? Can I think lightly of the past, or be careless any more? Is it not enough? Shall I go on to open afresh those wounds, and mock and wrong Him by new sin? Shall I even join with those who say, "Let Him be crucified"? Shall I not rather pray that I may behold that Man with self-reproach, and faith, and devotion? So can I ask God to behold His sorrows, and have mercy on me. So shall those sorrows brace me to shun sin, and to do and suffer well.

Almighty God, give me faith to behold the Man Christ Jesus as my Lord and Saviour, Whom my sins have wounded, and through Whom alone I can draw nigh to Thee for pardon and salvation.

> Why is Thy form so wasted and so worn;
> Why dost Thou bleed, with thorns and scourges torn;
> Why is the cross upon Thy shoulders borne?
> My pride, O Lord, has brought Thee down so low;
> My selfishness has made Thee suffer so;
> My sins have filled Thy cup of awful woe.

Good Friday.

"His own self bare our sins in His own body on the tree."
—1 Pet. ii. 24.

WHO is He Whose body hangs upon the cross? He is more than a sinless man. He is the Almighty, holy God. That body so outraged, that soul, whose mysterious sorrows even that face fails to reveal, are God's. The Son of God made them His own. Why is He there? His death is more than the triumphant close of a lifelong championship of good and protest against evil, the crowning act of a perfect example. He has lifted on Himself the load of man's sin, that He may bear sin's curse, and take sin away.

A man's body writhes on the cross. A man's soul looks out through those sad, patient eyes. A man is mocked and taunted, and bears all. Faith knows that God is one Person with that form, and with the human spirit that shares its woe, and that this death of the Incarnate is for me. The power of such a death must pass my thought; I dare not put bounds to it. I ask not *how* this sacrifice changes my state before God, or whether God might have saved me otherwise. Enough that the love of the Trinity willed thus to atone for sin, and come before my heart and conscience with mightiest claim. On the cross I see the end of the life of self-surrender, and I see what gives power to the life of intercession and blessing Christ lives for me now. I see more than the last victory of a brave, pure soul. I see the work of my sin in one Who loved me to the death, and the work of His love to save me from my sin. I see something done before God as well as before me, able to plead with Heaven as well as draw and hold my heart.

O Lord Jesu Christ, grant me faith in Thee, and in Thy work for me, that Thy death may atone for my past sin, and that Thy grace may keep me faithful evermore.

> As Jesus bows His head,
> Have I no tears to shed,
>   When I look up and see
>   Those loving arms spread wide
>   To draw me to His side,
>   My ransom thus to be?

Easter Even.

"And there was Mary Magdalene, and the other Mary, sitting over against the sepulchre."—MATT. xxvii. 61.

THE body of Jesus sleeps at last. Its weariness and pain are over. Taken down from the cross by loving hands, and wrapped in fine linen, it is laid in Joseph's new tomb. It hallows the grave, for it is the body of the Son of God. The Spirit is welcomed in Paradise. There it carries on the work of the Divine will. It bears to waiting souls the glad news of their Saviour's work. The way is being opened by which His people may pass after Him, through death, to life and glory.

I must be thoughtful beside any grave; more so at the fresh grave of a friend. Old memories crowd the mind. My heart blames me for any coldness or wrong. I would recall hasty words, and ask forgiveness, if I could. What if in any least way I blame myself for his death, if care for me has worn or broken the heart that beats no more ! Let me kneel in thought at the tomb of my Saviour. Why is that form lifeless and outraged? What mean the silent pleadings of these wounds? I know all; let me try to feel it. Let me learn, in the solemn quiet, the malice of my sin, and what Divine love has done and borne. Let me bring what has grieved my Saviour—my pride, and greed, and self-will—and lay them deep in His tomb. Here let me grow familiar with the grave, and learn to look on it as a resting-place for my body when its work is finished and its cross is left. Let me see that my flesh is crucified, ere my spirit leaves it, that I may go after Christ to the rest of Paradise.

Grant, Lord, that by the power of Christ living in me, I may so crucify the flesh, and die to sin, that I may pass without fear through death to go to Paradise and Thee.

> While the saints on earth are weeping,
>   While their heart within them dies,
> Happy souls in God's safe keeping
>   Welcome Him in Paradise.
> Death no longer can alarm us,
>   Christ has robbed it of its sting;
> In the grave no power can harm us,
>   There He reigns the victor King.

Easter Sunday.

"The Lord is risen indeed, and hath appeared."
—LUKE xxiv. 34.

EASTER is bright with a sudden startling joy. The sepulchre is empty. Angels in white tell that Christ is risen. His soul has come from the unseen world. Body and soul have united again by the Divine power in both. None saw Him rise; but the stone is rolled away, that friends and foes may see where the Lord lay. Christ shows Himself alive to those who seek the tomb as mourners. He is proved to be the "Son of God with power." He appears as the conqueror of sin and death. He lives to be the holiness and life eternal of those for whom He died.

Am I a disciple—a follower and a learner? Is Christ my Lord and Master Whom I serve? Have I been in spirit with those who mourned under the cross? Have I in loving faith opened my heart to receive my crucified Saviour, and made ready my best devotion and sacrifice to do Him honour? Have I known Him, and put before me all my sins against Him, all my cowardice and denials? Then is Easter gladness mine. The angels speak to me. I am one of those to whom Christ sends His own message, going before to the place of meeting. My Saviour's agony and shame are past. He lives to die no more. He lives, as He died, for me. Faith's trial ought not to be hard now: for I fear not, I doubt not, while One Who has passed triumphantly through death leads me on. I am one with the ever-living. Sin need not overcome me. Death cannot hold me. Friends in Christ cannot be lost. Sorrows only lead towards the better life, when all my scars shall, like Christ's, tell of victory, and like Him, I shall be risen to die no more.

Almighty God, Whose blessed Son rose the conqueror of sin and death, grant me such penitence, and faith, and love, that His triumph may be my joy, and His resurrection a pledge to me of everlasting life.

> Thou hast conquered in the fight,
> Thou hast brought us life and light;
> Thou hast opened Paradise,
> And in Thee Thy saints shall rise.

Monday in Easter Week.

"It is I Myself: handle Me, and see."—LUKE xxiv. 39.

THE risen Christ is the same Who died on the cross, and Whose body lay in Joseph's tomb. He is changed, but He is not another. He speaks with the well-known voice. He shows the wounded hands and side. The same soul looks out through the same eyes. He has laid down what belonged to His old life of humiliation; He is equipped for the glorified life. But He can look back through the past, and know that He has been by Himself in it all, apart from other men, with His own separate history. His life has gone on as one, and shall go on for ever.

I have begun a life that does not end. I am indeed changing day by day. I shall pass through the great change that comes at and after death. But death shall not make me cease to be the person I am now. I cannot get rid of myself, and feel as if the life I live as the days pass had not been lived by me, but by some one else. I shall stand on the farther shore, and shall feel that "it is I myself." I shall look back through life and recognise myself. I shall see in myself the marks life shall have left, as plainly as Christ saw the wound prints on His hands and feet. Shall I feel,—"This is the heart that has been hardened against God; these are the feet which have been swift to evil; these are the hands slow to good and busy in wrong-doing; this is the tongue set on fire of hell to speak sin; this being has been yielded to ungodliness"? Or shall my wounds of soul be all healed? Shall my nature have grown glorious like Christ's? Shall I see in myself the crowning of God's work of grace in time, that I may rejoice in my immortality?

O eternal God, teach me to keep in mind that "I myself" shall live for ever the life I now begin. Give me grace so to live like Christ, that I may rise from death in His likeness, and be glorified with Him for ever.

> I must shake off the dust of sin,
> And daily grow in grace,
> And more of Jesus' likeness win
> Before I see His face.

Tuesday in Easter Week.

"As in Adam all die, even so in Christ shall all be made alive."—1 Cor. xv. 22.

IN some way known to God, those who share Adam's nature share his sentence. We are born to toil and die. Our souls need a new gift of life, else they perish. In some way known to God, all who are joined to Christ share His reward. We are new born that, one with Christ, we may live for ever. We must indeed toil. Soul and body must part. But toil becomes a means of grace. What is called death, is going out of death's reach. Death becomes our slave to open the way to true life, in which glorified body and spirit have everlasting union with God.

I feel the blight that comes from Adam's fall. I am dying all through life. There is a second death, the beginnings of which alarm my soul. I am "in Adam;" but I am "in Christ" also. I can by faith realise my part in Him, and by love show myself a living member of the second Adam, into whom I have been baptized. I may feel in me the fruit of what Christ has done, the working of His own risen nature. I may know that the life of the Incarnate God grows daily stronger in me, and that though dying I am for ever. I may face death as a foe whose sting is gone; the grave may only remind me of Him Who giveth me the victory. So shall toil, and care, and strife now bring me closer to Him in Whom rest and peace are found. I shall go from earth, leaving behind me the mortality and sin I have from Adam, and, in full union with Christ, shall learn what true life means. It were death to live for ever apart from Christ's life. May my eternal portion be in Him.

Almighty, ever-living God, grant that I may be so one with the life of Christ that the evil of my old nature may be overcome, and that I may pass through death to everlasting life.

> Maker and Redeemer, Life and Health of all,
> Thou from heaven beholding human nature's fall;
> Of the Father's Godhead true and only Son,
> Manhood to deliver, manhood didst put on,
> Hell to-day is vanquished; heaven to-day is won.

WEDNESDAY IN EASTER WEEK.

" Reckon ye also yourselves to be dead indeed unto sin, but alive unto God through Jesus Christ our Lord."—ROM. vi. 11.

CHRIST'S death was a death unto sin once for all. He conquered sin, being obedient unto death. He atoned fully for all sin. He passed out of reach of sin's temptation. The life He lives is the free, glad life of glorified man glorifying God. As the Head is, so may and must the members rise to be. We are called to realise our state "through or in Jesus Christ." Temptations must find us deaf, blind, dead to them. Sin, for which Christ died, must find no power in us that it can use. All we are must be alive, quick, ready for God's work and glory.

Why did Christ die and rise? Not that I might live unto sin safely. Not that I might, though dead to God on earth, yet go to live for ever with Him. Not that I should spend life falling and repenting, living half for sin and half for God. Not, in the first place, that daily pardon might be ready for my daily sins. Not so much for time past as for time passing and to come. Christ died and rose that I might be in Him, and risen with Him from the grave of sin, die no more, but live to God. Can I be called "dead to sin" in any such way as a dead man is to the things around him? Am I even dying to sin? Do I feel the need of being done with it so thoroughly as the word "dead" implies? Do I try to have no ear or eye to let in temptation to my soul, no will to yield to it, no power at the service of sin. How far am I alive, ready, active for God, watching for each sign of His will, living my whole life before Him under the guidance and in the power of Christ living in me?

O Lord Jesus Christ, grant that all my love and will may be so purified by Thy grace that evil may have no attraction for me, and that my heart and life may be for God and righteousness alone.

> Lord, Thou art in my nature more mine than is my sin,
> Fulfil me with Thy presence, and make all new within;
> Let body, soul, and spirit be so indwelt by Thee,
> That of Thy life within me they may the organs be.

Thursday in Easter Week.

"If ye then be risen with Christ, seek those things which are above."—Col. iii. 1.

THE words speak of an unquestioned fact. They are—"Inasmuch as ye were raised with Christ." St. Paul tells us when,—"buried with Him in baptism, wherein also ye are risen with Him" (Col. ii. 12). By the Spirit's work in baptism we were made members of the Head, one with Him in His risen life. Old sin was buried, and a new power of life was given. Christ rose to die no more, but to ascend. We are called not to go back to the death of sin, or to seek rest on earth, but to lift up our hearts, and to rise in the whole aim of all our being toward things above, where Christ in glory prepares our home.

A change was wrought in me at my baptism which the Bible calls being "raised with Christ." I was given my own part in Christ's work and triumph for mankind. I was saved from the power of things below, and set free to love and long after and reach things on high. Hence my encouragement to strive upward: hence my shame, if sin hold me or earth content me. My spiritual life needs nourishment and care, if it is to last and thrive. My soul will die from Christ, unless I keep up union with Him by faith, and loving work, and the use of means of grace. It will be perfected, if in heart, and mind, and will, I yield to Christ, that He may raise me towards where He is, and by His grace prepare me here for His presence in glory. Only the things above can satisfy me. They must be sought for, else they never shall be mine. Am I seeking them in my daily duties and devotion, looking, aiming, praying, pressing towards them? If I seek truly I shall find a glad foretaste now, and fulness of joy for ever.

Almighty God, grant that being raised together with Christ I may abide in Him, and in my heart and life rise towards things above till I am with Him where He is.

> Baptized into your Saviour's death,
> Be dead to sin, and things beneath;
> Since ye, through grace, with Christ are risen,
> Seek things above—the things of heaven.

Friday in Easter Week.

"If we believe that Jesus died and rose again, even so them also which sleep in Jesus will God bring with Him."—1 Thess. iv. 14.

WE sorrow when those we love leave us. God knows we must. He has given the love that feels pain. He would have us love on in hope. They who have lived in Jesus have rest in Him when they depart. They are in Him more wholly, being away from earth. If we are in Him, we are still one with them. They are not out of sight for long. We know where they are, and can be sure that our love for them shall one day be a new source of joy. God will bring them with Him, or call us to rest with them "in Jesus."

Christ wept for Lazarus, though He was soon to raise him. He wills my love to reach after those whom He calls to Himself. He tells me where they are, that my love for them may lead my heart more close to Him. As surely as Christ died and rose again, those whom neither life nor death parts from Him shall be restored to one another. The hope Christ gives me in bereavement would mean nothing, were I not to know again, and be known by those for whom I sorrow. Let me abide in Christ: so shall I one day see them, and more than the joy of the old love shall be mine. They are gone from earth, but I must love them still. They grow more lovely and more loving where they are, and I may be purified by loving those who live in Paradise. Home in this world of trial empties, that home in the world of peace may fill, and that my heart may be drawn from here to there. They who rest in Jesus wait for me. One with the same Jesus, I long for them, and fight and struggle after them.

Almighty Father, grant me in the sorrow of my partings to trust Thee, and look forward. Bring me closer to Him in Whom the redeemed on earth and at rest are one, and through Whom they shall meet to part no more.

> Those who are one in Christ, hid in His heart,
> Death cannot sever, nor hold long apart.
> Soon they clasp hands again, all partings o'er,
> Where the Lifegiver has gone on before.

Saturday in Easter Week.

"Saved by His life."—Rom. v. 10.

CHRIST was made man, and died to be our Saviour. He lives to make salvation ours. He is the conqueror of sin and death, the giver of life and holiness. He washes our souls with the blood He shed. He blesses us with the Divine love which His toil, and woe, and death made known. The love that brought Him to die makes Him our Saviour still. In Him all grace is stored for all man's need. By His life for us and in us we can live unto God, and grow fit to live with God.

I dare not doubt the power of Christ's death, and refuse to come to God as a reconciled Father. I dare not doubt the power of Christ's life to save me to the end. Because He lives, I can live also. I am not alone, pleading by myself Christ's sacrifice, aiming by myself to grow like Him. He has sent the Holy Spirit, and by that Spirit I am baptized into Him. I am a member of His body, and His life is in me. I can gain ever fresh incomings of His life through those means of grace which He uses to quicken faithful souls. He gives His body, and His blood. The ministrations of His Church have, through Him, spiritual power. He pleads His death on high; and my prayers, which His Spirit guides, are heard as His. He is my strength to follow Him; and as I will and do in His name, God accepts me for His sake. He is my advocate when I fall. He guards me from foes, and makes my way safe. He is in me the hope of glory. He died for me; He does not will that I should die, but gain the full salvation He lives to make mine.

Almighty God, give me faith in Thee as my Father and Friend in Christ. Grant that by the power of His life for me and in me I may be saved.

> Our great High Priest and Shepherd, Thou
> Within the veil art entered now,
> To offer there Thy precious blood,
> Once poured on earth a cleansing flood.
> And thence the Church, Thy chosen bride,
> With countless gifts of grace supplied,
> Through all her members draws from Thee
> Her hidden life of sanctity.

Low Sunday.

"Peace be unto you."—John xx. 19.

SO Christ comforts and calms the misgiving hearts of the disciples whose faith had failed. More than this—He came to be "our peace." Now, by the blood of the cross, He has "made peace." His words impart that peace, as well as assure of it. What angels sang of at His birth, the risen Saviour gives. There is peace with God now made known as a Father and Friend, Whose love can reach and bless man. There is peace among men now bound together and made one in Christ. There is peace for man's own nature, its warring passions calmed, its every part ruled by the peace of God.

God in Christ comes to me with this word "peace," after the cross and grave, after all my forsaking of Him. He speaks, and it is done. This peace is a reality for my faith to grasp. Let me put away distrust, and be sure that God wills only my peace. Let me know Him in Christ, and I shall find Him all love. The sin that parts me from Him shall be done away, my pardon sure, all grace I need made mine. Though life be dark and rough, and sore temptations try to shake and overwhelm me, I shall be kept in perfect peace while my mind is stayed on Him and I trust in Him. Yielding to His gentle control, my rebel nature shall be restrained, and rising powers of evil stilled. I shall have calm, in a conscience God will help me to watch and keep. I shall live peaceably with all, by the power of Divine charity. Holding fast unto the end, I shall be able to lay me down in peace and take my rest. He will bring me safely to the quiet land where I shall feel and fear no evil for evermore.

Lord, grant me peaceful trust in God, grace to rule my nature, faith to be calm in trial, love to be gentle towards all men. May the peace of God be mine now and for ever.

> O Saving Victim, opening wide
> The gate of heaven to man below,
> Our foes press on from every side,
> Thine aid supply, Thy strength bestow.

Monday after Low Sunday.

"As My Father hath sent Me, even so send I you."—John xx. 21.

THE Father sent Christ. Christ, before He ascended, passed on a commission to chosen men. The Holy Spirit came down on Christ at Jordan. He breathed on His disciples, saying, "Receive ye the Holy Ghost." Again He said, "All power is given unto Me in heaven and earth, go ye *therefore.*" During the forty days He spake to them of the "things pertaining to the kingdom of God." So He provided for the building up and ruling of His Church. Those whom Christ sent have sent others. Still the power of God given to the Son of man works through men, for man's good and God's glory.

Few words of the risen Christ are written. There must be great meaning in those few. I might be sure that the God of order would not leave the ordering of His Church to chance. He set apart men to serve in holy things in the Jewish Church. It was likely that He would do the same in the Christian Church. Whatever need there was for an authorised ministry in the first days, is as strong to-day. There are now stewards of God's mysteries who have His commission. They hold their office by spiritual descent, not as members of one chosen family. Let me not question Christ's right to do as He wills, or the meaning or the wisdom of what His words say. Rather let me be thankful that I am in God's hands, and not dependent on man's worth or goodness. I trust in the power and promise of the Almighty, Who uses men, as in the sacraments He uses water, and bread, and wine. It is still as if Christ Himself were seen and heard. My faith looks to Christ, Who, by the voice and hand of men, imparts Divine gifts.

O Lord, Who, as Thou wast sent by Thy Father, dost send Thy ministers to bear Thy message and Thy gifts, grant me in faith and thankfulness to use, according to Thy will, what Thy will ordains for my good.

His twelve apostles first He made His ministers of grace,
And they their hands on others laid, to fill in turn their place.
So age by age, and year by year, His grace was handed on;
And still the holy Church is here, although her Lord is gone.

TUESDAY AFTER LOW SUNDAY.

"Whose soever sins ye remit, they are remitted unto them; and whose soever sins ye retain, they are retained."—JOHN xx. 23.

SO Christ stamps as real the whole work of His Church. None can forgive but God. "God was in Christ reconciling the world." The Son of man had "power on earth to forgive." The risen Christ had "all power in heaven and earth." He did not hand over any of this power so as to part with it. He provided for putting it forth. He sent men not only to speak about God's forgiveness, but to convey it. He has no pardon for the impenitent. He gives no one power to withhold pardon from the faithful.

God's messenger of old could say, "The Lord hath put away thy sin." So now, but in a more blessed way, God speaks through His Church and restores the fallen. The needs of sinners are what they were when Christ spoke. The provision has not failed. The Saviour is as near as ever in power and love. He gives might to man's weak words to rouse the sleeping or dead soul to the activity of faith. "Jesus Himself baptizeth not, but His disciples," yet baptism is more than an outward washing; it is a means and token of an inward blessing, because He is the baptizer. He makes the words of peace be a power of peace when sinners pour out their own soul's confession in the public acknowledgment of sin. He invites the anxious doubter to come for comfort and counsel, and when the heart's grief has been opened, bids him, by the voice of His minister, go in peace and sin no more. He makes the Holy Communion a spiritual feeding on His very self, and a means of renewed life. Let me be glad and thankful that, as God cares for my body through those whose work He blesses, so He provides through His Church for my soul's need.

O Lord, Who alone givest power to whatever is done in Thy Church for the good of souls, grant me faith so to seek Thy grace that I may rejoice in Thy salvation.

> Lord, Thou hast made it sure,
>   By Thy dear promise to Thy Church and bride,
> That Thou, on earth, wouldst aye with her endure
>   Till earth to heaven be purified.

WEDNESDAY AFTER LOW SUNDAY.

"Believe on the Lord Jesus Christ, and thou shalt be saved."
—ACTS xvi. 31.

JESUS CHRIST is man's only Saviour. Unbelief bars the soul against Him. Faith opens a way for Him, that He may come and apply the saving power of His work. To believe in Him is so to trust Him as to yield heart and will, and the whole being to be saved from evil, and purified and trained for good, in His way. Salvation must go on through life, till the soul is pure in a pure world. He who will be saved must go on to the end, believing in Christ as his atonement, his example, his teacher, his sure strength.

I need to be saved from the doom of sin, and from sin itself. I look to the cross, and believe and know that Christ by His death has won my pardon. I look to the living Christ in heaven, and know that He is able and willing to save me from all that stains, and weakens, and shames me. I live in faith, pleading, as my one plea with God, what Christ has done, watching and striving to be with Him in what He is doing for my soul now. I seek His grace in the means of grace and sacraments, to which He has bound His promises. I use in faith the helps He says are needful and useful for me. Trusting to His sure aid, I am diligent in works, which He tells me to do for the world's good, for God's glory, and my soul's training. Faith keeps me calm, and yet careful, lest I lose what I am thankful for and hope for. I believe that He Who has begun wills to save me to the end. I pray that my faith fail not.

O merciful Father, grant me always so to believe in Thy Son Jesus Christ, that I may be saved from the evil one, and the evil world, and the evil in myself, and at last may be among the saved in heaven, through the same Jesus Christ.

> Rock of Ages, cleft for me,
> Let me hide myself in Thee;
> Let the water and the blood
> From Thy wounded side which flowed,
> Be of sin the double cure,
> Save from guilt, and make me pure.

Thursday after Low Sunday.

"Work out your own salvation with fear and trembling: for it is God which worketh in you both to will and to do of His good pleasure."—Phil. ii. 12, 13.

GOD has wrought salvation. Each man must claim his own part in the gift, must fear lest he lose it, must persevere till its full blessing is safely his. God wills that the good work His grace begins should go on to perfection. He works in man to will and do. Here is sure hope; for all can be done when the Almighty gives the power. Yet here is ground for solemn carefulness lest man fail to unite his will with God's, and to put forth energy as God moves him.

If I am to be saved at last, I must work out my own salvation. God warns me plainly, that if this is not done by me it will not be done at all. I am helpless without God; but I am not without God. I can do all things, if I will; I am right to fear and tremble lest I come short. God saved me from sin's power, and set me free as His Son when I was baptized into Christ, my Saviour. Now every true desire, every high aim, every shrinking from evil, is God's will working in me. Every power I feel to refuse the wrong and do the right tells of the Holy and Almighty Presence. I grieve the Spirit when I make in vain the desires and power in me. When I work with the Divine will and strength, I grow in heavenly habits, and form the character of holiness. As I strive against sin, I am lifted out of its reach, and the triumph of my perfect salvation draws more near. How serious and awful my responsibility as a "worker together with God!" How great my glory, that God thus commissions me to overcome evil. How assuring the hope, that while I humbly watch and work, I am strong in the Lord to fulfil His good pleasure.

O Lord, Who hast made me an heir of salvation, grant me, with zeal and holy fear, to will and do of Thy good pleasure, till Thy work of grace is finished in me.

> Be Thou each day my power and consolation;
> Guard me from sin that merits condemnation;
> Lead me in paths that end in full salvation.

Friday after Low Sunday.

"The way of Balaam the son of Bosor, who loved the wages of unrighteousness."—2 Pet. ii. 15.

BALAAM was a prophet who knew God's will, and the worth of God's favour. He wished to die the death of the righteous, and yet loved the rewards of sin. He schemed how to win the bribes Balak offered, and curse God's people safely. God let him go where his heart was set on going. He wished to deceive himself, and was allowed. He taught the Midianites to tempt Israel to provoke God. Balaam was slain, and lost the earthly reward for which he had sold his eternal hope.

Only by living the life of the righteous, can I hope to die his death. No pleasure or gain is meant for me, if the way to it be doubtful. First thoughts are safest. The path of God's will is a straightforward one. When a commandment stops my way, I must not try to get round it. To argue with my warning conscience may be to silence it. To long after forbidden joys, and try to find how to have the gain of sin without its loss, is to tempt God to leave me. If I wish to deceive myself, I can always find a way of doing so. Satan will help me, and God will not hold me back by force from the path of danger I choose. What seems worldly success may indeed prove that I have been able to harden myself against God, and so to get what His love refused, but His wrath has given. If the heart be let go after the bribes of evil, the will soon follows, then the life. God's reward is sooner or later lost. The soul finds the wages of sin, which is death.

Almighty God, keep my heart from longing after sin's rewards, lest my steps go in sin's ways. Make me watchful to learn Thy will, and honest in obeying it, that I may live the life of the righteous, and gain the gifts of God.

> All, all in vain
> He seeks, to earth who clings,
>   To soar aloft in seraph's strain,
> Or speed his flight to heaven on angel's wings.
>   Let not thy voice
> To heavenly song give birth
>   The while thy carnal heart by choice
> Grovels unlifted from the dust of earth.

SATURDAY AFTER LOW SUNDAY.

" Leaving us an example, that ye should follow His steps."
—1 PET. ii. 21.

GOD not only tells men how to live: He has shown them a model life. Christ lived in childhood, youth, and full age, as man's example. His life teaches those for whom He died and rose again, how He would have them aim to live. It makes clear the path by which His words call them. It assures of what they may become if they will. It attracts men to Christ, and gives power to walk in the steps which mark where He has led. His death is in vain for those on whom His example is lost.

The Son of God lived that I might live like a child of God. He did not only die to save me from perishing as a prodigal. His whole life was meant to mould and influence my whole life. In Him I see the beauty and glory of all that is good, and high, and strong in man. I am drawn to copy the courage, truth, purity of One Who wins my love. Alas! how much of that life has failed for me! How faintly have I even tried to profit by it! Has the holy childhood made its attractive power felt in early years? Has the youth of Nazareth been before me as my model while I grew towards maturity? Have I gone on seeking to learn obedience, and to be made perfect in the way of God's will where Christ led? Do I try now to show Christ's spirit, and to act in all things as my Saviour would act were He in my place? If in the end it be found that Christ has lived in vain for me as an example, how can I hope that He shall not be found to have died in vain as my sacrifice?

Almighty God, give me grace to learn obediently from Christ's example, and to follow patiently in His steps, that, trusting in His merits and mediation, I may attain to everlasting life.

> Lord, draw me after Thee by Thine own ways
> Of prayer, of work, of patience, and of praise;
> And when, dear Lord, my days on earth are o'er,
> O call me whither Thou art gone before,
> To gaze upon Thy face for evermore.

The Second Sunday after Easter.

"I am the good Shepherd: the good Shepherd giveth His life for the sheep."—JOHN x. 11.

CHRIST is the one good Shepherd. Those whom He sends to care for His flock, act only in His name. For His sheep He spent His life on earth, fighting with their foes, resisting those who led them astray, and gathering them together. He went after them through paths of sorrow where their sin had led them. For them He laid down His life at last. His life now is for them. He knows and watches over every one in all the flock. He goes before, and guards from danger. He feeds and refreshes them, giving His own life to them, that they may be strong to follow to the heavenly fold.

I have been brought into the flock of Christ. Am I of those who in simple faith listen for the good Shepherd's voice, that I may follow Him whithersoever He leads? If so, then I shall lack nothing, I need fear nothing. He Who gave His life for me lives to care for all my wants, and keep me safe from harm. The love that found me as a sheep going astray, and folded me carefully, will not fail me now when I am one of His own flock. He leads me to the springs of comfort, and gives my soul the nourishment it needs. In His own means of grace He imparts His own life to strengthen and refresh me. Obeying His calls, keeping in His footsteps, I shall be safe under His care. He will warn me, lest I wander. He will lift me when I stumble. He will cheer me when the way seems weary, and I am sore and weak. Let me only in faith keep Him in sight and press after Him, He will lead me to the quiet fold where there is rest for ever.

O Thou good Shepherd, Who didst give Thy life for me, pardon my wanderings; call me after Thee, and lead me in safe ways, that I may be upheld by Thy grace, and brought safely to the heavenly fold.

> Shepherd most careful, warn us when straying,
>   Guide us in paths where Thine own feet have trod;
> Led by Thy call, Thy dear voice obeying,
>   Bring us in peace to the fold of God.

Second Monday after Easter.

"Come unto Me, all ye that labour and are heavy laden, and I will give you rest."—MATT. xi. 28.

CHRIST offers rest to all who feel their need, and will come for it. He is true; He is able and willing to give what He promises. Is the heart tired? Does life's toil wear the strength? Does sin lie heavy on the burdened soul? He says, "Ye need not sink under your load. Yield to the Father's drawing and the Spirit's influence. Leave other hopes; bring your whole self to Me, and find rest." The call and the power to come are from God. Man must obey the call, and put forth the power.

Am I weighed down with work and care? Do I long vainly to be able to go on with a quiet spirit through life's rough ways? Does a sin-laden conscience keep me back from God? Is my struggle with evil only a labour that wearies and disheartens, but brings no fruit? To me Christ says, "Come, come at once without delay, as the beginning of all. I will relieve, uphold, cheer you with what you cannot have away from Me; I will make your whole life restful." How am I to "come"? Owning my sin and sorrow, believing His word, trusting in His love and atonement, laying heart, powers, and life before Him, drawing near in all means of union which He offers. Perhaps I have been brought to Him in Baptism, have come to Him in the Holy Communion, and in other ways, and have gone back. The word "come" still promises pardon and restoring grace. In the fears and doubts, and trials and falls of daily life, this word has its message of comfort and strength. "Come," says Christ, "unto Me, after Me, closer to Me, come to be at last with Me where I am in My rest."

Grant me, O Saviour, so to come to Thee that I may lay down my soul's burden, and forsake sin's hard service, and in all the weariness of this tempted life may have the rest which Thou dost give Thine own.

> I came to Jesus as I was,
> Weary, and worn, and sad;
> I found in Him a resting place,
> And He has made me glad.

SECOND TUESDAY AFTER EASTER.

"Take My yoke upon you, and learn of Me."—MATT. xi. 29.

THE rest Christ gives is not the dull quiet of idleness or ignorance. It is for those only who come to work and learn, who are ready to own Him Lord, and in meekness believe and obey Him. Only to the true does Christ give pardon, and peace, and power. The soul has found rest when it has found forgiveness, when it is set free to serve its rightful Lord, to learn from Him Who is the Truth, to grow in God's wisdom and strength, and to be sure of its Saviour in all life's doubts and trials, and in the hour of death.

Have I seemed to come to Christ, and yet to find no rest? Is my soul still unquiet, burdened, weary, sinking? How is this? The fault is mine! The word of Christ has not failed. I may be bearing other yokes along with, or instead of, Christ's. I may be learning from other teachers more than from Him. Do I take Christ's yoke with ready will and single heart, resolved to know and do the work He gives me? Am I diligent in learning from His Word, His example, and His Spirit? Do I meekly wait for His teaching, and use the sacraments and means of grace in faith, making my proud thoughts bow to what He says? The yoke must be carried all through life, that I may be saved from other masters and be faithful. The learning must go on till Christ is seen, and I am educated for His presence. Christ bids me "come," not that I may be relieved of labour, but may find rest in working: not that I may be spared the use of means, but may learn with Him as teacher. Toiling for Him and learning from Him, I shall have a foretaste of the rest of the perfected.

Grant, Lord, that coming to Thee in faith I may receive Thy yoke, and learn from Thee, and serve Thee with my whole heart. So may I enjoy rest in my soul now, and grow fit for the perfect rest of heaven.

If I find Him, if I follow, what His guerdon here?
Many a sorrow, many a labour, many a tear!
If I still hold closely to Him, what hath he at last?
Sorrow vanquished, labour ended, Jordan past!

SECOND WEDNESDAY AFTER EASTER.
" My yoke is easy, and My burden is light."—MATT. xi. 30.

WHAT is a heavy cross to the old nature is light and easy to the new. Faith willingly takes Christ's yoke, and Love bears His burden gladly. His service is felt to be no humiliating bondage, but freedom from hard task-masters. Christ fits the load to the strength, and gives more power as He adds weight. Those who bear His yoke and burden are brought near Him, and knowing Him better, love Him more. Love lightens labour. They welcome claims upon their love. They view their burdens as signs of their Lord's trust, and pledges that He is training them for a service of perfect joy and freedom.

I cannot be free. I can have nothing but at the price of something else. Sin's pleasures are bought dearly. The world's good things are won only by care and self-denial. So Christ tells me frankly that I must be under rule, must work, must endure, if I would have the joy of purity, and be rich, and wise, and great with God. But the sacrifice He asks is small beside the claims of the world and sin. It is nothing to what He gives instead. Faith can know Him near, ready with comfort, lavish in blessing. Hope can look forward to the end. Love can be glad of new ways of proving its reality. Each claim Christ makes on me gives me a new claim on Him for grace, and is a pledge of larger reward. The yoke will gall unless I brace my strength, and lift it with a will. The burden will weigh me down, if I carry it languidly. Let me pray for more faith, and love, and hearty will, more freedom from other lords. Let me see that the yoke and burden I bear are Christ's, borne for Him. He will give His strength to feel them light and easy.

O Lord, may Thy grace uphold me, and Thy love lead me on, that I may gladly bear Thy yoke and burden till I reach Thy presence, and enter into Thy rest.

There is joy in sorrows borne, where thy Saviour trod,
When thy path of pain is worn by the feet of God.
There is rest, when hour by hour, as thy will obeys,
Comes Divine, Almighty power, failing strength to raise.

SECOND THURSDAY AFTER EASTER.

"So is the will of God, that with well-doing ye may put to silence the ignorance of foolish men."—1 PET. ii. 15.

CHRISTIANS in the first days were watched closely. Jews and heathens hated them. The faults of any one Christian were seized on to discredit the name of Christ and Christianity. So each life had its great importance. Patient care in well-doing, according to the will of God, was needed to keep faithful against such odds. There was a further aim—to disarm hate, to silence slander, to remove ignorant prejudice, and win men to Christ.

If unfriendly eyes are on me, let me watch myself more closely. Let accusations warn me where to be on my guard. God knows me, though man's judgment be groundless and unfair. Let me be true before God and myself. God wills my well-doing, for my own growth to perfection, and for His honour. He wills to help me to set right those who in ignorance mistake me and my religion, and to convince the foolish by the power of the "wisdom that cometh from above." I may be in knowledge a weak champion of the truth, little able to defend my faith in words. I may shrink with a right lowliness and godly fear from speaking much of my Saviour and my Holy calling. Did I argue, I might lose my charity, or provoke others to sin by reviling me or blaspheming the truth. In their "ignorance" they might not understand me; truth might seem foolishness to the foolish. But I can, with God's help, give the testimony of a blameless godly life. In time this will shame slander into silence, and gently overcome ill-will. Moreover, it will draw men to ask the secret of it, and lead them to own God Who wills their well-doing.

Almighty God, may Thy Holy Spirit so lead me in the steps of Christ, that my life may win men to believe Thy truth and seek Thy salvation.

>   Lord, may I show Thy Spirit within,
>   Which cleanses me from fleshly stain,
>   Unspotted from the world and sin,
>   My faith's integrity maintain;
>   The truth of my religion prove,
>   By perfect purity and love.

Second Friday after Easter.

"Blessed are the poor in spirit: for theirs is the kingdom of heaven."—Matt. v. 3.

THOSE only are blessed whom God blesses with the good things of His kingdom. The ease of plenty and the cares of want may alike harden man in pride against God. The poor in spirit, whether he have much or little here, feels unholy before the Holy One, helpless before the Almighty, unworthy of the goodness on which he is dependent. In lowly trust he waits on God. This gift of poorness in spirit is the beginning of all blessedness—the opening to him of the treasures of the kingdom of heaven.

I may be unblessed, however rich in friends and wealth and all the world gives. I may be blessed though bare of earthly consolations. God does not bind up blessedness with these things. It depends on my part in the kingdom of heaven, and how far my spirit bows itself aright to receive the pure and everlasting good which God bestows. In my prosperity, do I feel my unworthiness, and remember the deeper needs of my nature which the world leaves unfilled? In loss or want, do I bow in humble submission to a lot made by my Father's wise will more like Jesus Christ's? Do I take what God sends of cheer and help, with thankful acknowledgment of mercy more than my due? Do I look, before all else, for the wealth of Divine grace that is given to the lowly who forsake all trust in self, and "count all things loss for Christ"? Then God knows me blessed, for He makes me so. All things are mine, for I am in His hands. God prepares me to receive the uncounted blessings that He has prepared in the kingdom of heaven.

Almighty God, teach me my need of Thee; save me from trusting in earthly good. Enable me to bow to Thy will, and wait on Thee in lowly faith, that I may be blessed with the good things of Thy kingdom.

> Jesus, on me the want bestow,
> Which all who feel shall surely know their sins on earth forgiven;
> Give me to prove the kingdom mine,
> And taste in holiness divine the happiness of heaven.

SECOND SATURDAY AFTER EASTER.

"*Blessed are they that mourn: for they shall be comforted.*"
—MATT. v. 4.

HOW can he be blessed who mourns not when so much is mournful in him and around? The world is evil, and therefore sad. All have sinned. God's love is wronged. Christ has died, and is scarce remembered. Blessed are our sorrows which sober us, and warn of that of which they are the sign. God will bless true mourners who seek His consolation. He will use them to make the world less sad. He will give them pardon and peace now, and in the end the joy of perfect holiness.

I dare not ask that my life should be always calm, and bright, and free from care. Then I might forget my sin and need of a Saviour. This world might seem enough, and I might fail to seek a better. I must mourn while there is so much cause. I cannot be careless in a world where Christ mourned and bled for me. If I can feel, I must mourn for Him Who died, and for those who brought Him to the cross. How mighty is sin's hold on men! What woes crush them! What wrongs cry to heaven! How cold I am towards God! how untrue, how slothful! What deep-rooted evil shames me! How far off my unbelief keeps God! How slowly and unevenly I grow in grace and holiness. The love of God and the hope His patience gives only tell me to mourn more deeply for my unworthiness. Idle mourning will not help. I must labour and pray that what is saddening may be changed. So God will bless me while I work with Him. His comforts shall refresh my soul and cheer me, till I am blessed, where Divine love triumphs over all sin and sorrow.

Almighty and merciful God, give me a heart to mourn for my sin, and for the sin and sorrow of the world, and for all that made my Saviour mourn. Give me Thy comfort, and make me the means of bringing it to others, that we may be blessed together.

Jesu, friendless and forlorn, bowed with woes for sinners borne,
   Feeling still with all who mourn;
Show us why we ought to grieve, may we in Thy Word believe,
   And Thy comfort now receive.

The Third Sunday after Easter.

"Blessed are the meek: for they shall inherit the earth."
—MATT. v. 5.

THE meek learn from the meek and lowly Master. They draw into them and show forth His Spirit. They take quietly from God's hands what He sends, in whatever way He sees good to send it. They are not surprised by trials, for they are humble. In love to God and man, they bear willingly for others' sake. They bow to God's truth and God's will. So they gain the blessings He means for them. They win men to peace, and have quiet in their own hearts. So they have, even here, an earnest of the rest that awaits them in the new earth where dwelleth righteousness.

Like Christ, I have trials. As with Him, much that tries me comes from men. Let me learn and gain power from Christ to bear as He did. Why should I fret or rebel when my Father proves me. Why should it seem strange that men should think hardly of me, or treat me with unkindness? I deserve more than I suffer. I have many faults that only God and myself know. God understands all, and I may quietly leave my cause with Him. Wrongs against me are sins against Him. Why should I lose my calmness, and tempt others to new sin? If the world be evil, let me not help to make it more so. Pride that looks down on enemies is not meekness. Nor is the dull hardness that feels no hurt. True meekness comes from humility, love, and faith. The meek has power over his own spirit, and rules self by the grace of the strong calm God. Bearing meekly for God's sake and man's, I shall gain God's blessing, if not man's good will. Even in a troubled world I shall have much peace. Quiet from fear of evil, I shall be able calmly to prepare for the world where the meek shall be tried no more.

Almighty God, grant me so to bow to the mysteries of Thy Word and providence, that yielding meekly to Thy loving will, I may enjoy Thy blessing now and evermore.

Meeken my soul, Thou heavenly Lamb,
That I in the new earth may claim my hundredfold reward;
My rich inheritance possess,
Co-heir with the great Prince of Peace, copartner with my Lord.

Third Monday after Easter.

"Blessed are they which do hunger and thirst after righteousness: for they shall be filled."—Matt. v. 6.

CHRIST does not speak of being treated as if righteous, or being covered so as to look righteous, but of having righteousness, so as to be filled with it. God gives the want that welcomes His gifts. This craving is the first sign of the soul's life, when it awakes from the dull sleep of spiritual death. He who has it will wait on God in faith, and prayer, and work. As he uses the strength given, his desires will enlarge, and God will give more largely, till he is filled with the fruits of righteousness.

What a grand hope is mine! I may be filled with righteousness, so that evil can find no room. I may be right in my whole being—all loftiest aims reached—all pure, deep longings granted—Christ my righteousness so formed in me as to show in all my life what He is! Blessed indeed am I, if I am on my way to reach this state. But have I any such hunger? Is my highest aim perhaps to be called righteous and treated as if righteous when I am unrighteous; or only just not to starve in soul and die? Is "my meat and drink to do my Father's will" aright? Do I crave, as a parched, starving one, to receive into myself from God that by which man's higher being lives and thrives, and becomes God-like? Alas, how far I am from being "filled with righteousness!" I need to seek the bread of God and the streams of life. I need the "meat indeed and drink indeed." I need to gain, in all ways, closer union with Christ, that of His fulness I may receive what will make me like Him—righteous. God gives the craving as the beginning of blessedness, which has in it the promise of full satisfaction.

Almighty God, grant me to feel my soul's want, and long for Thy righteousness, and seek it in Thy ways till, satisfied with Thy likeness, I hunger and thirst no more.

> Me with that restless thirst inspire,
> That sacred infinite desire,
>   And feast my hungry heart;
> Less than Thyself cannot suffice,
> My soul for all Thy fulness cries,
>   For all Thou hast and art.

Third Tuesday after Easter.

"Blessed are the merciful: for they shall obtain mercy."
—Matt. v. 7.

MAN is helpless at the feet of mercy. But it is Divine mercy, always lavish, and enduring for ever. He who obtains it in the day when nothing hinders its work shall be blessed with all possible good. They are blessed in the beginning and the hope of this, who show that Divine mercy changes them, and makes them merciful. God's mercy is given that it may be passed on. They who are made the bearers of God's kindness, show by freely giving that they have freely received.

God has cared for me, borne with me, given me all things in Christ. God sets vast hopes before me, and gives grace to bring me on. All is in mercy. Whatever I am or have that is good proves God's kindness to one not worthy. I must ever be like those who sought Christ when He walked on earth, and cast themselves on His compassion. God's greatest mercy is the change of my heart, and the gift of His own loving, merciful Spirit. If I refuse that, all other mercies only add to my condemnation. Shall I dare to be hard and cold, keeping back the mercy which God would make known through me to others? Surely if I do, the flow of mercy to myself must stop, and I shall turn even the Divine mercy against me. God gives me the high privilege of making His mercy felt beyond myself among those who are His care. While doing this I draw down the power of God's love into my own soul. The harder the trial the more of that power comes, which fits me to receive mercy in that day when all shall know their need of mercy.

Almighty God, on Whose mercy I depend for pardon, and grace, and all things, grant me to feel my need of Thy mercy, and so to live guided by Thy loving Spirit, that I may be blessed through Thy mercy now and evermore.

> Mercy who show shall mercy find;
> Thy pitiful and tender mind
>   Be, Lord, on me bestowed:
> So shall I still the blessing gain,
> And to eternal life retain
>   The mercy of my God.

THIRD WEDNESDAY AFTER EASTER.

" Blessed are the pure in heart: for they shall see God."
—MATT. V. 8.

GOD desireth truth in the inward parts. Clean hands are not enough. The issues of life are from the heart—the seat of the affections and the will. There God's grace implants that purity before which what is impure passes away, till there is nothing between the soul and God. The pure in heart see God by faith now, a witness of every thought, feeling, and wish, a helper against evil. They know Him truly, though in part; and grow purer, living consciously in His presence. They shall see God when their imperfections that hide Him no longer cloud their souls, when they know as they are known, and are made like God—pure.

I can see God in His Word and works. I may, even now, know Himself. As God purifies my heart by faith, faith sees more clearly and grows more sure, God becomes more real to the soul. On earth this blessedness may be mine only in part, and as earnest of what is promised. Have I this purity? It is more than blamelessness of life. It is a state of the inner being to which uncleanness is painful, and by which the whole nature is refined and raised towards God. My soul should be as an eye, looking up to heaven through earth's mists, straining towards clearness of vision, quick to feel the touch of the least dust-spot of impurity. God reveals Himself as the soul can bear. Let me pray for this Divine gift. Let me aim to show a single-minded, guileless spirit. Let me realise God's nearness, and meditate on Him as Christ has shown Him. Let my only thoughts be such as will bear God's eye. Let me wish nothing against His will. Purity is heaven in the soul; a dwelling is prepared by God for Himself. Purity prepares for heaven, and for the vision of God which will perfect it.

O Lord, purify my heart by faith, that I may know and love Thee now, and live in hope of seeing Thee as Thou dost reveal Thyself where all are pure.

> Lead us daily nearer Thee,
> Till at last Thy face we see,
> Crowned with Thine own purity.

Third Thursday after Easter.

"Blessed are the peacemakers: for they shall be called the children of God."—MATT. v. 9.

THE Son of God brought the peace of God to earth. He laid down His life to take away the sin which parted man from God. He strove to win man from his distrust by making known God's love. He gave the law of love, and grace to obey it, that men might live as children of one Father. He brought a Divine power into man's fallen nature to reign there, that its rebel passions might be stilled, and the old harmony restored. They are blessed as the children of His Father, who labour with Him for His great ends of love.

Have I peace with God? Does my heart yield to Him in willing trust? Have I the peace God gives to those who bring their sin and care to Him through the Peacemaker? Is my nature swayed by the Spirit, and made to move in order? But I must do more if I am to be blessed indeed. My Father calls me to point others to the same peace, and to pray for them, careful not to reproach in a proud, unloving spirit, nor to speak peace when there is none. God bids me pray, and do my part against war and its sins, and against the strife and misunderstanding that rend the Church. When provoked, I must not alone bear meekly, but try to win foes to goodwill. When others strive, I must do all to set them at one, careful to act and speak gently, with judgment, and looking for God's help. I have God-like work to do. How blessed to be used to help one troubled, sin-tossed soul into the quiet of God's peace; to check the growing evil of one quarrel; to lead one heart from hate to love! How blessed if God owns me thus His child.

O Lord, the Prince of Peace, grant me peace with God and in my own nature, and zeal for the triumph of Thy love, that I may be blessed as a child of Thy Father.

> Lord, give me that pacific mind
> Which spreads Thy peace throughout mankind,
>   And knits them all in one.
> So shall He own me for His child,
> Who all through Thee hath reconciled,
>   And take me to His throne.

Third Friday after Easter.

"Blessed are they which are persecuted for righteousness' sake: for theirs is the kingdom of heaven."—MATT. v. 10.

GOD blesses sorrow which comes from righteousness, as well as that which leads to it. Those who take Christ's side openly, and go straight on, will be slandered and persecuted by a world which their lives reprove. Hardships and loss borne for God and truth are signs of grace. They prove the power that God has given. They drive the soul closer to Him to gain more grace. They are a pledge of reward. When endured in Christ's Spirit, they are blessed to form His image in the sufferer. So the persecuted faithful gain firmer hold on the blessings of the kingdom now, and a surer, happier hope.

How far have I a right to the comfort of this blessing? It is only for those who suffer for their faithfulness, and who, for Christ's sake, are spoken evil of falsely. Do my persecutors only punish my sin, and visit on me my awkwardness, carelessness, selfishness, or pride? Is the evil said against me true? Do those who upbraid me brand plain faults, of which my own heart is well aware? If I suffer as an evil-doer, I have no blessing till my sorrows lead me to repentance, and I take up my cross as a Christian. If I tread in Christ's steps, and am true to Him, I need fear no foe. No slander need move me. I have a part in the kingdom, and am lifted out of reach of the worst that men can do. Christ is with me: He will not let me lose by being on His side. In peace, I owe Him praise for the shelter of His arm. In trial, I may leave my cause with Christ, Who thus lets me share His cross and shame, that I may share His glory.

O Lord Jesus, grant me to be only careful to follow Thee, and to suffer as a Christian, not as an evil-doer. So may I through my sufferings on earth obtain more of the blessings of Thy kingdom.

> All they who would in Jesus live
> A daily death must die;
> His portion upon earth receive—
> His portion in the sky.

Third Saturday after Easter.

"When ye pray, say, Our Father, which art in heaven."
—Luke xi. 2.

HE through Whom prayers are heard gives us words. The only-begotten tells us to call His Father ours. God is a Father—fatherly as no earthly parent is. His children must not shrink from Him, but draw near with confidence, sure of kindness. God is in heaven; none may forget His awful holiness and majesty, or fail in godly fear. God is *our* Father; none must pray selfishly, or while unforgiving, or unmindful of others' good.

How could I dare to come unbidden before God, or, without His promise, hope to be heard! He is so great and holy; I am nothing. But He draws me near to Him, as a member of His only-begotten Son. He assures me of all good when He bids me call Him Father. To use that name, and, as a child, to open my heart to God, is not presumption, but faith. The great God in heaven, Who can do all things, is my Father. My Father, Who wills my welfare, is the Almighty God in heaven. Let me not be afraid of God, but reverence Him as a Father, and be drawn to Him by His glory. Let me not presume on God's goodness, but trust it, fearing to grieve that great love. Alas! how often have I dared heaven by thoughtless, unreal prayers! How often have I thrown away the blessing of my right to come near to that Almighty tenderness! How often have I pained my Father's love by bringing before Him a heart cold or hard against my brethren! He is still my Father, unworthy though I am. He waits to bless me, and to hear my prayers for those who, with me, call Him Father.

Almighty God, give me grace to worship Thee and live before Thee with lowly reverence, with childlike love and trust, and in charity to my brethren. Let Thy Fatherly blessing be over me now, and bring me to Thy home at last.

> Lead us, Heavenly Father, lead us
> O'er the world's tempestuous sea;
> Guide us, guard us, keep us, feed us,
> For we have no help but Thee,
> Yet possessing every blessing
> If our God our Father be.

The Fourth Sunday after Easter.

"Hallowed be Thy name."—MATT. vi. 9.

"THE honour due unto God's name" is the honour due unto God as He reveals Himself. "Holy is His name;" none can make it more or less so. But the world does not yet join in the full "Holy, holy, holy," of the Church on high. They do not hallow God in thoughts about Him, in worship of Him, in life for Him. Our first prayer breathed with all other prayers, must be that we and all men may be one with those who give God praise in heaven. When we pray, we offer ourselves as workers towards the end we pray for.

It is the first prayer of a child whom love makes jealous for his Father's honour. In it God points the aim of my heart and life. How far do I wish and try as I pray? How far do I endeavour to be in harmony with those who stand before the throne? Do I seek to gain and spread knowledge of God, that all minds may own Him in His love and holiness. Do I labour that all hearts may unite, with true devotion, in pure and reverent worship? Am I in earnest, that God may be glorified in the inward character and outward life, not of myself alone, but of all who are called by His name? God's truth, and all that makes it known, God's sacraments and worship, and all that has to do with them, God's will in all its parts, give me ways of hallowing God's name. God claims me on His side when He gives me this prayer. I cannot go on to pray till I make this prayer mine. I am happy and holy, and grow like those in heaven, according as it speaks the longing of my heart, and the effort of my life.

Enable me, O Lord, to think of Thee, to feel towards Thee, and live before Thee as I ought, earnestly labouring that all men may be one with the heavenly hosts in giving Thee the honour due unto Thy name.

> Father of earth and sky,
> Thy name we magnify;
> O that earth and heaven might join
> Thy perfections to proclaim,
> Praise the attributes divine,
> Fear and love Thy awful name.

Fourth Monday after Easter.

"Thy kingdom come."—MATT. vi. 10.

GOD is King; His power sways all things; men do not know or own His rule. God's kingdom of grace has in one way come; in another it goes on coming till Christ appears. Satan is still prince of this world. Men rebel against their true King. God's armies are discouraged and divided. The laws of the world, the wishes of the flesh, the promptings of the devil, are obeyed rather than God's will. The prayer of the faithful is that, in each man's being, God may be enthroned; that all nations may be one Church, ruled by one Spirit, worshipping one Lord; that Christ may come in power, and reign in glory.

Christ comes surely and soon. I shall share the triumph of His kingdom, or be cast out with His foes. I could not dare to pray for His speedy coming, did I not pray in the same words, that I myself and the world might be ready. I ask God to reign without rival over all I am. I seek grace to crush down each rebel thought and wish, to break wholly free from Satan, to cast off the yoke of self and the world. I vow to be a faithful soldier, winning others to the standard of my King, and enlarging His kingdom in the world. I declare myself on God's side. Oh, to act up to what these three short words say! They are solemn for the truest; what are they on the lips of one whose life says, "I will not have this man to reign over me," and who hinders the cause of truth and grace! If I can pray them honestly, I know that God has begun to set up His kingdom firmly in me. He will call me to higher work and trust, till His kingdom come, and I share its glory.

O God, set up Thy throne in my heart, and rule my life. May Thy grace triumph over evil in the world. Give me zeal for Thy kingdom, and a part in its glory.

<blockquote>
O quickly come, great King of all,
  Reign all around us and within;
Let sin no more our souls enthral,
  Let pain and sorrow die with sin.
Oh! quickly come; for Thou alone
Canst make Thy scattered children one.
</blockquote>

FOURTH TUESDAY AFTER EASTER.

"Thy will be done in earth, as it is in heaven."—MATT. vi. 10.

GOD'S will is done in heaven; for there all are holy and know God. All have full blessedness; for they gladly leave themselves in the hands of the wise Love that wills their highest good. They find true rest in the activity of loving obedience. On earth men choose what is evil, and turn from what is best. They shrink in unbelief from God's forming, restraining hand. They slothfully leave undone work by which God's will would educate them. They wilfully refuse God's guiding, and go their own way. So they miss their true good now, and risk it for ever.

I know not what is good for me. Divine love sees all to the end, and wills my true eternal welfare. I am only safe so far as I put myself out of my own hands into God's, that He may shape me in His own way, after His own plan. I am only safe when I bind my will to God's, that He may rule my life. When I pray this prayer I condemn my remaining ungodliness, I reprove my sloth, I warn down my self will, I lay hold of comfort in my sufferings. In spite of the flesh I cling to God, and ask Him not to leave me, but answer the prayer of the Spirit praying in me. Fearing self and sure of God, I would not have the fire burn less painfully, or the moulding hand press more lightly. I would be formed after God's likeness at any cost. I would not go my own way, or have slothful, useless ease, but watch for the indications of God's will, and be roused to do it. As for myself, so for all others, I am bound to long and pray that, in them and by them, God's will may be done, for their good and God's glory.

Grant, O Lord, that Thy people may so patiently trust and actively obey Thy will on earth, that they may do it perfectly and joyfully in heaven.

He always wins who sides with God, to him no chance is lost;
God's will is sweetest to him when it triumphs at his cost.
Ill that He blesses is our good, and unblest good is ill;
And all is right that seems most wrong, if it be His sweet will.

Fourth Wednesday after Easter.

"Give us this day our daily bread."—Matt. vi. 11.

OUR Creator, by Whom we live, teaches us to ask Him for all needful things. Our souls need Christ, His truth, His grace. Our bodies need what God has chosen to be means of nourishing and guarding their life. We pray for what we are without and we want. We bring before Him what we have, owning it as His gift, that we may receive it anew from Him with added blessing. We ask strength for labour, which is man's lot, and a true way of waiting on God. We plead for others as well as for ourselves.

If it be God's will, I would be free from the temptations of want. I dare not ask for wealth with its temptations. To-morrow may never come for me; I must not be careful for it, or boast myself of it, by asking for hoards to lay up. I pray not for encouragement to sloth, but for power to work, and for a blessing upon diligence. If I am idle, this prayer is presumption. When I pray for the daily supply of my soul's need, I do not look for it to come by special miracle; I must seek it in the way of faith and obedience, in the careful use of the means by which Christ gives knowledge and grace. I cannot ask daily provision for myself, and be careless how others fare. If I am selfish, this prayer is mockery. When I plead with my Father for His children, whose souls and bodies want, I bind myself to show by what I do that I mean what I say. I pray that I may receive, as part of my Father's bounty, a spirit of love, leading me to impart freely to my brethren.

O Lord, by Whose grace the souls and bodies of Thy creatures live, grant me what Thou knowest needful. Give me will, and faith, and patience, and strength to labour, a blessing on what Thy love bestows, and charity to care for the souls and bodies of my brethren.

> Daily, O Lord, our prayers be said,
> As Thou hast taught, for daily bread;
> But not alone our bodies feed,
> Supply our fainting spirit's need:
> O Bread of Life, from day to day,
> Be Thou their comfort, food, and stay.

FOURTH THURSDAY AFTER EASTER.
"Forgive us our debts, as we forgive our debtors."
—MATT. vi. 12.

WE need daily pardon, as we need daily bread. Duties owing to God and man are left unpaid. Wrongs are marked against us. We cannot wipe out old debts; for each day brings its own claims. There is nothing to spare for other days; our utmost always is only our duty. God invites us to come for mercy; but only if we feel our need of it, and show mercy. The unforgiving must not dare to pray what in his mouth means "Forgive me not." The words Christ gives are for those alone who are humbled by their own sin, and seek God's mercy for their foes and themselves.

The more honest I am, the more I must be shamed by my load of debt to God and my neighbour. Alas, that I should again and again have to own what I cannot pay! Alas, for laws broken, work not done, time wasted, love withheld! Alas, for thoughts, feelings, acts, stained by sin! Alas, for the poorness of my best offering, and all the hidden faults plain to God! What shame to fall from a state of pardon, and though so often forgiven, to need day by day fresh mercy! How great the love not yet tired! Would that the grace which waits to lift me up might be in me a power to keep me upright, and rule my life before God and with men. Knowing my need of mercy, I dare not deny it to my fellow-sinner. I cannot ask that my sin be forgiven, without asking God to forgive the wrongs of others against me. This would be to throw away my own hope of mercy, and to prove and to keep myself unpardoned. May I never condemn myself and call down God's wrath by praying Him to forgive me "as I forgive," while my heart is unforgiving.

Almighty God, grant me to live before Thee in lowly penitence and thankful faith, and to show to others the forbearing, forgiving love I need for myself, and seek through the merits of Him Who died for all.

My Father, for the sake of Him Who died,
Pardon me, wash me clean from guilty stain;
And let me never wander from Thy side,
Or fail in faithfulness and love again.

Fourth Friday after Easter.

"And lead us not into temptation."—MATT. vi. 13.

THE sins for which we ask forgiveness warn of evil within us and in the world. Taught our weakness, we dread temptation, and pray against it. Trial will come; but sin need not. Temptation well met, leaves us proved and trained, purer and stronger. We pray to be spared that temptation which is the punishment of sin, and that which is beyond our strength. We pray that we may not risk our souls by self-trust and presumption, or despondency and unbelief. We are safe if we are lowly, watchful, and true, strong in the help of a faithful Saviour.

My past falls tell me that I may fall again. I do well to dread temptation: I am so frail, the power against me is so great; to fall is so fearful; to rise again is so hard. I must take heed lest I go wilfully where I ask God not to lead me. If I yield to one temptation I open the way for others, and put God's help from me. I seek temptation if I go into evil company, listen to evil, look at what rouses evil in me, let Satan or the world gain advantage. I must draw back from the first snare, drive back the first onset, check the wrong desire at once. My falls must rouse me to show charity to others who are tried like me, in prayer for them, and kindly judgment of them. If I tempt them, or do not help them, what mockery is this prayer! Watchful and lowly, I must be brave in faith. If life's trials or evil without me be allowed to tempt, I must strive, as I pray, that the trial may leave me more faithful and sure of God. When my own evil will tries me, I must see that God's will triumphs, and is more firmly enthroned in my nature.

Almighty God, make me watchful and lowly, lest I fall by my own fault. Give me grace for every time of need, that trial may leave me purer, and more strong to resist evil.

O leave us not above our power, above our patience tried,
But turn aside the dreaded hour, and from temptation hide:
Or if we fall into the snare, let us our Lord behold,
Whose hand doth through the furnace bear, and bring us forth as gold.

Fourth Saturday after Easter.

"Deliver us from evil."—MATT. vi. 13.

WE feel the strength of evil in ourselves, and in the world, and in the malice of the evil one. We have made the evil in us worse by habits of sin. We often make what is good evil by using it wrongly. Even when forgiven, and under God's care, we are ever being reminded of the hold that evil has gained, and the struggle still before us if we are to be free. We feel the smart and the dread of those things which sin has brought into the world—pain, woe, death. Only God can deliver us; we cry to Him in sure faith that our Father will.

All round me and within me evil and good are mingled. I often can scarce tell where one begins and the other ends. In my blindness and helplessness I throw myself on God's care. I ask for God's grace, and take His side in the cause of my own soul and others. I pray Him to keep me under His wise, loving rule, and to bring me safely on in His own way past all that is evil in His sight. He can use even evil for His good ends, and make it serve me instead of enslaving me. How blessed to be freed from the evil in my nature that betrays me and welcomes sin! How blessed to be wholly at one in all things with God's good will; to find only good in the joy and work God gives me; to fear no evil when sorrow or death comes! I look forward, and in God's power I press forward to the time when no evil thought or wish shall ever rise, when the bad mysterious work of evil shall be overthrown, and nothing shall mar the peace and purity of life where all is very good.

Almighty God, grant that by the power of Thy grace I may overcome sin, and gain good from trial, and may go forward in the sure hope that Thou wilt deliver me from evil until evil is destroyed.

> The world, the flesh, and Satan dwell
>   Around the path I tread;
> O save me from the snares of hell,
>   Thou quickener of the dead.

The Fifth Sunday after Easter.

"Ask, and it shall be given you; seek, and ye shall find; knock, and it shall be opened unto you."—MATT. vii. 7.

OUR Father knows our needs, but bids us ask. He seeks us that we may seek Him. He knocks at our heart's door, that we may knock for mercy's gate to open. We ask what we have not, and wish to receive. We seek what has been ours but is lost; what is hidden, or but partly found and known. We knock, as still outside where we would be, and are promised welcome. God enlarges our desires, that He may give more. He adds earnestness to our seeking, that we may find Him more perfectly. He enables to go on knocking till all that bars our way to Him has been left behind.

I need not lack God's gifts, or presence, or consolations. Every one that asketh receiveth the spirit of prayer, and the good things promised to prayer. God waits to bestow till, by earnest asking, I prove that His gifts shall not be wasted. He that seeketh findeth the strait gate at which he may knock, the narrow way in which he may walk, the one Guide Whom he may follow. Let me be a true seeker, and I shall not seek in vain. Mercy's gate seems closed against me; but only that it may ever open to my knock, and let me in nearer to God, where richer gifts of grace are stored. These words of promise cheer and warn me when I am moved to pray my first true prayer for penitence and pardon, while God is still unfound, while all ways are dark, and the door of hope seems shut. They beckon me on, till all wants are satisfied, till God is not only known of, but known, till the door of heaven is shut, when I have passed in with burning lamp to the marriage feast on high.

Grant, Lord, that I may earnestly ask Thy good gifts, diligently seek Thy grace and truth, and knock where Thy love waits to bless, till I have all in heaven.

> Ask, and it shall be given unto you,
>   More than ye think, and better than ye ask;
> Seek, ye shall find that I am just and true;
>   My powerful love ye cannot overtask;
> Knock, and it shall be opened. Lord, I knock,
> I seek, I ask; do Thou Thy store unlock.

Rogation Monday.

"O Thou that hearest prayer, unto Thee shall all flesh come."
—Ps. lxv. 2.

GOD is a living God. He rules His own world. He watches over and cares for the creatures of His hand. He is Almighty and All Good. He bids us pray, and gives us the instinct of prayer. He promises to hear and answer. We are sure that our Father does not mislead His children. As God is real in His love, and power, and freedom, as we are real in our want and dependence, so prayer is real. God has chosen to make prayer a power. Those who trust God find Him true.

How good, to turn from the world and bow myself before my God! In that presence I feel what I am. My soul is humbled and solemnised, and owns its need. The power of things unseen is felt, and I am prepared to receive blessing. But when I pray I do more than seek thus to do myself good. I knock, that heaven's door may open; I ask, that One Who hears may give; I unburden my heart to a Parent. What a thought, that God sees me, by myself, among all the beings He has made, calls me to Him, listens, waits to help, asks me to ask Him, and owns my claim upon His love! He knows my needs; but His will is to hear them from me. He sees the future; but He gives my prayer a place in His plan. My poor desires join me with the Worker of All. God tells me to pray for myself and others, and He means me to act upon His word. I do not understand how this or any means leads to its end. I believe God, and my prayer is turned to praise.

Almighty and merciful God, give me the true spirit of prayer, that, asking in faith and reverence, I may receive the blessings which Thou art always waiting to bestow.

> There is a power which man can wield
>   When mortal aid is vain,
> God's eye, and arm, and love to reach,
>   God's listening ear to gain.
> That power is prayer, which soars on high,
>   Through Jesus to the throne,
> And moves the hand which moves the world
>   To bring salvation down.

Rogation Tuesday.

"*Lord, teach us to pray.*"—LUKE xi. 1.

POWER to pray aright comes in answer to prayer, and grows by careful use. A sinner must not come rashly before God, or speak unconsidered words. He must prepare himself and his prayers, lest his worship be "an abomination," and he bring "the sacrifice of fools." His heart must say to God what his lips say. He must desire and look for an answer, and mean to use the grace he seeks. The aim of his life must agree with the prayer of his mouth. He must not rush into God's presence, neither must he rush from it, but live still before God as one who has prayed.

It is no light thing, to call on God in the name of the Crucified. God is not mocked, or won by flattery. He knows how far my heart and life are like my words. Are my prayers those of one to whom the Lord's ears are open? Are they more than a short hurried look towards God, now and then, while I am far from Him? Do I mean my words, and pray with a clear aim; or do my words go on, while thoughts wander and desires flag? Does the solemn meaning of what I do rouse heart, and mind, and will, to earnestness? Do I wait God's answer, and feel my responsibility? My life should give meaning to my worship, and my worship give tone to my life. I should pray as a living dying creature to a living God, on Whom I depend wholly. I should pray thoughtfully, earnestly, simply, humbly, in faith, in hope, in patience, perseverance, and submission. If I use a form, it need not be a dead form; I should put it into mind and heart before I pray it. I should rise from prayer feeling that I have anew grasped God's promises, and pledged myself to God's service.

Grant me grace, O Lord, so to live and pray that I may always enjoy Thy favour, and daily be brought nearer to Thy presence through Jesus Christ.

O Thou, by Whom we come to God!
The Life, the Truth, the Way!
The path of prayer Thyself hast trod;
Lord, teach us how to pray.

Vigil of the Ascension.

"If ye loved Me, ye would rejoice, because I said, I go unto the Father."—JOHN xiv. 28.

LOVE that thought not of self might well rejoice that Christ was past all sorrow, and in glory with His Father. The disciples might forget their loss in sympathy with His triumph. But their love of His presence is ground for joy in His going away. His departure is needful, that He may come again to be with them in a new manner, a giver of larger blessing. He leaves them that He may send the Holy Spirit to be the means of His abiding Spiritual presence, and that so He may give them peace and joy which none can take from them.

I may seem less privileged than those who saw Christ on earth. I am tempted to long to meet His eye and hear His words of comfort, when I come and open my heart before Him. But I dare not wish Him back, and refuse to be glad that His conflict is ended. And it is better for me that He has not stayed on earth in the old way. He comes nearer now than He did even to the beloved disciple. He has gifts to bestow which were not in His hands till He passed beyond the cloud. I have a new hope in prayer, and a new hold on the sources of grace. I need not now to ask where Christ is to be found, nor to force my way through crowds to His feet. He is beside me, with me, in me always, everywhere, if I will know it. When I die I do not depart from where Christ is. I go to see, face to face, Him Whose presence on earth has been real to my faith. I go to receive a crown from Him Who cheers me now, and enables me to bear a cross well.

O my Saviour, give me faith to rejoice in Thy presence in heaven, and with me. Leave me not till, from having Thee with me where I am, I pass to be with Thee where Thou art for ever.

> I go from toil and care, and after life laid down,
> On heaven's high throne to wear the everlasting crown.
> Nor shall I leave you here alone and comfortless,
> My presence shall be near to guide, and help, and bless,
> The Spirit Whom I give shall make you one with Me,
> So ye, because I live, alive to God shall be.

Ascension Day.

" While He blessed them, He was parted from them, and carried up into heaven."—LUKE xxiv. 51.

THE life of humiliation was over. Sin was atoned for; death was conquered; the grave opened. During forty days the living Lord had spoken to those who were to order His kingdom. Then, while with lifted hands He blessed His disciples, He rose beyond their view. Faith could rejoice to see Him pass the gates of heaven. Angels who sang when God was born as man, now raised their triumphant songs when Man was throned on high as God. The disciples might well feel great joy; for angels told them where their Lord was gone, and that He would come again to receive them unto Himself. They knew that He cared for and blessed them still.

The ascension is Christ's triumph and is mine. It is the end of the long, hard, mournful way that began at Bethlehem; all my love is called on to be glad for Christ's sake. Moreover, what high glory it is that man sits on the throne of heaven! If I am a member of Him, I "sit in heavenly places in Christ." I need not fear to take up my cross, forsaking all; for He Who bids me follow Him, showing me His footprints on a rough and painful path, lets me see the end, and whither He leads. Through life's trials He calls me to go after Him, past death, on and up to heaven. Towards Him I lift up my heart, and He raises my life above the world that He has left. Now I can think of His hands lifted up to obtain gifts for me, and to pour them down in blessing. I can hear the angels tell me to labour for Him Whom by faith I see, and with Whom in love and thought I dwell. I know that He shall come again, that where He is I may be also.

O Lord Jesus, raise my heart and mind towards Thee. Grant that the grace Thou dost gain for me may lead me on till I am parted from all here, and carried up to heaven.

Borne on triumphal clouds, the King of Glory soars,
 While each tranced, faithful heart below in wondering love adores.
He hath not left His own: where faith illumes the light,
And love the dwelling-place prepares, there He abides in might!
Return into your hearts, and ye shall find Him there;
He hath but risen that ye may rise, and breathe of heaven's
   pure air.

FRIDAY AFTER ASCENSION DAY.

"We have a great High Priest, that is passed into the heavens, Jesus the Son of God."—HEB. iv. 14.

THE high priest of old went once a year into the holy of holies to offer the blood of atonement. Christ passed into the holiest heaven to plead His one sacrifice, which need not, and cannot be repeated. The power of that sacrifice prolongs man's day of grace, and wins him pardon and blessing. In union with it, all we do and all we pray reaches God, and is accepted. Our High Priest feels with us, for He still is man. He can help us, for He is Almighty God. He makes ready a place and welcome for us; He gains and bestows what fits us for the place.

The love that showed itself in the life and death of Christ is active in my behalf now. He Who died for me ever liveth to show forth His work for me. The whole value of what Christ did and bore is being pleaded always. He pleads Who knows all my want, and weakness, and distress, and remembers the days of His own flesh. He pleads Who is one with the Father in will, and love, and power. Shall I doubt or be discouraged? Shall I be careless, and slow to unite myself with Him Who is thus earnest for my good? Christ pleads with my heart and conscience, as well as for me in heaven. He points me to His work from Bethlehem to the cross, and to what He is doing now. Shall I not bring my soul, with all its sin, for cleansing? Shall I not be unwearying in prayer? Shall I not strive that all my life may be an offering of living service, hallowed by Christ's offering, and that I myself may be so one with Christ as to lose none of the fruit of His pleading for me?

O Lord Jesus Christ, Who dost plead for me, plead in my heart, and win me to penitence, and faith, and prayer; and grant that my whole life may be so devoted that it may be accepted in union with Thy sacrifice.

O Priest, O Victim, Who Thy prayer dost pour
For me as for the ransomed gone before,
Grant me by faith that sacrifice to see,
And thus my whole heart, Lord, to offer up to Thee.

SATURDAY AFTER ASCENSION DAY.

"I say not unto you, that I will pray the Father for you; for the Father Himself loveth you."—JOHN xvi. 26, 27.

CHRIST does not contradict His promises to pray for His people; He ever liveth to make intercession. Nor does He only mean that He need not assure them of what they know. He means that He does not say that He will pray for them, as if the Father had no good-will, and must be won over to kindness; or as if they stood in no relation to Christ, and through Him to the Father—as if He were Christ's Father, but not theirs. The Father Himself loveth, for He is Love; He is loving unto every man. He specially loveth those who welcome His love made known in Christ.

In Christ I see God as Love. God claims my trust and love through Christ; He gives, through Christ, the power to love Him. Christ is the Saviour specially of them that believe. God is the Father specially of those who believe in Him Whom He hath sent, and who, in union with Christ, are God's children by adoption and grace. If I am far away from God in sin and loneliness, yet God is not to be my terror, but my refuge. I must not flee from Him to Christ, but flee to Him through Christ. If I believe in Him, and love Him, this is because He has first loved me; and He loves me as His faithful child, not only with a love that longs after me, but with a love that can rejoice in blessing me. I am cheered in my work and prayers by knowing that I can join all with Christ's pleading on high. And I am cheered by knowing that as the love of God, the Father, Son, and Holy Ghost, provided the sacrifice, so the pleadings for my pardon and salvation are according to the will of God.

Almighty Father, Who art loving unto all, and dost make known Thy love in Christ, give me faith to receive Thy grace, that I may love Thee, and so enjoy that love with which Thou dost love Thy faithful children.

I love and trust Thee, holy Lord, Almighty as Thou art!
For Thou hast stooped to ask of me the love of my poor heart.
No earthly father loves like Thee, no mother half so mild,
Bears and forbears as Thou hast done with me, Thy sinful child.

The Sunday after Ascension Day.

"Hitherto have ye asked nothing in My name: ask, and ye shall receive, that your joy may be full."—JOHN xvi. 24.

NO one prayed in Christ's name till, by the work of the Holy Spirit, His disciples became His members. Christ is more now than an Intercessor pleading for us. He is the Mediator through Whom we are joined to God. We can not only draw nigh and pray to be heard for His sake, we are brought near in Him; we can know that God hears us as members of His Son, and grants our prayers as His. So one with Him we may ask and receive what no man can take from us, till our joy be full.

Though I be the least in the kingdom of heaven, I am greater than John the Baptist. I have a privilege higher than that of the saints of old, or of the disciples while Christ was with them; for I am baptized into Christ. I can dwell in Christ, and have Him dwelling in me. I can live animated by Christ's life, guided by His mind and motives, showing His Spirit. When I pray, realising my union with Him, uniting myself to Him in what He does on high, throwing my will into His purpose and desire, my prayers are offered in Christ's name. All the resources of the Eternal are open for my good. Only let me take heed that I abide in Christ by those means which He has given, and that His words abide in me, ruling my thoughts and life. Then I may ask, and go on asking, till my joy is full, till even in the world's worst tribulation I may be exceeding joyful. I shall know that He Whose name I bear, in Whose name I labour, and endure, and pray, is my great reward, and that His Father is mine, and loveth me.

Make me, O Lord, so one with Christ, that all my life and prayers may be guided by His Spirit, and that I may receive ever larger blessing till my joy be full.

> Look, Father, look on His anointed face,
>   And only look on us as found in Him;
> Look not on our misusings of Thy grace,
>   Our prayer so languid, and our faith so dim;
> For lo! between our sins and their reward
> We set the merits of Thy Son, our Lord.

MONDAY AFTER ASCENSION DAY.
"This man receiveth sinners, and eateth with them."
—LUKE XV. 2.

THE Saviour welcomed the sinners who met His love with trust. He sought them, and was among them as a friend. He was drawn to them, not because He was like them, or loved the sins they loved; He longed to make them like Him, and lead them to love the holiness taught in His words and life. He is the same Saviour now. He invites sinners to come near and be with Him for the same end. He receives them to very close communion. They may not only feast their souls in His presence and enjoy His love; they may even receive Himself, to dwell in them and be their soul's life.

Christ is still the Friend of sinners. His ways of making His goodness felt are as winning as of old. He does not shrink from me, sinner though He knows I am. My sin grieves Him, but He asks me to come that He may receive me and take my sin away. He seeks to be with me in all my life, that whether I eat or drink, or whatsoever I do, I may do all with the glad yet solemn feeling of His presence. He would have me not dread, but trust Him. But why does He, the All Holy, thus come to be my friend? It is that I may cease to be a sinner, that He may change me to be like Himself, that I may take my spirit from Him, and learn how to think, and feel, and live. He ever comes to my side; He draws near when I come in answer to His drawing. Virtue goes out of Him to heal and ennoble me. He spreads a heavenly feast, that I may share even His own being. All this He does that He may at last receive me, no more a sinner, to His table, in His kingdom.

O Friend of sinners, draw me to Thee, and receive me, that I may be saved from sin and prepared to take my place in Thy presence among Thy holy ones.

> Just as I am, poor, wretched, blind,
> Sight, riches, healing of the mind,
> Yea, all I need in Thee to find;
> Just as I am, of Thy free love,
> The breadth, length, depth, and height to prove,
> Here for a season, then above,
> O Lamb of God, I come.

TUESDAY AFTER ASCENSION DAY.
"This is My Body. . . . This is My Blood."—MATT. xxvi. 26, 28.

MOST solemn words, spoken at a most solemn hour, most solemnly! Surely most true words! On the eve of His death, while keeping the farewell Passover, Jesus blessed and brake bread; He blessed wine; He gave to His disciples, saying, "This is My Body; this is My Blood." So He taught them how to "eat the flesh of the Son of man, and drink His blood." Now they have the reward of patient faith. They see the bread and wine; faith knows of the Body and Blood of the Lord. It is enough.

The Bread which the stewards of Christ's mysteries break, "is it not the communion of the Body of Christ?" The Cup of blessing which they bless, is it not the communion of His Blood? He who has the words of eternal life speaks nothing vainly. He tells me these things are; He does not tell me how. Not for me to go beyond or fall short of what His words bid me believe. Not for me to be offended and go away because His saying is hard. Not for me to presume to explain away what He has left a mystery for faith and devotion. Christ was God veiled in flesh. He was the "Vine" and the "living Bread." He multiplied the loaves, and made water wine. He can do what He will in His own way. Enough for me to know that Christ, in His sacrament, has provided a means of making His presence sure, and of giving His Body and Blood to be my soul's food and cheer. Let my care be not to ask how He comes, but to come with a right love and awe, and so gain what He gives.

O Lord Jesus, give me faith to welcome Thy words with loving joy, that through Thy Body and Blood my soul and body may be preserved unto everlasting life.

> I ask not, Lord, the mystery hidden
>   Beneath those words so dark and deep;
> I would but do as Thou hast bidden,
>   In simple faith Thy mandate keep.
> The bread I eat, the cup I drink,
>   I know Thee present and adore:
> I look into myself, and shrink,
>   I look to Thee and want no more.

WEDNESDAY AFTER ASCENSION DAY.

"As often as ye eat this bread, and drink this cup, ye do show the Lord's death till He come."—1 COR. xi. 26.

CHRIST died to gain for us pardon and grace. He ever pleads that death before God in heaven, and in His Church on earth. The Jewish sacrifices showed His death, in type and figure, till He came to die. Now the sacrifice, finished on the cross, is continually proclaimed to man, and presented before God, till He come again in glory. Christ is the priest; it is He that is offered. Faith knows of His broken body and poured-out blood. Showing Christ's death before God, as Christ has taught us, we unite our prayers with His pleadings.

My only hope in coming before God rests on Christ and His work. When I pray, I ask to be heard through Him, for His sake. When I have sinned, I plead His atonement. When I offer praise or thanksgiving, or whatever I do and hear in His cause, I trust in His merits as my one ground of confidence. A special way is given me by Christ Himself, in which I may join with Him in showing forth His finished work, and may present all my devotions in union with what He does before God. Along with my Saviour, I offer my Saviour. Along with the whole Church, everywhere and always, I plead the Church's hope. Here are, indeed, greatness and joy, and assurance of the Divine favour. What faith, and hope, and love should be mine! How thankfully should I "do this," as often as I can, till Christ come! Oh, that through those merits which I plead I might be less unworthy of my calling! Oh that, made more one with Him by Whom my soul lives, my praise and thanksgiving, and I myself, might be acceptable!

O Lord Jesus Christ, grant me full and thankful faith in Thy merits and mediation. Teach me with earnest, lowly devotion to show Thy death, and to present all my devotion in union with Thy finished sacrifice.

    Thou didst once for sin atone,
Ever in Thine offering shown, perfect, finished, and alone.
Lamb of God, enthroned on high, Saviour wonderfully nigh,
    Thus we show Thy "memory."

Octave of the Ascension.

"He that eateth My flesh, and drinketh My blood, dwelleth in Me, and I in Him."—JOHN vi. 56.

WE can do and be all things if we dwell in Christ and are dwelt in by Him. Christ tells us that we have this union by eating His body and drinking His blood. At the Last Supper He said of the bread and the wine which He blessed, "This is My body, this is My blood; take, eat, drink ye all of this." So we know that He hallows the sacrament of His body and blood as a means in which He comes to receive His faithful into closest union. We believe and obey His word, and the outward pledge assures us of the unseen gift bestowed.

I can draw nigh to Christ in faith, and prayer, and love, and obedience. But here is something to which all these lead up, more full of mysterious blessedness. I can be made in an unknown but most true way, one with Him Who is God. The Holy Communion is spoken of by itself as nothing else is. In it Christ gives me not some grace or gift, but Himself, in Whom is all grace. He unites my being with His own. So He is a Saviour, not without but within me, not to look up to only, but to possess. His holiness becomes mine; His strength enables me for all high work. Out of His perfection all my failings are supplied. Surely in this sacrament I am brought into very solemn nearness to God. Each communion should be a new incoming of the life of God, and should send me forth to show more plainly the power of Christ living in me. No hope of mine can go beyond the greatness of the blessing offered. No care can be too much, that I may draw near as one to whom the blessing will be fully given.

O Lord Jesu Christ, grant me love and faith to long for Thee, and come to Thee as Thou dost bid me, that I may know Thy words true, and feel the joy and power of Thy indwelling presence.

> Jesu, Who through bread and wine
> Blest by mighty words of Thine, dost impart Thy life divine,
> Live within us day by day, guide our spirits when we pray,
> Lead us on our heavenward way.

Morrow of the Octave of the Ascension.

"*Wherefore whosoever shall eat this bread, and drink this cup of the Lord, unworthily, shall be guilty of the body and blood of the Lord.*"—1 COR. xi. 27.

NO one can be worthy to gather the crumbs of God's rich gifts. But no one need come to the Divine feast unworthily. They do this who fail to "discern the Lord's body," so as to know what God sets before them; and who fail to "examine themselves," so as to mourn what they are. They are like the men who took part in Christ's death, and cared not who He was or why He died. They who, hearing with lowly devout heart God's true words, long for the spiritual food God gives through His Sacrament, and who by close self-searching learn to come as sinners to a merciful Saviour, eat and drink worthily.

What am I, so weak and sin-stained, that I should dare to come so close to God and ask Him to dwell in me! Yet He calls me, and I dare not, I cannot hold back. If I wait till I feel worthy, I shall stay away for ever, or else come as a self-deceiver. Only by coming can I gain the worthiness I have not. God sets before me not a new risk, but a new power of salvation. He bids me not to give, but to be gifted; not to show any fancied goodness of mine, but to gain His. I will seek grace. I will meditate in thankful awe and faith on the great mystery of love in Christ's whole work, and in this way by which He feeds and gladdens souls. I will search my heart and life, and spread all my unworthiness before my Saviour. I will resolve in God's strength to live for God. I will come in faith to Him Who "receiveth sinners and eateth with them." So shall I find not danger but salvation, and be fed with "the meat indeed and drink indeed."

O Lord, grant me to receive Thy sacramental gifts with such penitence, and faith, and true resolve, that I may be strengthened and cheered, and, in union with Christ, made worthy of Thee.

> All my evil I deplore,
> Help me to desire Thee more, and with truer faith adore.
> Purge me from the taint of sin,
> Make my spirit pure within, eager all Thy gifts to win.

Whitsun Eve.

"We being many are one bread, and one body: for we are all partakers of that one bread."—1 Cor. x. 17.

MEN may be of one mind, have one faith and hope, join in prayer and praise, love one God, and so be at one. To be one is something more. We cannot make ourselves one. God alone does that, when His power joins us to Christ. "By one Spirit baptized into one body," "partakers of that one bread," we have one common life in Christ. Members of Him, we are joined to each other, branches of one vine, parts of one living body. Unity in faith, and love, and work, shows this oneness, and puts forth the power of it, but does not make it be.

In the Holy Communion God renews my oneness with Christ, and with all who are one with Him. This union depends on God, not on man. It *is*, whether I know it and act on it, or not. To disown it does not free from what it binds me to. I cannot part from those who are in Christ, unless I am cut off from Him. There is but one Christ. Time and distance do not divide Him. There is but one bread of God, upholding and building up the spiritual being of all living souls. In Christ's own sacrament I receive Him Who is the one living Bread, no other than that received by all Christ's faithful in all ages and all lands. Christians who know me not, and, perhaps, would own me not, are yet one with me. Friends far away on earth are not indeed separated. Friends gone to be with God are one with me still, in more than memory and love. Surely I lose much of help and cheer in my communions, if I fail to grasp this great truth in its full meaning, and to use it as a motive. What consolation for times of loneliness and sorrow! What ground for courage and hope! What a call to charity, and forbearance, and oneness of heart!

O Lord Jesus, grant that, sharing Thy life, I may live for Thee, and for those who, with me, are Thy members.

Though a stranger and pilgrim, I am not alone,
   I belong to the household whose home is above;
One with Christ, I have union with each of His own,
   And God's loved ones love me, and claim part in my love.

Whitsun Day.

"The Comforter, which is the Holy Ghost."—JOHN xiv. 26.

THE Holy Spirit gave life and order to creation; strove with fallen man; made known God's truth; guided the Jewish Church. By Him the Word took flesh. He lighted on Christ at Jordan. He was breathed on the apostles. At Pentecost He came in a new way, which answered to the Incarnation of God the Son. He was before with men; now He is in them as a person. He applies Christ's work, and unites men with it. He builds up the body of Christ. He makes sacraments real. He unfolds the Scriptures He inspired. He strengthens, comforts, pleads, warns. He inspires prayer, and gives will and power to become holy.

It was expedient for me that Christ should go away and send the Comforter. He abides, and is not instead of Christ, but a means of His presence. By the Holy Spirit I share the fruits of Christ's work. I am a "member of Christ" because I am "born of the Spirit." I am "strengthened and refreshed by the Body and Blood" of my Saviour, the Holy Spirit's power giving the unseen presence. All I learn and feel of the truth of God, I owe to the teaching Spirit in the Scriptures, in the Church, and in me. All union with all souls on earth or at rest is through Him by Whom the mystical body of Christ lives and is one. Every thought, and wish, and act of sin is in spite of the enlightening, restraining grace of the loving Spirit. Each right desire, each longing after holiness, each effort of faith, each comfort of hope, each movement of love, witnesses to the presence of the Holy Ghost. Let me hail and cherish the coming of Him by Whose Divine work in me I enjoy the grace of a Saviour, and the love of a heavenly Father.

Almighty Father, grant me by the power of the Holy Spirit the gifts which my Saviour received, that I may be prepared to follow Him to Thy presence.

Life-giving Spirit, o'er us move, as on the formless deep;
Give life and order, light and love, where now is death or sleep.
Great gift of our ascended King, His saving truth reveal;
Our tongues inspire His praise to sing, our hearts His love to feel.

Whitsun Monday.

"When He is come, He will reprove the world of sin, and of righteousness, and of judgment."—JOHN xvi. 8.

THE Holy Spirit breaks up the false peace of sinners by showing, in His love and power, the Saviour Whom unbelief rejects. He lays bare sin in its true form to the mind, and quickens the heart to feel shame and sorrow. He rouses the soul to hunger for that righteousness which the ascended Saviour, seen by faith, imparts to man. He warns of the judgment, when the prince of this world shall be doomed with those who are on his side, and Christ's faithful shall share their Lord's triumph.

The Holy Spirit speaks to me through the Church, the Scriptures, and the words of my fellow-men. He speaks in me, preparing me for His message and work. In His light I see truth; He makes my conscience tender. I learn the sin of putting away Christ in unbelief, or denying Him in my life. I feel how unbelief is the root of all sin, and shuts out light, and stops the flow of grace. I learn how vain is the hope of building up any righteousness of my own apart from Christ. I am given a craving for righteousness, and a sure hope, founded on Christ's going to His Father, that I shall be filled with it. I look to gain Christ's righteousness, not merely called mine, but put within me, making me a living, holy member of Himself. I shrink from the temptings of him whom God has doomed. I fear to be drawn from God's favour and safe keeping, and condemned with the wicked. It is well to hear the voice and yield to the power of Him Who guides to the one Giver of rest those whom He makes weary and heavy laden.

O Holy Spirit, reveal my Saviour, that I may hate my sin. Give me faith in Christ's work for me on high, and enable me so to be filled with His righteousness, that I may have boldness in the day of judgment.

And His that gentle voice we hear, soft as the breath of even,
That checks each fault, that calms each fear, and speaks of heaven,
And every virtue we possess, and every conquest won,
And every thought of holiness, are His alone.

Whitsun Tuesday.

"*Your body is the temple of the Holy Ghost.*"—1 Cor. vi. 19.

GOD has created and redeemed man for Himself. He has taken possession. The Holy Ghost has come to dwell in man's nature. He sets up His shrine there, that all the parts of man's being may be hallowed, and that every power may show forth God's praise. The "temple of God is holy." Sin must have no place where the Divine Presence is. Body, soul, and spirit must be a meet pure temple of God. What if He be forgotten, insulted, grieved, wearied, at last quenched!

God is more than near and with me. By His Holy Spirit He is in me. He comes to be a new Presence and power of life, ruling what I am by nature, guiding and inspiring thought, feeling, will, action. What glory is mine! How glad and hopeful may I be! Yet with what reverent awe must I live in this closeness to the Holy God! How can I rise to a worthy cleanness of heart and purity of life? How can I feel enough the seriousness of all I do? Alas, for the evil and mean things that cling to me, and defile God's temple! Alas, for the foolish and foul idols that have their altars there! Well might I cry in fear, "Depart from me, for I am sinful." But God comes to make me other than He finds me. He scorns not to cleanse and hallow me for His service, unworthy though I be. He asks me but to yield to Him, and let Him loose my heart from sin, and train my will and powers to do Him holy service. He is patient, though so often and sorely grieved. He will build up my ruins, and make me worthy of God.

Almighty God, grant me always a thankful, solemn remembrance of the indwelling of the Holy Ghost, and make me earnest, that body, soul, and spirit may be purified and devoted to Thy glory, through Jesus Christ.

> Heal our wounds, our strength renew,
> On our dryness pour Thy dew;
>   Wash the stains of guilt away,
> Bend the stubborn heart and will;
> Melt the frozen, warm the chill,
>   Guide the steps that go astray.

WEDNESDAY IN WHITSUN WEEK.

*"We know not what we should pray for as we ought: but the Spirit itself maketh intercession for us with groanings which cannot be uttered."—*ROM. viii. 26.

MAN knows not his true good. He often desires most what is worst for him, and feels his greatest need least. He knows not how to speak to God. God, Who bids him pray, provides help for his infirmity. Christ pleads on high for man. The Spirit in man prompts and guides the desires. Devotions beyond what human lips can utter rise to God, through Christ, from the soul in which the Spirit dwells. He who trusts himself to the Divine helper, gains, for Christ's sake, what the indwelling Spirit asks.

I have a twofold ground of humble boldness in prayer. Before the throne He stands Who died for me. I am accepted in the Beloved. The prayers I offer through Him need not be what my own ignorance of what is right and good, and of the way to ask, make them. The Holy Spirit comes to be one with my spirit. He imparts godly fear and childlike trust. He guides and guards my prayers by Divine wisdom, raising them towards better things than I could ask or think. He prays in me, so that what He prays is heard as mine. If I am earnest, I need not be cast down because my spirit is slow to rise, and my prayers seem cold and poor. Knowing my infirmity, let me always pray, looking for the presence and help of the Spirit, and trusting in Christ's intercession. Let me doubt myself, and lean on Divine help, asking to be saved from my own shortsighted wilfulness, and blessed as God knows well. Thus "praying in the Spirit," I shall seek what Divine love wills for my good, and through Christ's pleading I shall receive it.

Almighty Father, teach me what to pray for as I ought, and grant that what the Spirit asks according to Thy will may be heard through Jesus Christ.

> His breath inspires all prayer that doth rejoice
> To rise like incense to the central sun;
> All praise is the intoning of His voice,
> Swelling from whispers in the heart begun.

Thursday in Whitsun Week.
"I am the Way, and the Truth, and the Life."—John xiv. 6.

CHRIST shows the one narrow way, and leads lost souls in it. He teaches the truth of God's work and will. He gives to dying men hope of life for ever. More than this, He is the Way; only by Him can man far off in sin find God. He is the Truth in Whom God is made known. He is the Life, joined to Whom men live with the life of God. Those who trust to Him are borne on surely and safely. They find Him the Truth Who does not mislead. One with Him in His sufferings, they are one with Him in His risen life and ascended glory.

Without Christ, I am far from God, and unable to draw near; I am blind and deceived; I am perishing and have no hope. In Him I am brought to God, and go towards heaven. The truth makes me free from the power of sin and folly. I know that because Christ lives I shall live beyond death. I was joined to Him in baptism. If I have wandered, have I been careful to come back? Do I trust myself to Him, and watch lest I stray, and abide so that He may bring me on, step by step, safely and surely towards God's presence? Am I earnest not only to learn the truth Christ has spoken, but to know the Truth He is, and to know more of God as Christ reveals Him to devout, obedient souls? Do I feel the need of renewing and deepening my union with Christ by all the ways of which His true Word tells, that there may be a full flow of ever-fresh life to me from Him? Is He living in me the guide of all I do, my power in temptation, my hope in sorrow and in the prospect of death?

Almighty Father, Who hast sent Thy Son to save the lost and dying, grant me to seek and find Thee by the one Way, to learn and love the Truth made known in Christ, and to show in my life that Christ living in me makes my life one with Thine.

> Thou art the Way, the Truth, the Life:
> Grant us that way to know,
> That truth to keep, that life to win,
> Whose joys eternal flow.

Friday in Whitsun Week.

"*God is no respecter of persons: but in every nation he that feareth Him, and worketh righteousness, is accepted.*"—Acts x. 34, 35.

THE Jewish Church was God's Church. In it were privileges not to be had outside. There was one way of entering it. By obeying its rules, men kept their place and rights in it. But God left no men uncared for. All could know Him more or less clearly, and, using well the light and grace within reach, be accepted. Still, they were bound to own the claims of the Church, and seek her special blessings, when put before them. Their wish to learn more full truth, and gain more sure grace, was a test how far they were indeed accepted.

God has set up His Church, and made known rules of membership. In and through the Church God commonly blesses men and gives grace; but, as of old, love overflows its channels. God can bestow His goodness in His own way; I am not free to seek it in my way. I dare not think light of my place in God's Church, because many who are not in her yet fear God and work righteousness. I dare not undervalue means of grace, on the plea that God often gives grace without them. The lives of unbaptized persons or non-communicants may shame mine, and plainly show God's guiding; but I do not know all their case; I may not claim to be free from seeking and serving God in the ways He points out. While I thank God that His love goes forth beyond Jerusalem, I must not the less be thankful for my high calling, and humbled that I am proved so unworthy of it. Cornelius was bound to believe the fresh truths and seek the new privileges God sent him by St. Peter. I must earnestly seek all light and grace, thus showing fear of God, and a true will to work righteousness.

O Lord, Who art loving unto every man, give me love and holy fear, that, in union with Christ's body, I may so work righteousness as to be accepted, for Christ's sake.

> Where I am right, Thy grace impart
>   Still in the right to stay;
> Where I am wrong, oh, teach my heart
>   To find that better way.

Saturday in Whitsun Week.

"If I have told you earthly things, and ye believe not, how shall ye believe, if I tell you of heavenly things?"—JOHN iii. 12.

BY earthly things, Christ means works which God does on earth, and marks by outward sign. He asks faith as One Who "knows" the truth, and "testifies what He hath seen." For He is God, and can trace the working of the Spirit on man's soul. What He "tells" of earthly things let none doubt, else how can they receive the higher mysteries of the being of God in heaven—the Almighty, All-Knowing, Ever-living, Three in One. Those who trust Him will trust what He says. Faith can grasp what the mind cannot search out.

The world around is full of mystery; so is my own being. I do not know the how or why of much. My thoughts and will are guided, and in turn guide my words and life, but I cannot tell in what way. If I refuse to believe and act upon whatever I do not understand, I can scarce move in my daily life. Thus I am prepared to find mystery in God's ways and working. I do not look to know all about what God is and does. Because He is God, and I am not God, I must be unable to find Him out by any searching. There are many things which I cannot know till God tells me. He reveals enough to make plain my way, not to explain His ways. My reasonable course is to act in my religious life as in my common life I must act, if I act at all. Satisfied that a truth or duty is made known by God, my part is to believe and obey. What faith receives, experience proves true. Faith grows sure and strong, as it guides the will; it becomes able to welcome and rejoice in higher mysteries.

Give me, O Lord, a wise and lowly faith, that I may not stumble at Thy Word, but thankfully receive and obey what Thou dost reveal of Thy truth and will.

> Why seek to know what God hath sealed?
>   Faith were an empty sound,
> If nought but what our sight revealed
>   Around our course were found.
> Lord, I believe; increase my faith,
> To take on trust whate'er the Spirit saith.

Trinity Sunday.

"The grace of the Lord Jesus Christ, and the love of God, and the communion of the Holy Ghost, be with you all."—2 COR. xiii. 14.

GRACE is God's love working freely for and in us. Grace "came by Jesus Christ," when God the Son joined our nature to His. The Father Who loveth the Son loved us, and sent the Son that through Him we might have the adoption of sons. The Holy Ghost, the bond of love between the Father and the Son, was the agent by Whom God the Son was made man. Christ in His glorified manhood is still the Mediator, through Whom we draw near to the Father, and grace comes. The Holy Ghost joins us to Christ, and keeps us one with Him, that we may live as those who know the love of God.

God the Son, through His man's nature, joins me to God, the first source of all good. Through Him the love of the Father reaches me. One with Him, I can do all things, and become what I am called to be. One with Him, I am a son of His Father; I can draw upon the heart of God, and look humbly for all the good God has for His children. By the work of the Holy Ghost I was born into Christ, and my oneness of life with Christ is upheld. I share the one spiritual life, which is the same in all Christ's members. The Holy Ghost gives holy desires, and will, and power to put forth the grace that comes from union with Christ, and which is the outgoing of the love of God. Oh, to long for, and make mine, and use in full, the grace of the Lord Jesus Christ! Oh, to let the love of God, Who first loved me, win my love, and do with me what it wills. Oh, to yield my whole self to the indwelling and the leading of the Spirit!

Almighty and all-loving Father, Whose blessed Son, by the power of the Holy Ghost, was born to be my Mediator and Redeemer, grant me by the same Spirit so to receive the grace of Christ, that I may enjoy for ever the love of God.

I believe in God, Who all things made;
I believe in God, Who the ransom paid;
I believe in God, Who makes men pure;
And I hold my faith with a courage sure.

FIRST MONDAY AFTER TRINITY.

"Except a man be born of water and of the Spirit, he cannot enter into the kingdom of God."—JOHN iii. 5.

"BORN of water and of the Spirit," explains "born again," or "born from above." Christ is more than a "teacher come from God." He brings the life of God to souls; He is founder of a kingdom. Those who are to have part in it must not only learn, but receive a new nature, which God, in common cases, gives in baptism. Those alone who are "born from above" can "see the kingdom," and "enter into the kingdom," so as to know and share its privileges. The wisest must come as a little child, and begin humbly in God's way.

Through my parents I was joined to Adam, and received an evil nature. Without any act or knowledge of my own, I was born of the flesh. Christ provided that while yet in infancy, before my will was active, I might be joined to the second Adam, and "born again." I was "born from above," "born of the Spirit," when I was "born of water." When in faith and obedience Christ's promise was claimed for me, by the Spirit's power the new life came; for there was no power of unbelief or impenitence to shut out God's free grace. The outward sign told of what God did unseen for my soul. I became a child of God and heir of the kingdom through membership in Christ. Like natural life, my spiritual life was a free gift before my power to believe, or love, or labour. Like natural birth, my birth from above was the first gift of a life which might return to God Who gave it. It is a gift full of hope and promise, but needing care to nourish and employ aright, lest I lose it and die.

O Lord, by Whose grace I have been born of water and the Spirit, renew me daily, that I may so live as a member of Christ, a child of God, in Thy kingdom on earth, as to become fit to share its glory on high.

> We bear to Christ the helpless child,
> The words are said, the acts are done,
> Which He has taught: the sin-defiled
> Is cleansed, and made God's new-born son.

First Tuesday after Trinity.

"The Lord, having saved the people out of the land of Egypt, afterward destroyed them that believed not."—Jude 5.

GOD chose and called the Jews to be His own people. They were all "baptized in the cloud, and in the sea." The waters destroyed the power of their foes, and set them free. The pillar of cloud went before them, and the fire gave light. Moses, sent by God, led them towards the promised land. They had enough faith to leave Egypt, but not enough to go on to Canaan. They doubted God, and in heart turned back. So they were "saved out of Egypt," and perished in the wilderness.

I have been saved with a greater deliverance than that of Israel, and from a worse bondage. I have passed through the Red Sea of baptism, and been washed in my Saviour's blood. I need serve sin no longer. He of Whom Moses was a type is my leader. Christ's own footsteps mark my way, and His voice cheers me on. He proclaims the law of love and liberty. He gives me the true bread from heaven, and refreshes me with living waters. The light of the Holy Spirit is in me, and in the Church which teaches me. The heavenly Canaan is before me, beyond the wilderness, across the narrow stream. But my pilgrimage is not yet over, my battles are not all won. I must take heed lest I fall after the example of Israel's unbelief, and in heart forsake God. Let me press on in faith and patience. Let me be brave in God's might against God's foes, and use the help and cheer He gives by the way. I shall not think the way long or the fight hard, when I look back from heaven.

O Lord, Who hast called me into a state of salvation, enable me so to use Thy light and grace in following my Saviour's steps, that I may safely reach the heavenly land, and for ever glorify Thee, through Jesus Christ.

> May we the heavenly influence know
> Of baptism and its solemn vow;
> Born from above, and kept, and blest.
> So passed Thy people through the flood;
> So guided by the shadowing cloud,
> They gained the promised Canaan's rest.

First Wednesday after Trinity.

"Prove all things; hold fast that which is good."—1 Thess. v. 21.

A CHILD believes anything on the word of any one. A man can weigh the claim on his faith, and ought to know whom he trusts, and why. Faith must grow in wisdom, if it is to grow in favour with God and influence on men. Often it is made perfect by suffering. Reason and knowledge prove faith reasonable. When that is done, the wisest and best taught will, with the most child-like spirit, hold the truths, use the privileges, and obey the rules of God's kingdom. New proof comes from experience. Men hold fast what they have found good.

I believed first as a child in years and understanding. My mind has gained knowledge, has grown and strengthened. The truth has taken new forms: the old words mean more to me. I have fresh ground for my faith. God still asks a childlike faith, but calls on me also to know and to be able to say why I give it. I am not to be a self-trusting doubter, asking God to make unbelief impossible, and leave no room for faith. I am to learn the rightness of the claim made on my faith, to be sure of the foundation on which my hope is built, to be able to keep safe what I feel dear and sacred against my own doubts and the assaults of others. I cannot judge by reason what is above man's reason; but I can prove the claims of the authority I am asked to bow to. When I know that God speaks, or guides the voice I hear, I show truest wisdom by becoming as a little child. If I long to know what is good that I may hold it fast, pure from all that is evil, God will send me His light, and lead me. What I begin by taking on His word, I shall know by my own experience proving it good.

O Lord of truth, make me to grow in wisdom and knowledge, that I may be able to prove what is good, and to hold it fast, being a man in understanding, and trusting Thee with the faith of a little child.

<blockquote>
All the world is against me, with scoff and with sneer,
  And within me doubts throng till faith seems to be lost;
But the clouds break away, and the light is more clear,
  And the truth is more loved for the care it has cost.
</blockquote>

First Thursday after Trinity.

"Earnestly contend for the faith which was once delivered unto the saints."—JUDE 3.

THE one faith is from God. It was given to the Church once for all. It may be seen more fully and clearly; but none may change, or add to, or take from it. God claims belief for His truth as He claims obedience for His laws. Man finds it hard to hold God's truth, as he finds it hard to do God's will. He must strive against his own pride, and sloth, and wilfulness, and taking firm stand upon the faith, defend its full purity from those who deny or corrupt it. He must strive, but in a Christ-like spirit; not for his own fancies, but for what God has said.

If God has spoken, I listen and believe with lowly thankfulness. I dare not judge His words, setting aside one part as strange and another as trifling. God knows the meaning and the worth of all. Enough for me that it is all from Him. Against my own evil self I must be firm, making sure that I have and keep the whole faith. I must not be silent through shame or fear, if new views of man try to take the place of the old truth of God. To hold back is to bring harm to myself and others, and to be false to God's cause. I contend not for the triumph of my opinions, but for the faith which is alone the truth, and can have no rival. I contend not in proud self-trust, but in true lowly zeal for God and love for souls. I must stand firmly myself, and grasp the faith with strong hold, if I would strive well to make its foes harmless. If I am not sure, I cannot help others to be sure. I must strive so as not to set men against the truth, but to win them to love and obey it.

Grant me, O Lord, so to learn and know the faith once for all delivered to Thy Church, that I may hold it fast, and contend for it as a precious treasure and a sacred trust.

> What the saints established, that I hold for true;
> What the saints believèd, that believe I too.
> We are not divided, all one body we;
> One in hope, in doctrine, one in charity.

First Friday after Trinity.

"Lord, I believe; help Thou mine unbelief."—Mark ix. 24.

WEAK faith may still be true. The newly born is not strong or full grown, yet he may live. The sick, when he begins to amend, learns his weakness. The first dawn shows how much the darkness hides. So man must have some faith, to be aware of his unbelief. The longing for faith shows faith. It is a sign that God has lifted the veil, and let light in on the soul. It is full of promise. The strength of faith is proved by how much its remaining weakness is lamented. The heartfelt earnestness of the prayer, "Help Thou mine unbelief," tests the faith with which a man casts himself upon the Lord.

I can only believe as God shows Himself to my soul. The least feeble beginning of faith, and the full triumph are alike from Him. Though it be as a mustard-seed, it is planted in me by God, and He can make it grow and spread. It lays hold on the power of the Almighty, and joins me to the exhaustless sources of grace. Let me not be cast down if faith seems hardly real in me, and God seems out of reach. While I feel this, and my soul longs and stretches towards Him, faith lives. God wills to make Himself known and to help me. He shows me how blind I am that He may make me see, and open out before my soul His goodness and glory. He leads me by my felt helplessness to long for strengthened faith. As faith grows clear and strong, I shall know better how it falls short. As I can say humbly but truly, "Lord, I believe," I shall feel urged to own my unbelief, and seek the Lord's help. My faith must be a growing, and so an imperfect thing, till it brings me into the Lord's presence.

O Lord, my faith is weak; help Thou mine unbelief. I thank Thee that I can call Thee Lord. Enable me to hold fast and to press near, that I may know Thy goodness, and prepare in a life of faith to enjoy Thy glory.

> If I have lost my way, oh, set me right;
> If going now astray, hold my hand tight.
> This labyrinth is intricate and long,
> Show me the right path, lest I choose the wrong.

FIRST SATURDAY AFTER TRINITY.

"If any man will do His will, he shall know of the doctrine, whether it be of God, or whether I speak of myself."—JOHN vii. 17.

WE know, in order that we may do. We learn God's truth, that we may obey God's will. He reveals doctrines that we may act upon them. He does not make faith easy to those who will not humble their pride or bow their wills. He gives more light to those who use heartily what they have. We learn by doing. Those who seek truth, who frankly accept it as God's word, prove it true in their experience. Doubts about doctrine cease to vex those who are candid and earnest in learning and following the way of duty.

God will not bless me with the knowledge of the truth unless I seek truth. While I try to prove true what I wish to be true, while I set my will against God's, I search God's Word blindly and in vain. I shall not be left to wander unguided, if I truly wish to be led where God would have me go. Hard sayings and mysterious truths shall not try me, if I am willing to learn God's will, and follow the steps of Christ. I shall grow in knowledge as the Spirit enlightens me, and the secret things shall be made clear; or I shall have the gift of faith, and shall feel and prize as true what is too high for me to explain. I learn virtues by practising them, so I know doctrines by yielding to their influence upon me. I grow sure of God's might and love as I obey Him. I need not argue about prayer; I find its value real, while it brings down blessings on my work. The doctrine of the Blessed Sacrament becomes less of faith and more of thankful, glad experience, as I devoutly draw near, and seek to show in my life the Divine grace gained by its means.

Almighty God, grant me to seek knowledge in the way of active obedience, and to find Thy truth more clear and comforting to my faith, as my life is guided by Thy holy will.

> He who inquireth with an earnest mind,
> "Lord, what is truth?" shall very surely find
> That which he seeketh. Man asks not in vain
> The way to heaven—God will make it plain.

The First Sunday after Trinity.

"We love Him, because He first loved us."—1 JOHN iv. 19.

WE could not love God, had not God loved us first. He is Love, and the source of all love. In Christ He joined us to Himself, making us "partakers of the Divine nature." He gives us, as His children, power to love, and so to please Him. We can grow in love of Him, as we learn to know Him better, and yield to His love. We can enjoy His love more, as love to Him becomes the ruling influence of our lives among men. The power of loving God is the great fruit of God's work for us. It is the sign that God dwells in us, the witness of His love, the ground of our hope.

God made and redeemed me that I might know and love Him. His love did not forsake me even in my sin. He shows Himself to me in Christ. He gives me His Spirit, enabling me to know Him as a Father, and love Him with a son's love, not for what He gives, but for what He is. Do I love Him? Does love show itself in my life, drawing me towards Him, making me learn His will and seek to please Him? If so, it is because God first loved me. This love proves that God dwells in me, and wills to remain till His work of love is done. Have I no love for God, or longing for it, only a selfish fear, selfish gratitude, selfish care for safety? This low state of soul need not be. I need not thus be as a slave, when I am a son. I need not thus make God's love vain for its true end. God first loved me, and asked my love. He has done, and does all still, to come near and win my heart, that He may be to me a God known and loved.

O God of love, Who hast loved me, grant me to know Thy love, and to love Thee for what Thou art, and to grow worthy of Thy love, through Jesus Christ.

> Poor, unworthy though we be,
> Thou dost deign to will that we
> Should be blest in loving Thee,
> Not from dread of wrath or woe,
> Not for all Thou wilt bestow;
> For Thyself Whose love we know,
> Help us, Lord, to love Thee.

SECOND MONDAY AFTER TRINITY.

"Perfect love casteth out fear."—1 JOHN iv. 18.

LOVE gives boldness to do and bear all things for God's sake. Love to God casts out fear of God. It is a result and a proof of God's love. It removes the dread of those who would hide from God if they could. It changes slavish obedience into the glad desire and effort to please a Father. It makes fear needless as a motive. It is the witness of the Spirit that we are under the care of One Whose love changes not, and are being formed into Christ's likeness. It gives child-like boldness in looking up to God, and looking forward to the day of judgment.

All my love to God is because He "first loved" me. All I do and bear for love of Him proves that He dwells in me. I have ever new assurance of the goodwill of the Eternal, as His work grows more strong and perfect in me. I do not shrink from Him. Love wins away distrust. I delight in His nearness. I no longer need to be warned from sin, or urged to holy work; love draws me on. I ask not, what must I do lest I sin? but what can I do to please Him best Whom I love? I lose even the dread of grieving God, as I need it less, and love becomes the ruler of my life. I grow calmly sure of love that will finish its work. I gain fuller trust, as I know God, and feel His power. Death shall bring me where His love shall fulfil its work in me, and I shall know Him and love Him, as I long to do. I lose all fear but the fear of reverence, which shall grow more like that of the angels as my love becomes like theirs.

Almighty Father, Whose love has made me a partaker of the Divine nature, which is love; dwell in me more and more, that Thy love may be perfected in my heart and life, and that I may love Thee with a sure and child-like love.

> O draw me, Saviour, after Thee,
> So shall I run and never tire;
> With gracious words still comfort me,
> Be Thou my hope, my sole desire.
> On Thee I'd roll each weight and fear,
> Calm in the thought that Thou art near.

Second Tuesday after Trinity.

"The beggar died, and was carried by the angels into Abraham's bosom."—Luke xvi. 22.

THERE seemed a great gulf between Lazarus and the rich man, at whose gate he lay hungering for crumbs. The lot of one seemed all good, that of the other all evil. Soon "the beggar died," and the worn body was put away. Lazarus did not die; his name was known in heaven; angels bore him away to be comforted in the bosom of the father of the faithful. All along he had been God's care, healed of his spiritual wounds, fed with heaven's good things. He had been rich in faith, and heir of the promise, which, after patient waiting, he received.

One day it shall be said of me that I have died. My dying may be only my release from the pain, the wrongs, the loneliness of life. Bare of earthly riches, I may have wealth stored in heaven. Sick in body, I may be strong in my true self. Forsaken of men, angels may befriend me. Homeless now, I may be sure of rest in Paradise, and a place in the home of God. But I shall share the comfort of Lazarus, not if my sorrows are like his, but if I am like him. He did not pass to peace because he had suffered. He endured in faith. He mourned so as to gain God's consolation. He hungered after righteousness. So must it be with me, else my griefs are a warning, not a ground of hope. I may reach the rest of Lazarus, though my lot here is not like his. For I may be poor in spirit, and lay up treasure above. My joys may draw me nearer to Him Who gives them. I may weep with them that weep, and, while lightening the pain of their evil things, may gain the good things which are the blessing of true mourners.

O Lord, grant me grace so to do and bear Thy will on earth, that death may bring me to the comfort and the good things of a better life.

<blockquote>
Sorrow's long lesson o'er, death's discipline gone through,
Thou wilt unfold to me what joy can do.
Glad souls are on the wing; from earth to heaven they flee;
At last Thine hour will come to send for me.
</blockquote>

SECOND WEDNESDAY AFTER TRINITY.

"The rich man also died, and was buried; and in hell he lift up his eyes."—LUKE xvi. 22, 23.

THE rich man was called away from all that he had made "his good things," and had received in full. He did not die when his body was left lifeless. He lifted up his spirit's eyes to see the true worth of things. He found himself where the unsaved wait their last doom. He saw the rest he might have gained, but far off, across a great gulf. He had no fitness for it. He was what he had become on earth. All he thirsted for was out of reach. None might bring him a drop from the springs of mercy he had despised.

The rich man does not seem to have been or done what man blames; but he did not become or do what God requires. Nor was he lost because he was rich, but because earth's "good things" filled his heart. A poor and lonely Lazarus may be as earth-bound in having what he has not, as the rich in selfish pride of what he has. Health, friends, money, do not prove me rich, for death may any moment strip me of them all. My life goes on, and I am rich if I can call mine what lasts for ever. Earth's good things, like earth's sorrows, may be used so as to gain eternal good. If I bind my heart to what is here, my desires shall go with me to the world beyond, and there shall be nothing to quench their burning. What I have no taste for now, God will not give me hereafter. If I try to make my rest here, no "rest remaineth" for me. If I only live for time, God will not give me eternity. If I make not friends of the mammon of unrighteousness, none shall greet me in the unknown world. If I put away the angels now, they will not be at hand to bear me to Paradise.

Lord, grant Thy grace with earth's good things, that I may be poor in spirit, and rich towards God.

> In having all things and not Thee, what have I?
> Not having Thee, what have my labours got?
> Let me enjoy but Thee, what further crave I?
> And having Thee alone, what have I not?
> I wish not sea nor land; nor would I be
> Possessed of heaven, heaven unpossessed by Thee.

SECOND THURSDAY AFTER TRINITY.
"*Son, remember.*"—LUKE xvi. 25.

TO bid him remember, was to bid him despair. The past rising before him accused, condemned, tormented him. It darkened all the future. He looked back as a son of Abraham, whose birthright was sold, and the price of it gone. Memory pointed to grace wasted, privileges and power for good made vain, duties undone, joys lost for ever, hopes to be His no more. He was tormented as he tracked his downward path. He might have hoped, had he been able to forget.

I may forget now, and live thoughtlessly from hour to hour. One day the past shall spread itself before me. I have it all. I am ever adding to the store laid up by memory. How shall my life look when I see all clearly, in its true form and colour, from the world to which I go? Shall memory help my joy as I trace the work of God's wise love, and the leading of a will loved, and trusted, and obeyed? Shall memory heap reproach on my sad tormented soul, as I tell over the dark tale of a life's sin and shame? Shall my last hour be darkened by apparitions of sin long forgotten, but remembered then? Shall my joy in believing be dimmed by the memory of manifold, dark unworthiness? How can I be thoughtless, who shall remember! Think, my soul, when tempted, that the memory of sin will stay and burn when the pleasure is all gone. Live a life that you need not fear to remember. Lay not up store of what will make hell within you. Lay up what you can remember in Paradise. Remember your sins now, while you may do so and hope. Remember them, so that God may remember them no more, and that you may think of them as forgiven and forsaken.

Make me, O Lord, to keep in mind Thy goodness and my sin; that I may obtain Thy pardon, and find grace to keep my soul from all that it would be shame to remember.

> Our brief hours travel post,
> Each with its thought or deed, its why, or how;
> But know, each parting hour gives up a ghost
> To dwell with Thee.

Second Friday after Trinity.

"If they hear not Moses and the prophets, neither will they be persuaded, though one rose from the dead."—LUKE xvi. 31.

PROOFS, motives, helps are vain, where candour and earnestness are wanting. No man is "persuaded" of truths unless he attend to them. A man may be fully persuaded, and yet remain unchanged in heart and life. He who will not hear Moses and the prophets and Him of Whom they spake, is set against, or careless of truth. Special miracles would only add responsibility and condemnation. God does enough to leave mind, and heart, and will without excuse. Man is alone to blame, if he is not persuaded and converted. To question this is to contradict Christ and to slander God.

I have Moses and the prophets; do I hear them? One has risen from the dead; am I "persuaded" of the truth taught through Him? Am I being "converted" under the power of the truths I accept, the motives that urge me, the grace at hand? Or do I wait for some startling interference, which, with no humbling or effort of mine, will make my faith, and life, and character what they should be? Do I blame God as if more ought to be done for me, and I should be asked to do less, as if I could do my part better, did God not fail in His? Are my questions rather about God's wisdom and love, than my own spiritual state? I may have become blind, and dull, and hard, through past neglect or sin, however candid I may feel or wish to be now. If I remain unpersuaded and unconverted, it is because I am not in earnest. If I am not doing my best with the light, and grace, and means I have, no change in God's dealings would change me. If I am doing my best, God's help and blessing shall more and more be mine.

O Lord, give me an earnest mind and will, that I may be persuaded of Thy truth, and may receive it to the conversion of my heart, and the sanctification of my life.

Lord, Thou dost give me light and truth, that I may never stray;
The clouds and pillars march before, and show me Canaan's way:
I bless my God, Who is my guide, I sing in Zion's ways;
When shall I sing on Zion's hills Thine everlasting praise?

SECOND SATURDAY AFTER TRINITY.

"All with one consent began to make excuse."—LUKE xiv. 18.

ALL were glad to know of the feast, and to be invited. None were ready, when told to come at once. They gave various excuses, but with one spirit, as if they had agreed to put off the messenger. Other joys and interests held them; they would not be interrupted. Perhaps they thought the feast would wait, or that another would be prepared, which they might enjoy when there was nothing else to do. This was their last call. No place was kept for them. They were shut out.

God calls me to share the good things ready in the Church. He offers now, in the way of duty and the means of grace, a happy foretaste of the never-ending feast. Do I persuade myself, and think to persuade God, that I cannot or need not come? Do I know myself in the wrong, and try to lull conscience, or plead that God's call may wait till it suits me to attend to it? God weighs the worth and the motive of each excuse. He sees if I love the world more than what He offers, and feel no honest wish to have the way of right-doing made open. The duties of wealth, the claims of work, the cares and joys of home, need not keep the soul or the life from God. Every state of life has its own temptations, which God provides grace to overcome and turn to good. Anything may be pleaded as an excuse for doing any wrong or neglecting any duty. It is better to seek power to obey, than to seek excuses for disobedience. Excuses are worth now what they will be worth in the hour of death and the day of judgment. Be it my firm rule to force all things to give way to the claims of duty and the calls of God. May God, Who knows my difficulties, in mercy excuse my shortcomings.

O Lord, Who dost call me to share what Thou hast at great cost provided, may I so desire the blessings of Thy kingdom, that nothing may tempt me to lose them.

Thou hast loved me, O Lord, and I have not loved Thee;
Thou hast made me Thy child; I have wandered away;
There is nought I can plead, but that Christ died for me,
And what warns of my sin is my hope when I pray.

The Second Sunday after Trinity.

"He that keepeth His commandments dwelleth in Him, and He in him."—1 JOHN iii. 24.

FROM God, through Christ, comes all holiness in all. The life of His Spirit can alone quicken us to do His will and become righteous. Where there is loving obedience, we recognise the work of "the Spirit which He has given," and can assure our hearts before Him, knowing that God "abideth in us." While we keep His law in our hearts and obey it in our life, we cherish the Divine indwelling. The earnest and faithful find union with God grow to be a surer strength. As they put forth the power it gives, they have ever new cause for hope in what it enables them to do and be.

Obedience is a sign of grace. If I see in my heart love for God's law, and in my life firm care to obey it, I trace what God is doing. I am, by myself, slothful, careless, and prone to evil. The love of good I have, and the good I do, show God's work in and by me. Obedience is, moreover, a means of grace. In order to obey, I must draw upon God for will and strength. So while I prove God's indwelling, I receive more of the power of His presence, and am united more closely to Him. Grace gained for a special need stays with me, and makes me more able to meet all claims. Only from living union with God come strength and hope. All depends on whether I dwell in God and He in me. Let me test my state of soul by my life. Let me watch for outward signs of heartfelt love for God's will. Let me search for the one motive and power of all true well-doing, even love, which is God. Let me devoutly strive to make the flow of God's life to me more full, by putting it forth in ever larger efforts of love.

Abide in me, O Lord, that in the way of loving obedience I may seek to dwell in Thee more perfectly, and know that Thou dwellest in me, my salvation and my joy.

On the cross of my Lord I hold fast in my pain,
   Till the flesh strives no more, and its pleadings are still;
And the Christ living in me that soul-calm shall gain,
   When the nature's desires are all one with His will.

Third Monday after Trinity.

"Charity suffereth long, and is kind."—1 Cor. xiii. 4.

ST. PAUL does not name all the works and fruits of charity. He points out some signs of its presence that never fail. Charity is not, where these are wanting. He in whom this Divine love lives seeks the good of all men, and is not lightly turned from his aim. He bears wrongs with unmoved patience, though the trial last on, and is sore. He is careful lest he provoke new sin, or sin himself. He proves and calls out the power of love in him, by being kind to the unkind, and showing good will in word and deed. So the love, which is God, grows strong in him, while it bears with and blesses all.

Am I firm, so as to be still the same, though foes wrong me, friends prove false, and those I have trusted betray me? Can I go on without growing hard, or bitter, or revengeful, though my trial be long, and blow fast follows blow? This is not all! Do I meet scorn with gentleness, taunts and slanders with good words? Am I ready to show kindness to those who have caused me grief or loss? Perhaps few have gained the power to rise freely and fully to this height of love. I need not be cast down if I am aware of sad shortcoming, and if I find the fight with my pride and selfishness still needing much watchful prayer and use of grace. But do I own myself bound to aim at this power? Do I honestly pray and try thus to feel and act so as to have a good right to hope that God's love indeed dwells in and rules me? If so, my will is on the side of God and His love. If I am making no such true and lowly effort, I have not charity; for charity always shows itself by these signs. If I have not charity, I am nothing; I am without God.

O Lord, Who dost win me by Thy kindness; teach me what I owe to Thy patience, and give me of Thy love, that I may bear with my fellow-sinners, and do good to all for Christ's sake, Who died for those who slew Him.

When we wrongly suffer pain,
May we Jesus' spirit gain, and from angry thoughts refrain ;
Give the love divinely strong,
Moved not, though it suffer long, kind to those who do the wrong.

Third Tuesday after Trinity.
"Charity envieth not."—1 Cor. xiii. 4.

WHEN God's love shines into a man with its warmth and light, it shines from him. He who has that love is always glad when his neighbour does well. He never grudges him his gifts of body or mind, his good name, or the place he wins. Far less does he feel sore when he sees him take the lead in work for God, and gain triumphs for the Church's cause. He thinks not of self, but of what best helps the end for which all should live and work. He rejoices in what others show power to do well. He does not wish to drag them down where he is, but to reach the height of their example.

Does the bad spirit of envy overcome my charity, or do I force down and crush, in God's name, the mean, hateful thing that rises? With what feelings do I look upon the welfare, and joy, and honour in which others are before me? Would my own lot seem less hard, if theirs were as poor and lowly? Could I bear my own want of personal gifts and talents better, were they without them too? Do I let myself be tempted to make little of those who surpass me, so that their merits may seem less above and beyond mine? Do I slight others' work, instead of being roused by it to more earnest work myself? Do I in heart blame God, as if He dealt more hardly with me than others, and murmur that I cannot come to the front. Do I fret because others seem to have a lighter cross to bear, fewer temptations to master, a more quick and easy way to holiness? Do I murmur that my soul's growth is slow, and my work for God falls short, while envy is killing out of me that love to God and man, without which nothing good thrives?

Almighty God, fill me with that love of Thine which rejoices in the good of all. Give me such zeal for Thy cause, that I may be glad when others help it, and may seek grace to become a less unprofitable servant.

I envy not their hap whom fortune doth advance;
I take no pleasure in their pain that have less happy chance.
To rise by others' fall I deem a losing game;
All states with others' ruin built, to ruin run amain.

Third Wednesday after Trinity.

"Charity vaunteth not itself, is not puffed up, doth not behave itself unseemly."—1 Cor. xiii. 4, 5.

HE who has charity always shows it by being modest and courteous. He is thoughtful of others' feelings, and takes care not to wound them needlessly. He does not talk much of himself. He never boasts of his powers, or uses them so as to make those who are less gifted feel made little of or set aside. He works, not for his own credit, but for God, and for man's good. He moves among men with a kindly tact, which God's love gives, and of which the world's politeness is a poor copy.

Some men boast of powers which they have not, and of deeds which a true man feels it shame to be charged with. Some put on a bold, pushing manner, in order to hide felt weakness, and to be thought what they know they are not. But even God's best gifts may be turned to my loss, and used so as to tempt others. Satan cannot take them from me; but he tries to make them tempt me to pride and display. Do I guard my soul from this danger? Am I never vain of the means and powers with which God trusts me, thinking more of showing them than of doing my duty with them? Do I never put myself forward rudely? Am I never rough and overbearing in word or manner to those I think beneath me? Am I always watchful not to pain even the over-sensitive? Am I, when at home with those whose love and faithfulness I take for granted, the same courteous, refined person strangers find me? Thoughtfulness about others in the small things of daily and home life is a surer sign of charity than any great effort of patience, or forgiveness, or benevolence. To fail in courtesy is to fail in charity; that is to fail in religion.

O Lord, give me grace to use Thy gifts with a lowly, simple aim, to praise Thee, and help my neighbour's good, that I may show Thy love in each part of my daily life.

<blockquote>
Let grace our selfishness expel,
Our earthliness refine;
And kindness in our bosom dwell,
As free and true as Thine.
</blockquote>

Third Thursday after Trinity.

"Let no man seek his own, but every man another's wealth."
—1 Cor. x. 24.

GOD has made us members one of another. He puts us in one another's care; each has rights in the rest, and is bound to do his part for the good of all. He who seeks selfishly his own well-being, without thought of others, is without God in the world, and surely fails. He who thinks to push his lonely way to heaven, and has no heart, or voice, or hand to help others on, is without God in the Church. His "religion" is vain.

Do I grasp my "rights" with a hard hand, heedless how others lose, if I gain? Is my heart full of care for self, leaving no room for thought about my neighbours? If so, I act against God's plan for the world's good. I may get my own way; but God's way alone leads to that in which man's heart can rest. Even on earth, selfishness is a mistake. What is called self-love is not, indeed, wise care for one's own true good: for He in Whose hands all things are has willed that the large-hearted and sympathising win happiness. Am I busy, as I think, in seeking to "save my soul," while cold about the souls around? Do I pray for self, and neglect intercession? Am I selfish in claiming what pleases me or seems to help me, even though it bring loss or hindrance to weak souls? Do I abuse my knowledge, by doing what may lead others to act against the misgivings of conscience? God will count among His own no religious misers, or greedy self-pleasers. Christ pleased not Himself. If my religion is to profit me, it must be full of that love which will make me ready to give up all but God, for God's glory, and for the souls He loves.

O Lord, save me from vainly seeking my own selfish ends in this world or for the next. Grant me to find happiness, according to Thy will, in helping the joy and the eternal good of those for whom Christ died.

All that seeks self-profit first rather than another's good,
   Whether foe or linked in blood,
Let me hold such thoughts accurst, and my heart henceforward be
   Ruled, inspired, O Love, by Thee.

Third Friday after Trinity.

Charity "thinketh no evil; rejoiceth not in iniquity, but rejoiceth in the truth; beareth all things, believeth all things, hopeth all things, endureth all things."—1 Cor. xiii. 5, 6, 7.

HE in whose heart God puts His love loves God and man. He wishes God's love to have its way, and long's for man's true good. He is on truth's side, and is glad of all that shows its success. He is unwilling to find others in the wrong. He loves not fault-finding. He bears much before he gives up faith in the right motives of his neighbours. He welcomes all that tells for them, or explains what has looked bad. He holds fast the hope that things seem worse than they are.

Have I this actively loving spirit, or is my religion without it, and so proved worthless? Do I act at times as if eager to find proof that evil holds sway where truth ought to rule? Am I ready to brand a life or a character, because of a doubtful deed or word, or even look? Do I catch myself putting the worst meaning on what will bear many, and, among all possible motives, imputing the lowest? Do I feel a hateful satisfaction when others fall or are found out, as if their sin raised me? Is it pure, generous joy to me, when others do nobly and are proved true? Am I slow to change a kindly judgment, or can my charity bear little without being shaken? Am I glad to hear what may be said to clear away suspicions, and quick to believe the best? Do I cling to the most hopeful view, even when guilt seems plain; or do evil speakers find my ears waiting to receive, and my tongue loose to spread, slander? The meanest, basest forms of uncharitableness hide themselves. I may be in most danger from those which are so shameful that I shrink from owning them even to myself.

Almighty God, make me unwilling to judge others, and glad to welcome whatever shows the spread of Thy truth and the triumph of Thy love.

> The froward heart, the haughty eye,
> The slanderous tongue, be mine to fly;
> Those whom Thou lovest I would love,
> And here dwell with them, and above.

Third Saturday after Trinity.

"Casting all your care upon Him; for He careth for you."
—1 Pet. v. 7.

MAN must not be careless. God would not have him be unthinking or unfeeling. He ought to feel care for those he loves, for the Church, for all mankind, for his own good here, for his soul's growth in holiness, for God's glory. He must not care as if he were alone. God cares for all these things. Sure of God's watchful love and power, man may be calm. Each care and all cares must be laid on God as they arise. Let man take care to do his best with grace given, and in quiet faith leave the care of the result to God.

God careth for me with a care which follows me through all the least changes of my life. Do I care for myself? I cannot cast on Him what I have not. It will not do for me to be careless and slothful, trusting that God is in earnest, and will do all. I may not stand aloof from the rest of men, as if their lot were nothing to me. I am meant to have care, that I may cast it always upon God. I am meant to feel with the care He has for my good and the world's well-being, as He feels with mine. He bids me not lose heart or calmness under a sense of my weakness, and the greatness of the interests that are in my care. He gives love, and zeal, and power to do my part. Let me only care that my work be done earnestly and in dependence on Him, and that my prayers fail not. He will take care that I am not over-tasked or left unhelped, and that in the end all shall be well. Each new care laid on me is a new call to come more near to Him in Whose love and truth I can find rest.

Almighty God, care for me always, and make me always sure of Thy care, that I may go on calmly in the way of Thy will, leaving the end with Thee, in Whose power all things are.

When obstacles and trials seem like prison walls to me,
I do the little I can do, and leave the rest to Thee;
I have no cares, O blessed will, for all my cares are Thine;
I live in triumph, Lord, for Thou hast made my triumphs Thine.

The Third Sunday after Trinity.

"And go after that which is lost, until he find it? And when he hath found it, he layeth it on his shoulders, rejoicing."—
LUKE xv. 4, 5.

THE Good Shepherd knows His sheep, and calls each by name. No one can stray and be forgotten. He has made it His own at great cost. He seeks it as if it were His whole wealth, and He were poor without it. He goes after it with the same love that led Him to give His life. When He finds it He is glad. There is no harsh reproach, no rough driving back. He cleanses stains, He soothes hurts. With joy He lifts the trembling one, that His own strength may bear it safely to the fold.

I have gone astray like a sheep that is lost.. I have wandered from the safe fold and the Good Shepherd's care. I have left the pastures where He led me, and sought in self-chosen paths what my foolish heart craved. And have I not felt my soul tire, and grow weak to face danger, and helpless to return? Has not the voice of Christ called to me often, and been unheeded? What am I, that He should so follow me, and try to find me willing to own His care? How patient and untiring His love! How tender His healing, cleansing hand, when He finds me stained, and wounded, and humbled, where my wilfulness has brought me! How kindly He bends over me to lift me from my low lost state, and lay me on the firm support of His own human sympathy and Divine power! Alas, that I should break loose from His kind arms, and grieve His love by new far wanderings! If He rejoices when He finds me, is there no loss of joy to Him when I am lost, and His seeking grace fails to bless me? Shall I not give Him the joy of keeping me safe and glad?

O Lord, Who didst come to seek and save the lost, make me hear Thy call; bear me in Thy strength above the world's perils and temptations to the heavenly fold.

> If I have wandered, call me by my name,
> Make known to me Thy goodness and my shame;
> From evil cleanse, from every foe defend,
> And bear me onward till my trial end.

FOURTH MONDAY AFTER TRINITY.

"And when he cometh home, he calleth together his friends and neighbours, saying unto them, Rejoice with me; for I have found my sheep which was lost."—LUKE XV. 6.

THE shepherd lifts the lost sheep on his shoulders. It is a burden, but one that he loves. Back over the rough ways he bears it till the fold is reached. Those who sang Christ's going out into the wilderness, and are the glad ministers of His mercy, feel with His joy at the first answer of each lost one to the seeking Shepherd's call. They rejoice indeed with Him over each wanderer brought safely home to be made glad for ever.

The angels know me as one whom their Lord loves, and wills them to befriend. They share His joy when I stop in my wayward course, when I feel myself lost, and in the mourning of repentance let my Saviour find me. They rejoice to minister to me as an heir of salvation, while Divine love heals and purifies me, and keeps me faithful, and bears me heavenwards. The full joy is not yet. It will begin when I have passed within the gates of home, beyond reach of foes, out of danger from my own foolish waywardness. Then I shall know how great the love and goodness of my Saviour, and how rich I have been in friends whom He taught to care for me. What sure hope there is in the mercy that calls me "His sheep," and seeks me even when by my own fault I am lost! What comfort in the love that "finds" me, and owns me His, while still but a "sinner that repenteth!" What joy in the love that bids all heaven be glad when I am safely brought home to stray no more!

O Thou Good Shepherd, Who hast gone after me when lost, bind me to Thee, that I may never go from Thee, and may be upheld till I am welcomed among those who rejoice with Thee in the triumphs of Thy love.

> O Shepherd good, how hard this heart of mine;
> To wound and grieve Thy tenderness divine;
> O may my soul Thy dear-bought blessing gain,
> And give to Thee the fruits of all Thy pain.
> Be Thine the holy joy of saving me,
> Be mine the bliss of being saved by Thee.

Fourth Tuesday after Trinity.

" Rejoice with me; for I have found the piece which I had lost."—LUKE xv. 9.

THE coin is still silver, and bears the mark which tells its worth. But it is lost. Where it fell it lies useless and rusting. Such is man when he is no more in God's hands for use, when he is down among earthly things, heedless of his fall, and of the high end of his being. Dust gathers over what is precious, and God's likeness and name are hidden. The Holy Spirit in the Church holds up truth's light, and seeks one by one those who are still God's wealth, till they are given back to God for the holy uses of His kingdom.

If, like the prodigal, I leave my Father, I may find myself grown dull and helpless like the wandering sheep; I may at last sink to be like the lost coin, without longing for help or feeling of my fall. I may be without spiritual power to arise and seek my Father, or even to welcome the seeking Shepherd. Let me dread the first step from being a son loved and loving, to being a creature learning its need of God in the misery of wandering, and so downward to being God's property, knowing nothing of His rights and of His value for me. God claims the lost and dead in evil as His handiwork, which may regain its brightness and beauty. He calls His Church and each member of it to share His work of seeking, in order to share His joy in finding. The Spirit gives love and wisdom to search the dark places, to bring heavenly light into them, to sweep away what defiles souls and buries them from their God. So far as I am guided by the Spirit, I will be diligent in making a way for God to lay His hand on His lost ones, making them a joy to all who love Him, and love the souls He treasures.

O Lord, may I never leave Thee, lest I become as those who know not their lost state away from Thee. Give me Thy Spirit to labour, that there may be joy in heaven over souls saved from darkness and sin.

My soul lies cleaving to the dust;
Lord, give me life divine!
From vain desires and sinful lust,
Oh! turn this heart of mine.

FOURTH WEDNESDAY AFTER TRINITY.

"The younger son gathered all together, and took his journey into a far country, and there wasted his substance."—LUKE xv. 13.

HIS heart went first. He tired of the pure joys of his home. He chafed under his father's wise rule. He longed to take his own wilful way through life, and taste the world's pleasures freely. His father would not hold him back by force, when his heart was gone, or destroy his will by binding it. With all he had he went where his father, who had given him all, was forgotten. Now he was master of his substance, but not of himself. His unruled desires ruled him. No thought of old days, or of the future, checked his life of waste.

In Adam, I am God's child. In Christ, I am His child in a more blessed way. Have I valued His strong, wise, Fatherly care, and been glad to be near Him in trustful obedience? Or has my heart left Him? have I gone away from Him in life? Have I craved for what He withheld, and received unthankfully what He gave? Have I set my judgment and will against His, and chosen my own way, heedless how I pained my Father's love, broke His laws, and cast off His firm protection? Have I impatiently thrust aside the restraints of Providence, as if to force God's will to set me free? Have I removed from God's control the gifts, and powers, and means I had from Him! Am I living now for earth and time, with no thought of my Father, and laying up nothing for my everlasting future? It is sad to have gone away, even though I have returned. What if I still am wasting my all! What if famine find me far from my Father, and I have spent all, even my power to arise and go to Him!

O Divine Father, teach me to love Thy will and use Thy gifts as a faithful son. May I never waste upon my ruin what Thou dost give to make me rich for heaven.

> We grasp at joys that end in pain,
> We strive for rest—no rest we gain,
>   And still we wait to live;
> The earthly good that stirs desire,
> The earthly aims that hope inspire,
>   No satisfaction give.

FOURTH THURSDAY AFTER TRINITY.

"And when he had spent all, there arose a mighty famine in that land; and he began to be in want."—LUKE xv. 14.

WANT soon came as the end of waste. While his "portion of goods" lasted, he could drown thought in sinful pleasure. When that was spent, he was without the means of enjoying what he had made his all. Those who had helped him to throw away his "goods" failed him in the hour of need. He tried to be as those who were at home where his father was unknown. He sought, by plunging into coarser sin, to quiet the craving within him. No man gave to him; no man could. Only in the home he had forsaken, might his want find help. Away from his father, he could only starve.

Time, health, strength, do not last. The portion of goods God gives His sons, if spent away from God, is wasted. Each day leaves the spiritual spendthrift poorer. The world loses its charm; the body fails in its power to enjoy. He who has lived for these feels the sore pain of want. Sometimes, when sin's pleasures pall and tire, the sinner, with lowered taste, seeks grosser joys, and tries to be as if he were formed for nothing higher. But ere long the soul finds that away from its God there is famine. Well for him who early learns that the promises that drew him away are false. Well for him who waits not for the time of famine to force him to think of a forgotten Father. Well for him who returns before all is spent, before his conscience is dulled, and his nature debased. Am I spending my hope and joy, and laying up shame and misery for coming days? Do I "begin to be in want," and act so as to go more far away, and sink more deeply into dishonour? Or do I let my soul's hunger warn me, and draw my desires homewards?

O heavenly Father, save me from trying to find rest away from Thee. If I wander, call me back before I have wasted Thy gifts, and lost the power of loving Thee.

How vain, and poor, and little worth,
Are all these glittering toys of earth that lure us here;
Dreams of a sleep, that death must break,
Alas! before it bids us wake, we disappear.

FOURTH FRIDAY AFTER TRINITY.

"I will arise and go to my father."—LUKE xv. 18.

AT first the prodigal felt want only in his lower nature. He would fain have found enough where he was. He tried long to do so, until he "came to himself." Then he thought of all he had thrown away and left. His first feeling was selfish and unspiritual. He remembered the "bread enough" of his home, and longed to be as the hirelings of his father. The name father reminded him that he was no alien, but still a son. Then came thoughts of heaven, and conscience made him see his life as sin. He resolved to arise from his shame, and to go and lay all before his father.

If all the world gives fail to satisfy, this is because I am a son of God, and need what is higher. If the world's good things are mine no more, God makes the famine, that He may draw me back from the far land by thoughts of home and of my Father. If my religious life seem no path of peace, may it be that I am still going to my Father through the wilderness, where all reminds me of my wanderings, and I am still sore and weak from my old life? If I seem so stained and unworthy after going from God, that I scarce dare look towards home, let me not be tempted to delay. I can only grow worse and more helpless where I am. Only by arising, can I break loose from the ways and the companionship of sin. Only by going as I am to my Father, can I find pardon. Only He can make me fit for His presence, and give me back what I have thrown away. My motives may be mixed, so that I shrink before His soul-searching eye; He will give me better, and show me my sin in the light of His love. He will own me as His child, shamed and unworthy though I am.

O merciful Father, draw my heart to Thee in the sorrow of my sin. Help me to arise with earnest will and go to Thee humbly, trusting Thy Fatherly love.

    Thou art my only hope : I have no claim
      Upon Thy mercy, I am so defiled;
    But I will dare to call Thee by Thy name,
      I am a prodigal, but still Thy child.

FOURTH SATURDAY AFTER TRINITY.

"When he was yet a great way off, his father saw him, and had compassion, and ran, and fell on his neck, and kissed him."—LUKE XV. 20.

THE father's heart went after the prodigal, and would not let him go. He mourned his son as still loved, though lost and dead. At the first sign of returning he hastened to show him kindness, and to lead him home. So God in Christ went out to win man to feel and own a Father's love. So now the Divine Father meets each humbled prodigal when he first rises in answer to the call of grace. While still afar off, arms of Divine compassion are stretched out to welcome and uphold.

Though I forsake and forget my Father, His love all the while tracks me, and wills not that I should be lost. God seeks to rouse in me a right sense of my sin, and to make me long for Him as He longs for me. He sends grace to help me to arise and return. He comes to meet me that I may not tread the way of penitence alone. At once He freely gives the assurance of pardon, and the pledge of all that His Fatherly love will do. He will take away the soiled dress of old habits, that bear the marks of my shameful past. He will clothe my inmost being with the robe of divinely-imparted righteousness, and outfit me for a holy life. He will restore me to a place among His sons and daughters, and admit me to the strengthening and refreshing feast of joy. How heartless is my sin against this Father! How tender is the love I wound when I go from this God! What good I cast away! What shame I surely lay up for myself, whether it be the shame of the penitent, or the shame of the despairing who perishes in the far country!

Almighty Father, Who art ready to restore Thy erring children who arise and come to Thee, draw nigh to my soul and take me under Thy loving care, that I may love Thee as my Father, and fear to wander from Thee.

> I know Thy love will follow to the last
> Thy children who have wandered far away.
> Thy love has taught me how to hate the past,
> And in my shame it teaches me to pray.

The Fourth Sunday after Trinity.

" Why beholdest thou the mote that is in thy brother's eye, but perceivest not the beam that is in thine own eye?"—LUKE vi. 41.

MOST men are quick to search out their brother's least faults, slow to be aware of their own great sin. They behold—gaze closely on another's blemish, but overlook their own deformity. They are ready to set others right, while what is wrong in themselves is left to grow more wrong. No man can give good excuse for so acting. He who would be tender and skilful in helping others, must first know and cast off his own sin.

Am I self-contented and officious in correcting my brother's failings? This is itself a "beam;" it is one of many. It proves me spiritually blind, and makes my sins more: I wrong my brother, deceive myself, and provoke God. My brother sinner has a claim on my help and prayers. But I must fear lest I wound and harm him, while with dim sight and rough, clumsy hand I try to do him good. His sin should warn me to know my own sin and be healed, that I may be used to bring healing to my brother. Evil nearest home calls for greatest watchfulness. My conscience should be tender to feel painfully the least touch of lightest evil, and to shrink at its approach. I should be first of all jealous for my own soul's health and purity. I should be most sharp-sighted in marking my own faults, and most prompt in removing them. So, as I grow pure, charity will cover the faults of others. I shall not judge rashly, or meddle roughly, or touch in a way to give pain. Divine Love, which guides me in casting off my sins, will guide me in helping those to whom I would bring God's healing.

O Lord, Who seest all hearts and judgest all men, show me my sins, and save me from them. Grant me lowliness and charity, that I may be used according to Thy will to bring Thy help to my brother sinners.

Speak kindly to the erring. Thou yet mayest lead him back
With holy words and tones of love from error's thorny track;
Forget not thou hast often sinned, and sinful yet must be;
Deal gently with the erring one, as God hast dealt with thee.

FIFTH MONDAY AFTER TRINITY.

"Himself took our infirmities, and bare our sicknesses."
—MATT. viii. 17.

CHRIST had no sin or sickness of His own. His nature, one with God, was pure from taint, free from evil and the power of death. When He died He gave up His life: no one took it. But He read the evil of each heart and life, and felt in a true way the sin of each. And by His perfect power of sympathy, every sorrow of every tried one helped to add to His load as the Man of Sorrows acquainted with all forms of human grief, and touched with a personal, painful feeling of them all.

I may be lonely in a hard world. Even in the midst of friends, only my own heart knows its bitterness. Even the tenderest human sympathy falls short. But the God-Man knows and feels with all. He understands how each part of my trial presses, and where I am weak and quick to feel. In a true way, He is with me. I can know that there is One Who knows me, Who weighs all I have to bear, Who measures the hardness of my task, and the soreness of my pain and weariness. No pang of heart, no sad looking back, no dread of what is to come, is passed over, or made light of. All is before His mind and in His heart, as His own. He does not spare me all grief, for He longs most to free me from sin, that worst sorrow of which my trials warn. But He makes His love felt: He puts Himself under my cross that its weight may not crush me. He cheers my faith, and makes me strong in His own might. He gladdens me with hope of the time when all my soul's wounds shall be healed, and my body shall be glorious, and my load of care shall be laid down for ever.

O Lord Jesu Christ, save me in my sorrow, save me from my sin, give me faith to know the love which bore grief, and pain, and death for me, and to be sure that Thou art with me now, the same always.

> Strive thou in soul to sympathise with Him,
>   The infinitely Great;
> For He has stooped to understand and share
>   The weakness of thy state.

Fifth Tuesday after Trinity.

"No chastening for the present seemeth to be joyous, but grievous: nevertheless afterward it yieldeth the peaceable fruit of righteousness unto them which are exercised thereby."—Heb. xii. 11.

GOD is a wise Father. He knows how grievously we feel all trial. He sends or allows it that we may gain more of His holiness. It may only harden in sin and unbelief. It promises good to those who are trained by it in faith and steadfastness. Righteousness comes to them from the Father, Whom they seek and hold firm to in their time of conflict. They enjoy this fruit when the strife is past. They have the peace that comes from growth in spiritual power, and faith in a God proved true. When righteousness is ripened for heaven they have sure peace there, around as well as within them.

The nature God has given me shrinks from the pain He wills me to bear. God means pain to be felt as pain. It is good only as a means to an end which I cannot gain as well without it. If I miss that, my pain is only grievous, and harms me. I am taught to view sorrow as the training of a Father, and to bear and use it so as to see joy set before me coming from it. It should bring low my pride, and turn my thoughts to God and my endless future. It should rouse me to search heart and life, and to seek light and grace, that I may be firm in faith and patience, and may know and do as my Father wills. So shall the holiness of my Father be made mine, as the fruit of my sad days of toil and strife. I shall know, indeed, that God is with and in me. In the peace of sure faith and hope, of a quiet conscience, of a nature ruled by God's grace, I shall have the first-fruits of the harvest of peace, when perfect righteousness shall be the crown of those who have endured to the end.

O merciful Father, Who dost care for Thy children's good, enable me so to endure in patience, that my griefs and trials may yield the fruit of righteousness to be enjoyed in peace.

I should not have to bear my pain, and grieve so many days,
If what I need my soul could gain by easy pleasant ways;
For Thou art love, Thou lovest me, and Thou art wisdom too,
And sorrow does not work for Thee what happiness could do.

FIFTH WEDNESDAY AFTER TRINITY.

"Waiting for the adoption, to wit, the redemption of our body."—ROM. viii. 23.

THE sons of God are not free yet. They have the earnest of the Spirit which tells them they are redeemed and made members of God's family. The Holy Spirit works in them to purify even their lower nature. But they groan and are burdened while tabernacling in a mortal body. Even when freed from the burden of the flesh, they hope for their manifestation as sons of God. When they are clothed upon with the "house which is from heaven," they shall, in body as well as spirit, bear the image of the heavenly.

Though redeemed and made a child and heir of God, I share the sorrows under which the rest of creation groans. I feel the burden of a body sinking to its decay. I groan under the temptings of evil, and my weakness to hold firm against the inroads of that worst death. My spirit in its efforts to rise feels its bondage galling. But the Holy Spirit's work is a pledge that the burden is not for ever. All I am has been redeemed, and joined to the Only-begotten. For the perfecting of all I am grace works now. For that I wait, not in fretful gloom, but in patient faith and hope; not idly, but as one who knows a purpose in all life's hard restraints, and would be made fit to use and enjoy his freedom. I wait for the holy liberty which the children of God shall have in the glory of their Father. I look not to be "unclothed," but to have a body worthy to be the fellow and the organ of a purified spirit. I wait till God takes down this tabernacle, and builds it up anew, a spiritual body in which I can appear among the redeemed in my Father's home.

Almighty Father, grant that by Thy Holy Spirit I may be upheld in faith and hope, till I gain in body and spirit the liberty of the glory of Thy children.

> Oh, how glorious and resplendent,
> Fragile body, shalt thou be,
> When endued with so much beauty,
> Full of health, and strong, and free;
> Full of vigour, full of pleasure, that shall last eternally.

Fifth Thursday after Trinity.

"*Whatsoever a man soweth, that shall he also reap.*"—GAL. vi. 7.

THE farmer stores at harvest the same kind of grain that he sowed. The amount bears some proportion to the much or little seed sown and work done. Ground left to itself bears weeds, as surely as if weeds were planted. Men can nearly always see in their past the cause of what they are. Health, sickness, wealth, want, wisdom, ignorance, purity, corruption, happiness, woe, honour, shame—are the fruits of their doing or not doing. So, when the part of life spent on earth ends, what is reaped tells what the sowing has been.

Now is the seed time. On the way I use it depends what I am to be and to have hereafter. All I do or fail to do in thought, feeling, word, or act, bears on that life that has no end. I can choose what to sow; but, when harvest-time comes, I cannot choose what to reap. I can sow now to the flesh or to the spirit. The crop will be like the sowing; I can only gather that. I cannot sow in unrighteousness, and hope to reap in mercy. I cannot sow in sloth, and reap the fruit of earnest toil. I cannot sow in uncleanness, and reap purity. I cannot plant thorns, and gather grapes; or sow sparingly for God, and reap plenteously from Him. I cannot sow nothing good, and hope to be given all good. I cannot sow evil, and expect God to root it out, and enrich me with ripe holiness by a miracle. What I put into the soil of my nature and cherish there, I shall have full grown. As surely as early days, improved or misspent, tell on the whole after-life here, so does my life now make me, in good or evil, what I shall find myself, and lay up for me what shall be my store in the life to come.

Almighty God, grant me grace to sow in repentance, and faith, and loving obedience, that I may reap the fruit of holiness and joy, through Thy mercy in Jesus Christ.

> Heaven is a place of rest from sin;
> But all who hope to enter there
> Must here that holy course begin
> Which shall their souls for rest prepare.

FIFTH FRIDAY AFTER TRINITY.

"Be ye therefore perfect, even as your Father which is in heaven is perfect."—MATT. v. 48.

GOD is love; so all find Him loving. Even the unthankful and unholy share His goodness. His love in Christ sought to win foes to let Him bless them. Those who wish to be indeed His children must aim to have His love in them, and to love as He does. It is unnatural to love no one, natural to love friends, supernatural to love all. Divine love shines forth in blessing because it is love, not because its objects are worthy, or will give back love. It overcomes evil with good.

Godless men love those from whom they get or hope to get a return. Even lower animals show love to their kind. As a member of Christ, I cannot be content with what is but a form of self-love. How dwells the love of God in me if this is all my love does! The Samaritan, who was not within God's Church, did not ask what the wounded Jew felt towards him, or whether he would have helped him in a like case. He acted as neighbour to him. Had Christ waited to love us till we loved Him, we should have been left to perish. His love that sought me, and bears with me, must show itself in me, or I am none of His. Alas! the old, proud, selfish heart does not yield easily to the Divine will. I can only set an aim before me, and reach after it. The love of God in me gains power as I force myself to do its bidding. What my own love cannot do, that higher love can. Though unable to feel as I ought, still I can be gentle and kind in deed, and word, and look, refusing to let my weakness hinder what God wills to do by means of grace.

O Divine Love, dwell in me and rule me; overcome my selfishness, and sloth, and weakness, that the love of my Father in heaven may be seen in all I am and do.

> God only knows the love of God;
> Oh, that it now were shed abroad
>   In this poor stony heart!
> For love I sigh, for love I pine;
> This only portion, Lord, be mine—
>   Be mine this better part.

FIFTH SATURDAY AFTER TRINITY.

"Lift up the hands which hang down, and the feeble knees; and make straight paths for your feet."—HEB. xii. 12, 13.

STRONG Christians are rare, who seem sure of what they do, and on what firm ground they stand, and where they mean to go. Some long, but fear to begin, to live godly. Some start well, but soon tire and yield. Some spend life in gaining and losing the same ground, never getting really forward, but growing weaker and more faint-hearted. So hands that ought to be lifted in prayer, or busy in God's work and war, hang down useless. Every blast of vain doctrine shakes the trembling faith. Every trial upsets the feeble purpose. Life is wasted in wandering which brings heaven no nearer.

Do I raise my hands in prayer with small heart or hope? Am I weary in well-doing, or holding back from God's work? Have I dropped or loosed my grasp of the weapons given to arm me against sin? Is the stand I take for God timid? Am I neither fixed in faith nor steadily upright in life; but weak in purpose, with no clear plan or course, easily daunted, turned aside, upset? This need not be, or go on. The blame is mine, not God's. I fail thus, not from lack of grace, but of will. I must not wish idly for God to do more for me. I must do more with what I have from God. I must wait on God in hearty, bold, trustful doing. I can pray, work, conquer, if I will. I can stand firm for truth and holiness, and press straight on in a plain course. God is pledged to give grace for what He tells me to be and do. His grace is sure. I am not alone. My Maker, and Father, and Redeemer, and Sanctifier, is with me, and seeks my highest good. I will take His grace for granted. I will brace my will, and put forth my strength as one whose will and strength are almighty through God.

O Lord, make me strong in faith, and zeal, and hope, that I may stir up Thy power in me, and ever gain new grace to will and do Thy will more perfectly.

> Go, labour on, your hands are weak,
>   Your knees are faint, your soul cast down;
> Yet falter not; the prize you seek
>   Is near—a kingdom and a crown.

The Fifth Sunday after Trinity.

"Kept by the power of God through faith unto salvation ready to be revealed in the last time."—1 PET. i. 5.

SALVATION is given now, so that all may be free from sin's yoke, and live as God's children. In the last time, what hinders its fulness and joy shall pass away. Meanwhile, man must use what he has in order to gain what he hopes for. In God's power is his sure trust. That is on his side, and is almighty. Faith grasps it in all needs. God's power keeps safe those who do not in unbelief let it go. He whose faith lives and works is strong in God to do, and bear, and conquer to the end.

God has saved me, and given me the pledge of full salvation. I have grace that I may win glory. The power of God is the power of love. He Who has begun can alone finish, and He wills to do so. It is the part of my faith to yield to God's strong tender hand, and put forth the power He puts in me. So shall that power free me from my own evil, and enable me to drive back the sin that assails me. So shall I on earth be kept and prepared for the inheritance that is kept and prepared for me in heaven. The power of the All-powerful is pledged to guard me till the last time. What need I fear but my own unbelief, which would set me alone in my helplessness? Through faith I learn the ways in which grace comes. Through faith I draw nigh, and keep nigh, that I may be strong in God. Through faith I follow where God leads in safe ways of obedience, and grow in holiness. Through faith I see Him Who is invisible; I am lifted above earthly things, and live for what is ready to be revealed, and is eternal. I fear not while I know that God's power is on my side. I faint not while I know what God's power keeps for me.

Almighty God, Whose power can alone keep me safely, give me faith to gain and use Thy grace in reaching towards the full salvation to be revealed in the last time.

> Lord, be ours the faith that saveth,
> Hope that every trial braveth,
> Love that to the end endureth,
> And, through Christ, the crown secureth.

Sixth Monday after Trinity.

"Depart from me; for I am a sinful man, O Lord."—LUKE v.8.

THE disciples saw a promise in Christ's command. Christ filled the nets their faith let down at His word. The plain signs of God's nearness overpowered St. Peter with a feeling of his own littleness as man, and guilt as a sinful man. He saw, as he had not before, how great and holy his Lord was, and how unworthy he was of such close companionship. He could not flee from that presence; he feared to go away; for to whom should he go? He fell at Christ's feet, asking to be relieved from what was more than he could bear. His words spoke lowliness. Christ bade him "fear not."

When signs of God's nearness flash on me in some new way, I am tempted to lose calmness. I am awed when what is grand or lovely in nature seems to bring me in my littleness face to face with the might of nature's God. Or, for the first time, faith shows me the closeness and majesty of the Divine Heart-searcher, before Whom I have lived so thoughtlessly, to Whom I have prayed so idly, against Whom I have sinned with so light a heart. I fear, when I am shown how dread a thing it is to have to do with God in any way; I am apt to wish that He might withdraw farther from me, and to think it safer not to risk drawing nigh in the ways He tells me of. But I cannot flee, and only near Him am I safe. He is to be feared, but as the God Who is Love. His power is on my side. His holiness may be made mine. God in Christ is man, and the Saviour of the sinful. Because I am a sinful man I pray Him not to depart, or let me leave Him. He can fit me for His presence, and give me such fear as angels have, and such love as casteth out all fear that has torment.

Give me faith, O Lord, to know Thy holiness and glory, and be sure of Thy love, that I may press near to Thee with lowly trust, and gain the love that casts out fear.

 Draw near, O Lord, and bid my sin depart
  Before Thy power divine;
 Renew me, Lord, and cheer my wounded heart,
  And make me wholly Thine.

SIXTH TUESDAY AFTER TRINITY.

"In everything by prayer and supplication with thanksgiving let your requests be made known unto God."—PHIL. iv. 6.

THIS is the way to be "careful for nothing," and to have the "peace of God." In prayer, heart and mind turn towards God, rest in Him, feel and think in His presence with faith, hope, love, and adoration. In much true "prayer" nothing is asked. Prayer may be the posture of the spirit "always," "without ceasing." In supplication wants and wishes are made known. Thanksgiving is part of all true "prayer" and "supplication." He who seeks mercies must acknowledge those already given. He will give thanks in everything who trusts the Love that guides all for his good.

My mind and heart can be kept in peace only by being stayed on God. If I live a life of prayer, I am never by myself. I hold communion with God; my thoughts and feelings are hallowed by Him, and drawn towards Him. I bear nothing apart from God. I desire nothing without laying it before God, that His will may be known. I need not to look for God in restless alarm when cares come; I can quietly spread everything, at all times, before a near tried Friend, Who careth for me. I do not seek God only in times of fear or want; I make known my requests, as I make known in prayer all else that is in mind or heart. I thank Him Who allows me to draw thus near, and Whose loving-kindness I feel more when I need sympathy and help. I thank Him for past mercies, and for the hope of mercies yet in store. I thank Him for the love that grants, and for the love that wisely denies. I thank Him that He is my Father in Christ Jesus. When I have made known my requests, I can leave them with Him in peace.

O Lord, grant me to live before Thee in faith and love, and to make known to Thee at all times everything that is in my heart and mind, that I may have Thy peace.

> Lord, let my soul Thy goodness always see,
> And with strong confidence lay hold on Thee;
> Prepared to kiss the sceptre or the rod,
> While God is seen in all, and all in God.

Sixth Wednesday after Trinity.

"Our light affliction, which is but for a moment, worketh for us a far more exceeding and eternal weight of glory."—2 Cor. iv. 17.

ST. PAUL bore long a heavy load of trial. Yet he speaks of all as nothing; for the longest, saddest night on earth is but as a moment to the everlasting day that follows. The world's worst counts not when weighed with heaven's glory. He who has good hope that his griefs are doing in and for him God's work of love, faints not, nor is weary. With the eye of faith he looks to the eternal things he longs for. All that God's will allows to make his sorrows more keen and lasting, helps him on to glory, boundless and for ever.

My cross is often painful, and must be borne long in hard ways, with no rest. If I think only of earth and time, I surely lose heart and give way. But my life goes on when all here is left. I may have the fruit of what I bear now, in glory, which God from His full treasures adds to for ever. One thing only need be my care—that what God wills me to suffer work in me what God wills. Then to my faith and hope, my griefs may be felt light and passing. I can fix my soul's eye on things unseen, and their untold, unknown worth shall make me grudge no cost to win them. If a fiercer flame be needed to burn away my sin, and make me pure for God, what is it all to having the clear glory of holiness brought out in me at last? If God in wise care lengthens my slow-moving hours of trial, I would not wish to risk any loss of endless glory for a little fleeting ease. Let God mould me and refine me after His own likeness, in His own way, in His own time. Enough for me to be found at last a perfect work of His love, fit for the glory which His love prepares in heaven.

O Lord, grant me faith so to bow to Thy will, that my affliction may be a means of grace, and a pledge of glory.

Lord, since our griefs on Thee were laid, and Thou hast felt their sting,
Help us in holiest calm to take our turn of suffering;
Thou didst look on unto Thy joy, and so by grace will we,
But we would clasp Thy cross, and feel we owe that joy to Thee.

SIXTH THURSDAY AFTER TRINITY.

"To do good and to communicate forget not; for with such sacrifices God is well pleased."—HEB. xiii. 16.

HE in whom God's love dwells, does all good he can with the means God gives. In Christ's members he sees Christ, Who gave life for him. Beyond the "household of faith" he sees those whom God pities. He will not offer what costs nothing. He gives alms in help for soul, mind, and body, not to be seen of men, or rewarded by God, or praised by himself. That were vanity, trading, selfishness, not love. Yet he is glad that God counts gifts to His poor as loans to Himself, and welcomes the least sacrifice of a guileless heart.

I have gifts from God to pass on. If I use all on self, I miss what makes them good gifts indeed. If I show the love shown me, I work with God; I gain new blessing, and am a means of blessing others. Of all good things, the best is that indwelling love that acts with the generosity of God. Wanting that, all else I have is worthless. Do I give? What do I give? How do I give? Are my money, my knowledge, my religion any help to those around me? Do I give only because I must, and asking grudgingly how much is my bare duty? Do I give what costs no trouble or self-denial? Do I give for gain in this world or the next? Do I give in a way to humble those who receive, and to exalt self? Or does God's love in me flow forth in its free course? Do I in love to God bring my best gladly, and make my dearest sacrifice with humble thankfulness? I owe all to God; but He in mercy looks on what I give for His sake as lent to Him. He is well pleased with my little blemished offerings of what is His right. He will reward me for what His love enables me to do and give.

O Lord, from Whom comes all I have and am that is good; stir up in me love for others, which will make Thy gifts be felt beyond myself, and bring me new blessing.

Largely Thou givest, gracious Lord,
Largely Thy gifts should be restored;
Freely Thou givest, and Thy word is "Freely give,"
He only who forgets to hoard has learned to live.

Sixth Friday after Trinity.

"By thy words thou shalt be justified, and by thy words thou shalt be condemned."—Matt. xii. 37.

WORDS are thoughts and feelings in outward form. They show what is in mind and heart. They are the outcome of the character. If a man be foolish, false, impure, unkind, or wise, true, pure, gentle, such will his words be. He may deceive his fellowmen or himself; but God traces his words to their source, and gives them their true value. By means of words, good and evil pass from man to man, and work is done for or against God. A man's words will at last show what he is.

My whole way of using my power of speech tells what I am. By the words of my lips I can know what God sees in my heart, and how like or unlike Christ I live. If I am careless about what I say, I am careless about all. What a power for good or evil words are! I may speak so as to harm and shame my soul, or so as to train myself in what is good. I may mislead, and give pain, and wrong my neighbour, or I may cheer, and help, and bless him. I may bring him God's food for mind and heart, or poison him with sin. I may spread peace and good-will, or stir up strife and every evil work. I may glorify God, and make known His truth and grace, or blaspheme Him, and tempt men from Him. My words show in myself, and spread among men, to God's glory or dishonour, truth or falsehood, wisdom or folly, virtue or vice. How closely should I watch my words, to learn the state of my heart! How carefully should I guard the use of so great a power for good and evil! How solemn the thought that, by what I speak or write God judges me, and shall justify or condemn me at last.

Almighty God, give me grace so to guard my thoughts and heart, and keep the door of my lips, that I may speak no idle or corrupt word, but only what is good to the use of edifying, according to Thy holy will.

At Thy feet our thoughts we lay,
Make Thine own the words we say, make our lives more pure
each day;
May our lips our faith confess,
Teach us when reviled to bless, conquering by gentleness.

Sixth Saturday after Trinity.

"They loved the praise of men more than the praise of God."
—John xii. 43.

THAT only is good which God counts good. What men praise may be of no worth with God. Man is not to be dressed so as to look right, but to be changed so as to be right. God made that which is without and within; He claims that both be holy. The shining before men must not hide, but show what the man is. A fair outward life may leave the heart foul; inward holiness always makes the life pure. Hypocrites are boldly sinners before God. They live a lie, lest men should find them out. They dishonestly take credit meant for such as they seem to be.

It is pleasant to have man's good word; but I can spare that if I am right before God. My hope rests on what God knows, not on what man thinks. God sees the spring and aim of my life, and weighs each least part with the rest. Man judges my heart by my life; God judges also my life by my heart. Man marks what I do and say; God knows what I am. Praise got by false pretences is shame; it warns me that it would be turned to scorn could men see the truth. I am base, if I care more for a good name than a good conscience. I insult God, if I am more careful to order the life by which men judge me, than the thoughts and feelings which He reads. I add sin to sin, if I cloak over with false virtue what is wrong in me, instead of setting it right. The old man and his deeds must be put off, not disguised. Do I pray more reverently, give more largely, live more purely, when men watch me, than when only God is by? If so, do I not trifle with Him Who loves and will judge me? Must I not fear the portion of the hypocrites?

O Lord, to Whom all hearts are open, make me true in my inmost being, that I may please Thee, and that my life before men may prove that I grow holy in body, soul, and spirit.

    Thyself despise,
Thou knowest well thy weakness and thy shame:
    Above man's censure calmly rise;
Be true to God and right, unmoved by praise or blame.

The Sixth Sunday after Trinity.

"Ye are all the children of God by faith in Christ Jesus. For as many of you as have been baptized into Christ have put on Christ."—GAL. iii. 26, 27.

MAN'S faith welcomes the faith revealed by God, and seeks a share in the grace and truth given through Jesus Christ. In baptism, by the One Spirit he is made part of the "Only-begotten," "God's dear Son;" he is "accepted in the Beloved" as a child of God. Now he is no more a slave, but a son, with new duties, new motives, new power. He is not driven by hard laws against his will. As he puts on the new man more wholly, and grows after the image of Christ living in him, it becomes his nature to live godly in Christ Jesus.

What God has done for me, warns of what I ought to do. What God has made me, warns of what I ought to be. I am God's son; only He could make me that. Perhaps the Church's faith brought me to Him ere I knew that I was born in sin. He gave me, not in name, but in truth, a share in the Divine nature of the God-Man. All the good things made known in the faith of Christ are ready for my faith to take and use. My sins are sins of a son of God. I can sin only with the members of Christ, using powers which are a part of Him. If I go on in sin I throw from me the rights and hopes of a joint-heir with Christ. The new man has been put on, but the old nature is still strong, and slow to give way. My faith must grasp the truth of what by God's free grace I am, and may grow to be; to what state I may rise, and what height I fall from if I fail. I must more and more put on the Lord Jesus Christ, that His mind in me may keep down what is evil. So shall I love God more with a son's love, and trust His will.

Almighty Father, give me faith to know the place and hopes to which Thou hast called me, and to live as Thy child, growing ever in living union with the Only-begotten.

> At the font we were marked with the Cross on our brow,
> Of our grace and our calling the sign,
> And the weakest is strong to be true to his vow,
> For the weapons we wield are divine.

SEVENTH MONDAY AFTER TRINITY.

"Except your righteousness shall exceed the righteousness of the scribes and Pharisees, ye shall in no case enter into the kingdom of heaven."—MATT. v. 20.

THE scribes and Pharisees were looked up to as the most learned in God's truth, and the highest models of blameless life. They felt sure of a foremost place in the kingdom of God. With many knowledge was unfruitful, motives were not pure, aims were not the highest. Even the true and earnest knew not of the gift of God's righteousness by the Spirit through union with Christ. This all can and must have now.

I must have a righteousness, not outside myself, not from myself, but put within me and so made mine. It must equal that of scribe and Pharisee in the careful doing of duty carefully learned. It must go beyond that of the deceived and deceivers among them in being heartfelt and for the eye of God. It must exceed any the truest ever had or taught; for it can. More is given me, and more is asked. The Holy Spirit has come. I am a member of Christ, I have ways of union with God unknown to the best saints of old. I may dwell in Christ while He dwells in me, making His power mine, changing my nature and guiding my life. His righteousness, the righteousness of God, is my perfect pattern. Imparted to me it is my power to live as He did, and to grow like Him. Have I any righteousness—even as much as scribe and Pharisee? Am I tempted to think of Christ's righteousness as set to my account instead of any I need have? Or do I prize it as the infinite source from which I may draw in faith, while in humble trust I use means of grace, and will and try to do righteousness?

Almighty Father, Who hast given me union with Thee through Christ, grant that He may so dwell in me as the source of righteousness that I may gain Thy kingdom.

> Fain would we Thy Word embrace,
> Live each moment in Thy grace,
> All ourselves to Thee consign,
> Fold up all our wills in Thine.
> Think, and speak, and do, and be
> Simply that which pleases Thee.

Seventh Tuesday after Trinity.
"Thou art the man."—2 Sam. xii. 7.

DAVID fell from a height, and sank deeply. He went down from sin to sin, growing more hard and dull. Not till the prophet roused his anger by a story of another's guilt, did he see what his own deserved. He confessed his sin, and it was put away. But he could not undo its work, or forgive himself, or escape unpunished. He was never afterwards a free man, but in the power of those who knew his shame. His children's sin darkened his days. Sorrows crowded on him to the last. He learned that, though God is merciful, sin always finds the sinner out, and punishment is sure.

I have not the large gifts of grace, or the high calling that David had. I may well doubt myself, and fear the first yielding to temptation, lest I sink as low as he. I dare not ask God to let me sin once, and save me from falling farther. I cannot count on stopping when I will, or on ever being brought back to the state whence I cast myself down willingly. What if I should be left to go down into sin, and to lie down in it, till I lose the dread of sin and even the feeling of it ! I may well fear lest I be blind as David was to sin in myself, which I would abhor in another. I do well to look on the evil around me as perhaps a parable of my sin, and to try myself as before God. Forgiven sin does not mean forgotten sin. Rather must I remember it with more sad shame, when its baseness is shown in the light of God's forgiving love. God is very pitiful and gracious, but He is not mocked. His laws cannot be safely trifled with; sooner or later they avenge themselves. If my sin does not find me out here, I shall find it hereafter.

Almighty and merciful God, give me an enlightened conscience and a firm will, a holy dread of sin, and a humble feeling of my weakness, that through Thy grace I may be saved from the guilt and sorrow of sin.

I want a godly fear, a quick discerning eye,
That looks to Thee when sin is near, and sees the tempter fly;
A spirit still prepared and armed with jealous care;
For ever standing on its guard, and watching unto prayer.

Seventh Wednesday after Trinity.

"Confess your faults one to another, and pray one for another."—James v. 16.

HE whose brother has aught against him must own the wrong and ask pardon. He who sins against God must confess his fault, that it may be forgiven. It is good to open the soul's grief to a wise, kind friend. The act humbles; it tests the penitence; a fairer judgment than one's own is gained, with the help of advice and prayers. If the need be felt great, or the soul's questions be hard, the burdened one will naturally go to some discreet and learned minister of God's Word.

If I wrong my neighbour, confession is due to him, to myself, and to God. Justice, honour, and religion claim it. When I bow before God, and tell my sin, He hears me, and bids me go in peace and sin no more. Yet He teaches me to lay bare my faults before a fellow-sinner, and ask his prayers. I may own sin to God with no true sense of dishonour or humbling of my pride. My shame that man knows my sin warns me what my shame ought to be under the holy eye of God; the effort it costs to tell him how I have sinned warns me what pains I should take not to sin. A friend's voice may speak to me God's counsel and comfort. A friend's prayers may quicken mine, and call down an added blessing. What friend can I choose so fit to help me, as one who has a charge from God to watch for souls, and must give account of them to God? God will not fail to give him grace to guide and care for me as a sheep of Christ's flock who has strayed. He is sent to speak the word of pardon, and to bless in the Lord's name. To sin is shameful. I disown it when I own it.

O Lord, Who knowest my heart and life, make me so to hate sin that I may be quick to own my faults against my fellow-men and Thee, and may use all means to be delivered from the guilt and stain of sin.

> Lord, when we bend before Thy throne,
>   And our confessions pour,
> Teach us to feel the sins we own,
>   And hate what we deplore.

SEVENTH THURSDAY AFTER TRINITY.

"The kingdom of heaven is like unto treasure hid in a field; the which when a man hath found, he hideth, and for joy thereof goeth and selleth all that he hath, and buyeth that field."—MATT. xiii. 44.

WHILE toiling for daily bread, he found what would make him rich for ever. All he had seemed nothing; he sold it that he might buy the field where the treasure lay. So, to man bowed over the world's toil, is made known the wealth that is in Christ. He hides the new-found prize. Joy makes him fear lest he lose it. He grudges nothing if he may feel sure that it is safely his own. It is enough. He buys the whole field for the sake of it. Outward things and means of grace, which before were barren and a weariness, have treasure in them now.

The wealth of God is hidden from the careless idler; it is often found by the earnest, even when he seeks it not. While toiling for the best ends I know of, a higher good is shown me. I can have it if I will, but not without cost. Beside that treasure all else is of no worth. It gives all joy and power. It grows larger and more full of blessing the more it is drawn upon and used. To have found this, and to know that it may be mine, is indeed joy. Not for me to boast, but with lowly care to hide it, while I do all, and, if need be, give up all else at once, to make my right to it sure. Have I toiled in earthly tasks, thoughtless of heavenly good? Now, God shows me that as the great end to be sought in all labour. Have I prayed, and used means of grace with small gain, as if digging round the treasure without reaching it? Now I know the worth of the "field." Hidden in it there is a treasure I can make my own. For the sake of that, I joyfully part with what I have prized most. I count all things but loss, that I may win Christ and be enriched by Him.

Grant, Lord, that in all I do I may seek the true riches, and that I may spare no cost to make them mine.

> Whate'er I fondly counted mine,
>   To Thee, my Lord, I here restore;
>   Gladly I all for Thee resign;
>   Give me Thyself, I ask no more.

SEVENTH FRIDAY AFTER TRINITY.

"I know thy works, and tribulation, and poverty (but thou art rich)."—Rev. ii. 9.

TO the Ever-living and All-Knowing all things are present. He knows them that are His, and how His life in them is put forth. No least work of those who live in union with the Lord, fails to follow them when they die in the Lord. He measures the trial and need which make their strife with sin hard, and their gifts like the widow's mite. He notes how they work in taking up the cross, and carrying it, and in lowly patience. They are blessed, and heirs of the kingdom, who have suffered for His sake, and been rich in faith.

My Maker and my Judge knows what I am, and what I do. He sees my past and what is before me, in all their meaning and value. He marks as my works the working of His life in and by me. He knows what helps I need, and gives as is best. He understands my difficulties, and my want of means to serve Him by what men call great deeds. He owns my efforts in spite of hindrances. He feels with me in my cares, and knows the strain of prayer and patience it costs to keep down self, and bow to the Divine will. He remembers each trial and victory of faith, though I toil and fight as a matter of course, and forget, as soon as it is past. When I mourn my unworthiness, He longs to bless, and His mercy sees His own worthiness in what I feebly do. Though I feel myself poor, and miserable, and blind, and naked, yet, if I am earnest, He lays up store for me above, and sees me rich towards God. No least part of my life is trifling, or need be lonely or in vain. Thus, under God's eye, I must live carefully, yet hopefully. I need fear nothing while He knows me true to Him.

O Lord, Who knowest all my path, grant me grace to labour and suffer gladly according to Thy will, and to be rich towards God, and an heir of the kingdom.

Thou wilt do all I have undone, remake what I have marred,
My foolish hindrances the while wilt gently disregard:
And when the work is all complete, then Thou wilt call it mine,
And I shall hear Thee say, "Well done! henceforth My joy is thine."

SEVENTH SATURDAY AFTER TRINITY.

"Thou art careful and troubled about many things: but one thing is needful: and Mary hath chosen that good part, which shall not be taken away from her."—LUKE x. 41, 42.

BOTH sisters loved Christ, and were loved by Him. Love led each to do what she did. Martha sought to give her best; Mary to feed her soul with the Lord's words. Martha, in her restless care about many things, was not herself what Christ would have had her be. She grudged Mary her calm, and blamed her to her Lord for not trying to honour Him in her way.

Some are called more to active work; some more to a quiet life of thought and prayer. Martha must not envy Mary, nor Mary look down on Martha. Christ's work needs both. Each calling has its own blessings and its own dangers. I may leave work undone while seeking what gladdens my own soul, and so make my religious life an idle self-pleasing. I may welcome the Word that tells of rest, and be glad to learn, but unready to bear the yoke. Or I may so live in the whirl and bustle of work as to leave my soul without what it needs for growth and vigour. Even work for Christ may draw and keep me away from Him. I may be so eager to give as to forget that I must first and always be a receiver. I may be careful and troubled in many schemes to do Christ honour, and yet fail to find and know Him, or have in His service rest for my soul. I need times of quiet sitting still at my Master's feet, to gain love and calmness, that I may do Martha's work in Mary's spirit. I am bound to go forth from hearing the Lord's words to use for Him what I gain from Him.

O Lord, lead me to choose the good part which fails not, and so to learn at Thy feet, that I may ever with quiet loving spirit work for Thy glory.

> Be heaven my spirit's calm abode,
> Hid be my life with Christ in God,
> My spirit, Lord, be one with Thine;
> Let all my works in Thee be wrought,
> And filled with Thee be all my thought,
> And in myself Thy likeness shine.

The Seventh Sunday after Trinity.

"Whence can a man satisfy these men with bread?"—MARK viii. 4.

THERE was no money, and no place to buy. They laid their small store in Christ's hands. He gave it power to be enough for all. So year by year men wait on God for what is not and they cannot bring into being. They trust the seed to God, as He has taught. God gives it back multiplied. So in obedient faith men seek their soul's food. What they lay before God becomes in His hands means of grace and support of spiritual life.

God can feed with manna, or as He wills. He is not bound to one way of working. His power is as real when He provides for me in what I call the course of nature, as when He works what I call a miracle. I must not forget Him because He is so sure that I can count on what He will do when I plant and water. I must look to Him for increase, and praise Him when I reap. He blesses weak means in weak men's hands, to help tired starving souls. My work for men fails unless I bring it to Him to be made His work. When my soul wants cheer and strength He sends help, sometimes straight from Himself, often in His chosen ways through the ministry of men. He blessed means which had no look of promise, when in my baptism He took me into union with His own life. As I wait on Him in faith and prayer, He upholds my soul's life, through what I do, and men do for me. In the Holy Communion bread and wine are brought to Him; He gives them back, blessed to be my meat and drink indeed, so that I partake of Him Who is the Bread of God and the eternal Life of souls.

Almighty God, teach me in faith, and prayer, and obedience to wait on Thee for all good things I need for soul and body, that all my blessings may come to me as tokens of Thy power and love.

> He cares for all who are His own,
> He never lets them be alone,
> But always waits to give;
> Their daily needs He will supply,
> And nothing will His love deny
> By which their souls may live.

EIGHTH MONDAY AFTER TRINITY.

"If ye then, being evil, know how to give good gifts unto your children, how much more shall your Father which is in heaven give good things to them that ask Him?"—MATT. vii. 11.

NATURE guides fallen men to seek their children's true good. God is better than His creatures. From Him come all Fatherly love and wisdom. In Him is no selfishness, caprice, partiality. He knows each, whom He bids call Him Father. He knows how best to give what is best for each. He grants more good than is asked. He withholds evil things though asked. He gives the Holy Spirit—the sum of all "good things," assuring of His wise love in granting or refusing.

All fatherly love and wisdom of all best earthly fathers tell me of my Father in heaven. He as God is perfectly what they as men can only be imperfectly. Though sinners, they still show something of what God implanted in them. God Who has made me His child pledges Himself to do a Father's part. He wishes my true improvement and well-being, and will provide for it. He calls on me to show the trustful asking spirit of a child. He does not scorn my least prayer. He will deny me no good thing. I would not have Him grant all that in my wilfulness or foolishness I ask. I trust Him to withhold what He knows would be to me the useless "stone," or the dangerous "serpent." So I ask freely, sure of His firm true love, and knowing that if He denies me what I think good, He will grant me what He knows good. I ask, with all things, and above all things, for the Holy Spirit—to make my will more one with my Father's will, and make His gifts be indeed blessings. Without this, nothing is good for me. With this, all is good.

Almighty Father, teach me to pray as Thy child. Grant me what is good, though I fail to ask it: deny me what is evil, though I ask it: give me Thy Holy Spirit.

> Not to my wish, but to my want,
> Do Thou Thy gifts apply;
> The good unasked in mercy grant,
> The ill, though asked, deny.

Eighth Tuesday after Trinity.

"When ye were the servants of sin, ye were free from righteousness. What fruit had ye then in those things whereof ye are now ashamed? for the end of those things is death."—ROM. vi. 20, 21.

MAN may so disown God's right over him as to obey no call of duty, and feel no check of conscience. This freedom from God's law means the loss of His care and blessing. Life's powers are spent in laying up shame, and in going on to death. The spirit is blighted and dishonoured till it is parted from God, its life and glory. Even if sin's service be forsaken, shame is not escaped. Sinners must feel the shame of the despairing soul that perishes, or of the humbled penitent.

I am able to sin freely only so far as I have shaken off God's careful, guiding hand, and have ceased to love and fear Him. I am happy in sin so far as I am falling towards shame, and the utter loss of Him Who is the life of souls. I must shrink from that state in which the soul is out of sight and hearing of the God of righteousness! Well for me when conscience makes the way of sin hard, and forbids me to obey my tempters and my own evil nature. Blessed are the shame and self-reproach which warn me when I have failed, and send me for pardon and renewal. Thus God claims me for righteousness, and shows that He has not let me go. He protects me from sin, and holds me back from the way of dishonour that leads to death. Alas, for the days when I broke loose from His kind Fatherly rule, and to bear the yoke of sin! Alas, for those fruits of unrighteousness which bow me before myself and God, and seem more shameful the more sure I am of Divine forgiveness. Let me be thankful that my soul lives, and feels, and can still love the restraints of righteousness.

Almighty God, grant me such an abiding sense of Thy claim upon me, that I may be ashamed of past sin, and guided by fear and love of Thee, may serve Thee for ever.

> I love, I love Thee, Lord, most high,
>   Because Thou first hast loved me;
> I seek no other liberty,
>   But that of being bound to Thee.

EIGHTH WEDNESDAY AFTER TRINITY.

"*Being made free from sin, and become servants to God, ye have your fruit unto holiness, and the end everlasting life.*"—Rom. vi. 22.

SIN is not our rightful lord. God has redeemed us for His own, and given us the freedom of His sons. He has pledged Himself to enable us to resist sin. We need not yield to its power. We are bound to serve God as our Father, Who guards and upholds us. In His service growing holiness is our reward. Day by day we become holy, as through God's grace we are trained in habits of right-doing. So we go forward to the end—fulness of life, in perfect union with the everlasting God.

I belong to God, and owe Him all my service, for He has saved me from the power of sin, which brings shame, and ends in death. He calls me to be faithful, not as a servant, but a son, that I may grow like my Father, and worthy to share His home. As I obey Him, evil loosens its hold upon me, and I am set more free from all that shames and kills. Yielding to His will, I am formed to holiness after His loving plan, and by the power of His grace I bring forth the fruit of holy living. But in this world I am still struggling free from the toils of evil. I have only the glad hope and foretaste of the glory to be revealed. I have the joy of knowing that God is my Lord and Saviour, and that His holiness is being made mine. I look on to the end,—life with God, life in God, life like God's—pure, perfect, and for ever. I will claim my freedom. Sin shall not usurp dominion over me. I will serve my Father as a faithful son. I will watch, and pray, and labour to bring forth that fruit which tells of growth unto holiness, and of the power of the life that is everlasting.

Almighty Father, Who hast broken the yoke of sin and set me free, give me grace to serve Thee with all my heart, that I may go forward in a life of righteousness to the reward of holiness and everlasting life.

A slave of sin and death was I, but Christ has set me free;
I live to glorify His love, Who died to ransom me.
My God I serve, to Him alone my loving homage pay;
I gain His likeness, and His will I joyfully obey.

Eighth Thursday after Trinity.

"As He prayed, the fashion of His countenance was altered, and His raiment was white and glistering."—LUKE ix. 29.

MOSES' face shone after speaking with God at Sinai. But, as Christ prayed on the holy mountain, His own glory shone through the veil of His humanity. Men saw that glory—the same which St. John saw afterwards in the Revelation. The voice from heaven and the bright cloud recalled the anointing to His work at Jordan. His human soul was newly braced for what was now near, of which His forerunners, Moses and Elias, spoke. The glimpse of His glory would help the faith of those who saw Him led to the Cross. It helps the hope of those who look forward to being like Him.

Let me be much with Christ apart, that I may catch some of the glory which lights on those who speak to God. Let me cherish Christ in me, that by the shining forth of His holiness my nature may be transfigured. It is good for me to enjoy the soul's vision of the Lord in His glory. But this cannot always be. Moses and Elias warned me of laws and truths which Christ came to fulfil, and to set before me with new meaning. Tokens of Divine favour and signs of the glory union with Christ gives, are foretastes of what is only reached in full beyond the cross and the grave. I must go down from the mountain top, bearing with me the strength they give. My Lord calls me after Him to lowly work, with prayer and fasting, that I may cast out evil in His name. I must be as sure of what He is when He leads me to Gethsemane as when He unveils His glory. Now I see Him as He is, only by faith. I hope to wear His likeness and share His glory, not in a tabernacle built by man, but in the eternal mansions He prepares on high.

Bring me apart with Thee, O Lord, and reveal Thy glory to my faith, till, being purified, I see Thee as Thou art, and know that Thou hast made me like Thee.

Not yet, not yet, to man is given to rest upon that height;
'Tis but a passing glimpse of heaven; we must descend and fight.
Beneath the mount, in toil and pain, O Christ, Thy strength
    impart;
Till we, transfigured too, shall reign for ever where Thou art.

EIGHTH FRIDAY AFTER TRINITY.

"Now we see through a glass, darkly; but then face to face: now I know in part; but then shall I know even as also I am known."—1 COR. xiii. 12.

WHEN the veil of unbelief falls, faith sees the glory of God in Christ and His work. But we cannot now know all. We must learn God's truths in man's words. We can think of heavenly things only as our experience of earthly things helps us to give them form. The mirror shows us a true reflection, but not the thing itself. Like children, we are taught what we do not yet know all the meaning of. When the veil of the flesh is withdrawn, we hope with pure spiritual eyes to see the things of God clearly. We hope to understand the speech of heaven, and to know God as truly as God knows us.

Christ is the shining forth of the Father's glory. I see Him in His words and works shown to me in the Gospel and by the Spirit. In Him I see God. But while in my earthly state I know only as far as is safe and good for me. Sin hides God's face. I have not power to put plainly even before my faith much of the glory I am told of. Enough is clear to draw my mind and heart, and influence my whole being. What Christ said and did and is can mould and change me, if I will. Grace comes from Him to work glory in me, that I may grow fit to look on Him as He is. God does not yet show me His glory, but makes His goodness pass before me. So I do not now trace the growth of glory in myself, but watch for light and grace. If my faith grasps the truths made known, and my will uses each new gift of grace, I may rejoice in hope of the glory of God to be revealed to me when I am pure enough to look upon it, and to be revealed in me as the finished work of God.

O Lord, make Thyself known to my faith, and pour out Thy grace upon me, that by the power of Thy goodness I may be changed till I can see Thee in Thy glory.

> May Reason my desires restrain,
> May Reason bow when Faith is sure;
> May I, through Faith and Reason, gain
> New light from Thee, desires more pure.

Eighth Saturday after Trinity.

"Jesus, beholding him, loved him, and said unto him, One thing Thou lackest."—Mark x. 21.

ALL was his that earth could give. He had kept what he knew of God's will. He did not make this world his all, nor did he feel content with himself; for he still asked how to gain sure hold on eternal life. Christ loved him as He looked into his manly, guileless heart. He saw his high gifts and calling, and what he lacked that he might be free to rise. The claim laid bare what made it hard for him to seek God's kingdom first. He went away sad, to count the cost of following the Good Master and the call of God's love.

Christ tells me that God's law marks the way of life. Till I try from the heart to do God's will, I have not set off towards life. My aim to be perfect proves how far I do this. Christ loves to see in me a true will to lack no grace, and fail in no work of love. He loves to see me bold to own my wish for light and help to take the highest path. I have no love which Christ will love, if I do not seek to be perfect, and ask how. I must let Christ take me at my word; I must not wonder or be sad, if He bid me part with what tempts my trust and love from God. The self-denial and work to which He calls me may seem more than are laid on others; but they are only my needful duty. The cross He gives may try me with its weight and sharpness; but I have asked for it; without it I cannot be what I have prayed to be. Christ may seem to lead me through rough, hard ways, but it is not for me to choose His course. My care must be to follow whithersoever He goeth, Him to Whom I have come as a seeker after eternal life.

Look on me, O Lord, and make me what Thou lovest. Make me glad to do all and bear all at Thy word, that I may lack nothing to fit me for life with Thee.

>Is there a thing beneath the sun
> That strives with Thee my heart to share?
>Ah! tear it thence, and reign alone,
> The Lord of every motion there!
>Then shall my heart from earth be free,
>When it hath found repose in Thee.

The Eighth Sunday after Trinity.

"Make the tree good, and his fruit good."—MATT. xii. 33.

THE fruit shows of what sort the root is. Words and deeds tell the state of the heart out of which they come. From an evil source, evil flows. Only by the outward life can men judge. God sees the heart, and knows how far what seems good is good. Man's will is free to put away evil and to choose good, so as to become good. He can lay hold of offered grace, and yield his will and affections to Him from Whom all goodness comes. He only is good who is grafted into the true Vine, and abides in Him. He only can bear much good fruit.

My words and deeds tell me much of what I am. Thoughts and feelings are a surer, fuller, plainer test. It is not enough to watch my outward life. Let me search down in my heart for the roots of evil, and take heed that the springs of my thinking and doing be made pure. Let my will be bent strongly towards good, and the force of evil in my nature, in myself, be firmly mastered. Let the healing, renewing grace of God be humbly, truly sought for each wounded, weakened power. Then good words and works will follow. If I am loving, I will live in love. If I am pure, I will not say or do what is impure, but what is holy. If I am meek, my manner will show it when I am tried. If I am good before God, such will my life be with men. There is none good but God; yet I may be good with God's goodness implanted in me. Only God can make me good; yet it rests with me whether I become good or not. He does not force an entrance to my nature, but He stands at the door and knocks.

O Lord, the one source of holiness, renew me and rule my whole being by Thine indwelling Spirit, that I may be made good in Thy sight, and that so all my words and deeds may please Thee; for Jesus Christ's sake.

Oh! what peace when the body of evil has died,
    And its wants and its weakness alarm me no more!
And I yield to my Father a spirit supplied
    With the gifts which from Christ's opened heart ever pour.

NINTH MONDAY AFTER TRINITY.

"The Spirit itself beareth witness with our spirit, that we are the children of God."—ROM. viii. 16.

THE Holy Spirit speaks in our hearts for God. He imparts peace and hope to those whom He warns and attracts away from sin, in the steps of Christ. He gives faith in a Father's love, and hope of the great inheritance. His alarms and pleadings tell of a God Who claims His child. In each shrinking from sin God's clinging hold is felt. Each longing and effort to do well tells of His inspiration. Devotion and praise show the Divine love that kindles them. Each temptation overcome, each evil way forsaken, each grace gained, is the Spirit's work, witnessing that our Father owns us as His.

To know myself God's child indeed, is to have all joy and hope. The favour and blessing of a heavenly Father are the pledge and earnest of full bliss to be. Perhaps I fail to realise the calm deep peace that some find? I cannot rise to their height of joy in prayer and communion with God? This need not grieve me. My Father may keep me lowly and watchful, that I may be safe. He may, by withholding joy, lead me to gain more cause of joy. I can have surer ground of quiet rest than my own shifting feelings. Is sin a grief? Do I fear its most far-off approach, and strive with each form of it? Do I will and try to obey the Spirit of my Father and my Saviour? Do I watch for light from heaven to lead me on? Do I pray and seek for all grace? Do I aim at holiness, humbly resolved to rest not till the fruits and works of the Spirit are shown in my nature and my life? If so, I have ground for joy in God, whether I feel joy or not. Otherwise I have ground for fear, lest my joy and peace be only self-deception.

Almighty Father, cheer me with such peace and joy as is good for me, and grant that I may ever show those fruits by which the Spirit witnesses to Thy true children.

The blood which made our conscience pure full confidence imparts;
Thy testimony, Lord, is sure in all Thy children's hearts.
The Spirit of Thy Son within, Who "Abba, Father," cries,
Redeems the faithful soul from sin, and wholly sanctifies.

NINTH TUESDAY AFTER TRINITY.

"*As many as are led by the Spirit of God, they are the sons of God.*"—ROM. viii. 14.

ALL were not Israel that were of Israel. So all that have been given a place in God's family are not in a true sense sons. Born into the world, men are God's offspring. Born into the Church by the new birth of water and the Spirit, they can call God Father in a new way. All is in order that they may use, as the Spirit guides, the powers they have by nature, and their powers as members of Christ. Those only have the freedom, and blessing, and hope of God's sons, who yield themselves to be led by the Spirit to that perfection which their Father wills for them.

It is vain to be called by a heavenly Father's name, and to be given the powers and rights of a son, if I live not as a son. I am bound to show in my life and character the gifts I have from God, and to grow daily into His likeness. My path is beset by snares. I cannot guide myself. If I go my own way, led by the will of the flesh or the mind, I pass from under my Father's care, I lose His help; I grow to be as if I were in no way a partaker of the Divine nature; I am in the world as if I had never been born into God's family, and had no place or hope as His child. Shall I not gladly yield to the leading of the Spirit, Who renews in me my divine Father's life, and brings His love near to win and draw me. He does not drive or force. If I am willing, He will guide my every thought and wish, and uplift and purify my whole nature, and lead me in safe ways to my Father's home.

Almighty Father, grant me to prize aright my calling as Thy child, and to follow the loving leadings of Thy Spirit. So may I always be safe under Thy care, and grow to be like Thee and meet for Thy holy presence.

> Send forth the Spirit of Thy Son,
> O God, into my wayward heart,
> That governed by Thy love alone
> I never may from Thee depart,
> But, following my celestial guide,
> Be numbered with the glorified.

Ninth Wednesday after Trinity.

"Not every one that saith unto Me, Lord, Lord, shall enter into the kingdom of heaven; but he that doeth the will of My Father Which is in heaven."—Matt. vii. 21.

CHRIST does not make little of right faith and open confession. Men "do well" to know and own Him as their Lord. But those alone who in secret heart and outward life do His Father's will are heirs with Christ of the kingdom. Faith is dead, unless it work by love. Obedience proves prayer and praise true. If the life be rebellion, homage of the lips is mockery. Right thoughts and good words cost less than an always-yielded will. He who from the heart does God's will grows in faith, and power to confess Christ in word and work.

I am sure that Jesus Christ is Lord. I call Him Lord. I profess to be His servant and disciple. Yet I may be of those to whom the Judge will say, "I never knew you." I may work iniquity instead of doing God's will; and out of my own mouth be proved to sin wilfully against One Whom I know, and Whose claims I grant. My hope is not good because my mind is clear, and I think rightly about Christ. He is not pleased by flattery. Words of homage and devotion insult Him and harden me, if they do not speak what my heart feels, and if they are out of tune with my life. Christ warns me to ask how far His Father's will is my rule of life. By this test He will judge me. By doing God's will I am formed after it, I show faith in my Saviour and Example, I offer the truest praise. My hope depends on what love leads me to do, and give up for Him in Whom I believe; not on what I can say to Him, or feel towards Him now and then, but on what I am before Him in the steady aim of my whole inward and outward life.

O Lord Jesu Christ, enable me in heart, and word, and life so to own Thee Lord, to the glory of God the Father, that, doing His will, I may inherit the kingdom.

> To Thee we bring, Who art the Lord,
> Ourselves to be Thy throne;
> Let every thought, and deed, and word,
> Thy pure dominion own.

NINTH THURSDAY AFTER TRINITY.

"I will put My fear in their hearts, that they shall not depart from Me."—JER. xxxii. 40.

DEVILS tremble before God, Whom they believe in, but do not love. Wilful sinners have no fear of God before their eyes; or in their hearts they shrink from Him Whom their lives dare. Fear may warn men from the sins that hide God and His love. God's true children see His power and holiness in the light of His love. Fear of sin draws them close to their Father. Reverence grows as they love with a more happy trust. As they learn to prize God's favour, they are careful of it.

If I have no fear of God, I have no hope; I am without God in the world, and when I am forced to fear Him shall flee from Him. Better to dread Him in His might and holiness, than to sin on unchecked, and go farther from Him. But my prayer must be for the holy fear which He gives to those whom He teaches to know Him as a Father, and draws close in child-like love. So faith, as it brings joy and peace, will deepen right fear. Fear will keep me where joy and peace are. I will not trifle with the love that becomes more precious as I know it. I will watch lest I stray from Him Who alone can make me safe. All I do, and say, and think, and am, shall be to please Him. Fear shall be in my heart, where God is loved. I shall not love God less, but more, because He is greatly to be feared. I shall not fear Him less, but more, as love grows jealous for Him. Fear and love shall help one another. I shall learn the spirit of those who never depart from God, but find their full joy as they bend adoringly before the holy loving Presence.

Almighty Father, make Thyself known to me in Thy holiness and love, that I may always seek to enjoy Thy care and goodness, and may take heed not to wander.

How dread are Thine eternal years, O everlasting Lord,
By prostrate spirits day and night incessantly adored!
How wonderful, how beautiful the sight of Thee must be,
Thine endless wisdom, boundless power, and awful purity!
Oh, how I fear Thee, living God, with deepest, tenderest fears,
And worship Thee with trembling hope and penitential tears!

NINTH FRIDAY AFTER TRINITY.

"Let them that suffer according to the will of God commit the keeping of their souls to Him in well-doing, as unto a faithful Creator."—1 PET. iv. 19.

GOD cares for all whom He has made. While they keep in the path of His will, nothing can harm them. God is true, for His name's sake, to those who suffer for His sake, and through being true to Him. As God is faithful, His creatures may be sure. They can go on boldly, trusting all to Him, Whose they are. Only they must take care that while they bow to the will that allows them to suffer, they obey the will that marks the one safe way. Trusting the true God, faithful to the faithful God, they can go on in well-doing, sure of well-being.

God is love. He made me for good, not for evil. He changes not. He does not mislead me: He tells me to plead His pledged word. He has shown His love for me by the cost at which He won me back when I was lost. I dare not wrong Him by the thought that perhaps He made me, and will leave me, to be the helpless sport of sin and woe. He made me, and trains me for a higher, better state than that in which I am now. This I take for granted. If I let Him guide my life, He will guide all things for my good. Only by leaving Him can I lose His care. He knows best what I ought to do and to suffer. I need not be cast down by what tries me now, or be careful about what may come. Enough if I know myself in the strong, safe hand of my God, Who will not scorn or forget His own work. I trust Him to show me the way of well-doing, and to keep me in it. I watch for the leadings of His will, and use the helps of His grace. I am sure that in the end I shall find all well.

O merciful Father, keep me in the way of patient faith and well-doing, that, led always by Thy wise, loving will, I may become what Thou didst create me to be, through Thy grace in Jesus Christ.

> Lord, give me grace my cross to bear,
> And grant Thy peace in heart and mind;
> Be this my aim, my only care,
> To serve Thee well with will resigned.

Ninth Saturday after Trinity.

"The wisdom that is from above is first pure, then peaceable, gentle, and easy to be entreated, full of mercy and good fruits."—James iii. 17.

TRUE wisdom is from above. God gives it freely to all who ask aright, with true desire to know and do His will. It grows as truth is learned and acted on. By it man sees and chooses the better way and end. It makes man pure in what he loves, and wills, and does. It keeps mind and heart at peace, and gives skill to win men for a patient God. It gives a candid spirit ready to learn truth, a loving spirit fruitful in works of mercy.

God alone can give me wisdom to know my lack of wisdom. He sends wisdom from above in answer to the heart's prayer. I seek to be wise, not in my own eyes, but in God's. Wisdom learned from the world, and with no view beyond it, leaves me foolish before God. By itself it is no help for eternity. Mere knowledge of all truth does not make me wise. Wisdom is God's light in me, enabling me to use well the truth I know, to judge the worth of things, to choose the best, and seek it in the right way. I am not wise if I leave out of sight God and my soul's needs, and plan only, or chiefly, for my body and this world. Wisdom is shown by its fruit in heart and life. Am I pure, aiming at freedom from all that is false and unclean? Do I seek to make peace lest purity of truth and life suffer from the "evil work" that comes with strife? Am I so firm and sure as to be gentle always with all, able to work for God and man without rough haste? Am I ready to hear others, and, if I am wrong, to set my judgment right? Do I give the world the fruit of the mercy I have from God, and show that Christ is "made unto me wisdom"?

O Lord, grant me wisdom from above, that in all my life I may choose the good and pure, make known Thy peace, and bring forth the fruit of love and holiness.

> Come, Thy light and grace bestowing,
> Make me willing, make me wise;
> Day by day more steadfast growing,
> Till I win the heavenly prize.

The Ninth Sunday after Trinity.

"*Give an account of thy stewardship.*"—LUKE xvi. 2.

MEN are not owners, but stewards. Time, powers of thought and speech and work, position in the Church and the world, money, influence, knowledge, grace, all belong to God. Men are not free to use, or neglect, or waste them. God lays His hand on them in many ways, warning that they are His, and asking how they are being used. Sooner or later, the stewardship of each on earth ends. That of the unfaithful shall be taken away. The faithful shall receive a higher trust.

I have a trust from God. Each day is given, that in it I may grow wiser and holier, make the world more bright and good, and bring God praise. My gifts of mind and body, my place in life, my power to lead others, are part of my Lord's capital. Knowledge of truth, union with Christ through means of grace, the Spirit's help, are treasure which I may not hoard, or waste, or enjoy selfishly, but must turn to profit as God's. A day of reckoning comes, when I shall receive honour or disgrace. God marks how far I am faithful. He warns me to know also, by His voice in my conscience, the calls of His Word, the changes of my life. He asks how it is with me, and summons me to His presence to give account. Am I honest in the care of what God gives to my keeping? Do I use it well for Him and for myself, that I may glorify Him in what I do, and in what I grow to be? To go on blindly, is to trifle with myself and God. I am wise if I face the truth in time, and have my books always ready; so, whenever the last call comes, I shall not be taken by surprise, but shall give account with joy.

O Lord, without Whom I am nothing and have nothing, teach me so to use my life and powers in Thy service, and so to turn to profit Thy truth and grace, that I may at last be found faithful, through Thy mercy in Christ.

No faithful life is lived in vain;
Our work shall live, although we die,
And all our powers revive again
For greater, holier work on high.

TENTH MONDAY AFTER TRINITY.

"The children of this world are in their generation wiser than the children of light."—LUKE xvi. 8.

THOSE who are of the world, at home in it, living only for it, know not their true good. Their wisdom is folly. But, as far as their hopes and aims reach, they are wise. They form plans with shrewd forethought. They grudge no toil, or care, or self-denial. They even part with hope of heaven. Those who say they live for true and lasting good, seldom show themselves as far-seeing and earnest in planning and doing. How unready they are to lay out now for the sake of good to come! How weak in will, how sparing of self, how easily daunted, how slow to grasp and use what brings success!

I believe in Christ's work, and the value of the good and hope it gives. I profess to seek things above. How does my wisdom for eternity show beside the worldly wisdom of men, whose aims reach not beyond earth and time? Am I, in providing for my future, as careful to find out the best course, and as earnest in carrying out a clear plan of life? Do I as readily let go what holds me back, and with a like force press on past difficulties? Do I make sure that I have the best helps, and use them with the same thoroughness? Do I, like the world's workers, take hard toil and self-rule for granted, as part of the cost of success? Do I set aside temptations, as the wilfully ungodly refuse to hear conscience? What a grand, sure hope mine is! How worthless, when weighed against it, is all the world can give? What ruin, if I fail! What folly, not to act wisely where my all for ever is at stake! God is ready to give wisdom, and strength, and will, that all things may help to make my place sure in the homes of the saints in light.

O Lord, Who hast called me to know Thee and receive Thy grace, send out Thy light and truth to lead me, that I may always choose and act wisely for my eternal good.

> For the world's love we live not, its hate we defy,
> And we will not be led by the throng;
> We'll be true to ourselves, to our Father on high,
> And the bright world to which we belong.

Tenth Tuesday after Trinity.

" Let him that thinketh he standeth take heed lest he fall."
—1 Cor. x. 12.

SOME think they stand who have never been lifted from their fallen state. They do not test how far they are upright before God, and firm to withstand evil and do good. Some who stand are prone to fall, and are weak through self-trust. They do not watch in lowly, careful faith, ever drawing down fresh grace, so that what comes to shake them may leave them stronger. He who will not walk cannot stand. He who only thinks he stands is sure to learn in shame how false his hope is. He who stands must fall, if he fail to take heed.

Does God know my state to be what I think it is? Do I take heed to judge from the signs of grace working in and by me? Have I risen from my fallen earthbound state, and grown strong in God, or do I only take for granted that I stand, while heart and thoughts lie low on the earth? Through false hope I may fall hopelessly. But though I stand, and have stood through long, sore trial, I yet may fall. I surely shall fall unless I take heed that my soul live and sleep not. I stand firmly if my faith is active, if I cling fast to Him Who can keep me from falling, and lead me on steadfast to the end. I fail if I forget what it cost to raise me, and what I need to hold me up. If I prize not God's gift and work, I lose their blessing. If I think to stand in my own strength, I part from the one source of strength; I am in danger of being left to fall, like St. Peter, to rise again and stand firm in watchful lowliness; or, like Judas, to rise no more. I will keep near God, that He may hold me up, sure in faith and true in life.

O Lord, in Whose strength alone I can stand upright, and keep from falling, give me faith and lowliness, so earnestly to seek Thy grace and take heed unto my ways, that I may ever grow more firm and true.

May I wish a spirit lowly, feel my weakness, own my sin ;
Leaning on Thy mercy wholly, may I labour heaven to win.
May I fear without despairing, watchful lest I fall from Thee ;
Give me courage, all things daring, in the might Thou givest
    me.

Tenth Wednesday after Trinity.

"God is faithful, Who will not suffer you to be tempted above that ye are able; but will with the temptation also make a way to escape."—1 Cor. x. 13.

ALL are tempted; none need fall. No man is forced to sin, or can plead weakness as an excuse. God's word is sure. Temptation gives a new claim on God's faithfulness. It assures of fresh grace ready, and of a way open to new triumph. It warns to grasp the grace, to find the way, and to escape. No man must dare to court temptation, or be careless when tempted, or by excusing his sin cast doubt on God's faithfulness.

God knows me, and what I am able to bear. He is my Father, and wills my good. He never forgets, or breaks His word. He rules all things. He will not let my strength be overstrained by too hard tasks. He adds grace when he adds duty. He gives more power as He asks more work. He arms afresh, when He calls to meet new foes. He never suffers evil to close all round me. He keeps a way open, and is ready to lead me safely through it. Sins do not prove that my task has been too heavy, my fight too sore, or that God has forgotten. They prove that I have failed to seek and use God's help. Temptation is sad and dangerous. I may not presume in it, or make light of it. My part is to make it a means to joy and safety. God is true; let me not be false to Him and to myself. Let me bow to the will that proves me, and put forth God's might in me, to escape from sin by the way God makes. So shall each temptation make my faith, and love, and courage stronger.

O merciful Father, Who hast promised that I shall not be tried beyond my strength or left alone, grant me in every temptation to use Thy grace to escape from sin by the way which Thy faithfulness provides.

Temptation's billows round my soul are fiercely rolling,
The Crucified gives peace, their power and rage controlling;
I fear not, while I feel His arms of love enfolding;
I sink not, while I feel His arms of might upholding.
Lord, make and keep me true, whatever storms assail me,
So shall I live unharmed, for Thou wilt never fail me.

Tenth Thursday after Trinity.

"The Lord was angry with Solomon, because his heart was turned from the Lord God of Israel."—1 Kings xi. 9.

SOLOMON was the wisest of men; yet he sank to be all that his own writings say makes a "fool." He built God's temple; yet he became an idolater. He wrote words of the loftiest devotion; yet he was false to God. He warned of the vanity of earthly good; yet the world and passing joys enslaved him. He went down from sin to sin; and we read of no awakening of his conscience in sorrow for the wrong he did to God and himself, and the ruin he prepared for Israel. He chose the way of sin, and sin dislodged God from his heart.

The rarest gifts and the grandest calling are vain, if the heart be not true. I may be skilled in all wisdom to speak of truth and to guide souls, and yet lose my own way. I may have clear signs of Divine favour, so as to seem like Solomon—the "beloved of the Lord," and yet be a castaway. I may know well what the world is, and what its joys are worth, and yet lose all for it. I may be able to kindle holy thoughts and devout feelings in others by my glowing words of devotion, and yet turn in heart from God. I may be known far and wide for great works done in God's cause; yet all may but serve to hold me up more clearly as a warning. If I let my heart be turned towards what God forbids, it will be drawn away so as to forsake Him. If I give room to evil, God will not find room in part of my nature. Shall I not use my gifts of knowledge and wisdom to teach and warn myself, lest I wander from God, and throw away my own hope? Shall I not use my gifts of grace to keep my own soul true, and to grow in holiness?

Almighty God, make me careful, lest, being lifted up by mercies and privileges, my heart be turned from Thee, and I provoke Thee in judgment to withdraw Thy grace.

    Remould my inner man in every part;
      Reknit these broken ties, resume Thy sway;
    Take, as Thy throne and altar, this poor heart;
      Oh, teach me how to love! Oh, help me to obey.

Tenth Friday after Trinity.

"Nevertheless I have somewhat against thee, because thou hast left thy first love."—Rev. ii. 4.

THE Ephesian Christians had at first strong devotion to their Lord. Love made them jealous for His truth, zealous in His cause, ready to suffer for His name. They still did and bore as much. All still seemed well to man. But Christ saw their works and knew they were not as "the first works." Love had grown cold. It was no longer a living power and motive. Their works told only of what had been. They were dead works of those out of whom life had gone, and which would soon cease, unless by repentance love could revive.

God asks my love. He comes to be in me a power of love, enabling me to love Him, and to show my love in holy life and patience for Him. That love ought to grow as God is more known. Becoming greater than my first love, it should lead to better than the first works. Can it be that I have grown cold, as if God were found less to be loved? Can it be that I have fallen, without knowing it, from even my first place? Has my religion become a matter of form, without heart, telling of lost life, and love once in my soul? Has my Judge and Saviour this "against me," that though there is no outward change, what made my works acceptable and promised perseverance is gone? Love always shows itself in works; but there may be works for a while, where love is of the past. What if even the light that shone before men has grown dim, as well as that inward flame of love which God kindled! Let me watch and judge myself, that I may repent when I have failed. Let me seek abiding union with God, and pray for more than the first love, to do better than the first works.

Almighty God, grant me so to know Thy love, that my whole life may be guided by a love to Thee, ever growing stronger, and making me more zealous for Thy glory.

> Return to me, my oft-forgotten God,
>   My spirit's true, though long forsaken rest;
> Undo these bars, re-enter Thine abode,
>   In Thee and in Thy love alone would I be blest.

Tenth Saturday after Trinity.

" I know thy works, that thou art neither cold nor hot: I would thou wert cold or hot."—Rev. iii. 15.

THERE is hope of him who has never learned God's claim or felt God's love. He may be born to give God the service of an active mind, a true heart, a warm zeal. He provokes God less than the man who prays, but with no fervour; who uses means of grace, but without faith or desire; who works, but with no heart. The lukewarm seem to say that what they give and do is enough for God. They lull themselves; they set a low aim before others.

God's truth claims that I learn, and uphold, and spread it diligently. God's work claims to be done with my might of mind, and heart, and will. God's gifts claim to be received with thankful devotion, and put to earnest use. God must be loved and trusted fervently. How can I be indifferent, if I know at all the meaning of the great truths of God, and of what God asks of me? How can I be half-hearted in taking God's side, if I feel at all what interests are at stake? How can I be content to offer God a love which is only not forgetfulness, or is at best but a languid feeling? If my heart is warmed by a living flame from heaven, I shall never think any devotion I offer enough. If my love be true, I shall always mourn and blame my failure in love. God seeks to make known His love in me, that my devotion and zeal may burn with an ever brightening glow. Let me beware lest I reject this coming near of God, and provoke God to reject me. I should help to kindle earnestness in others, for God's glory. Let me not have the sin of chilling them, and encouraging them in lukewarmness.

Almighty Father, grant me such love to Thee that I may be zealous for Thy truth and faithful to Thy cause, and may live for Thy glory and my perfection.

> I have not loved Thee as I ought,
> Nor valued all Thy love of me;
> Thy presence I have coldly sought,
> And feebly longed Thy face to see.
> Lord, give a pure and loving heart,
> To feel and own the Love Thou art.

The Tenth Sunday after Trinity.

"*There are diversities of gifts, but the same Spirit.*"
—1 Cor. xii. 4.

NO two men have like gifts. The first germ of faith in Christ, and the most rare grace or power tell of the same Spirit, Who works all in all, as He wills, for the good of all. Each part of the body has its own place and gifts. All are meant to work for the perfection of the whole, one making up what another lacks. God sees not as man sees. Who can tell what place the least known may have in the Spirit's great plan for the Church's good and God's praise? Gifts which all souls need, all souls can have. God will make a great claim on those whom He trusts with great gifts.

All I am and all I can do that is good proves the Holy Spirit's work. All light, and love, and power are mine by His will, for the growth and joy of the whole Church. It is for Him to choose how to gift and to use me. My part is to find out my place, and to fill it well, to grasp the gifts God trusts me with, and to put them forth in true, well-done work. It matters not where I am put or what I have, so long as I know that I do what God sets me, and am a means to His wise good ends. I have no cause to boast if my gifts seem to me large, nor to fret if men scorn them. They are the Spirit's powers in me, not anything of my own. They are not for selfish use, but to help God's work as a whole. I am put where I am wanted. I have what the Church has need of in me, and what best makes me fit into my place. I know not what gift is highest in God's eyes. I can spare those which men covet. I cannot spare the homely graces which God withholds from none. I gain my crown by what the Spirit wills to work in me and by means of me.

O Lord, enable me with meekness and zeal to fill my place in the body of Christ, and to use my gifts for my own soul's growth, the Church's good, and Thy glory.

All growth in wisdom, all pure love's increase,
All noble daring and endurance meek,
All battles for the truth, all sighs for peace,
The presence of the Comforter bespeak.

Eleventh Monday after Trinity.

"Well done, thou good and faithful servant: thou hast been faithful over a few things, I will make thee ruler over many things: enter thou into the joy of thy Lord."—MATT. xxv. 21.

THOSE to whom Christ gives a trust are "His own servants." The spiritual gifts they have from Him are "His goods"—the fruit of His work for them. He gives to each "according to his ability." He takes into account the natural powers He has already bestowed, now to be changed and reinforced by grace, and hallowed for holy uses. He goes away, so as to leave man's will free, till the time of reckoning. The "faithful," who have "well done" in their lowly place, are given power and blessedness, which may train them for yet higher trust and fuller joy.

I am God's, and my natural ability is all from Him. He made me, and not I myself. Christ has won for me new spiritual powers. He gives me a work to do, and leaves me, out of His own store, the means with which to do it. He seems away in a far land. He is out of sight; but faith can know Him near. He cometh one day to ask me how I have profited. He has suited my spiritual to my natural gifts. In His claims He will consider both. He knows how much I am bound to do for His kingdom in myself and in the world. He will not ask ten talents, if He gave me only two; if I have received five, He will ask other five. The time till the King appears is long enough to do well in, but there is no time to spare. Let me see to it that I take and use to the utmost all that is committed to me. My Lord will not take from me what I gain, but make it my own, and add His blessing. In His mercy He will call me "good and faithful," and my work "well done." I shall enter into His joy, and be newly gifted for a yet greater calling.

O Lord, may I so use Thy gifts and grace that my work may be well done, and that, numbered with the good and faithful, I may serve Thee in Thy joy for ever.

My faithfulness I cannot see, my goodness is unknown to me,
   And be it, Lord, unknown;
So Thou, the Giver of all grace, in that great day Thy servant
   praise
    For what Thyself hast done.

ELEVENTH TUESDAY AFTER TRINITY.

" Unto every one which hath shall be given; and from him that hath not, even that he hath shall be taken away."—LUKE xix. 26.

POWERS of mind and body grow by use. More grace comes to those who do well with their first gifts. To have talents and opportunities, so as to keep them and make the most of them, is to thank God for them, and to wait on Him for more. Those whose gifts are used for no good end, lose them. Those who are as if without grace, soon have none. Those who will not hear God, grow deaf to His call, and hard against Him. The earnest and true step into the empty place. They are newly gifted for the new work, and win the crown.

I can be said to "have" only so far as I take and keep what God gives, in a way to profit by it. That is not indeed mine which leaves me as if I had it not. God does not need me or my work. His love gives me a trust, that I may win blessing, and rise ever towards what is most good. Do I try to "have" what God gives me, with the sure, firm hold of a thinking, responsible being? Do mind, and heart, and will, and hands grasp and use them for God? If so, I do more than keep them safe. They enlarge and are added to. I am on the way to a higher place, for which God fits me. Or do I persuade myself that it is enough to think I have, or to seem to have, what only marks me as unfaithful? Am I burying grace in my earthly nature, content to say, "I do no harm," though I do no good? Am I using my will to force and hold down the talent which will bear fruit of itself if left free? What I have in vain, God will take back. I shall lose it, and the reward of its right use. Others will take my work and crown.

Almighty God, from Whom all good gifts come, make me earnest in my calling, that through Thy grace I may be found faithful, and be given greater powers for a higher place in Thy kingdom.

The hope of Thy redeeming love, oh, give me, Saviour, to retain,
To use and carefully improve one talent till the rest I gain:
On me, if still I clasp Thy feet, Thou wilt bestow the Gospel peace,
And then Thy righteousness complete, and then the crown of
    righteousness.

Eleventh Wednesday after Trinity.

"He that had received one went and digged in the earth, and hid his lord's money."—MATT. xxv. 18.

HE had but one talent, while others were given more. He thought the little he could do was not worth doing. It seemed as if in his case his Master had not sown, and had no claim to reap. He shrank from the hard work needed to make the most of his small gifts. His lowly tasks seemed to promise little honour. He gave himself to earthly toil, and wilfully and sullenly hid the God-given talent of light and grace. He pleaded fear of his Lord's hardness; but true fear would have roused to careful work. What he failed to improve was taken away. He was cast out as "wicked and slothful."

My gifts may be small, my place among men lowly. I may have to work harder than others, and yet seem to do less for God. But God knows what I have from Him, and will ask only for the fruit of that. He looks not to the worth of what is done, but to the spirit in which I do it. He is no hard, grasping Master. He gives me the work and the help which are best for me and for His cause. Though I seem last in privilege, I may be first in faithfulness. I am "wicked and slothful" if I grudge others their larger talents, and have hard thoughts of God, and in slavish fear of failure will not make the most of what is mine. Have I been slothful, hiding what I was given to use for God, "digging in the earth," toiling only for time? Have I, perhaps, wickedly turned my talents to evil uses? Let me labour no more against the grace that stirs and strengthens me for holy work. Let me act with it, and in hope and love do what I can, where I can, as well as I can. So I can trust my work and myself to God.

O Lord, save me from sloth and slavish fear, lest I be unprofitable. Grant me, with glad will, and true heart, and sure hope, to use all my gifts well for Thee.

Time was I shrank from what was right, from fear of what was wrong;
I would not brave the sacred fight, because the foe was strong;
But now I cast that finer sense and sorer shame aside:
Such dread of sin was indolence, such aim at heaven was pride.

ELEVENTH THURSDAY AFTER TRINITY.

"Godliness is profitable unto all things, having promise of the life that now is, and of that which is to come."—1 TIM. iv. 8.

TO live godly is to live guided by the will of our Maker, Who is Love. He teaches how to seek our true good and happiness here and for ever. Were there no hereafter, godliness would save from or lessen most of life's ills, and lead to or increase earth's best joys. Its promise for eternity is so great, that even could it only be had at the cost of all man clings to here, these things would be as nothing. But it has the promise of both worlds. It gives a glad foretaste now of the unknown bliss of heaven, and prepares for the enjoyment of it.

I trust myself to Him Who knows my true good, and wills it for me. Did He ask me to part with all else that brightens life, I dare not doubt His wise care, and risk losing Him. But His will forbids only what would harm me, commands what trains me for good, tries me to make me strong and pure. Where His Word and Spirit lead nothing can harm me, and I can always look to a faithful God for all I want. He promises to make my life glad with His blessing, and with all good, pure, safe joys. While I am thus led on, free from what grief and loss my own wilfulness would surely cause, I know that I am on the way to a life where godliness shall be mine in full, and its promise shall be realised beyond my largest hope. I think not of godliness only for the life to come. To have it then I must gain it here. I cannot deny God glory now, hoping for pardon at last. I cannot deny my soul the help and blessing godliness brings to each day of life. Nor can I withhold from the love of God the joy of blessing me now and always.

O God, my Creator, and Redeemer, and Sanctifier, grant me always to seek for happiness in the way of godliness, that I may have day by day a fuller foretaste of the joy of perfect godliness in the life to come.

Then we begin to live indeed, when from our sin and bondage freed
    By Christ, our Lord and Friend,
We follow Him from day to day, assured of grace through all the way,
    And glory at the end.

ELEVENTH FRIDAY AFTER TRINITY.

"God is a Spirit: and they that worship Him must worship Him in spirit and in truth."—JOHN iv. 24.

GOD is, was, and ever shall be a Spirit. He never could be pleased with any worship that was not spiritual. In the Christian Church each place may be made a Jerusalem. True worshippers draw near through Him Who is the truth of all types. The Holy Spirit guides and inspires their worship, so that all the parts of the being join to glorify God. Christ used forms, He gave some to His Church, and put life in them. Sacraments, and words used in prayer or praise, are forms. Neglect of forms does not prove truth of spirit.

He Who is the Truth makes known God, and is the way to Him. I am but a form till the Holy Spirit quickens me with the life of God. He prays in me. I need not ask where God is, for His Church is in all the world. Salvation is not "of the Jews." Men of all nations "know what they worship," and have a place where they "ought to worship," and God reveals His presence. I have not to seek God through types and figures. The sacraments and means of grace in Christ's Church are spiritual realities. The Jews of old sinned when they drew near while their heart was far from God; how much worse is my sin, if what I say and do before God be not felt and meant! God asks me to worship with mind, heart, and will. When my knee bows, He asks if my soul adores. When my voice owns sin, or speaks in praise and prayer, He looks for lowliness of spirit, heartfelt thankfulness, and true desire. When I come to His house, He asks if my soul seeks Him. When I come to means of grace, He asks me to see in faith the inward reality of which the sign tells, and to long for it.

O Lord, give me Thy Holy Spirit, that I may know, and fear, and love Thee, and may worship Thee in spirit and in truth, so as to be accepted, through Jesus Christ.

When we come, our homage bringing, all the needful gifts impart;
When our lips Thy praise are singing, Lord, do Thou lift up our heart.
May we bow with spirit lowly, when before Thy throne we kneel,
Give desires devout and holy, grant us all we say to feel.

Eleventh Saturday after Trinity.

"Let us have grace, whereby we may serve God acceptably with reverence and godly fear."— Heb. xii. 28.

WE are always before God. Life should be one long act of worship, well pleasing to Him. We are bound to use all pains to "serve God acceptably," when with His Church we bring the solemn offering of worship. Grace makes us thankful for the right to draw near. In thankfulness we ask grace to adore worthily. Knowing and feeling what we are, we act and speak as if heaven were open, and we saw God's glory.

I worship to please God. His Word, not my own will, or sloth, or fancy, or the world's ways, must guide me. If my faith makes the unseen real, it does not fail to give me godly fear. If my worship be thoughtful, I cannot be irreverent. Freedom of access does not mean the right to make free with God. I draw near to God with boldness; but I remember that I owe all my hope to the humiliation of God's Son. If I treat God as an equal, I prove that I do not love Him as my God. A heedless manner shows an untaught or dull mind, and an unbowed hard heart. My God is the same before Whom Israel feared at Sinai, and Who taught His people rules of careful reverence, lest their worship should be sin. It is still "holy ground" where I meet His specially invited Presence. I have no less need for awe than the holy ones in heaven. I pray for grace to feel what I owe to God. I am all unworthy; but I do the best I can, and give the best I have. I unite all I do and give with Christ's pleading. Faith and love rouse reverence and godly fear. Body, soul, and spirit unite to "serve God acceptably."

Almighty Father, grant that seeing by faith Thy majesty and goodness, I may have the spirit of godly fear, and may worship Thee to Thy glory and my soul's joy.

> When shall I know Thee as I ought,
> And fear, and love, and serve aright?
> Not till, past earth's temptations brought,
> I safely reach the land of light.
> Lord, daily help me more and more,
> And fit me for that sinless shore.

The Eleventh Sunday after Trinity.

"I declare unto you the Gospel."—1 COR. xv. 1.

ST. PAUL declared to the Corinthians, as the Gospel which he had received, that "Christ died for our sins," "was buried," and "rose again." These are the central facts of Christ's work. The rest lead up to, or follow from these, the "first of all." They imply that Christ came down from heaven, and went up to "where He was before" to impart the gifts He had won. By these truths of the faith the Corinthians were being saved, so long as with true hearts they held them fast.

I believe in Christ, risen from the death He died for me, to the life He lives for me. God sets before me this Gospel. In His Word and by His Church He declares the faith, and asks my faith to lay hold of it, and keep it. The facts of God's work in Christ reveal His mind towards me. They show the love of the unchanging One, and at what cost it sought me. Heedlessness or neglect is sin. Belief opens the way for the blessings of redemption. Unbelief shuts off from me the grace offered. But I cannot be saved by mere bare belief in certain facts. I must believe as one interested in their truth. I welcome the Gospel as finding it meet the questions and supply the wants of my soul. With the heart, out of which are the issues of life, I believe in order to gain righteousness. I yield myself to the changing power and influence of those realities of which the truths of the Gospel make me sure. I unite myself in will with the purpose of God in the Gospel; that I may be one with the Incarnate, may copy His life and character, may die to sin, may rise to new life, and may persevere till my salvation is wrought out, and I am glorified with Christ.

O Lord, Who hast declared to me the Gospel, bestow the gift of faith, that I may hold it fast in my strife with sin, and may be saved by Him Whom it makes known.

Oh, that we Thy truth confessing, and Thy Holy Word possessing,
    Jesu, may Thy love adore;
Unto Thee our voices raising, Thee with all Thy ransomed praising
    Ever and for evermore.

TWELFTH MONDAY AFTER TRINITY.

"*The law was our schoolmaster to bring us unto Christ.*"
—GAL. iii. 24.

THE law was outside man, saying, "This do and thou shalt live; fail to do this and thou shalt die." It gave no help to obey. It laid bare sin, but did not heal it. Sin grew more sinful as it became more a rebellion against God's will clearly made known. The law might rule the life; it could not change the heart. The Gospel showed Christ as the End to which the law led up. It offered a Saviour, to free from the sin of which the law warned, and to be in man the righteousness which the law showed his need of, but could not give.

Only God can give love for His law and power to keep it. He helped souls always, and He helps me now in a new way. While I see God's law as a mere set of rules and warnings, I am tempted to rebel. In its light the sinfulness of my sin stands out darkly. I learn how far my whole self has fallen from the state which the law of its Maker willed for it. I feel my want and weakness; I long to be saved and renewed, and have in me a will in harmony with God's, and a spirit and power of righteousness. I find this in Christ. He comes, as faith receives Him, to master sin in me, and make me of one mind with Himself in love for righteousness. I can do and be all I will, and I will to do and be all I can through Him strengthening me. I am not awed by threats, or drawn on by promises, to do what I have no heart for, or to shun what I would do if I dared. I live in the presence of the truths of Christ's work, and inspired by His indwelling. I am trained to righteousness, as He Whom I love rules my nature by His own Spirit.

O Lord Jesu Christ, make known to me the truth and meaning of the law of which Thou art the end. Write God's will upon my heart, that I may fulfil it in my life.

Clothed in our flesh and blood, Saviour, Thou didst fulfil
The holy, righteous law of God, and do His perfect will;
And we may do the same, begotten from above,
Filled with the grace that comes from Thee, inspired with
    purest love.

TWELFTH TUESDAY AFTER TRINITY.

" Leaving the principles of the doctrine of Christ, let us go on unto perfection."—HEB. vi. 1.

WITHOUT a foundation there can be no safe building. It must be well laid and kept sure. From it all rises; on it all rests. But work begun is not done. Repentance from dead works not wrought by God's life in the soul, faith towards God, means of grace, the resurrection and the judgment—these are the alphabet which babes in Christ are taught, so as to be able to read and learn full truth. First truths are forgotten if not used. A foundation loosens if nothing is built on it.

I am as plainly called to go on unto perfection as to learn the root doctrines of Christ's religion. God makes known His truth, that I may be able to "adorn the doctrine of Christ," and teach others. If I think I know enough, I know nothing yet as I ought to know. The foundation is not good if I am slow to build. Till it is firm and sure, no building can rise towards heaven. Let me once for all see to that, and so not spend life in doubt, or in laying anew what is weak and apt to be overthrown. Shame on me if I am still a babe in knowledge of the things of God, with no settled foundation on which higher doctrine can rest! I need the full use of all my best powers always, if I would be rightly educated in divine things. The treasures of wisdom and knowledge hid in Christ are not opened to the trifling idler any more than earthly knowledge is. I do not find out what there is to learn till I am in earnest and begin. My knowledge is a way to know more. Let me go on from what I have gained—reading, hearing, meditating, praying, pressing near to Christ in a life of faith, and obedience, and hope of everlasting life.

Give me grace, O Lord, to hold surely the truth I know, and to act on it earnestly, ever growing in spiritual wisdom, that I may serve Thee in a holier life.

Give me faith to see more clearly what Thou art, what love is
    Thine;
Earnestness to press more nearly to enjoy Thy love divine.
Keep me patient, keep me lowly, ever learning more of Thee;
Make me day by day more holy, till Thine unveiled face I see.

Twelfth Wednesday after Trinity.

"God, I thank Thee, that I am not as other men."
—Luke xviii. 11.

THE Pharisee was not a hypocrite; he deceived himself. He came to the temple "to pray," and he meant what he said to God. He believed he was better than others, and he thought he gave God all the praise. He knew not how pride and scorn of others spoiled all he did, and were themselves sin, shutting off grace. He prayed "with himself," listening to his prayer as a new merit. He felt no need or sin; he asked nothing; so he went down to his house unpardoned and unblessed.

If I am free from some coarse sins, yet there may be evil in my heart as grievous to God. If I seem better than the openly wicked, how unworthy I am compared with the saints, how feebly I even try to be like Christ! It is right to praise God for the work of His grace, but I must always remember how far I have come short of what that grace was meant to do in me and by me. Self-content proves spiritual blindness and want of love. It stops progress, and makes even what God has done for the soul a temptation to sin. Pride puts grace away, and denies God His due honour. I dare not scorn others, for I cannot read any hearts but my own. Does God see me what I am tempted to think others are? Am I self-deceived? Am I perhaps a sinner like the Publican, and yet as blind to my true state as the Pharisee? Rather let me be as careful in outward life as the Pharisee, and as lowly before God as the Publican. While in the body I shall be a sinner needing mercy. The more I am enabled to love God, the more I shall feel my remaining sin, and long to be pure.

O Lord, the source of all my good, save me from blind self-trust, and scorn of others; make and keep me lowly, that I may be exalted in Thine own time and way.

> May I in self-distrust beware,
>   Nor think above what God hath done,
> Nor boastfully my state declare;
>   But magnify Thy grace alone,
> And thus my faith's true measure prove
> By soberness of lowly love.

TWELFTH THURSDAY AFTER TRINITY.

"The publican, standing afar off, would not lift up so much as his eyes unto heaven, but smote upon his breast, saying, God be merciful to me a sinner."—LUKE xviii. 13.

HE felt far off in his sin, and unfit to draw near with other worshippers to God's presence. He bowed his head, ashamed to look up. He stood smiting his breast, condemning his own fault. He sought no comfort in the sins of others. He was before God to answer for himself. He said nothing to hide or excuse his guilt. He urged no claim for favour. He felt himself "the sinner" above all men, whose one hope was in mercy. God pardoned him, and set him free to go and sin no more.

I may use the Publican's prayer, and yet be in heart a Pharisee. I may be proud of my penitence, and vaunt my humility. I may be tempted to judge, as boastful Pharisees, some in whom God sees the lowliness of the Publican. God knows me a sinner. It is well that I should know it, and own it, and lay all the blame upon myself. While I am on earth I shall need mercy. As my heart grows more true, and my conscience more wise, as I draw nearer to God and love His law, I shall feel deeper shame for what makes me still a sinner. My sense of sin must not keep me away in shrinking dread; my only hope is in the mercy I sin against. I dare not in God's presence turn my eyes on others' faults, or plead excuses for my own. I can only think of the ways in which I fall short and try the Divine patience. The more I know of mercy, the more I shall seek that its full work be done for me and in me. If I come before God in the Publican's spirit, I may know that I return to my place in the world justified—at peace with God, and newly strengthened against sin.

O merciful God, teach me to feel how sinful I am in Thy holy eyes, and grant me so to humble myself, that I may be justified through Thy mercy in Jesus Christ.

> All my past misdoing, teach me to confess,
> When for mercy suing give me lowliness;
> See me humbly kneeling, Thou canst make me whole,
> Bring Thy strength and healing to my weary soul.

Twelfth Friday after Trinity.

"*By the grace of God I am what I am.*"—1 Cor. xv. 10.

ST. PAUL had felt bound to do all against Christ. He became foremost in His cause. He might have been tempted to boast, but he saw God's work in all he was and did. Grace, the working love of God, won him to the truth. Grace taught and strengthened him, guided his will, and used his powers. He felt thankful, not boastful. Sure of Divine help, he went boldly where God sent him. He laboured diligently, careful lest through his failure God's work might be hindered or marred. For all good in him, or done by him, he praised God; for all evil he blamed himself.

Grace does not destroy my free will; it helps it to choose and follow right. Grace purifies and strengthens my natural powers, and gives powers above nature. What in me is good, and all that I do well, are the work of grace. My sins and failures are in spite of grace. To grace I owe my calling into God's family, and my power to grow in holiness and seek the things above. I have nothing which I have not received. I must not boast, as if I had made myself what I am, or worked by myself what I am the means of doing rightly. It is great ground for joy, and thankfulness, and hope, that God's love works in and with me, using me for its holy ends. I may find encouragement and comfort in each least sign that I am thus in the Almighty's hands. But my responsibility is great also. If the grace of God is thus with me, I am bound to work with the grace of God, and put forth the power I have in all the ways God's will makes known. By that grace I am bound to grow to be stronger and holier than I am, till I am perfect and my work is finished, according to God's will.

Almighty God, to Whom I owe all power for good; grant that I may so use Thy gifts, that Thou mayest be glorified in me, and in the work for which Thy grace enables me.

> Not mine the merit when I stand,
> Mine the dishonour when I fall;
> And if I reach the Holy Land,
> Thine is the glory of it all.

TWELFTH SATURDAY AFTER TRINITY.

"He that cometh to God must believe that He is, and that He is a rewarder of them that diligently seek Him."—HEB. xi. 6.

GOD is, whether believed in or not, whether thought of or forgotten. Almighty and All-Knowing, He judges now: He rewards now, as an earnest of what every man shall have in full from Him at last. Faith makes the unseen God real to the soul, and makes sure the good which the soul hopes for in seeking God. Worship may be words, thoughts, feelings, but not meant to rise anywhere, or offered as to One Who waits to hear. Much seeking of God is vain, because work is done and sacraments are used with no real trust in God's promises.

I profess to come to God and seek Him. Do I, as a fact, believe that "God is," and try to grasp what the fact means to me? Is God in any way as real to me as if I saw Him look at me, and heard Him speak? Do I live before Him, as watchful of the thoughts He sees me think, as I am of the words men hear me say? Do I speak to God with the care to know and say what I mean, that guides my words to fellow-sinners? Do I show faith that God is worth seeking and can be found? Do I seek Him in the ways He tells me of, and as One Who hides Himself from the heedless, but rewards the earnest by making Himself known? My whole life ought to be a drawing nigher to a God seen by faith always, and a seeking One Whose promises are felt to give a real aim to hope. If I press towards God, and reach after the hope He gives, He will make my faith more clear-eyed and true, He will be Himself my great reward. In Him I shall have all things assured to me even now. All things shall be mine indeed when coming and seeking are over, and I have come and found.

O God, give me faith to come to Thee, believing that Thou art my God, and that Thou art found by souls that seek Thee a never-failing and sure rewarder.

> Frail children of dust, and feeble as frail,
> In Thee do we trust, nor find Thee to fail;
> Thy mercies how tender! how firm to the end!
> Our Maker, Defender, Redeemer, and Friend.

The Twelfth Sunday after Trinity.

"*And, looking up to heaven, He sighed, and saith unto him, Ephphatha, that is, Be opened.*"—MARK vii. 34.

DID Christ sigh in prayer, or in breathing forth His power? Or did He sigh, knowing the sin and sorrow caused by open ears and ready tongues? Did He, while pitying the deaf and dumb, feel how the gifts of speech and hearing would place the man in new danger, and open new ways of sin? Men turn to their hurt what God means for good. They hear and speak the false and evil rather than the true and pure. They use to wrong God and man what they owe to God's goodness. So love withholds blessings, or gives them in sorrow, if not in judgment.

I do not know how much my sorrows save me from. A careful God may show most love when He seems hardest on me. Sickness or want may put me into shelter till some storm of temptation passes; health or wealth may bring me out to loss or shipwreck. Perhaps what I most long for my Father could only give me with a sigh. What powers I have are from Him, and to be used for Him. In each I have a way to praise Him, to do good, and to gain blessing. In each there is a risk lest I grieve Him by new sin. It is well at times to go apart alone with Christ, and in sight of heaven let Him lay His hand on me, marking each power as His gift. So shall I be warned to watch myself, and shall know that He feels for me in my trial as a helper always near. Speech and hearing open my soul to give and receive good or evil. Better be deaf, than let my ears be doors where sin finds welcome. Better be dumb, than let my tongue be lit from hell, and my mouth be open for what shames and defiles me to go forth.

Forgive me, O Lord, for past misuse of Thy gifts, and grant me grace to use them all hereafter for my own and my neighbour's good and for Thy glory.

> Lord, Thou hast sworn that every ear,
> Willing or loth, Thy trump shall hear,
> And every tongue unchainèd be
> To own no hope, no God, but Thee.

Thirteenth Monday after Trinity.

"Be thou faithful unto death, and I will give thee a crown of life."—Rev. ii. 10.

SO speaks the First and the Last, Who was obedient unto death, and liveth for evermore. He is the life of those who are one with Him, and are led by God's will. They have nothing to fear, if they trust themselves to the faithful God. They need not halt or swerve from the way of duty, though death confront them. When they die they are freed from what dies, they overcome death, the second death cannot hurt or threaten them. Christ gives them at once a crown of endless life, and at His appearing will give them a crown of glory.

I am pledged and called to be Christ's soldier and servant. He strengthens, arms, leads me. I need only fear my own unfaithfulness. Cowardice or sloth is ruin. To weary is to make past toil vain. To save life or the ease of it by being untrue is to fall back from union with Christ, and throw away the power and the triumphs already won. God fails not those that take Him at His word. His grace is sure. His promises are always kept. Counting on His help, I can be brave and strong to go where He calls, to do what His will lays on me, and to bear what His will sends. Each least trial is meant to strengthen the Life of my Saviour in me. Let me be always faithful to that Life, and to my own good. So shall I be always more than conqueror, and shall be unharmed by man's last foe. Death cannot part me from the Everlasting. I shall live on, though I die. I shall pass through death out of reach of death and all that leads to death. Christ will crown me with life, and keep me safely till the resurrection of the just, when I shall share His glory.

O Lord Jesus Christ, keep me faithful all my days and in all trial, even unto death, that having obeyed Thy will in all things, I may receive the crown of life.

> Though the warfare be weary, the trial be sore,
> In the might of our God we will stand.
> Oh! what joy to be crowned and be pure evermore
> In the peace of our own fatherland!

THIRTEENTH TUESDAY AFTER TRINITY.

"Whosoever shall keep the whole law, and yet offend in one point, he is guilty of all."—JAMES ii. 10.

AS God is one, His law is one. To keep it is to obey Him Whose will it makes known. Man is not free to obey what he likes, and set aside what seems hard or trifling. If God speaks, man must give careful heed to His least word. The spirit of true obedience is best shown in doing what costs most yielding of the will, and what only faith can see the meaning of. He who wilfully breaks what he knows is part of God's law, denies God's authority, and makes his own will his lord.

God asks for whole-hearted obedience. He asks me to learn His will and do it, trusting Him, and glad to be told how to please Him. It is not for me to ask why any rule is laid down, or to judge about the use and end of it. Enough if I am sure that it is part of God's law, given to guide me. The question is, not whether I can safely pass by any commandment, but whether I dare defy God, Who gives it. He has His own reasons for each law, and for hiding His reasons. What I think least, He may know to be greatest. Obedience in nine points does not make me free to break one. I am not to judge God's law, but in faith and love to bow my will to His will, because it is His will. If I only obey what I choose, I may well doubt how far my obedience is more than wilfulness. So it is with the means of grace which help obedience. I know not which God knows to be most needful for me. The one I am tempted to neglect may be that which I can least spare. All I do is vain while I keep back part of God's claim, as if saying, "In this one thing my will shall be done, not Thine."

Almighty God, teach me to know and love Thy law, and with a glad will seek and use Thy grace, that I may obey Thee in all things.

> Either resolve for all or else for none;
>   Obedience universal God doth claim.
> Either be wholly his, or all thine own;
>   At what thou canst not reach, at least take aim:
> He that of purpose looks beside the mark,
> Might as well hoodwinked shoot, or in the dark.

Thirteenth Wednesday after Trinity.

"Without Me ye can do nothing."—John xv. 5.

A LIMB has no life of its own, apart from the body. A branch lives only while life flows into it from the root. So man has spiritual life and powers, not of his own, but from God, through his membership in Christ. As that union which God has given is kept healthy and vigorous, as life is drawn ever freshly from the source, fruit of holiness will be borne to God's glory. Branches "in" Christ may be unfruitful, and be "taken away," and "cast out." Those who take no care to abide in Christ, lose what they have received, and wither.

Out of Christ what am I, what have I, what can I do? If I am in Him, He is in me; I have all things, and God's power works God's will through me. Christ gave me freely this oneness with Him, by the grace of the Holy Spirit. He shows me how to keep open and full the flow into me of the Divine life. I hold fast to Him in those means through which He meets my faith, and prayer, and the longings of my love. Keeping His commandments, I abide in His love, drawing into me that power of His which alone enables me to obey. I seek with special devotion that way of close communion by which He tells me that He dwells in me, and I in Him. I watch, and pray, and strive to put from me all sin that stops or checks the incoming and the activity of grace. I do all to stir up and yield to the power of God in me. New and nearer union shall be mine, as my life becomes more truly a showing forth of Him. As I grow more fruitful, He will train me to use fresh and larger gifts. The heavenly Husbandman will fit me for greater fruitfulness. I shall long to be more one with Christ, and to bring Him more perfect praise.

O Lord, apart from Whom my soul's life withers, grant me to abide in Thee, and to seek more of the power of Thy indwelling, that I may bear much fruit for Thy glory.

> Cling to the Bleeding One, cling to His side;
> Cling to the Risen One, in Him abide;
> Cling to the Coming One, hope shall arise;
> Cling to the Reigning One, joy lights thine eyes.

THIRTEENTH THURSDAY AFTER TRINITY.
"He is the head of the body, the Church."—COL. i. 18.

THE Son of God in His glorified Manhood is "head over all things to the Church." He is Head of the Church. He rules all for her good; He is one with her. On union with Him, through the One Spirit, her life depends. His thought and will guide and guard her. From Him come the grace and power that make her what she is. As in the natural body, the members live and move by the energy which comes from the head through the nerves, so each living member of Christ's body does his own work in obedience to Christ.

The life of the Head and of the Body are the same. The Holy Spirit, which is in Christ's Manhood, is from Him in all His true members. He cares for His body as for Himself. I am sure that the Church is safe. As the body is not without the Head, so is the Head not without the body. What God loves and cherishes, and fills with His own fulness, and uses to manifest Himself, cannot perish or fail. But, I prove with care my own part in the Church's life, and work, and blessing. She can live without me; out of her I die. Does unbelief, or sloth, or sin shut off from me the life of God in her? Am I like a withered or palsied limb, fastened indeed to the body, but out of sympathy with it; not feeling what the other members suffer, or caring for them; not conscious of the ruling of the Head, or answering to His will? Or do I hold fast to the Head, and keep fresh and full the flow of life that can nourish, and strengthen, and quicken me to do my part well? Do I obey the will that controls each member, seeking to grow into more perfect oneness with the mind of Christ?

O Lord Jesu Christ, by Whose life Thy Church lives, and Who, as the Head dost guide and rule Thy members, grant me always, in faith and love, to have living union with Thee, and to put forth Thy power to Thy praise.

> Of Thy Church the mystic Head,
> Life, through all Thy members spread,
> Living bond of quick and dead,
> Hear us, Holy Jesu.

THIRTEENTH FRIDAY AFTER TRINITY.
"My grace is sufficient for thee."—2 COR. xii. 9.

ST. PAUL besought the Lord thrice that his infirmity might leave him. The prayer was heard, so as to give him more good than he had asked. The thorn remained in his flesh, but he was so helped and changed in spirit, that sorrow was not the same to him. God's strength took the place of man's. Taught his own weakness, St. Paul found what grace could do. He gladly bore the trial for the sake of the new power of Christ that came with it, which gave him more peace and better joy than the trial took away.

I am right to bring before God all griefs from which body and spirit shrink. God does not always see fit to give me what I ask; but no true prayer of lowly faith is vain. God always hears, and gives what He knows best. If my trial is the same still, I am not; for God's grace changes me. His love rests on me and adds power to bear gladly what makes that love so felt. The more I know my own weakness, the more I learn how strong I am in Christ. Grace comes as I need and seek it. When the world is dark, light from heaven gives most cheer. When I am in pain, I learn to prize the comfort that calms and heals the spirit. When friends leave me, the Lord draws near, and proves Himself a friend that never fails or changes. When I am shamed by falls, and can scarce hope on, His grace can pardon the past and nerve me to go forward. His grace can make my lot on earth be, even in all its saddest parts, full of blessing, and a means of growing towards perfection. I can do and bear all things in the power of Christ. He bends all to my good, and often takes from me what I vainly trust in, that I may find my true strength in Him.

O Lord Jesu Christ, teach me to fly to Thee in all my griefs, that Thy love may relieve me, or may enable me to feel Thy power made perfect in my weakness.

> I could not do without Thee, I cannot stand alone,
> I have no strength or goodness, no wisdom of my own;
> But Thou, beloved Saviour, art all in all to me,
> And weakness will be power if I abide in Thee.

THIRTEENTH SATURDAY AFTER TRINITY.

"Be ready always to give an answer to every man that asketh you a reason of the hope that is in you with meekness and fear."—1 PET. iii. 15.

HE who desires to have a Christian hope should know what it is, and how he has it. Unthinking trust that God is good, and that all shall somehow be well, can give him no true lasting rest. He should be able to say what good he wishes for, and what reason he has to expect it. He should know how to answer his own heart's questions, and the cavils of unbelievers, for his own peace, for the instruction of others, and for God's glory. A good hope grows strong by proving. He who has it will show a meek and loving spirit, honouring man and reverencing God.

My hope is vain, if it will not bear testing. It will be tried one day; let me be glad if I am forced to put it to the proof now. Have I indeed any hope, rightly called so? Can I say what truths I believe, and on what ground I hold them true? Do I try to know Him in Whom I profess trust, and to have proof that I am going, with His help, in the way of His will, towards the good His mercy sets before me? If I am wise, I will often ask myself the reason of my hope, that it may be made sure, and be a growing consolation. I have a duty beyond myself. I am bound not only to be humbly sure that my hope is real, but to be able and willing to show others what it is, and on what truths it rests, and to lead them to desire the same. I dare not court controversy, lest I vaunt self, wrong the truth, harm souls, sin in spirit or word. But with lowly reverence I must make and keep myself ready to speak in calm, sure words my faith and my hope. If I am sure, I can be calm.

Almighty God, enable me in a life of faith and obedience to make surely mine the hope set before me in the Gospel, and in meekness and fear to be always ready to prove my hope well grounded.

Lord, on our hearts may lively faith celestial comfort pour,
With patience, lightener of our ills, and hope that looks before;
That we with Thy united Church may lift our souls above,
And with one mind and mouth proclaim Thy glory, God of love.

The Thirteenth Sunday after Trinity.

"*Go and wash in Jordan seven times, and thy flesh shall come again to thee, and thou shalt be clean.*"—2 KINGS v. 10.

NAAMAN prayed for health, but wished to be healed in his own way, with no trouble to himself, or bowing down of pride. He thought Elisha would come to him, and call on God, and cleanse him with a touch. He went away in a rage, when told to do something in which he saw no promise. Why bathe? Why in Jordan? Why seven times? There was no power in the means, but God chose to work by them, proving and calling out Naaman's faith and obedience.

I am unclean through the leprosy of sin, and am beyond all help but God's. He alone can make me clean. He does not ask me to do some great thing, which might tempt me to boast. He hides His ways of working with means. My part is to do what He commands, sure that He will keep His promise. Do I perhaps wait, far away from God, till my soul's sickness is very sore, and then look for God's messenger to come and call down healing on me by a few words of prayer? Do I despise appointed streams of blessing, and choose others which please my taste better, and seem to me as good? Do I turn from commandments which test obedience, and from means of grace which make a claim on faith? Do I, for instance, ask doubtingly why water in baptism should avail more than other water, and why bread and wine, blessed as Christ ordains, should bring my soul gifts more than common food? Do I treat God's rules lightly, as Naaman would, had he bathed but once, or six times? The soul's healing is God's free gift. He has the right and power to bestow it on His own terms. I have no right to question the ways of Him Who doeth all things well.

Almighty God, give me grace, and with lowly faith and full obedience to seek for Thy healing, cleansing gifts in Thine appointed way.

> The grace and might are His alone,
> God sends His gifts in hidden ways;
> Be ours the faith His love to own,
> Be ours the heart to tell His praise.

FOURTEENTH MONDAY AFTER TRINITY.

"But He said, Yea rather, blessed are they that hear the word of God, and keep it."—LUKE xi. 28.

SHE was blessed as no other was, from whom the Lord took flesh, and by whom His infant life was nourished. But this, in which she was alone, was not her chief blessedness. Rather was it that Christ was formed in her spirit, that He fed her with His truth, and strengthened her by His grace. She gave heed to His words, and treasured them in her heart. She did the will of God, and she rejoiced in God her Saviour.

Only one could be the mother of the Christ. Only one could feel that from her body His was formed and sustained. But I may share with blessed Mary that which Christ judged to be her highest glory. I need not long for the privileged nearness of those who were, according to the flesh, the kindred of the Lord. What He declares best is within my reach. I am joined to Him in bonds of holier relationship. I am a member of Christ, "of His flesh, and of His bones." My spiritual life is from Him. I am a child of His Father. The mother of Christ was blessed most because of her lowly, loving holiness. My privileges make me blessed only so far as I am faithful. Let me with care listen for the words of God, and lay them up in my heart. Let me seek the grace of Him Who is the Word of God, that I may show fruit in holy character and life. So shall Christ own me as partaker of the Divine life that is in Him. I shall know of His presence with me always, and enjoy His care and love. He will welcome me as one blessed of His Father when He comes in glory.

O Lord Jesus Christ, Who wast born of a human mother that I might be a son of God, grant that in hearing and keeping the Word of God I may be blessed.

> Blessed is the womb that bare Him—blessed
> The bosom where His lips were pressed;
>   But rather blessed are they
> Who hear His Word, and keep it well,
> The living homes where Christ shall dwell,
>   And never pass away.

Fourteenth Tuesday after Trinity.

"Thou shalt love the Lord thy God with all thy heart, and with all thy soul, and with all thy strength, and with all thy mind."—LUKE x. 27.

IT is the first; for where love is refused, obedience has no life or worth with God. It is the great commandment, for it has in it all the rest. He who keeps this fulfils all duty gladly. God proves His love by asking us to love Him. Our great glory is that we can love Him Who made and redeemed us, and dwells in us. God claims to take the first place, with no rival, in our heart's affection. He bids us find in Him rest for the soul's cravings, the noblest and most attractive object of thought, the inspirer of zeal to put forth strength in will and work.

It is high honour that God loves me. What glory, that He asks me to love Him, that He should seem to care how one like me feels towards Him! But will love come because I am told to have it? The law is a promise; it tells me of God's love, and of what grace He will give me. He makes Himself known by His Word, and will do so more and more by His Spirit, if I am willing. I was made for God, and in Him alone all my being can find its rest. As God is one, so must my obedience be one in the undivided devotion of my inward self and my outward life. He can draw my heart, so that I love all else in Him. He can make my will glad to rule all the powers of my being, so as to please Him. He can make all that interests my mind tell of His love, and help me to adore. He can make my life's great joy the putting forth of energy in His service. Oh, for more power to keep this law! When I love God, all other laws are but guides how to please Him Whose will it is my happiness to do.

Almighty Father, Whose name is Love, Who dost love me, and deign to ask my love, enable me so to love Thee that in all I am and do I may obey Thy holy will.

> Lord, show me more the love Thou art,
> Bestow the gift of love on me,
> That I may love with mind and heart,
> And soul and strength, all vowed to Thee.

Fourteenth Wednesday after Trinity.

"Thou shalt love thy neighbour as thyself."—MATT. xxii. 39.

WE are given into our own care, and into one another's care. Selfishness is not true self-love. We ought to love ourselves as God's creatures who have His grace and are made for His glory. So we ought to love our neighbour. God Whom we have not seen asks us to show our love to Him in love to our brother whom we see. We are bound to have a care for our neighbour's goodness, and good name, and well-being, like that we have for our own. This love must be in deed and in truth, earnest, steady, active, prayerful. It is the due of the unthankful and unholy as well as the good. Christ is the example and the power.

God gives my neighbour rights. I owe him a debt, to do him all good, as well as not to do him any wrong. I see in him one who, like myself, is God's care. If I love God, and God's love lives in me, I will be one with God in caring for him. The good I ask for myself I will pray God to bestow on him also. I love him for God's sake, not because he seems to me worthy. God is kind to me in spite of what I am. My neighbour's sin must not shut off my good-will. If he does wrong, I must still do right. I must still love him as my neighbour, though he tries my love in new ways. The Samaritan in the parable acted as a neighbour to the wounded Jew, foe though he was in race and in religion. Christ bids me go and do likewise, and thus be like my Father in heaven. If I am His child with His nature in me, I shall not only love those who love me, but ask how I can best be the means of bringing the blessing of God's love to all.

O God, Who art kind to the evil and the good, may Thy love dwell in me, that I may always seek my neighbour's good as I seek my own, to Thy glory; through Jesus Christ, Who loved me and gave Himself for me.

> Be ours to choose the path of lowly love
> And patient work our meek Redeemer trod:
> Are we provoked? it all is known above,
> And we may bear what is endured by God.

Fourteenth Thursday after Trinity.

" I exhort therefore, that, first of all, supplications, prayers, intercessions, and giving of thanks, be made for all men."—
1 Tim. ii. 1.

GOD will have all men to be saved from evil and to gain all good. To pray and give thanks for others is to unite with God in caring for man. Thus charity is exercised, and is made strong and ready to work in all ways. He who before God makes himself one with his neighbour will show the same spirit in his whole life. He who, in love to God, prays for men, will try, for God's sake, to show God's loving-kindness.

God calls me to a share in His love's work and triumph. In prayer and praise sympathy with my neighbour is hallowed as part of my religious training. I draw near with what is on my heart, I have it along with God, and catch His feeling of it. I learn how best to show love to God in work for those whose good is His joy. I gain the spirit of Him in Whose name I pray. Selfishness and envy are shamed away as I plead for my brethren with our Father, and thank God for their success as for my own. I cannot but forgive one whom I ask God to pardon through Him Who died for us both. I cannot withhold my love where I ask God to show His. I must pray for each, as God wills the good of all. I must praise when man is blessed, and God is glorified. The farthest from good need my sympathy most. If my love has no other means, prayer can lay hold on the help of the Almighty. If the happy care not for my sympathy, I can have it with God. I best bring the needs and joys of others before God when with the Church I "show the Lord's death," and offer thanks for the fruits of it.

O Lord, Who willest the good of all, give me of Thy love and unite my will with Thine, that I may pray for Thy triumph over evil, and praise Thy goodness when my neighbour is blessed.

> For all we love, the poor, the sad,
> The sinful, unto Thee we call;
> O let Thy mercy make us glad;
> Thou art our Jesus, and our all.

Fourteenth Friday after Trinity.

"It is more blessed to give than to receive."—ACTS xx. 35.

THE world gives in order to get as much or more in return. Christ teaches to receive in order to have wherewith to give. God is pure love. As men grow like God, they manifest more the love that delights to give freely. The selfish seek a lonely joy in their own gain. The generous have a part in others' happiness, and by sharing the good they have, make it a larger source of blessing to themselves. It is nobler to help than to be helped. God calls the givers, not the receivers, happy, and His children.

I am a true child of God, so far as I love generously and live to do good. God loves me, that I may have His love in me, and show it forth. All good things are from Him, and for Him I am bound to use them. I gain a new blessing when I impart of God's gifts. I am in the true safe way to happiness when God's love has won me to devote myself and all I have to Him for His own sake. I can have a divine joy in freely giving, as God does, where no return comes, and even the giver is unknown. The pleasure of helping the needy is nobler than that of gaining or keeping to spend on self. It is better to bring comfort than to be comforted, to uphold the weak than to be upheld. I am blessed if God's light shine on me; I do well indeed to be happy, if it shine from me to make the world around me good and glad. I can be blessed if I will. I can give some money, much kindness in word or deed in many ways. I can give prayers, and thus call down gifts waiting in God's hands for those in whose behalf He bids me pray. I may receive from God, and be unblessed; I am surely blessed when I give for God.

Almighty Father, from Whom all good things come, give me Thy love, that I may be always glad to do good, and to give freely to others of what I freely receive from Thee.

> We lose what on ourselves we spend,
> We have as treasure without end,
> Whatever, Lord, to Thee we lend,
> Who givest all.

Fourteenth Saturday after Trinity.

"If there be first a willing mind, it is accepted according to that a man hath, and not according to that he hath not."—2 Cor. viii. 12.

GOD does not ask how much men give or do, but with how much good-will. He loves the cheerful giver who finds joy in taking from self for God's service. Large gifts from a grudging heart, great works done "of necessity," are promised no blessing. Offerings made to gain man's praise bring only that reward. The widow's mites given simply, from a loving heart, have more worth in God's eyes than the rich gifts of those who stop where self-denial begins. The poor widow need not be discouraged because her means are small. The wealthy must not think to put God off with two mites.

God Who loves me asks my love. All I have is from Him : He invites me to show my love by giving to Him out of His gifts. The best is but like the presents a little child gives its father. Whether I have much or little, I can win the full blessing. I can give plenteously of my abundance, or give gladly of my small store. God looks to my willing mind. He marks the diligence I use that I may do my best. He counts the cost of my sacrifice. God is not mocked, as men are, by what seems much, but may be nothing to me. Nor does God despise me when I feel as if I had nothing worthy to lay at His feet. If my work is easily done, and my alms leave my comforts untouched, I need to ask how I would act were this changed, and how far I am giving according to that I have. If I can ill spare even a little, if my powers are small, and want of education or influence make work for God hard and humbling, God knows all, and values the effort of my willing mind. Enough if He says of me, "He hath done what he could."

Almighty Father, Who givest what is best for me, and trustest me with what I can best use for Thy glory ; fill me with love and zeal, that I may so offer my much or little as to be accepted in Thy mercy.

If with honest-hearted love for God and man,
Day by day Thou find us doing what we can,
Thou Who giv'st the seed-time wilt give large increase,
Crown the head with blessings, fill the heart with peace.

The Fourteenth Sunday after Trinity.

" Were there not ten cleansed? but where are the nine?"
—LUKE xvii. 17.

THE ten had faith to go at Christ's word and to receive cleansing as they went. Only one had faith to come back to Christ to thank God, and to gain the further spiritual blessing, so as to be made whole. Christ saw the hearts of the nine go away. They were eager only to press back again into the world. They sought nothing more from Him. So men are loud in asking, but silent when they have gained. They take and use gifts, without coming for God's best and perfect blessing.

My praise for mercy granted should be as earnest and open as my prayer for mercy needed. I cry to God when none but He can help; I must not act as if His boons were sought to enable me to go from Him. Each gift recalls me to the feet of the Giver, that I may own it, and may gain grace to use it well. I have been often saved from harm, and blessed with many a good in the things of this life. These mercies are meant to bring me close to God, that while I thank Him I may receive higher gifts. Christ brought healing to mankind when He was made man, that He might live, and die, and rise for man. I was cleansed in baptism. Christ has had restoring mercy ready when, through my own fault, I have again and again become unclean. Is it my manner to take God's grace for granted, and to go away after each gift, as if I needed nothing more? In all my life I should tell my Saviour's praise, ever coming to His feet in lowly, thankful trust; waiting for Him to bid me arise and go my way under His guidance; laying hold in faith upon that grace that can make and keep me whole.

O Lord, from Whom all good comes, grant me, with each mercy, grace to thank Thee in heart, and word, and life, that so I may ever wait on Thee for new blessings, and become what Thou wouldst have me be.

O may our Saviour stay through all our lifetime near us,
With ever joyful hearts and heavenly peace to cheer us:
And keep us in His grace, and guide us when perplexed,
And free us from all ills in this world and the next.

FIFTEENTH MONDAY AFTER TRINITY.

"They that are Christ's have crucified the flesh with the affections and lusts."—GAL. v. 24.

THOSE who were baptized into Christ were united to Him in His death. They were crucified with Christ, that the body of sin might be destroyed. The old evil nature was not then slain and cast out. It was fastened to the cross with all its clinging to sin and longing after sin. Christians gained grace which they undertook to use in holding the strong evil on the cross in spite of its struggles, till it died. Crucifixion is painful and lingering. Earnest souls find it hard to persevere unto the end. The sure hope of glory upholds them.

I have nailed my evil nature to the cross, and vowed to keep it there. Its blind, unruled passions and desires are strong. It will break free if it can, and overpower the new life of the spirit. Slowly and painfully it must die. Only by watchful firmness can it be held down and forced to yield. I need not wonder, or lose heart, or weary, because to be true costs much, and evil, after all my efforts, still seems ready to rise up strongly. I have undertaken a crucifixion; I cannot hope that the cross will kill without pain, and at once. I am warned what it is to be Christ's; I am cheered by the sure promise of grace and triumph. He Who bore His cross for me is my strength. I dare not take down the evil nature from the cross; that would be to crucify Christ in its stead, and make His sorrows in vain. I may take courage from the hardness of the struggle, if only I am steadfast. The pain proves that Christ in me is active, and that the death of evil is being hastened. I will not flinch till I leave my evil nature lifeless on the cross, and rise to the full freedom of God's children.

Be with me, O Lord Jesus, and be my strength to hold my evil nature on the cross till I have wholly died to sin, and, one with Thee, am free to live the risen life.

Lord, may Thy agony, Thy tears, Thy pain,
Thy stripes, Thy shame, Thy wounds, Thy death transfuse
Their hidden virtue that the soul renews,
Till all my sins with Thee be crucified and slain.

FIFTEENTH TUESDAY AFTER TRINITY.

"*The flesh lusteth against the Spirit, and the Spirit against the flesh: and these are contrary the one to the other; so that ye cannot do the things that ye would.*"—GAL. V. 17.

TWO natures strive in man for mastery. The old fallen nature goes wilfully or blindly after evil. The new nature has holy aims. The strong man armed is not yet dislodged. "His goods are *not* in" peace. "All his armour" is not yet taken from him. Those in whom God's Spirit is most perfectly a law and power of life still strive against proneness to sin and slowness to good. The restraints of the better self forbid to live after the flesh freely. Each struggle brings the flesh or the spirit nearer to its triumph.

I am drawn upwards, and dragged down. I aim at what is high and holy. I find in me what clings to low delights and follows sin. I fail to do the good I wish; for evil is strong in me, and I am weakened and weighted by old habits. I cannot obey fully or freely my ungodly desires; for the Christ in me shrinks, and the Holy Spirit pleads and warns. I must make up my mind to this strife while I am in the body. Only let me make sure which gains ground. Well for me if the power of evil in me is felt, from the spirit pressing strongly against it and forcing it down. Well for me if sin is hard to do, and my failures shame me. Well for me if in spite of wars within and temptings from without, I am true to the aim God sets before me. If I am on the side of good, God is on my side, and I shall gain the peace of holiness. I fear the state of those who can do all evil, out of whom all good has gone, who have no will to be holy. I seek to be of those who in God's might have fought their way to freedom, and who will and do good perfectly.

Make strong in me, O Lord, the new man, that my flesh may be subdued to the Spirit till I am all pure, and only will and do what pleases Thee.

Lord, our spirit clings to Thee, will not, dare not, let Thee go,
Till Thy power have set us free from the bonds that cause our woe;
By Thy dying we were bought, ransomed from the world and sin;
By the work that Thou hast wrought, Jesu, make us pure within.

FIFTEENTH WEDNESDAY AFTER TRINITY.

"Strait is the gate, and narrow is the way, which leadeth unto life."—MATT. vii. 14.

ALL go by one of two roads towards one of two ends. He who lets himself be borne along with the crowd, or by his wilful unsteady desires, keeps the broad path. No care is needed to find and follow that. It leads to the wide gate which shuts off from God. The way of life is fenced in by God's law, and marked by the steps of Christ. Only careful seekers find it, and get out of the broad way into it. All but the lowly and watchful stray and lose it. None reach the gate of life where Christ waits with welcome, but by this way.

I am on the way to "life" or "destruction." The gate of one or the other shall soon shut behind me. Whither does each step bring me on? What road do I travel? If I am one of the careless crowd, guided by no clear rule, all is wrong. I cannot be right while I leave myself thus to drift or be driven any how. The door that opens into "life" is not gained without care and effort. The way to life is hard to find and to follow. Many a smooth, pleasant by-path that seems to lead to the same place tempts me to stray. Many an easy downward slope tempts me to turn from the steep climb up. Often the way is lonely, and many a voice bids me join the thoughtless throng of wanderers and loiterers. But the rough and narrow path of faith and obedience where God's will guides is the only safe one. Christ is with me to hold me by the hand and cheer me on. The narrow way is broad enough for me, if I walk warily and firmly in my Saviour's steps. The gate is wide enough to let me in. He who has gone before me in the way will open the gate, that I may pass to life with Him.

O Lord, Who in love hast warned me how narrow is the way of life, send me Thy light and grace, that knowing Thy holy will, I may steadfastly obey it after the example of my Saviour.

> Hold me fast, and guide me in the narrow way,
> So, with Thee beside me, I shall never stray.
> Daily bring us nearer to the heavenly shore;
> May Thy love grow dearer, may I love Thee more.

FIFTEENTH THURSDAY AFTER TRINITY.

"Strive to enter in at the strait gate: for many, I say unto you, will seek to enter in, and shall not be able."—LUKE xiii. 24.

SO Christ calls back from questions of idle curiosity to the soul's own work. He seems to say to each, "Ask not how many or few shall be saved, but live that you may be one of them." There is only one gate, and it is narrow. None can pass in by it who do not "strive," "agonise." Many shall "seek to enter" without striving, or by ways of their own choosing, or when too late. Those whom the Lord has never known as gatherers with Him shall be shut out as workers of iniquity.

Questions which can have no sure answer, and do not bear on my own duty, are worse than vain. They tempt me to pry into God's secrets, and to waste my short time. Light comes best to clear up dark things, while in lowly faith I do God's known will. I wish to be safe in the land of life, but slothful wishes leave me where I am. One way leads to the one gate. Christ warns me to make sure that I am of those who pass in, and that I do all to help others. I mock my soul and God if my "seeking" be in truth a looking about for a broader, easier path. He who has opened the one way tells me that such seeking ends in failure. Do I "strive" with will and might to learn the way, strive to gain all help of grace, strive to press forward, strive to know and be known by God, and to work with Him against iniquity? Am I careful not to put off any part of the needful striving, lest the door be shut, and I begin too late. I can only enter after patient striving; but I can strive if I will, and, by God's grace, add one to the number of the saved.

O Lord, let me not waste my short time in vain questions, too hard for me, but strive, in Thy strength, to follow the way of Thy known will, that I may at last enter in by the strait gate among Thy saved.

March, march onward, soldiers true, take through cloud and
    mist your way;
Yonder flows the fount of life, yonder dwells eternal day.
March, though myriad foes are nigh, forward till ye reach the
    shore:
Then when all the strife is done, rest in peace for evermore.

FIFTEENTH FRIDAY AFTER TRINITY.

"They that are whole have no need of the physician, but they that are sick."—MARK ii. 17.

IN the words of a common saying, Christ met those who blamed Him for eating with sinners. He was the good Physician, come to heal the stricken souls of men. His right place was among the sick, making known the nature and cause of their diseases, and using in each case the right means of cure. Those who felt whole would not have His help. He turned to those who owned their need, and longed for health. To them He is not a Judge, but a tender Physician, doing all to make them whole.

I am sick in soul beyond all aid but God's. To forget or deny my state is to grow surely worse, till I am past hope. If I feel and own it, I can draw near to One Who longs to heal me. Christ mercifully looks on me, not as a wrong-doer to be punished, but as a sufferer to be cured. I cannot check the inroads of disorder, and bring back my soul's vigour: Christ can, and will. Souls, like bodies, have many sorts of ailment, due to many causes, showing themselves in many ways, needing various treatment. I must learn what ails me, that I may tell the Divine Physician, and put my case in His hands. He will show me my true state, and how to regain health. He does more than bring good news of life and health; He gives help, and tells me what course to follow, that I may profit by it. If I believe His word, I will show my faith in Him by taking and using what He gives, and doing all that He prescribes. His medicines may be bitter, and seem unlikely to help; His rule of life may be hard. But the good Physician knows what each case needs, and deals with it in His own wise way.

O Lord Jesus Christ, Who dost not shrink from the worst who in their souls' need seek Thy care, show me my danger, and draw me in faith to Thee, that I may leave myself in Thy hands, to be made whole in Thy way.

> Gentle Physician, mortal ills healing,
>   Bending in love o'er each sin-stricken soul;
> Come, all Thy care and goodness revealing,
>   Strengthen my weakness, and make me whole.

Fifteenth Saturday after Trinity.

"*If thine eye offend thee, pluck it out, and cast it from thee.*"
—Matt. xviii. 9.

ALL that a man hath will he give for his life. He to whom his soul's life is dear will keep it safe at all costs. He dare run no risk of harm to that. If he finds anything tempt him to sin, or check the work of grace in his soul, he acts at once, and so as to leave no doubt. He faces pain or loss to make sure. What he parts with may be dear to him as a right hand or right eye, and as great a means of gain or joy; but if he is in earnest, the sacrifice is made as a thing of course.

I would lose an arm or eye, to live a few years more on earth. I would not flinch from the pain, or think the price too great to pay for life. My state for ever is being fixed now by the way in which God's grace grows strong in me, and leads me on in the narrow way of holiness. I can spare all but God's grace. Though my life be one long sacrifice, I triumph if in the end heaven is mine. I am in earnest, I am wise, so far as I feel and act on this truth. Everything must be made to give way to the one aim I set before me. I clear from my path and put far away whatever holds me back, or draws me aside, or makes me stumble in the onward upward course. These companions make me worldly; this business cannot be carried on honestly or without harming others; this pleasure stirs up sinful thoughts and spoils my prayers,—the sacrifice is great and sore, but God asks it, my soul's safety demands it. I seek grace to make up my mind to bear loss of friendship, or good name, or promotion, or money, for the sake of that which I make my highest good and my first care.

O Lord, make me jealous for the safety of Thy work in my everliving soul; give me will and power to put from me at all cost whatever hinders me in loving and serving Thee, and in seeking eternal good.

Jesus calls us from the evil in a world we cannot flee,
From each idol that would hold us, softly, clearly—" Follow Me."
Thou dost call us ! may we ever to Thy call attentive be ;
Give our hearts to Thine obedience, rise, leave all, and follow
    Thee.

The Fifteenth Sunday after Trinity.

"God forbid that I should glory, save in the Cross of our Lord Jesus Christ, by Whom the world is crucified unto me, and I unto the world."—GAL. vi. 14.

ST. PAUL warned those who were circumcised in order to escape persecution. The cross which they shrank from in fear and shame was his one glory. It told him of his Lord's love. The cross he bore proved his faithfulness to the Crucified. Suffering in the cause of the Lord Jesus left honourable scars showing Whom he served. The Cross shamed the world which slew Christ. From the Cross came his power to crucify all those leanings and desires by which the world tempted.

The world glories in what is indeed shame; be it mine to glory in what the world counts shame. But for the Scorned, the Outcast, the Crucified, what could I be but sin's slave, toiling helplessly in dishonour for sin's sure wages of lasting shame? Through Him I know myself the care of the Almighty Father, purchased for His own, an heir of glory. It is my highest honour to be counted worthy to bear the reproach of the Cross. To suffer for faithfulness to the Crucified marks me as His follower, under His strong, sure care, on the way to where He is. What is the world to me? Did not its pride and selfishness bring my Saviour to the Cross? How can I love or welcome its praise? How can I live for its bribes? For Christ's sake I must look upon the world in its sin and enmity to Christ as dishonoured, and powerless to tempt me. The Cross warns me to keep down and kill the worldliness and evil longings of my nature. From the death borne on the Cross and the grace won there, I gain power to become in heart dead to sin.

O Lord Jesus Christ, may the power of Thy death enable me to die from the world's evil, and rise to new life free from its temptations. May it be my glory that Thou hast died for me, and that I suffer for Thy name.

> Forbid it, Lord, that I should boast
> Save in the Cross of Christ my God;
> All the vain things that charm me most,
> I sacrifice them to His blood.

SIXTEENTH MONDAY AFTER TRINITY.

"Faith which worketh by love."—GAL. v. 6.

FAITH sees the work of God's love, and its claim on man. Faith meets the love of God that is ever coming forth seeking to find a place in the soul. Thus he who believes asks how he can show love to God Who has so loved him. By faith he seeks and receives grace to do works of love for God and man. True faith never fails to show itself in a life of love. As faith is clear, love is strong. As love gains power, it does more, with more glad will and free hand.

Only one sort of faith is of any worth or use for my salvation. There need be no doubt whether I have it or not. Its signs are plain. My heart and life show them, or want them. If the truths about God and the work of His grace are real to me, they cannot but make me feel in a new world, and live in a new way. I cannot look with cold eye on the Cross, or be untouched in heart by the love that bore it. I must at least long to love Him Who thus loved me, and to prove my love in true ways. I must try to be drawn close to God, that He may be in me the love of which I feel my need. That Divine love comes with power where it is let in. It is God. It will not rest till it rules all I say and do. So faith will work by love, in zeal for God's cause, in self-denial for others' good, in Christ-like patience under wrong, in care for all whom God pities in their need and sin. If what I call my faith leaves me without God's love working in me to help others and bring God praise, it avails me nothing. What I do and bear for God proves how far His love is in me: my love is the measure of the faith which receives God's grace.

Almighty God, give me faith to know Thee, and to receive Thy grace, that I may love Thee indeed, and may prove my love in a life of earnest work according to Thy holy will.

The crowd of cares, the weightiest cross, seem trifles less than light,
Earth looks so little and so low when faith shines full and bright;
Thy choice, O God of goodness! then I lovingly adore;
O give me grace to keep Thy grace, and grace to gain it more.

SIXTEENTH TUESDAY AFTER TRINITY.
"No servant can serve two masters."—LUKE xvi. 13.

MEN cannot be their own masters. They must serve, either as sons or slaves. They may own God's right to rule heart and will and life, looking to Him for all good. Or they may turn from God to seek what seems good in their own way. He who loves God will not love what God hates. He who holds to God will despise the bribes with which Satan tempts his heart away. He whose heart is the world's will hate God, Whose warnings disturb sinful joy. He who holds to the world makes light of God and His reward.

I am God's, not my own. He has all right in me, all claim on me. So long as my heart is His, and my life is spent for Him, I am free, safe, and at rest; for I move as my Maker wills for my good. The world with its passing delights tries to rival God and rule my life. I must not serve it, but make it serve me, using it under my Father's eye. I must love God as my highest good, and hold to Him as the one source of true blessedness. My heart may be faithful though I feel my love weak. The aim of my will may be steadfast, though my life fail. The world's joys must be sought, not by leaving God's service, but while serving Him in the way of His will. They must be used, not so as to draw the heart from Him, but as tokens of His love. I am not true to God if I think to have some good from Him, and the rest from His rival, in spite of or apart from Him. I love and serve God, if to please Him is my first great aim, and to grieve Him is my great grief. I hold to God and despise mammon, if I count the world's best not worth buying at the cost of the least sin.

Almighty Father, Who hast made me, and in Whose service alone I can be free and blessed, grant me to love Thee with undivided heart, and to hold fast to Thee with a firm will, letting nothing turn me away, or tempt me from Thee.

> Work for Him truly in life's daily task,
> And what the future hides, nor fear, nor ask;
> Seek His will only, leave to Him the rest,
> And toil or suffer as shall please Him best.

Sixteenth Wednesday after Trinity.

"Seek ye first the kingdom of God, and His righteousness.
—Matt. vi. 33.

THOSE who know not of heaven seek this world as their all. They are full of care, for they know not of God's help, and strive alone. Those who have a Divine Father to trust in, and eternal good to grasp, must not be as the heathen. A sure part in God's kingdom is more than high place among men. Righteousness is the one possession none can do without. These must be sought always in all things, and, if need be, at the cost of all else. God gives them to those who show their value for them by earnest seeking. He adds blessing on true honest work for this life's ends.

Which has my first thought, my best strength—earth or heaven, time or eternity? Am I more careful of my body's health or my soul's purity? Which grieves me most—loss of money or of grace—of man's praise or God's blessing? Do I seek first what may help me on in life, or what lifts to a higher place among saints? Do I spend my power in toil for this world, trusting that what my soul needs shall be added? Do I act as if the world's work must be done, and its good gained, at all risks, and that the leavings of time, and strength, and heart were enough to spend in providing for my eternity? Do I live as if the full blessings of the kingdom could be gained without righteousness; and as if heaven, and fitness for it, would come with no seeking? Or do I in all my seeking keep heaven in view, that God's righteousness may prepare me to share God's glory. If I live for time, I lose both worlds; if I live for heaven, I gain both. I seek this world best while I seek the other first.

O Lord, bind my heart to Thee, and reign in my nature, that I may seek first for a sure place in Thy kingdom, and for growth in Thy righteousness, trusting Thee for all I need till I am holy in Thy Church on high.

The soul that fixes upon earth unsatisfied desires,
Forgetful of its heavenly birth and what that birth inspires,
That soul shall mourn itself too late, its wingèd nature gone,
Degraded from its higher state to that it feeds upon.

Sixteenth Thursday after Trinity.

"Where your treasure is, there will your heart be also."
—Matt. vi. 21.

CHRIST does not say, Have your heart in heaven, that you may have treasure there, but, Lay up treasure in heaven, that your heart may rise to it. What we love matters more than what we have, for it shows what we are, and makes us what we are to be. Our affections should be in heaven before us. There must be treasure there, with God to draw them up. Earth's good things may be thankfully used as cheer by the way, and as means to lay up more wealth in the heart's true home. A lot growing bare and lonely may leave the heart more free to go where its all is fast being stored.

Treasure of friends and of earth's good need not hold my heart down. God means me to think much of all His gifts. It is as ungrateful to slight the smallest mercy He sends to cheer me now, as to forget eternal blessings. I do not think less of earth, but more of heaven. I do not count heaven only better than what is worthless, but so good, that all I thank God for now is nothing beside it. I am glad now as one who belongs to a higher world, and lives for ever. I love friends gone where I am going, and I love those still here as part of what will make the joy of life there. I do my best by prayer and work to gather friends for that life. I use money and power as means for God's ends, and make each least gift bind my love more fast to the Giver. When friends go up from earth, there is less to love here, and more to reach towards there. When I lose health, or money, or any earthly comfort, I feel more the need and worth of treasure laid up in heaven. My heart can find rest while I know that to be surely mine, though not yet enjoyed in full.

O Lord, teach me to use the blessings of this life and the gifts of Thy grace so as to lay up treasure in heaven and be lifted up in heart to things above.

> God takes our precious things away,
> And lays them up for us in store,
> That in the realms of endless day
> We may have treasure sent before.

SIXTEENTH FRIDAY AFTER TRINITY.

"Sufficient unto the day is the evil thereof."—MATT. vi. 34.

TO use foresight is a duty. To give way to foreboding is sin. Each day has its own work and care. God gives grace as we need it. He does not send it beforehand, so as to leave nothing for faith to do. We prepare best for to-morrow by doing well to-day's work, and going on bravely under to-day's load. If we stop to brood, we waste time and power; we are tempted to lose heart, and to question the truth of Him Who is pledged not to fail us. What threatens is not sure to fall. If it does, help and strength are sure to come too.

I know not what shall be on the morrow, or whether there shall be any to-morrow on earth for me. I dare not boast, or put off to-day's work. Nor must I let fears of what the morrow may bring take up the time, or daunt the courage, or weaken the power I need for pressing duties of to-day. God gives now what I want now, not what I may want hereafter. The right use of the gifts I have, in the work before me, will train me best to do well in days to come. God, in kindness, veils the future. Nothing is hidden from Him. He would have me trustful and calm, diligent and brave. His loving kindness and mercy shall follow me all the days of my life. Each day shall bring its own light and power for each new need. I may feel unequal now for what is in store; but, if I am true to God, I shall find myself made strong when the trial comes. I may dread dying, and wonder how I shall bear the last hard struggle; but, if I care for the days of life as they go by, God will take care of my day of death. He will bring me safely through the dark valley, if I hold fast to Him now.

O Lord, let not fear of the future tempt me to unbelief and idleness; enable me to go on cheerfully in the way of faith and obedience, sure that, as each hour of need comes, Thy help will not fail.

> Before our Father's unveiled face, in heaven's clear day,
> Our happy souls may love to trace this long dark way;
> There, knowing as ourselves are known, it shall be plain
> That we have never been alone, or worked in vain.

Sixteenth Saturday after Trinity.

"He that spared not His own Son, but delivered Him up for us all, how shall He not with Him also freely give us all things?"
—Rom. viii. 32.

GOD is love; He changes not. He made man to be something for Him to love. He loved man even when he sinned, but with the love of pity and forbearance. He spared not what cost dearest, to make man again "very good." He gave His own Son, that we might be His sons, unworthy though He knew we would be. He will deny us nothing needful to make ours all the fruit of the work of Christ. The Love that grudged not that unspeakable gift will give freely the daily blessings that help to make life good and bright.

What must be my worth in the heart of God, Who for my sake spared not His own Son! I cannot know what the sacrifice cost, or measure the love that made it. These mysteries are above the reach of man's thoughts. God can do no greater thing to win my trust. How can I dare to wound His love by doubt? How can I neglect my soul, for which God has done so much? How can I yield to sin, when God at such a cost offers me holiness? It is not His will that all He has done should be vain, or should bring me only part of its power and blessing. He does not tell me of a Saviour, and mock my longings to be saved. He does not tell me of grace, and leave me unable to gain or use it. He gave His Son, though fallen man did not ask, and could not have dared to hope for such a gift. Now He bids me come for all I need. He will give penitence, and faith, and love, that the risen Christ may live in me, and that, having Him, I may have all things for this life and the next.

Almighty Father, grant me to believe and rejoice in the changeless love that gave Thy Son, that, seeking Him above all things, and all things in Him, I may have the full blessedness Thou dost will to give.

> What will He not bestow
> Who freely gave this mighty gift, unbought,
> Unmerited, unheeded, and unsought,
> What will He not bestow?

The Sixteenth Sunday after Trinity.

"God so loved the world, that He gave His only begotten Son, that whosoever believeth in Him should not perish, but have everlasting life."—JOHN iii. 16.

GOD loved because He is God, and God is love. He loved the world—not a favoured few. God's love is in deed and in truth. He gave, freely and unasked, His only Son. "So" He made known His infinite love. It appeared in the form of self-sacrifice. God loved in order to save. He is always the same. He willeth not that any whom His love seeks to save should perish. Whosoever will can have the gift of faith. Whosoever believeth on Him Whom God gave is given life through Him, and in Him shall live for ever.

God is everywhere, and is always love. I dare not ask if God loves me. He is loving unto every man in the world for which Christ died. He loved me when He saw me in my sin; He gave His Son that I might not perish but have life. This giving was in some way a real cost to God. I am taught to think of Abraham's sacrifice and of the feelings of a human father, that I may be helped to know the love that passeth knowledge. The love that gave Christ to die for me, gives Christ to be eternal life in me. What sin, to pain that love by doubt! What sin, to treat the gift as if of small worth! What madness, to perish while life is within reach, and the patient love of God waits to bestow it! Do I believe in Christ as One given for me, and given to me? Do I trust in the work of Divine love done through Him, and take for granted the work He is ready to go on doing now? Is my faith a life-long looking for His grace, and leaning on His strength? Do I prove my faith by putting forth His grace in love and faithfulness?

O God, Who hast loved me and given Thy Son for me, grant that believing in Him I may have eternal life, and show for ever my love to Thee.

O Holy, Holy, Holy, I flee unto Thy breast,
Upon Thy stainless justice let a lost sinner rest!
By mystery o'ershadowed, by boundless love constrained,
I yield myself adoring, for glory to be trained.

SEVENTEENTH MONDAY AFTER TRINITY.

"The Son of God, Who loved me, and gave Himself for me."
—GAL. ii. 20.

ONLY God had that to give which Christ gave. Only God could so love those who loved Him not. He could give no more than Himself, and He gave no less. He devoted Himself to save the fallen. As Man, He died in man's stead. As Man, He pleads man's cause with God, and passes down God's love. All souls were embraced by that vast love. The whole might of God went forth in love to each. Only God knows the worth of His Son's gift. Every one may say, "It was all for me, and I can have its unknown good if I will."

The Son of God loved me before He gave Himself to become Man for me. He loved me not as one lost in a crowd, but as if the only one. He is God still, and His love changes not. He was giver and gift. I did nothing, and was nothing, that could make the gift less free. Christ did not send something He had; He gave all He was. The Son of God, Who is always all love and might, did for me what I read of in the Gospels. For me He bore man's hard lot, and fought with man's foes. He felt the weight of my sins, and died for them. For me He rose again and went to His Father's house. There He prepares a place and pleads for me. He does not withdraw now from the work of my salvation. He gives Himself ever. I may count upon all that Christ is for the supply of my soul's need. All things are mine if the Son of God in all His wealth of love is mine. Let me give myself to Him Who died and lives for me. Let me throw myself upon His true word, learn and do His will, use in glad, thankful faith those means by which He bestows the unspeakable gift of Himself.

O Lord Jesus Christ, Who in love for me didst give Thyself to be the Son of man and to die, that I might be made a son of God, fill me with Thy love, that I may die to sin, and in a life of faith live for Thee alone.

Deep in His heart for me the wound of love He bore,
That love which He enkindles still in hearts that Him adore.
Hide me in Thy dear heart, Jesu, my Saviour blest,
So shall I find Thy plenteous grace, and heaven's eternal rest.

SEVENTEENTH TUESDAY AFTER TRINITY.

"To know the love of Christ, which passeth knowledge."
—EPH. iii. 19.

GOD is love, and Christ reveals Him. The love of Christ is the showing forth of God Who cannot be fully known, but Who may be truly known and rejoiced in. All pure natural love on earth is of God. Christ gave man union with God, Who is love. Christ's love is seen in all Christian charity and tenderness. All tells of Him Whom love led to Bethlehem and Calvary. He reveals Himself now to the faithful, loving them, and giving them love. They shall find delight for eternity in ever fresh discoveries of His love.

So far as I know the love of Christ, I know God. I can trace God in all the goodness written on creation. I can find Him in all pure human love that brightens and blesses the world. I can learn, in the Gospels, of the love that is now what it always was, and can study its various forms. Faith opens ways for Christ to show Himself and dwell in me. I can make claims on His love. I can, with the love He gives me, love Him, and love others for His sake, and thus study His love made known in me. More may be mine than the knowledge of what others have found Him. I can learn His love shown to myself in giving pardon, comfort, and peace, in guiding my life, in changing my nature, in using me to make known His love. This knowledge, as it grows clearer and fuller, makes me strong against sin, and glad with a joy that cannot be taken from me. Even when the veil of sin and unbelief that hides God is withdrawn, I shall still find new depths of glory in the love of Christ that passeth the knowledge of the blessed.

O Lord Jesus Christ, Who in Thy person and work dost reveal God, make Thyself known to my faith; be in me, and guide my life. So may I learn for ever among Thy holy ones the glories of Thy love.

O Love Divine, how sweet Thou art,
When shall I find my willing heart all taken up by Thee?
I thirst, I faint, I die to prove
The greatness of redeeming love, the love of Christ to me.

Seventeenth Wednesday after Trinity.

"Blessed is he, whosoever shall not be offended in Me."
—Luke vii. 23.

CHRIST makes Himself known to faith. Faith always has work to do, and is often sorely tried. Christ did not seem what He was, when in the manger, at Nazareth, at Gethsemane, on the Cross. His sayings were full of strange, deep mystery. So He tries men still. Those are blessed ones who can adore Him like the shepherds and the wise men, in whatever form; who keep and ponder His hard words like Blessed Mary; who own their Lord though His cause seems lost.

I do not expect God to make known His truth or give His grace as I might think best. I do not expect God's ways to be plain to me. There must be mysteries deeper than my thoughts can reach. It is folly to stumble because God does not answer all my questions of how? and why? or make my understanding like His. The reason of many duties is kept back. Why should I question God's right thus to test my obedience to His will clearly made known? If Christ comes near and works in sacraments and means of grace which seem common and homely, this is but what His lowly life and manner while seen on earth prepare me for. If He leads me in ways of sore trial, I must not wonder that my earthly path is not all unlike His own. If His body, the Church, seems helpless in the hands of foes, I must not say, "Let Him come down from the cross, and I will believe." Blessed are they whose faith knows that He is the Christ, and that His words are the words of eternal life. He will bless those who thus believe, preparing them to see Him as He is, behind the veil.

O Lord, grant me to hear Thy Word and believe it; to take Thy grace thankfully through Thy means of grace; to learn Thy will and do it; to follow Thee patiently in humble faith, till I see Thee as Thou art.

> I do not ask my cross to understand
> My way to see—
> Better in darkness just to feel Thy hand,
> And follow Thee.

SEVENTEENTH THURSDAY AFTER TRINITY.

"Grow in grace, and in the knowledge of our Lord and Saviour Jesus Christ."—2 PET. iii. 18.

GRACE must grow in a soul, or else weaken and die out of it. He who does not gain more, loses what he has. True knowledge of Christ always gives a longing to know Him better. He who is not learning is forgetting. The grace that comes from Christ helps to the knowledge of Him. The more Christ is known, the more His grace will be sought, that He may be worthily copied. Man needs to grow on in grace and knowledge till he is like Christ, and knows as he is known.

Christ is ready to give me new grace day by day. I despise what He has already bestowed unless I use it so as to add to my store. Christ draws near to make Himself known in ever new ways, with greater clearness. I slight Him, if I am content with the knowledge I have. Let me beware not to tempt my Saviour to withdraw His gifts, and to hide Himself from me. If I would keep grace I must work with it, so as to make my hold on it firm, and make it strong in me. I must add to it by waiting on the one Giver of grace in all the means of grace He provides. To know about Christ is not to know Christ as my Lord and Saviour. He reveals Himself not to cold curiosity, but to lowly, earnest love and faith. As with an earthly friend, I get to know Him by holding converse with Him, by loving attention to His words, by studying His example, by working with Him in His cause. Above all, in the communion of the Body and Blood of Christ, by which He dwells in me and I in Him, can I find grace and knowledge. Am I growing to the fulness of both?

O Lord Jesu Christ, by Whom grace comes, Whom to know is eternal life, reveal Thyself to me, and dwell in me more and more, till I wear Thy likeness.

Lord, may I never turn away, or waste the grace Thou dost provide,
But live more near Thee every day, and by the faith of Him Who died.
Let every word of love Divine my comfort and my warning be;
My hope to be made wholly Thine—my only dread to fall from Thee.

SEVENTEENTH FRIDAY AFTER TRINITY.

"The wise took oil in their vessels with their lamps."
—MATT. xxv. 4.

GOD calls men to be light-bearers, letting inward holiness shine forth while they watch, ready to hail Christ's coming. The light is from God; so is what feeds the flame. The wise seek ever fresh supplies, and look well to their store. So, however sudden the call, they are ready. The foolish forget their need of continual renewal. When the time of testing comes, the light from God has gone out in their souls. It is too late to gain the grace by which it might revive.

My nature is but as a dry lamp. The grace of the Holy Spirit is as the oil by which I can shine as a light in the world, and be fit to share the joy of Christ's union with His Church. My life should be a going forth from a world of sin to meet Christ, a glad looking for Him, a preparing to do Him honour. If I am wise with the wisdom of faith, and hope, and love, and self-distrust, I will not rest content with what seems just enough to keep my soul's light from dying out. I will not delay to "buy" what I need at any cost. I will watch my religion, lest that which feeds its flame get low, and it burn feebly. I will provide for days to come, and, above all, for that day when all must depend on my readiness. I will use all means of drawing from the one Divine source a full store of all grace. As I spend I must receive. It is not enough to have been once lit, or to shine brightly now. I must gain what God gives to keep the fire of heaven burning. So, whenever the "Bridegroom cometh," I shall only need to trim my lamp, and pass in with Him to the eternal feast.

Almighty God, make me wise to watch and pray for the grace of the Holy Spirit, that my life may shine to Thy glory, and that my faith and love may always burn brightly while I wait for the coming of my Saviour.

> Grant us, O Christ, this grace to win,
>   Thy ransomed flock implore Thee;
> With oil-fed lamps to enter in,
>   And stand unblamed before Thee.
> So may we in Thy triumph share,
> Caught up to meet Thee in the air.

SEVENTEENTH SATURDAY AFTER TRINITY.

"He that believeth in Me, though he were dead, yet shall he live: and whosoever liveth and believeth in Me shall never die."
—JOHN xi. 25, 26.

CHRIST, though He died, was still the Life. Death never had Him in its power; nor can it hold His members. He rose that men might live in Him, and never indeed die. Man's natural life lasts only till soul and body part. His true life is from God, through spiritual union with Christ. Faith receives this in the ways by which God draws nigh. The perishing of the outward man leaves it untouched. He in whom it is outlives all changes of his state; his inward man is renewed, day by day, till he appears with Christ in glory.

Out of Christ I am dead, though I live; in Christ I live on, though I die. If Christ lives in me I can pass unharmed through the grave and gate of death, where He has gone before. If I have the Son I have life, even the everlasting life of God! I must indeed cease to be on earth, with soul and body joined as they are now; but I shall live on, leaving behind only what belongs to this humbled state. My body shall die, that it may be changed to share the glorified spirit's everlasting good. Have I this right to be reverently sure that I shall not die? God has given the eternal life that is in His Son. I am "baptized into His death," "buried," "risen with Him." But do I live my life in the flesh "by the faith of the Son of God"? Do I make mine, by a living, working faith, God's work of grace towards me? Do I abide in Christ as a believer who learns from Him how to "abide in His love," and to "dwell in" Him? Is my life a dying to sin, a burying of the old nature, a rising to ever more full active union with Christ's risen life?

O Lord Jesus Christ, increase my faith, that I may have closer union with Thy life, and may so abide in Thy love that nothing may ever separate me from Thee.

> O sovereign Love, to Thee I cry,
> Give me Thyself, or else I die!
> Save me from death, from sin set free;
> Death, hell are but the want of Thee!

The Seventeenth Sunday after Trinity.

"There is one body, and one Spirit."—EPH. iv. 4.

CHRIST is not divided. His Church, which is His body, cannot but be one. Into this one body, by one Spirit, we are all baptized. Whatever spiritual life we have comes from union with the life of the same Lord. Only so far as we are parted from Him is our union broken with others who are in Him. Our faith can rest only on One. Our hope can only point to one end of our faith. God sees us as His grace has made us—one.

God sees a unity which I cannot see, but which is an object of faith. I need not lose my trust in God through the envying, and strife, and divisions of men. Men have not owned, or acted on, their spiritual oneness. They have not been lowly and meek forbearing one another in love. So the "bond of peace" "has been broken." But brothers are of one blood still, though distance or estrangement part them. Members of Christ, who are not cut off from Him, are members of each other. A common life makes us all live. Be it mine to grasp this truth with my faith, and show it in my life. Let me pray and labour to bind up the Church's wounds, to remove mistakes, and calm strife. Let me take all pains to deepen my own union with Christ, and lead others to do the same, so that unity may be more valued and realised. I must have the truth, and hold it fast, and speak it out; but with meekness and fear, with patience and love, so as to win men, not to scatter them. It is God's truth; I dare not hide it, nor dare I vaunt myself while I know it and make it known. The cause of peace is not helped by unloving means. Wrongs against charity are not undone by new sins against it.

O Lord Jesu Christ, grant to me and all Thy members so to do our part by prayer and works of love, that Thy Church's unity may win the world to faith in Thee.

Elect from every nation, yet one in all the earth,
Her charter of salvation—one Lord, one faith, one birth;
One holy name she blesses, partakes one holy food,
And to one hope she presses, with every grace endued.

EIGHTEENTH MONDAY AFTER TRINITY.

" Walk worthy of God, Who hath called you unto His kingdom and glory."—1 THESS. ii. 12.

GOD has made us His children, and called us by His name. We have a place in His kingdom and a part in the blessings of it now. We are God's heirs, and have, as joint-heirs with Christ, the promise of fulness of joy when God's kingdom has come, and His glory is revealed. We should move on earth as children of the King of heaven, whom God's grace prepares for glory. God gives power to fill the place to which He calls.

What a pure and noble life I ought to live, who have such a calling, such hopes, and such help! Alas, how mournfully my life falls short! How little worthy I am even of a place in the Church on earth! How unfit I am to share the glory of the Church on high! How poor and unworthy is all I do, as the fruit of God's power working in me! How little I look like one on whom the Almighty has poured out such gifts! How unreal is my sense of the greatness of calling; how feebly and half-heartedly I try to rise to it! I need not go on in this life of failure. God wills and waits to make me what He calls me to become. I will set before me this high aim as something which I can reach if I will. I can be in thought, and word, and deed, worthy of Him Who made me, of Him Who died for me, of Him Who sanctifies me. I can live with God in light of my soul always. I can let His presence and power be seen in what I am and do. I can be more and more what I ought to be, to whom God has given rights in His kingdom, and whom He trains for its full glory.

Almighty and all holy God, Who hast called me into Thy kingdom on earth to fit me for the joy Thou dost prepare in Thy kingdom above; grant me grace and wisdom to use grace rightly, that my life may be worthy of Thee, and of the hopes Thou dost set before me.

I ask the gift of righteousness, the sin-subduing power,
Power to believe and go in peace, and never grieve Thee more;
I ask the blood-bought pardon sealed, the liberty from sin,
The grace infused, the love revealed, the kingdom fixed within.

Eighteenth Tuesday after Trinity.

"*Let us consider one another to provoke unto love and to good works: not forsaking the assembling of ourselves together, as the manner of some is.*"—HEB. x. 24, 25.

MEMBERS of the one Christ must have one heart, pray and praise with one voice, work with one mind and will. God claims open homage before men. Blessings are promised to those who meet in Christ's name, specially to those who come together to plead His death and take His body and blood. As "the day" draws near, men are called more loudly to provoke one another, not to envy, strife, and debate, but to love and all good works.

Public worship is a means of grace and a duty; neglect is loss and sin. I need to claim and keep my place as a living, working member of Christ's body. I need to acknowledge God among men, and to set an example of devotion. I have no right to ask God to give me by myself what He bids me seek openly with the Church, or to hope for inheritance in Canaan if I go not with the Church in the wilderness. Union in prayer unites for work. My religion will grow weak if it grow lonely. If Christ is indeed among those assembled in His name, I must be there. If in the Holy Communion He comes in a way over and above this special presence, no light cause must keep me away. How good to go apart for a while with Christ, one in spirit with the Church in earth and heaven! So I prepare for the time when I shall look on Him Whom now I know by faith, and shall see those heavenly ones who, unseen and unheard, share the worship of the Church on earth. So shall I catch the spirit and learn the songs of heaven. So shall I be roused to love those who worship with me, and to work for God's glory and their good.

O Lord, grant me so to hold living, loving communion with Thee and with my brethren, that I may, in the Church on earth, grow fit for the worship and work of heaven.

> One the object of our journey,
> One the faith that never tires,
> One the earnest looking forward,
> One the hope our God inspires.

EIGHTEENTH WEDNESDAY AFTER TRINITY.

" Ye know not what ye ask. Are ye able to drink of the cup that I shall drink of, and to be baptized with the baptism that I am baptized with?"—MATT. xx. 22.

CHRIST had spoken of "twelve thrones" and of His coming sorrows. James and John asked the places of honour in the kingdom. Perhaps they thought selfishly of being set above others; rather of being most worthy and near their loved Lord. The honour sought was not Christ's to give, as man, to human friends; only as one with God, to those for whom it was being prepared. It awaits those who, in willing love, have drunk deeply His cup of woe, and have come forth pure from the baptism of fiery trial borne for Him.

I am right, in love for Christ and holiness, to long for a place near His throne. But while thinking of the end, I must not forget the way to it. I owe all my hope of glory to my Saviour's shame and death. Life and work for Christ are not to be looked on selfishly as means of gaining greatness here or hereafter. Christ gives me hopes to cheer me on, but He warns me to ask what I do, and bear, and am now, rather than what I shall have. A heavy cross well borne prepares for a bright crown. Power grows by the grace given in hard, honest, proving work. The purest holiness is wrought in a soul by the keenest and most searching trial. I "know not what I ask," if I pray for glory and refuse to be fitted for it in God's way. If I am unready to share Christ's sufferings, I may not hope to share His glory. Be it my one care to follow the Lamb whithersoever He leads, to drink whatever healing, though bitter, cup He gives, to yield to whatever cleansing fire He wills to bathe me in. He will prepare the right place, and prepare me for it.

O Lord Jesu Christ, make me willing and able so to drink Thy cup and be baptized with Thy baptism now, that I may hereafter be found meet to share Thy glory.

>If Thou the cup of pain givest to drink,
>Let not my trembling lip from the draught shrink;
>   So by my woes to be
>Nearer, my God, to Thee, nearer to Thee.

Eighteenth Thursday after Trinity.

"Your sins have withholden good things from you."
—Jer. v. 25.

EVEN in this life men reap as they sow. God's laws, made known in nature and His Word, work so that men may count on them. The good God gives to bless man's life must be sought in the way of God's will. Most of man's woes can be traced to his own fault or folly. God does not work miracles to save men from the sure end of the course they choose. Sloth or want of thrift brings poverty. Selfishness puts away friends. Idleness stops success in life. Carelessness or indulgence breaks down health. So man's life is spoiled.

God makes fire burn; He does not force me into it. He makes sorrow sin's shadow; He does not make me sin. There are griefs of which I can say, "It is the Lord." But much that tries me shames me too, as the plain fruit of my own doings. I have brought it on myself, in spite of God's clear warnings. I know how my load has been heaped up, and how the good things God held out to me have been thrown away. I might have seen that the path I took could only lead to where I am. I must not add sin to sin by laying to God's charge trouble of my own making. God is not hard on me; I have been hard on myself. I must blame my own wilfulness in going against God's will. I have no right to ask that God's laws should change their course to spare me. I must be patient, but must be penitent also, for my sorrows tell of sin, and warn me that I have wasted and spoiled what might have been improved for God's use and my lasting joy. If sin and even want of thought bring sure loss on earth, I may well take heed lest in the time left me I put away eternal good.

O Lord of love, give me grace to seek, in the way of Thy laws, the good things Thou dost will to give me, that I may praise Thee in my life on earth, and go on towards the good things that are for ever.

> Lay Thy hand upon me when I rashly stray
> Into paths forbidden, choosing my own way.
> Ah! how much correction, Lord, I have to bear,
> Yet must take it meekly, for Thy hand is there.

EIGHTEENTH FRIDAY AFTER TRINITY.
"Every one that exalteth himself shall be abased."
—LUKE xviii. 14.

THE proud trusts in himself and surely fails. He forgets his need of grace, so is unhelped. He strives to get honour rather than to deserve it. He overlooks his faults, so they grow. He vaunts right-doing, so as to change it into sin. He looks down on others, so he is self-satisfied, and without high aim. He does not bow his mind to learn, or his will to obey; so he goes on in blindness and sin. He faces temptation alone, unarmed and careless; so he is overcome. He craves the world's praise, so he is unhappy when it is denied. Sooner or later God abases him, in mercy or judgment.

I must not force myself forward. If God calls me to go up higher, I must not be high-minded, but fear lest I fail in lowly trust on Him. I am in sore danger when my heart is lifted up, and I am tempted to look down on others. I am ready to lose what I have gained, and to fall from the place to which I have been raised. I check the incoming of God's grace, and shut out my soul from the light of His wisdom. The watchful tempter finds me off my guard, and an easy prey. I stop my growth in holiness and my onward climb towards heaven. I fall away from the meek and lowly Teacher, and provoke God to "resist" me. Pride may be hidden under a cloak of humility, and so work secretly my soul's loss. I may seem lowly even to myself, while proud of lowliness as my chief virtue. Well for me if God tears away, however roughly, the veil that hides the truth, and shows me how little cause I have for pride or confidence. Well for me to be let fall so as to be humbled now, rather than to go on blindly to destruction and everlasting shame.

Almighty Father, Whose mercy is my one hope, save me from pride or trust in self, lest I exalt myself before Thee, or against Thee, and lose the glory of holiness won for me by the humiliation of Thy Son Jesus Christ.

> Humble we must be, if to heaven we go;
> High is the roof there, but the gate is low;
> Whene'er Thou speakest, look with lowly eye,
> Grace is increased by humility.

Eighteenth Saturday after Trinity.

"He that humbleth himself shall be exalted."—LUKE xiv. 11.

THE lowly knows and remembers what he is without God. When he does right he gives God the praise; when he fails he blames himself. Christ's example shows him how far he falls short. The faults of others warn him of his own. He trusts God's word, and obeys God's will in child-like faith. He humbly comes for grace in all the ways God sets before him. He takes humiliations for granted, and does not wonder if he is kept low. He will not push himself where new temptations are. He toils in faith and patience to be worthy of higher service, waiting for God to exalt him in due time.

I am nothing without grace, which God gives only to the humble. The wisdom and strength I need come from the meek and lowly Master. All good and hope I have are mine through the humiliation of my Lord. Each gift that is the fruit of that warns me to be lowly. What wrongs I have done against God! How I have wasted His love, and misused my time and powers! What am I compared with what I might have become? What can I do to make up for all I owe? What is there in myself or my life that does not tell of grace more or less made vain? How the pure, brave life of Christ shames me! How feebly I try to follow or be like Him! My trials are less than I deserve; my blessings are far more. Shall I complain of being humbled, even by sore means, if God can only thus bring me to a right spirit and posture to be exalted by His grace. There is danger even in humiliations. Though cast down as low as Satan, I may bring my pride with me, and even be more hardened in it. Only if I "humble myself" under the mighty hand of God shall I be lifted up.

O Lord Jesu Christ, Who didst humble Thyself for me, make me willing to learn in Thy school, and to bear my cross in Thy steps, that I may hereafter share Thy glory.

O Lord, behold a sinner kneel before Thy gracious throne,
Confessing what he truly is, left to himself alone.
Within, without, I lean on Thee, on Thee for aid rely;
O still my outward life protect, my inward life supply.

The Eighteenth Sunday after Trinity.

" Whoso looketh into the perfect law of liberty, and continueth therein, he being not a forgetful hearer, but a doer of the work, this man shall be blessed in his deed."—JAMES i. 25.

SOME hear with no lowly, earnest will to learn and do. They forget what God's Word shows them of their sinful state and holy calling. Or they deceive themselves, by changing the outside look of life and character. Or they welcome words that promise pardon, not those which promise holiness. He who looks aright into the mirror of God's truth, searches to know perfectly what he is in himself, and can be in Christ. He finds more blessing as his will is more one with God's.

God's Word shows me what I am, and what God wills me to be. I see there a perfect law, claiming no less than the doing of God's whole will from a true heart. It is a law of liberty, for only willing obedience avails, and in doing of it I find freedom. It shows how to be strong to break sin's yoke, and to gain such love of God and holiness as to do my own will while doing God's. So it is no bondage, but a loosening of bonds. It bids me know myself free to live as a child, and be no more a slave. It shows God's light, to lead and cheer me while I go forward in God's might. It must be looked into till all its perfectness is known. Its promises warn; its warnings are promises. The full meaning will come out as I humbly bow down myself to search, and as I earnestly put to use what I learn. By learning and doing, I shall see more what God would have me be. I shall be more free as my will is more one with His, and Christ is more one with me. As I rise towards the standard of the perfect law of liberty, my blessing shall be larger.

Grant me, O Lord, the spirit so to search Thy Word that I may know myself and Thee, and, being made free in heart to do Thy will gladly, may have Thy blessing.

Our wishes and affections, our impulses and powers,
We yield unto Thy guidance, for they are Thine, not ours;
Our spirits we surrender, our purposes resign,
To be conformed for ever unto the will Divine.

NINETEENTH MONDAY AFTER TRINITY.
"He had this testimony, that he pleased God."—HEB. xi. 5.

ENOCH walked with God. He knew God and God's will. God was with him, as he did what pleased God, and so grew to be one in whom God was well pleased. We can know God from His works and Word, and see Him in Christ. We "have received how we ought to walk and to please" Him. We can do this, which we "ought" to do; for God gives grace for what He asks. He is pleased with the heart's first true wish to please Him. He adds blessing, as growing love and strengthening will find ever new joy in abounding more and more unto all pleasing.

I am an interest to God. He cares for what I do and how I fare. He gives me sure truth about Himself and His will, that I may know with Whom I have to do, and how to please Him. His fatherly love is pleased when I trust Him, and seek my true good as He teaches me. But can I be anything but evil to the All Holy? Can my life or my self be of worth so as to please God? God says I can. He gives what He bids me have. He does in me what He asks me to do. He forms me after the good pleasure of His will. He is pleased with His own work, the life and growth of Christ in me. As a father, He pitieth His children, and welcomes their offerings of love. Each honest fight with sin, each laying down of self for His sake, pleases Him. All I do has in it some want or flaw; but God loves to look on me while my heart and life show a true wish to please Him. Here is a motive able to stir and urge me on. While I do what pleases God, not from fear or self-interest, but for the sake of pleasing Him, I grow to the character which He loves to see perfected in His children.

Almighty Father, grant that my life's aim and joy may be to please Thee always in all things, and that, one with Christ, I may grow to be well-pleasing in Thy sight.

Surrounded by ten thousand snares, I shall not, cannot fall,
While clinging to the arm that bears my soul above them all.
That I may please Thee evermore, Thy blessed self impart,
And stamp in perfect peace and power Thy image on my heart.

NINETEENTH TUESDAY AFTER TRINITY.

"Thou hast a name that thou livest, and art dead. Be watchful, and strengthen the things which remain, that are ready to die : for I have not found thy works perfect before God."—Rev. iii. 1, 2.

THE soul dies which does not maintain union with the living God. A form of godliness deceives if the quickening power of God be wanting. A name to live may only give false peace to a soul that is perishing. There is hope while there is any hold on life. But there is only one hope—to awake from the sleep of self-content, and to seek grace carefully, that each failing, but not wholly lost power, may be renewed, and that in each work the strength of God may be heartily put forth.

I want life, not a name to live. I want all my spiritual powers to grow and strengthen towards perfection, and to do, in the best way, all the work God gives them. If my life is weak or languid, better to be roused and know the truth ere it is too late. Has the flow of life from God to me been checked? Is my spiritual vigour failing through want of earnestness in gaining grace, or in exercising it? Does the imperfection of my works prove that I am not living close to God, and drawing always from Him the needful strength? To be unwatchful is to be on the way down to death. To rest content with form and name among men, or with some poor, small service, is to trifle with God, Who searches the inmost heart, and Who claims to make all I am fully active by His living presence. If I have lost some powers, they may yet be restored. What little I can do I will do, as perfectly as God enables me. What powers I have I will seek to use with my might, humbly and prayerfully. I will watch, and wait on God in faith and well-doing, till all my nature lives by Him for His praise.

Almighty, everliving God, renew the life of my soul, and arouse me to watchful activity, that I may glorify Thy name, in the strength of Jesus Christ, my Saviour.

With all my small remains of grace, the blessing I implore;
Stir up my soul to seek Thy face, to seek it evermore;
To wrestle till the clouds remove, and Thou Thy name declare,
While all my happy heart is love, and all my life is prayer.

Nineteenth Wednesday after Trinity.

"*Her sins, which are many, are forgiven; for she loved much.*"
—Luke vii. 47.

THE Pharisee did not know the love his sin wronged, and his own want of love made him blind to the number and greatness of his sins. So he thought he had little to be forgiven. Love did not deepen penitence and encourage faith, so it did not show itself in gratitude and devotion. The woman felt herself a sinner against Divine love that waited to forgive. The more God's love in Christ attracted her faith, and won her love, the larger seemed the claim upon her devotion.

I cannot be rightly sorry for my sins till I learn of God's love, and my heart begins to feel what I owe to it. Faith draws me to God for pardon if He is seen as the God of love, winning my trust, and giving power to love Him. I am not forgiven because of my love. I love because God is made known to my faith as a forgiving God, Who pardons freely for Christ's sake. Love makes me feel how much I need forgiveness. What to a cold heart seems little, will be a vast debt to me if I am lovingly jealous for God. Love proves that I am in a state of grace. It is the sign of that living union with the Saviour on which forgiveness of sin depends. Love is tested not by what it seems in thought or feeling, but by what deeds show it to be in truth. I cannot wash my Saviour's feet, but I can be devoted to my fellow-sinner's good for His sake. If I am indeed, through His work, free from the sentence and the power of sin, my heart cannot but overflow with love to Him, and grief that I have grieved Him. I will ask how I can show my feeling that to me much is forgiven.

O Lord, show me Thy love, that I may see the sinfulness of my sin. Draw me to Thee in loving penitence and faith. Grant that all my life may prove how much I love Thee for Thy love and mercy.

> Naught can I bring, dear Lord, for what I owe,
> Yet let my full heart what it can bestow;
> Like Mary's gift let my devotion prove,
> Forgiven greatly, how I greatly love.

Nineteenth Thursday after Trinity.

"What shall I render unto the Lord for all His benefits toward me? I will take the cup of salvation, and call upon the name of the Lord."—Ps. cxvi. 12, 13.

GOD'S benefits are bestowed on His creatures for their good and His glory. Man is bound to ask how he can best acknowledge God's freely-given mercies, and offer worthy thanks. The lips must speak what the mind knows and the heart feels. But the most acceptable way of thanksgiving is to ask and take more spiritual benefits, to call upon the Lord's name with firmer faith and enlarged desires. Thus value is shown for gifts already received. Thus man becomes more what pleases God, and grows more able to glorify Him in his life.

What can I render to Him from Whom comes all I am and have that is good? Whatever I might give, is His gift to me. Each joy and comfort, each power, even life itself—all are from above, and remind me of my debt. I can lay all before Him, and own it His with grateful heart and voice. I can will and work to live for Him. I can do more—I can seek larger gifts of grace till all that salvation means is fully mine. I can gladly lay hold of all the Divine blessing He offers, drawing more largely on His store. So shall I please my Father, as I prove how I prize His gifts, and seek to be formed after His likeness. So shall I have greater powers to put forth in His service, and my life shall be a more willing and perfect offering to His praise. His love will rejoice as my holiness and joy increase, and as the fruit of all His goodness is seen in a child growing like that Son in Whom He is well pleased. I shall learn more what I am to my Father, and how to give Him the glory that is His due.

O Lord, the Giver of all good and hope, teach me to thank Thee with heart, and lips, and life; and to seek grace, that I may become what Thy love would have me be, and may grow in will and power to praise Thee.

> Be all my heart and all my days
> Devoted to my Saviour's praise;
> And let my glad obedience prove
> How much I owe, how much I love.

Nineteenth Friday after Trinity.

"I am not ashamed of the Gospel of Christ: for it is the power of God unto salvation to every one that believeth."—Rom. i. 16.

THE Gospel is the good news of what God in Christ has done for man, and does now. The world's wisdom sees no fitness in the way God has chosen. But the Gospel tells of a coming forth of God's power, planned by God's perfect wisdom, to save perishing man. Christ liveth, Who was dead. In Him God's power still puts forth energy, that the salvation of each may be wrought out. To unbelief the Gospel tells of no light or help. To faith it reveals God, willing and strong to save.

Only by God's power can I be saved from my soul's sin and foes. The Gospel of Christ makes known One in Whose person and work the wisdom of the Almighty has provided for my salvation. I cannot be ashamed to meet God's love with faith, and yield to His grace thankfully. I need not, as God's creature, fear to own that I owe all to His free bounty. It is no shame to lose my weakness in His strength, and, in my ignorance, to lean on His wisdom. God knows how to put forth power in my cause. In Christ that power worked for me, and strives to work in me. If I believe not, all is vain; I am not being saved, and so am perishing. If I believe the truths of the Gospel, what I believe becomes the power of God to gain my pardon and to make me righteous. I am in the hands of Divine love that wills to free me from the sentence Christ bore, and to impart the gifts He won. True faith forbids me to stumble at what seem the foolishness and weakness of the ways by which Christ leads me on to full salvation. I believe in Him, however He comes, whatever He commands or gives.

Almighty God, grant me so to believe the Gospel of Christ, that He may be a power working in me to work out the salvation I owe to Thy free mercy.

> I have no help but Thine; nor do I need
>   Another arm, save Thine, to lean upon;
> It is enough, my Lord, enough, indeed;
>   My strength is in Thy might, Thy might alone.

NINETEENTH SATURDAY AFTER TRINITY.

"We know that all things work together for good to them that love God."—ROM. viii. 28.

THOSE who love God have first been loved by Him. Their love is a fruit and proof of His love for them. Nothing can harm, all things must help those whom the Almighty loves. While they love and trust and serve Him, all things serve them. God gives to what seems most against them its own place in His plan for their true good. What looks tangled and dark to them is clear to Him, Who sees to the end, and lets go His hold on nothing. Those who love Him have a pledge that His love will lead them on, by means of all things, to the full blessedness which He prepares.

"All is for the best." Yes, for some; but is all for the best for me? All is for the worst, if I close my heart against God's love, and put away His guiding hand. Only if I let Him rule my heart and life, have I any right to hope that He will rule all things for my good. Only if I love God and live to show my love, can I say thankfully that God lives to show His love to me. What peace may keep my mind and heart, if my love to God tells of the Almighty Father's love watching over me, and wisely working out my highest good. He knows how each friend or foe, each bitter or pleasant thing, each bright or sad hour has its part in fulfilling the plan of His love for me. No least care or joy is vain in His hands. I know not what is well for me, but to love God and trust myself to Him. Whatever may befall, one question only is important—do I love God? If I can be humbly sure of this, then all is well. I know that the building up of the good to be in me, and to be mine for ever, is going on.

O God of love, give me such love to Thee, that I may find my joy in serving Thee, and may know that the love which enables me to show my love to Thee will make all things work together for my everlasting good.

> The worth and end of all our strife, and all our woes,
> The hidden meaning of our life, our Father knows.
> All things are guided to fulfil, we know not how,
> The purpose of that loving will we work with now.

The Nineteenth Sunday after Trinity.

"*When Jesus saw their faith, He said unto the sick of the palsy, Son, thy sins be forgiven thee.*"—MARK ii. 5.

THE sick man, and those who bore him, had faith. Christ, as man, saw proof of their faith in what they did. As God He saw the true inward faith of which their deeds told. Christ knew the deepest want and longing of the man. Perhaps sin was felt as in some way the cause of his sickness, adding bitterness to it. Christ spoke peace and cheer, calling him son. He healed his soul that it might rise and go forth in new strength. Then, to prove that God spoke with power with man's lips, He made his body whole.

In sorrow I seek the Son of man, Who feels with me and can help. Sorrow should tell of my most pressing need. I should come to Christ first, not as a sufferer, but as a sinner. If I have faith, nothing need stop my drawing near. If my faith is weak, and I know not how to come, others can help me, and bear me to His Presence in their prayers. I am unworthy to be called son; but He waits to speak the name that assures of a Divine Father's goodness. I can "be of good cheer," though my worldly sorrow lasts on, if my faith can grasp the gift of pardon, and I can rise and walk in spiritual health and power. I am called to new thankfulness if my affliction is removed, when it has done its work, and has brought me humbly to the Healer of souls. It is easy to believe that God in heaven forgives sins. The hard claim on my faith is that Christ puts forth on earth, through the ministration of His Church, that power He never parts with. If others are weak to draw near, I can help them. In love for souls and zeal for Christ's glory, I must lay them at Christ's feet.

O Lord, in all my sorrows show me my sin, and draw me in faith to Thee. Hear my prayers, and the prayers of those who plead for me, that I may gain the help best for me, and may be of good cheer as Thy pardoned son.

At Thy feet in faith we bow,
Good Physician, sure that Thou art as kind as ever now,
May the sorrows we endure
Be the medicine for our cure, be the fire to make us pure.

TWENTIETH MONDAY AFTER TRINITY.

"Who can understand his errors? cleanse Thou me from secret faults."—Ps. xix. 12.

EARTH'S purest are not stainless. The truest may err. Faults may be overlooked by the most jealous for God. No man dare trust his own judgment of himself, or his firmness. Sloth, pride, false self-love, his own habits, and the world's customs, help to hide truth. God is man's hope. He knows all in all. He sees the least fault in man's secret nature. Those who will to be what He wills can own the sins they see, and can ask the All-Seeing to make them clean in His holy eyes.

Though, like St. Paul, I "know nothing by myself" after honest searching, yet this does not prove me sinless. God is greater than my conscience, and of purer eyes. Though I search heart and life with true will to lay all before God for cleansing and grace, yet I dare not be sure that nothing deadly is left. My worst sins may have deep-sunk roots, or look harmless. They may mix with what is of God, or hide behind it, or wear its dress. I could not hope for purity, did the blood of Christ wash only the stains I see. Thanks be to God, He searches the secret workings of my whole being, and traces every stain with a Father's loving care. This is my comfort. I know He wills to cleanse me wholly. I can bring my unknown need before Him; but I must do all to drag to light my lurking faults, that I may be guided in overcoming them. I must not through sloth leave any hidden, which I might find out, and confess, and be saved from. I must not murmur at the means, however humbling and painful, by which God may see fit to answer my prayer to cleanse me from my secret faults.

Try me, O God, and seek the ground of my heart, prove me and examine my thoughts, look well if there be any way of wickedness in me, and lead me in the way everlasting.

Only long to be delivered from each remnant of disguise;
Only let Him lay in ruins all thy refuges of lies;
Only strive to say, "My Saviour," as thou liest at His feet;
He can from thy dust and ashes spotless holiness complete.

Twentieth Tuesday after Trinity.

"Bear ye one another's burdens, and so fulfil the law of Christ."—Gal. vi. 2.

IN one way each must bear his own burden; no man can shift his responsibility on another. Yet there are burdens which all may help to lighten. The law of Christ is the law which rules and guides the life of His body, the Church. It is the law of love which the Head gives, that the members should care for one another. Christ bore our griefs, and lifted from us the weight of our sins. He feels with and helps us now. His indwelling life stirs up and enables those who are one with Him to love in deed and truth. So they fulfil His law written on their hearts.

The law of Christ asks more than the law of Moses. I am not free to disobey, but to obey. Grace does not do away with duty, but enables for it. The claims of God and my neighbour are not felt a burden: to the new nature obedience is using its liberty and following the law of its life. Christ is in me a power of love to will and do. I can live as a part of Christ's body, and let His love be active in me always. I can go about doing good, bringing His healing to crushed weary souls. I can cheer the sad with kind words and deeds, help the poor and sick, teach the untaught, befriend the lonely. I can bear meekly and gently with the slaves of sin, while I pray and labour that their yoke may be loosed. I can deny self in order to aid the tempted to hold firm. Sympathising as a fellow-sinner and fellow-mourner, I can do my part to lift away some of the burden under which my brethren sink, and show them the love of Christ. Am I thus fulfilling the law of Christ, led by the love of Christ within me?

O Lord, Who hast joined Thy members in one body in Thee, and dost give them the law of love, teach me to help those in need or care, after Thy example and in Thy strength.

I need Thy mercy for my sin; but more than this I need,
Thy mercy's likeness in my soul, for others' sin to bleed.
'Tis not enough to weep my sins; 'tis but one step to heaven;
When I am kind to others, then I know myself forgiven.

TWENTIETH WEDNESDAY AFTER TRINITY.

"Like as a father pitieth his children, so the Lord pitieth them that fear Him."—Ps. ciii. 13.

GOD knows our frame and our state, what we are and where we are. He measures our weakness; He weighs all the sadness and hardship of our short tempted life; He knows the power of inborn evil, and the strong force of evil all around, that make well-doing hard. He bears with His children's childishness, and encourages them while they try, even with trembling hand, the task that trains them for their grown-up life.

As a dying sinner I feel for others' griefs, and am patient with their faults. God feels for and bears with me, because He is so great and holy. He is more kindly and forbearing to me than I can ever be to a fellow-man. For He is a strong, wise, perfect Father, pitying His child. God knows how short and tried my life is; how hard it must be to rise free from the evil and earthliness in me from the first, and to overcome the strong temptations that beset me. He understands my weakness and my burden. He takes into merciful consideration all my every temptation. He makes more allowance for me than He asks me to make for others. Only He can know under what drawbacks and disadvantages I begin and go on in my Christian life. Only His Divine tender mercy can be always gentle with my failures, and patiently help me still. I fear Him, knowing that His holy eye is ever on me. But I am quiet and trustful; for He is kindlier than any earthly parent, and will not judge me except as a Father Who is God. As I gain the child-like spirit, I am only careful to be in His keeping, and to judge myself more sternly than He in His mercy judges me.

O God of love and pity, give me child-like trust in Thee, that I may always be happy under Thy fatherly care, and may never presume upon Thy kindness.

> There is no place where earth's sorrows
> Are more felt than up in heaven;
> There is no place where earth's failings
> Have such kindly judgment given.

TWENTIETH THURSDAY AFTER TRINITY.
"Study to be quiet, and to do your own business."
—1 THESS. iv. 11.

HE who would work well must be quiet; he who would be quiet must have work of his own, and do it. The quiet is likely to work best. The diligent in his own business has the best hope of quiet. It is hard to work on steadily, free from inward unrest and outward fuss and meddling. Few quite reach what all are bound to aim at. Many are tempted from their place of duty to speak and do rash things, in unbelieving impatience or fear. So they lose their own peace, make the world more unquiet, waste time and strength, and hinder others.

In this troubled world I can make one more on the side of quiet. I can take care not to leave my own post of duty, to interfere with what is my neighbour's business. I cannot always make calm around me, but quietness of spirit is a gift I can gain, and a habit I can, with God's help, form. So I can go on with what God gives me to do, trusting Him Whose word stills life's storms, feeling that I work best for the world at large while busy at my own tasks. I escape running against others by keeping my own quiet course. Steady occupation saves from the many fretting temptations of idleness, and gives my spirit strength and calm. Time and strength spent in fuss are taken from work. God will ask how far I have made the most of my time and strength and opportunities to do well my own business, and fill the place in which He has put me. If I would get on in life, my wise way is quietly and thoroughly to do each day's duty. If I would be fit for the quiet land, I must learn the spirit now, in this unquiet world. If I would help others, a quiet, earnest, true life has its sure power for good.

O Lord, Who hast given me my place and work in life, grant me Thy peace in heart and mind, that I may not be drawn from my duty, or hinder others, but may study to follow the quiet path of faith and diligence.

When I have learned His name to praise, by labour here below,
When I have learned in sorrow's ways my Saviour's love to know,
Then shall I rise His face to see, the rest of heaven to share,
And learn to know His love to me in joy for ever there.

TWENTIETH FRIDAY AFTER TRINITY.

"Speak every man truth with his neighbour : for we are members one of another."—EPH. iv. 25.

CHRISTIANS are members of Him Who is the truth; they must be true. They are freed from the power of him who is a liar from the beginning; they must put from them all that is false. They are members one of another, sharing a common life, depending on one another; all have a claim on the rest to be what they seem, and to mean what they say. He who lies to a fellow-member in Christ's body, lies to Christ the Head.

As a member of Christ, I am bound to Him, and to those who in Him are one body with me. Wrongs against them wrong Him. Those who are joined together for a common end must be able to rely on one another, else their union cannot prosper. Without truth, trust and peace and harmony of movement are impossible. If I am untrue, I wrong Christ in His members whom I deceive, and in myself whom I make a liar. I dare not be false and base before God and my conscience, in order to seem better, or to escape blame before men. I dare not insult God by a lie, in order to please man. I dare not think to help God's cause, or man's welfare, or my own ends, by falsehood. God disowns all who would bring sin into His service. I further my neighbour's interests more by making a firm stand for truth, than by any advantage that any lie may seem to promise. It may be God's will that I should lose friends, or wealth, or life, or power to work for Him, or even what seems most good for my soul. It is never God's will that I should lie, as if the God of truth failed me, and I had to fall back on the help of the father of lies.

O Lord God of truth, make me true in word and deed, to myself, my fellow-men, and Thee. May I always mean what I say, and be in heart what I seem outwardly, and fill honestly my place among the members of Christ.

> Make me pure in thought and feeling,
> Kind and true in all I say,
> In my every deed revealing
> Jesus with me all the day.

TWENTIETH SATURDAY AFTER TRINITY.

"There be many that say, Who will show us any good? Lord, lift Thou up the light of Thy countenance upon us."—Ps. iv. 6.

THE cry of restless unbelief, and the quiet prayer of faith. Many turn here and there, asking from all but God what is good, and how to gain it. They try one or another of earth's streams, but thirst still. Pleasure, money, honour, prove vain. At last the soul asks in almost despair, if there be any good. Only in Him Who is the source of all good can man find what he wants. Those who trust the Good One are given what is best. His eyes are over them for good always, and His favour lightens even their darkest hours.

I ask not for some good, but for all good; not for what seems, but for what is good; not for passing, but for eternal good; not for what part of my nature craves, but for what God Who made me has provided for me. Nothing is good that does not come from Him, with His blessing. If I love Him and trust Him as my chief good, His love makes all things good for me. I listen not to the lies of Satan, or my own blind desires. I trust not the flattering promises of the world. I am not led away with the many, who wander, seeking they know not what. God is good, and He is ready to make known His goodness. I ask no more. Enough that the Source of all good is within my reach. I turn from all else to Him, that His face may shine down on me. He will give me light to know what is good, and how to follow it. He will make me good with His own Divine goodness, driving evil from me. He will keep my joys pure, and make my darkness to be light, giving sure peace in trial, and overruling all things for my true, eternal good.

O God, give me firm, happy faith in Thee as the One Good, and the Giver of all good! Let Thine eyes be over me for good, that all I enjoy, and all that seems hard or evil, may bring me what Thou knowest to be good.

> Thy love, and Thine alone, all joy bestows;
> Thy love, and Thine alone, all tears can dry;
> Thy Presence the perfection of repose,
> Oh! let its fulness all my loss supply.

The Twentieth Sunday after Trinity.

"O come, let us worship and bow down: let us kneel before the Lord our Maker."—Ps. xcv. 6.

GOD has made us, and has in Christ created us anew. As in the rest of life's work, so in worship; all our being—body, soul, and spirit—must join to do Him honour. The mind must not be idle or wandering; the heart must not be cold; the body must not be as if God had not made it for His service. Right knowledge and right feeling will guide to fitting posture of body. Even when no word is said and no boon is sought, it is good to bow down, silently adoring, while God's felt Presence moves the soul to devout thought and holy longing.

Want and sin bring me to God as my one helper. But worship is more than seeking what I can get. God calls me to draw near Him in faith, with those who behold His glory, and have a true feeling of what He is. Kneeling before Him, with bowed mind and heart, I can fix my soul's gaze on Him, till reverence and awe, and love and hope, find in Him their highest object. I can lay my whole self—body, soul, and spirit—at His feet, and join in the "Holy, holy, holy," of saints and angels. So, unworthy though I am, I can offer what God will not despise. I shall find myself more blessed when I come to give than when I come to receive. The power to admire God's glory and goodness will grow as I exercise it in adoration. I shall go back into the world under the solemn, grand influence of the Divine Presence; I shall feel more my own dignity, and the sacredness of my calling as a worshipper of God; I shall be hallowed, while I glorify the Holy One.

Almighty and most holy God, reveal Thyself to my faith, and give me the spirit of lowliest devotion, that I may adore Thee as I ought, and give Thee the honour due unto Thy name.

> Holy, holy, holy! though the darkness hide Thee,
> Though the eye of sinful man Thy glory cannot see.
> Only Thou art holy! there is none beside Thee,
> Perfect in power, in love, and purity.

Twenty-first Monday after Trinity.

"Sing unto the Lord, bless His name; show forth His salvation from day to day."—Ps. xcvi. 2.

ALL God's works praise Him, showing forth His wisdom and goodness. His saints rejoice in Him as their God. They make melody in their hearts, and with their lips they sing of His salvation. The voice of praise utters the soul's deep joy in God. It is an offering dear to God, Who loves to see His children glad in Him. It expresses the union of those who share a common blessedness. It proclaims God to those who know Him not. It joins in holy fellowship the Church on earth, and the Church whose whole life is praise.

With other sinners, I own my sins, and pray humbly to the Giver of all good. But as knowledge of sin and need saddens, knowledge of God lifts up with joy. With those in whose hearts are only love and gladness, I come before God. I count up His manifold free mercies, and proclaim the goodness to which I owe them. I tell of the holiness and glory which delight and awe my soul as my faith grows clear. I offer God a heart filled with His love, and eager to tell out its love for Him. I do not thank God only for what He bestows, but for what His mercy shows Him to be, and because He, so glorious in holiness, is my God. He welcomes me tenderly when I confess my sin, or ask His bounty; but He loves most to hear my voice tell that my heart is glad in Him, and that I am being set free from what parts me from Him. When I praise God I help, by sympathy of heart and voice, those who are cared for and blessed as I am, in the Church on earth. I learn to catch the spirit of the happy choirs that understand how to praise aright, and know better than I can, how worthy God is to be praised.

O Lord, make known Thy goodness, and open my lips, that my spirit may rejoice in God my Saviour, and that my mouth may never weary to show forth Thy praise.

'Tis Thine each soul to calm, each wayward thought reclaim,
And make our life a daily psalm of glory to Thy name;
A little while, and then shall come the glorious end,
And songs of angels and of men in perfect praise shall blend.

TWENTY-FIRST TUESDAY AFTER TRINITY.

"Is any among you afflicted? let him pray. Is any merry? let him sing psalms."—JAMES V. 13.

THE heart should turn towards God alike in grief and joy. The Father is with His children in both. He is a God of the hills where all is bright, and of the valleys where shadows darken. All care should be spread before Him. Apart from Him, no joy should gladden. Faith makes the sighing of the most heavy-laden have praise in it: hope tells of the thanksgiving to which it leads. Those who sing with joyfulness draw nigh to God in the highest, most unselfish way of prayer. The grateful love of a glad child-like heart wins new blessing.

I can bear grief well only by God's help. I can have pure joy only when praise marks it as God's gift. God calls me to Him, that I may tell Him all that is in my heart. He is so great in His Fatherly love, that nothing is small which has to do with my well-being. He bids me speak with child-like openness, taking His sympathy for granted. In my sorest trial I have this ground for praise, that I can pray; and my prayer, if true, passes into thanksgiving. There is comfort even in songs of mourning. In my gladdest hour I need to pray; and there is prayer in my drawing nigh, even when my one wish is to bless God's love. In sorrow I must sing, as I can, to remind myself of joy and hope still left, and to cheer my downcast soul. In merry hours I must pray, that my joy may not be that which ends in heaviness, but such as becomes a child of God. My words of prayer must tell of heartfelt need; my words of praise must be the outcome of melody in the heart. Prayer turns to praise: thanksgiving brings me to the God Who heareth prayer, so that He is at hand when trial comes.

Almighty Father, my one help in trial, and the source of all that cheers my path; teach me to spread my cares before Thee, and praise Thee for my every joy, that all my life may bind me to Thee in love and faith.

Through all the changing scenes of life, in trouble and in joy,
The praises of my God shall still my heart and tongue employ.
Fear Him, ye saints, and you will then have nothing else to fear;
Make you His service your delight, your wants shall be His care.

TWENTY-FIRST WEDNESDAY AFTER TRINITY.
"Giving thanks always for all things."—EPH. v. 20.

MAN knows not what is for his good. God guides all for him with perfect love and wisdom. Life, with its every power, and all that helps to make it glad, reminds of the Giver. The work of Christ and of the Holy Spirit makes known the Divine Father's love and mercy, and patient longing for His children's good. Trials and losses tell of God's care to warn and discipline and purify. Faith can see God's love in all things. So there is a ceaseless claim on the heart to feel thankfulness, and on the lips and the life to show it.

God's love gave me my being, and cares for me now. In His mercy He gives me a claim on His kindness and bounty, promising to hold from me, out of His infinite resources, nothing that is good. Whatever upholds and cheers my daily life is His free gift. I owe all my soul's good and my everlasting hope to Him. With His Son He gave all things. Hour by hour I am spared and borne with, and helped by new mercies. I share the life of Christ. I am taught and comforted by the Holy Spirit. I am strengthened by means of grace, and cheered by the hope of glory. My Father's firm, wise love seeks my true and lasting good in all the sorrows He sends, or allows to come. He waits to bless me by means of each. I will count up and think over my great debt, that my heart may be roused. I will try to own God's goodness in things great and small—in what I can see to be good, and in what tries faith. I can thank God best by using His gifts well. I will pray that in my whole self and life I may thank Him, Who is always in all things showing loving kindness.

O Lord, to Whom I owe my being, and all good and hope for time and eternity, grant me to see Thy love in all things, and to show in a life always lived to Thy glory the thankfulness of a devoted heart.

We thank Thee, Holy Father, for all that gentle love
Which leads these earthly, anxious hearts to peaceful homes
    above;
Which shows the passing vanity of worldly cares and joys,
And man's strong will and passion's might in tenderness
    destroys.

TWENTY-FIRST THURSDAY AFTER TRINITY.

"When the King came in to see the guests, He saw there a man which had not on a wedding garment."—MATT. xxii. 11.

HE was among the many called, but not among the few chosen. The wedding robe had been offered to him, as to the other guests. He chose to come in his own way. He passed among men without remark or blame. He did not doubt himself, till the King, Who had seen him all along, "came in," and, in His felt presence, he saw the truth. Speechless and shamed, he did not dare to say "how" he came without the wedding garment. It was too late to put it on, too late to ask for mercy.

I am called to share the joy of Christ's union with His Church. The feast of grace is spread now, to prepare for the feast of glory, when Christ takes to Himself His spotless bride. God welcomes me, poor and squalid, out of the highways of sin, that He may make me fit to take my place with saints. Only what He gives will do; I may not come as I like. My own best is as filthy rags. No mere outside covering can hide from Him my nature's inner vileness. He tells me to "put on the Lord Jesus Christ." The wedding robe is that spiritual character which comes from true, abiding, deepening union with Christ. It is not put over me from without: it shines forth from the centre of my being, a clothing of purity. Christ in me changes all I am, even where the searching eye of God alone sees me. Now is the time to see that I have that righteousness which does away with my own evil, and takes its place. Am I deceiving myself in self-will and carelessness? Am I wearing before men what leaves me unchanged in the sight of God? Or am I indeed putting off the old man, and being renewed after Christ's image? God "sees" me now, and knows.

O Lord, strip from me all false trust and wilfulness; give me that inward holiness which will glorify my nature and fit me to appear among Thy holy ones.

> Lord, Thou alone the grace canst give
> To fit me for the home on high;
> Oh, may I please Thee while I live,
> And in Thy loving favour die.

TWENTY-FIRST FRIDAY AFTER TRINITY.

"See then that ye walk circumspectly, not as fools, but as wise."—EPH. v. 15.

THE words mean, "Take heed how ye walk, strictly." Christian life is not standing still; it is a walk—a steady going forward. There is for each man one right path to the safe good end. It needs care to find, and pains to keep. The wise man knows this. He wishes to succeed, and fears to fail. He doubts himself. He has a rule of life, and lives by it watchfully. Day by day he seeks new light and grace, that he may go on with firm sure step where God's will leads. Fools have no rule, no clear aim. They drift anyhow, any whither.

In few and evil days I have a work to do for my eternity. I have to find and make my way through a world full of snares and foes. I can learn, if I will, how I "ought to walk and to please God." The will of God is plainly made known. The example of Christ is full. The truths of the Gospel make their strong claim on my heart and life. I have knowledge and grace within reach, and can know the worth of success, and how to make it sure. Am I wisely alive to my position, or am I among those whom God sees to be "fools"? Do I waste time and strength through want of a rule? Am I bringing on myself shame and grief through want of care to live by rule? Am I slow in studying truth so as to know what my faith is, and in learning how to act upon what I believe? Am I, perhaps, following a wrong rule, or following a right rule wrongly? Am I irregular in my reading and meditation, and prayer and communions, and other means of grace? Is my religious "walk" a blind, heedless wandering hither and thither, an aimless lounging, a series of stops and falls and goings back?

Almighty God, grant me wisdom to learn how I ought to walk through the perils of these evil days, and grace to rule my life prudently, according to Thy holy will.

> There are stony ways to tread,
>   Give the strength we sorely lack;
> There are tangled paths to thread,
>   Light us, lest we lose the track.
> Holy Jesu! day by day lead us in the narrow way.

TWENTY-FIRST SATURDAY AFTER TRINITY.
"*Honour all men.*"—1 PET. ii. 17.

GOD claims honour for all men, as their due from all. They are of worth in His eyes as His creatures, redeemed at great cost to be the temples of the Holy Ghost. Angels love to be their ministers. They are more or less spoiled by sin; but, even in ruins, God's handiwork is to be treated reverently. What seems utterly fallen, God's grace may yet build up again in more than its first glory. Authority, wisdom, goodness give men claim to honour, over and above what man has as man. He who fails to honour his brother man, dishonours himself and his Maker.

I honour God, and for His sake honour man. I honour myself, fearing what degrades, aiming to think and feel and speak and act as a son of God and an heir of heaven. I honour those whom God sets over me in the Church, the State, or the family, and those who show God's special light and grace in mind and character. But I own the dignity of man as man, even in his fallen state. I dare not scorn, in thought or word, him for whom Christ gave Himself, and who, by the power of grace, may be a saint on high. I cannot judge how far the sin I loathe has destroyed God's work in any soul, or how much God sees left there still. I dare not be rough where God is tender. I show honour to the sinner by doing my best to help him to cast off his sin. I am gentle with the weak, lest I break the bruised reed and displease God. I treat with reverent care the little ones for whom Christ is jealous. I cherish a right sense of man's worth, that I may do my duty honestly to God and man. So I grow to be thoughtful, courteous, gentle, always active in care for man's good in body, mind, and soul.

Teach me, O Lord, to live, with watchful, lowly self-respect, as a child of Thine, and always to show, in all things, a right sense of the worth of those whom Thou hast made in Thy likeness and redeemed.

> The world despise,
>   Account its honours and its pleasures nought;
>   Look on no man with scornful eyes,
>   He is thy God-born brother, by thy Saviour bought.

The Twenty-first Sunday after Trinity.

"Be strong in the Lord, and in the power of His might."
—EPH. vi. 10.

MAN has no strength of his own; but weakness is no excuse, for he can do and become all things, if he will. Nothing is too hard for the Lord, in Whose might man may be strong. He who remains weak, unable to do God's work, and beaten by his soul's foes, fails through unbelief and sloth. He has either not made his own, or not used the power offered. "Be strong" is a command, and it is a promise. God wills to give what He tells man to have. The Almighty wills to be in man the power He calls on man to put forth.

Strong foes are against me, with whom I must fight for my life. Hard work is set me, needing patient skill and great power to do it well. How can I crush down sin in my nature, withstand the evil around me, and fulfil my duty? I am weak, without will or force to succeed. I cannot know this humbling truth too plainly. But I can have a might not my own. In that I can be full of calm boldness, and more than conqueror. I can draw upon the almightiness of the same Lord Who makes the claim on me for what needs strength. I can abide in Christ, and He in me. One with Him, His power is mine; He Who is God does in me and through me the will of God. The fault is mine if I fail or am overthrown; for I can do all things in Christ Which strengtheneth me. O for a right knowledge of my danger, and my own utter helplessness! O to be strong in faith to take God at His word, and strong in hope to be glad and brave in Him! O to seek with true resolve more living, active oneness with man's only strength, and to be ever growing stronger in the Lord!

Almighty and merciful Father, lead me in my weakness to seek for Divine strength through Christ, that in union with Him I may be strong and brave to overcome evil, and to do my work for Thee.

> Strong in the Lord of Hosts,
> And in His mighty power;
> Who in the strength of Jesus trusts
> Is more than conqueror.

TWENTY-SECOND MONDAY AFTER TRINITY.

"*Take unto you the whole armour of God.*"—EPH. vi. 13.

GOD arms His soldiers. We need the whole suit of mail, and all the weapons He gives. Truth—sincerity of purpose, braces the man and holds the rest of the armour together. Righteousness keeps sin from reaching the heart. The peace of the Gospel gives readiness to tread firmly in active work. Against faith temptations strike harmless. The gift of salvation emboldens to stand upright and press on with brave hope towards its fulness. God's Word is a sword which the Spirit nerves man to wield against the tempter. Prayer keeps the flame of the soul's life burning.

God gives the armour. It is my part to take it thankfully, to put it on carefully, and use it boldly in God's name. I need it all. The stroke of death may find its way to my soul through the least opening, or where one weapon is wanting. Am I true, acting with honest single aim? Do I labour and pray to put between my heart and evil a breastplate of strongly-wrought virtues—even the righteousness that is from God? Do I seek from the Gospel that Divine peace which will keep heart and mind, and will and strength, ready for each call of duty? Are the truths of the faith so sure to me, that temptations of unbelief and sin are vain to shake my hold on God? Do I strive to realise what my Saviour has given, and will give, so that I can lift my head, and go on heartily towards the hope of full salvation? Do I make God's Word my own, so as to wield it readily, taught by the Spirit Who gave it? Does the same Spirit pray in me, and guide my desires towards God, that blessings always waiting may be always waited for? God means this state for me: how far is it mine?

Almighty God, may I so take and use the armour Thou givest, that I may pass unhurt through my time of warfare, and be crowned among those who overcome.

> Wield the great power of grace to win renown;
> Aim at the highest place, the brightest crown;
> Fearing the only loss—the shame of sin,
> Manfully bear the cross, till crowns you win.

TWENTY-SECOND TUESDAY AFTER TRINITY.

"Resist the devil, and he will flee from you. Draw nigh to God, and He will draw nigh to you."—JAMES iv. 7, 8.

NONE are in Satan's power, or need be harmed by him. He flees from all who withstand him. He will return, but he can again be put to flight. None need be far from God. He draws nigh to all who in heart and will meet His call to come to Him. Man is helpless to resist Satan till he has drawn nigh to God for strength. God will not draw nigh to souls that have no will to resist Satan. Those who draw nigh to Satan forsake and resist God. They provoke Him to resist them, or draw nigh in judgment, when they flee in vain before their enemies.

God has drawn nigh and given me the first power to come to Him and to resist the evil one. I depart from God when I fail to use that power, or to keep up the union from which it comes. I resist God when I break away from His protecting, guiding hand, and put forth the evil in me to meet Satan half-way. I can only stand firm against my foe by pressing close to my Father. I can only be free to draw nigh to God by thrusting Satan from me with all my strength of prayer and will. If I yield to Satan, I go out of God's safe keeping, and lose the peace He gives. If I wander from God, Satan finds me alone, without will or power to defend myself. As long as I am in the body, I shall need to watch and fight against the tempter. Till I see God, His call comes and His grace reaches out to draw me nearer to Him. How without excuse I am for my every sin and failure, for my faint-heartedness, for my slowness to repent, for my state still so far from God! But what hope is mine, if I will, even now, act upon God's sure word!

O Lord, Who hast drawn nigh to me in Christ and given me Thy Holy Spirit, enable me to persevere in resisting Satan and drawing nearer to Thee, till I am safe from evil in Thy presence.

> Quit you like men, be strong in God's great might;
> Resist the false and wrong, uphold the right;
> Fight for the home on high, as soldiers true;
> Think of the Father's eye that watches you.

Twenty-second Wednesday after Trinity.

"A bruised reed shall He not break, and smoking flax shall He not quench, till He send forth judgment unto victory."—
Matt. xii. 20.

IT is the day of grace. Not yet has Christ made known His power, and triumphed as Judge of all. Still He waits, and pleads, and helps. He bears with man's weakness; He deals gently with those who have fallen and are bruised; He seeks to heal their wounds; He is careful not to lay too much upon them, or let their trial be too sore. He does not scorn the least smouldering flame of right desire, or faith, or love. He cherishes tenderly the struggling life newly kindled in the soul, that it may burn brightly to God's praise.

How much do I owe to my Lord's patient gentleness! When sin has scarred and weakened my soul, He might have crushed me and cast me away. But He has borne with me, and dealt kindly with me, till my soundness might be restored. When my religious life has burned low and almost failed, He has not judged me harshly. He has not left me to myself, or withdrawn the fire from above, well nigh smothered by earthly things. He has waited patiently, trying how and when it might be quickened by His Holy Spirit into a blessed and blessing glow, and shine before men to His praise. Let me be thankful. Let the loving tenderness of Christ cheer me when I am cast down, and my soul feels weak and wounded, and cold and dark, and when grace seems only not quite gone out. Let me be more earnest to be made strong for His work, and to shine for His glory. Let His victory over me, which He must win, be a triumph of His love. Let me beware of being among the foes over whom He shall be victorious. Let me show His Spirit, and thus prove that His love has won me.

O Lord Jesus, give me thankful desire to serve Thee with firm will and zealous love, that evil may be judged and destroyed in me, and that I may share Thy victory.

> Thou wilt not break the bruisèd reed,
>   Nor quench the flame that feebly burns;
> In Thee is all the power I need,
>   The grace for which my spirit yearns.

TWENTY-SECOND THURSDAY AFTER TRINITY.

" Whoso shall offend one of these little ones which believe in Me, it were better for him that a millstone were hanged about his neck, and that he were drowned in the depth of the sea."— MATT. xviii. 6.

STERNLY Christ warns those who draw or drive the young and feeble from Him. Better to die, than dare the might of God's love by helping Satan to win those whom Christ died and lives to save. He "offends the little ones" who makes right-doing hard or sin tempting; who laughs down devotion or watchfulness; who leads astray by bad example; who discredits religion by his inconsistent life; who shakes faith, who daunts hope.

Each sin that hurts my soul, wounds my Saviour's love. But what I am and do tells on others who trust me, or watch my ways and mark my words. I help to lead right or to mislead the young, whose characters are taking shape, and whose course for good or evil is being fixed. My influence is more or less felt on some beginners in the Christian life. I may fail to hold up a stumbler, or cheer a trembler on past his trial. I may put temptation in the way, so that he falls, or turns aside and leaves Christ. I may add to the weight of some weak one's cross, so that he lays it down despairingly. I may plant unbelief in a simple mind by careless words, or by disowning God in my life. I may soil a pure heart by giving knowledge of sin. I may lead the guileless into doubtful paths, and help them to still the voice of God's warning love. How much grace I want for each step in life! Christ warns me to take heed lest I harm, not my own soul only, but the souls of my weak brethren. My guilt is great if I harm Christ's members by want of care; who can tell what it is, if I do so wilfully? What terror, to turn the Saviour's love for souls against me!

Almighty God, make me to live in holy fear, lest I fail of Thy love, or turn Thy love against me by causing to fall or go astray a weak brother for whom Christ died.

    He folds the little ones in careful arm,
      To make the feeble sure of safety there;
    To warn of judgment those who do them harm,
      To give them to His faithful people's care.

Twenty-Second Friday after Trinity.

"O thou of little faith, wherefore didst thou doubt?"
—Matt. xiv. 31.

ST. PETER felt his faith firm. He longed to prove it, and go to his Master and walk with Him. He did not presume to go unbidden; he prayed to be called. While he only thought of his Lord and of doing His bidding, the same power that bore up Christ upheld him. When he began to think of himself and look away to the winds and waves, his hold on God loosened and he began to sink. His weakened faith had still strength to cry for the saving hand, and to grasp it. He shows what faith can do, and how faith fails.

I dare not, unbidden, court danger and count on special help. Where my call is sure I may boldly go, whether in life's common way, or in some great venture of faith. Christ's will is my safe guide, not my own self-trust or self-will. At His word I can leave all that man seems most to need. While I look to Him and forget self, only seeking to obey His call, I shall not sink in any sorrow or temptation. I can go where no man can go without God. I can do what no man can do alone. Underneath shall be the everlasting arms. My feet shall walk firmly; and, though dangers threaten, there shall be calm within me. God's help never fails, but my faith may. Let me only think of Christ and His will and promise. What I am, and what my difficulties are, need not alarm me. These are not in the way of His power or love, unless they draw off my thoughts, and loosen the firm grasp of my faith. When I turn from Him, I doubt. When I doubt, I sink. Then my one hope is in the hand held out. I perish, if He save me not. It is well to be restored by His grace; it is better not to fail, and need His reproof.

O Lord, make me willing always to obey Thy call and go where Thou dost bid me, in undoubting faith, thinking not of my own weakness or my danger, but of Thee, and sure that I cannot perish while Thou art near to save.

My Saviour, Thou hast bid me come, O bid me come again,
And till I reach my heavenly home my sinking soul sustain;
While walking as at Thy command o'er this life's troubled sea,
O save me by Thine outstretched hand until I am with Thee.

Twenty-Second Saturday after Trinity.

"Which hope we have as an anchor of the soul, both sure and stedfast, and which entereth into that within the veil; whither the Forerunner is for us entered."—HEB. vi. 19, 20.

WHILE the soul is still out on life's unquiet waves, it has not the happy rest for which it looks and longs. Christ has passed in to the safe haven, where faith sees Him. Hope clings fast to Him. That anchor holds firm Rock which will not fail. But hope will let go, unless faith and love help to make it steadfast. The soul must be drawn on surely, till it comes where its hope is made fast. It is not enough that Christ is in His glory "within the veil." He must be in man the power to move heavenward, and so be the "hope of glory."

In my care and sin, tossed about and in danger, my soul desires the peace that is within the veil. Wish becomes hope when I know that Christ is there. For He was born as man, and died for me, and, still the same, He makes my cause His own care on high, and pleads His work in my behalf. My hope stretches up to Him. He makes heaven more desired, and assures me that He is there to bring me to be with Him. So love and faith make my hope firm, as Christ draws me towards Him in true devotion, and I learn more how sure His word of promise is. "Christ in" me yearns for the good things above, where the same Christ is at God's right hand. As He forms me after His pure likeness, I have better hope of that unknown blessedness which He prepares. I can wait in patience for what is yet unseen, if I am humbly sure that Christ draws me nearer to it, and that His work in me goes on. For my hope is not that of the hypocrite which shall perish, but a sure confidence that Christ has begun what He will perfect within the veil.

Almighty God, grant that my hope may be fastened to Christ Who has gone before, and that I may be drawn towards where He is, by His grace working in me.

Here faith is ours, and heavenly hope, and grace to lead us higher;
But there are perfectness and peace beyond our best desire;
Oh! by Thy love and anguish, Lord, and by Thy life laid down,
Grant that we fall not from Thy grace, nor cast away our crown.

The Twenty-second Sunday after Trinity.

"His windows being open in his chamber toward Jerusalem, he kneeled upon his knees three times a day, and prayed, and gave thanks before his God, as he did aforetime."—DAN. vi. 10.

DANIEL might have found many fair reasons for giving way. Why should he lose life, with his power to serve God and protect his brethren, when he might be safe by ceasing to pray openly for only forty days? But Daniel's mind was made up. No law of man could change his clear duty to God. He chose to face death, rather than lose God's favour. He could not live prayerless, or seem to do so. He made no boastful display, but went on quietly "as aforetime," leaving his cause with God.

Well for me if, like Daniel, I am open to attack, only through my faithfulness to God. Well for me if, like him, I take my stand, before the evil day, and am found ready. I must not go out of my way to provoke men to sin by wronging me. Nor must I save myself by sinning. Sloth and false prudence will offer many ways of sparing self. The bold, straightforward course is simplest and safest. God can take care of His own cause, and my cowardice or falsehood are no help. All that men say or do leaves God's claim on me unchanged. It is God's will that I bear what it costs me to do His will. It is due to God that I so love and fear Him as not to hide what I feel. It is due to myself to be true, and to seem what I am. It is due to my fellow-men to show that God is real to me, and to help them, by my example, to take God's side boldly. Let me learn to be sure of God, and gain fixed principles of duty. Then no trial shall take me by surprise. I shall not think I do anything great while I calmly hold fast to God, and go on "as aforetime."

Almighty God, Who never failest them that trust in Thee, give me the calm courage of sure faith and earnest love, that I may follow Christ in the plain path of duty, unmoved by any fear of man or longing for earthly good.

> Long as Thou shalt smile upon me,
> God of wisdom, love, and might,
> Foes may hate, and friends disown me;
> Show Thy face, and all is bright.

TWENTY-THIRD MONDAY AFTER TRINITY.

"Are not two sparrows sold for a farthing? and one of them shall not fall on the ground without your Father."—MATT. x. 29.

GOD cares for His least creatures. Till He allows it, no bird falls. He is not the Father of the sparrows; but He has made men in His likeness; at great cost He has redeemed them, that they might share His nature, and be His children. They are far better than the birds; they have a new value in God's eyes, and He has given them a new claim on Him. They need fear nothing while they fear Him with a child's loving fear. He often lets them be tried, that what makes them better than the birds may reach its full growth.

My heavenly Father's care for the creatures which know Him not, assures me of His care for me. He has made me able to learn of Him and love Him. The price He paid to give me the place of child proves how much He values me. I am safe in His keeping, and may go on where He calls. All His might and love are on my side. My one fear must be lest I forsake Him through fear or love of aught else. None can pluck me out of His hands. Sorrow and death cannot harm me while I am in His care. I am better than the birds, as God's child whose home is heaven. God watches over me, not only or mainly that I may live long or have rest here. He deals with me as one to whose high and eternal interests all else must give way. What looks like lost is often true gain. My Father sees all to the end. He cares for me as one whose life reaches on through eternity. Even the hairs of my head are numbered. He overlooks none of my smallest passing interests: how much more does He guide firmly what bears on my everlasting good.

Almighty Father, without Whom no sparrow falls, fill me with sure trust in Thy fatherly care and goodness, that no fear of man or love of sin may turn me from the straight path of Thy will.

> Can a child presume to choose where or how to live?
> Can a father's love refuse all the best to give?
> More Thou givest every day than the best can claim,
> Nor withholdest aught that may glorify Thy name.

TWENTY-THIRD TUESDAY AFTER TRINITY.

"I forgave thee all that debt, because thou desiredst me: shouldest not thou also have had compassion on thy fellow-servant?"—MATT. xviii. 32, 33.

WE are in debt to God for work undone, for time and talents wasted, or used against Him. We cannot make good any part of what is owing. All that is left us is only enough for the days to come, and may not be spent on the past. God spreads the account before us that we may ask grace, and find more than we hope. If we are hard to others, while we cringe before God, our penitence is proved to be only the selfishness of cowards. We put away God's love when we refuse to let it make us loving. We find no more mercy than we show.

I have received mercy, and I shall need mercy till the end. God only knows how much I owe, and shall owe, to His free grace. Beside all that debt which I can never pay, what trifles are the worst wrongs done to me! Is there no charge which might be brought against me by my fellow-servants? Who am I, that I should claim a right to withhold mercy? Can I dare to plead the Cross, while God sees my heart hard and unforgiving against those who in some small way hurt my pride, or spoil my ease. On God's mere mercy all my hope rests: I am taught to prove my hope good by my readiness to forgive. If I have gained, and not lost God's pardon, I shall be thankful, lowly, and loving: wrongs against me will remind me of my own great sins against God. So they will not rouse my pride, but humble me. When I forgive, I show that God's goodness has found a place in me, and gives me a power not my own. God forgives for Christ's sake, that I may, for Christ's sake, show myself loving. God's mercy is changed to judgment when I refuse mercy to others.

O merciful God, grant me to feel my need of mercy, and to be lowly and loving, and ready always to forgive, as Thou, for Christ's sake, dost forgive me.

Grace, all unmerited and free, Thy sweet, forgiving grace,
Instructs us, as embraced by Thee, our brother to embrace;
Since Thou our infinite offence dost pardon and forget,
His debt of scarce an hundred pence we cheerfully remit.

TWENTY-THIRD WEDNESDAY AFTER TRINITY.

"Sincere and without offence, till the day of Christ; being filled with the fruits of righteousness."—PHIL. 1. 10, 11.

MEN are called to bring God praise by willing and doing righteousness. He is "sincere" whose nature and life show no flaw, no stain, when held up to God's light; or who still is clear from fault even when shaken by hard, rough trial. He is "without offence" who climbs straight on after Christ, not stumbling himself, nor hindering others. He is filled with the fruits of righteousness, in whom Christ dwells, making the life abound in all holy works, forming the character by habits of right-doing.

St. Paul states what height God means me to reach; I must not rest below it. It is the end set before me and all those in whom the faithful God begins the good work. My hope for the day of Christ depends on how far in lowly, earnest wish and aim I rise to it, or fall short. I dare not say in plain words to Christ in me, that some faults must be left in my character, that I must go on yielding to some temptations, that there are some fruits of righteousness that I choose to do without. What does my life say? Am I led on by no high aim, content, perhaps, to think myself only as bad as others, or to hope that God will not quite cast me off? Do I look on sin as a thing of course, and a life full of good works done by Christ in me as a life I need not vainly try to live? Or do I become more blameless before God, and more harmless among men, showing that my heart grows pure, and my will is more true to God's? Do I watch to learn what is best, and rouse myself to do it with all God's might, that I may bring praise to Him Who worketh in me, and may have my fruit in being at last filled with His righteousness?

O God of holiness, make me pure in Thy holy eyes, and fill me with every gift of grace, that I may glorify Thee in all I do, till the day of Jesus Christ.

> Oh! for a heart that never sins;
> Oh! for a soul washed white;
> Oh! for a voice to praise our King,
> Nor weary day or night!

TWENTY-THIRD THURSDAY AFTER TRINITY.

"*If any man sin, we have an advocate with the Father, Jesus Christ the righteous.*"—1 JOHN ii. 1.

THE words do not encourage those who think lightly of sin to go on in carelessness. They give comfort to the true seekers after holiness, whose failures might tempt them to lose heart. The most watchful fall short through their own weakness. But so long as their life's aim is to sin not, they need not lose their hope. He Whose blood cleanses from all sin, ever pleads with His Father and theirs. The prayer of lowly penitence is heard, the sin is forgiven, and grace comes, enabling them to abide more closely in Him, in Whom is no sin.

He Who gave His Son for me is my Father. The Righteous One pleads for me according to His will. Always the power of the work of God's love in Christ is being exerted to save me from sin. My least fault is in spite of that, and makes it so far fruitless. Well may I dread sin. If I seek the holiness God seeks for me, I need to be assured that God does not cast me off when I sin; so He gives me this word of cheer. I must not doubt God, because I am proved weak and unworthy. Though I fall, God will make me stand, if with honest heart I own my fault and pray for cleansing. My sins warn me where I am weak and have been unwatchful; they show me what God knew before, and is ready to set right. Let me pray for a more firm will to sin not. Let me seek more abiding union with the Righteous One, Who can in His strength keep me from falling. Be it my comfort that when I fail, He is my advocate with a Father. Be it my fixed aim to be presented faultless before the presence of His glory.

Almighty Father, grant that by the power of Christ living in me I may be saved from wilful sin, and that when I fall or fail through my own weakness, Thy grace may restore me, through the merits and mediation of my Saviour.

> He Who for men their surety stood,
> And poured on earth His cleansing blood,
> Pursues in heaven His mighty plan,
> The Saviour and the Friend of man.

TWENTY-THIRD FRIDAY AFTER TRINITY.

"He Which hath begun a good work in you will perform it until the day of Jesus Christ."—PHIL. i. 6.

ALL good in men is God's work. The feeblest will or power to be and do right is a pledge that the faithful, unchanging God has begun what He is willing, as well as able, to bring to perfection. He begins without our choice; but He will not go on in spite of our sloth and unbelief. He calls on us to be workers together with Him, strong in the grace He gives, and cheered by His sure promise. He wills to carry on His work by us and in us, till we are found blameless, with our work finished.

God has begun His work in me. I have been baptized into Christ, and received the Holy Spirit. I have been made a sharer in the blessings and divine power at work in the Church of Christ. Each right wish and longing and effort is from God. What God has done is a promise and earnest of all He waits to do. His word cannot fail, His meaning cannot change; I may be calmly sure of Him always and to the end. But I must doubt and watch myself. Have I put God's love from me, or let His grace lie unthought of and unused? If His work in me is to bring me any good, it must go on. My faith must meet, and grasp, and make my own, God's grace. My will must yield to God's, and put forth the powers bestowed upon me. I must look up each day for needful daily help, that my character and life may show the handiwork of God growing towards perfection. There is no room for doubt or faint-heartedness while God is pledged not to fail me. There is no excuse for want of care, while so much is to be done "until the day of Christ," and I can make in vain the loving purpose of the Almighty.

Almighty Father, I thank Thee for the love which has blessed me, and which assures me of Thy unchanging good-will; grant that nothing in me may hinder Thy love from perfecting its work until the day of Jesus Christ.

He willeth not the death of one
For whom the Saviour bled;
The work the Spirit hath begun
He willeth perfected.

TWENTY-THIRD SATURDAY AFTER TRINITY.

"In the world ye shall have tribulation: but be of good cheer; I have overcome the world."—JOHN xvi. 33.

THE words are true for all disciples always. The world, which was against Christ, is against His members. They must be, as He was, while in the world, not of it. They have to bear its hate, and watch against its temptings. Christ does not free His followers from the common trials of life. But He gives them the cheer that comes from strength. He, as man, bore the worst of all that the world can do. One with Him, His members can have sure peace, and be strong to overcome.

I am not misled by vain hopes. I am plainly warned that through much tribulation I must pass after Christ to where He is. Besides man's common burden, I must carry the cross in a narrow, steep path: I must deny self, and suffer at the hands of my Lord's foes. But nothing need dismay or crush me. I can be of good cheer, with heart and mind at peace. The world's hate has been dared; its woes have been borne; its snares have been made harmless. Christ overcame for me; now He is ready to endure and triumph over again in me. He feels with me, having known in Himself what tries to cast me down, and, remembering the days of His fleshly weakness, He makes my cause His own. His strength, made perfect through His tribulation, is all for me. I will not shrink from what He sends me forth to meet. I forsake the world for Him; I will not leave Him for what the false world promises. I am careful only to abide in Him, that I may have the peace and good cheer of God. So shall I always overcome, till I am taken out of the world, and am safe from fear of evil.

O Lord, Who through sore tribulation didst overcome the world for me, be my shelter in storm, my strength in fight, my holiness when I am tempted; grant me Thy peace, till I follow whither Thou art gone.

> Be my strength in weakness, be my peace in strife;
> Come with Thine own meekness, quieting my life;
> When I faint in sorrow, bring Thy comfort near;
> When I dread the morrow, come with hope to cheer.

The Twenty-third Sunday after Trinity.

"*Our conversation is in heaven.*"—Phil. iii. 20.

THE words mean, our citizenship is in heaven, our country is there. Not only do we hope for heaven, we belong to it now. The Church on high and in earth is one. As members of that, we are fellow-citizens of the saints and of the household of God. Even now we enjoy much privilege and blessing, though the full glory is not yet ours. We are strangers and pilgrims, who seek their own land. We are blessed by the way, but are not at home. We are bound by the laws of a higher world.

With a great sum God obtained for me the freedom of the city which is above. Born an alien, I am free-born by His grace in Christ. What honour and responsibility are mine! I am enrolled among those whom God calls His, to whom He gives share in the rights and hopes of His kingdom. The holy ones around the throne acknowledge me. Though as yet far from my true home, fighting and toiling out in the world, I am given a claim upon the protection and bounty of the King. He cares for my good, and orders my state and duties on earth, to train me for the place He will call me to fill above. I must not join myself to the citizens of this country, whose whole care is for earthly things, and be as one of them. I must not guide my life by worldly rules, but show the character of one who belongs to heaven, and bears a noble name. Let me meet sorrows and temptations without surprise, knowing myself a stranger here. Let me be brave and patient, with my heart in the better country towards which I press, and looking for the Saviour to bring me there.

Almighty God, Who hast given me a share in the hopes and privileges of Thy kingdom, enable me always so to live on earth as a citizen of heaven, that I may look with joy for the coming of the Saviour.

Raise us up from earth to heaven, give us wings of faith and love,
Gales of holy aspirations wafting us to realms above;
That with hearts and minds uplifted, we with Christ our Lord may dwell,
Where He sits enthroned in glory, in His heavenly citadel.

Twenty-Fourth Monday after Trinity.

"We walk by faith, not by sight."—2 Cor. v. 7.

FAITH is a power which God bestows to enable man to receive His truth and grace. It opens up to the soul the realities of the unseen world, and gives sureness to hope in looking beyond things now and here. It enables to judge and act, not by what things seem, but by what in truth they are. It frees man's life from the fear of man, and the power of what is passing. It gives new motives, and makes a way for Divine and holy influences to act upon the will. It reveals to man God's dealings with him, and his life's true meaning and strength and aim.

The world I see is not all with which I have to do. The future need not be dark before me. Faith shows me a new world, with interests which concern me most nearly. Faith calls away my hopes from this life's good to that which is unbounded and unending. The look of things ought not to mislead. Faith shows me their true place and worth. By faith I know of a world unseen, with which I have to do, where my treasure is being stored, where my hopes shall find rest, whither my heart is drawn. I live, seeing by faith Him Who is invisible, owning His right over me, sure of His love, trusting His care. I take Him at His word in all things. I do His will, however strange it seems. I thankfully seek His grace, in whatever form He veils it. Faith weakens temptation, for by it I am aware of a God Whose eye is on me; I measure the worth of godliness and the loss of sin. Faith lightens sorrow, and cheers loneliness by making felt the presence and sympathy of God, and assuring of the truth of His promises. By faith I can be guided in a safe course, cheered by a sure hope.

Almighty God, save me from the power of things seen and passing; give me faith to feel Thy nearness always; and to seek in the way of Thy will the everlasting good which Thou dost promise.

> Give me joy or sadness, this be all my care,
> That eternal gladness I with Thee may share;
> Day by day prepare me as Thou seest best,
> Then let angels bear me to Thy promised rest.

TWENTY-FOURTH TUESDAY AFTER TRINITY.

"I am Jesus Whom thou persecutest."—ACTS ix. 5.

WORDS of comfort to the wronged, and of warning to those who wrong them. Christ is one with His people who suffer for Him. The Head feels with the members. Their griefs are His. His strength is theirs, to uphold them to the end. Wrongs done to them are sins against Him. Those who harm His least and humblest dare the Almighty. All sin is persecution of Jesus Christ. It makes His sorrows in vain. It wounds His love. It denies, rejects, dishonours Him. He pleads with sinners, showing His power, but speaking gentle words, and waiting to win the heart and will and life.

Am I called to meet loss and care for Christ's name? Do I try to bear life's common griefs in a Christ-like spirit? I may be calm and strong. He Who is my God is in a real way touched by what pains me. The unjust thoughts, the hard words, the acts of wrong or unkindness that trouble me persecute Him. What He bears I can bear with His help. I can forget my own hardship in the thought of what He endures for me, and of the sin of those who thus provoke Him. Does zeal for God's truth make me unloving and bitter? Let me beware lest my zeal, like Saul's, be blind; and prejudice or ignorance makes me war against Him Whose cause I think to champion. What if I scorn and revile those whom God loves? What if Christ be in those whom I cast out as evil? The Saviour's oneness with His people warns me against paining, even by little unkindness and want of thought, those with whom I live. My temper or roughness or other fault may help to purify them, but it is sin in me, done against Christ in them and in myself. I persecute Christ by tempting His weak ones to sin.

O Lord Jesus, make me watchful lest I persecute Thee in Thy members, and comfort me with the knowledge that Thou art touched with a feeling of all my sorrows.

God's justice is a bed, where we our anxious hearts may lay,
And, weary with ourselves, may muse our discontent away;
Muse on his justice, downcast soul, muse and take better heart;
Back with thine angel to the field, and bravely do thy part.

TWENTY-FOURTH WEDNESDAY AFTER TRINITY.

"Inasmuch as ye have done it unto one of the least of these My brethren, ye have done it unto Me."—MATT. xxv. 40.

CHRIST is one with all His members. The feeblest and most forgotten by the world are parts of Himself. He cares even for those who know Him not. Thus He is among men still, and asks their kindness. Thus men may have the joy and honour of ministering to their Saviour in the persons of His suffering ones. What is done for His sake, He counts as done to Himself. He does not ask great things, but great love. He prizes the simple deeds of brotherly-kindness which are in the power of all. What His people think trifling and forget, He remembers that He may reward.

If I have love to Christ, my life will prove it. In the power of the love He gives I can be as He was in this world of care. I can be His voice and hand to comfort and relieve. I can see in all want and sorrow, what Christ bids me feel for and try to make less. So I can not only do angels' work, but God's. More than this, I can hear in each sufferer's appeal the voice of Him to Whose griefs I owe all my hope. Those whom I help are not alone. I do more than entertain angels; I minister to the Lord of angels. What I do for Him, He accepts as done to Him. A cup of water given in His name refreshes Christ, Who thirsts to find in me the fruit of His work. The pleasantness I am able to add to the life of others, by the manner and the little words and deeds which He inspires, pleases Him. The more His love in me is strong and pure, the more simply and naturally will I show love, the less will I seem to myself to do what is worth naming. But He takes note of all, and will let nothing be unrewarded.

O Lord Jesus, use me to make known Thy kindness in this sad world, and grant that what Thy love gives the will and power to do may be accepted as done to Thee.

I want the unreflecting love, which simply Thee obeys,
Content, if Thou at last approve, nor on the action stays;
Still would I my own good forget, which is not, Lord, my own,
Till Thou Thy servant's works approve, and praise what grace has done.

TWENTY-FOURTH THURSDAY AFTER TRINITY.

" Who shall change our vile body, that it may be fashioned like unto His glorious body."—PHIL. iii. 21.

CHRIST humbled Himself to be made flesh. He wore a body which was in the power of pain, weakness, and death, showing His state of humiliation. He now has a body in which His glory appears. He became as we are, in all but sin, that He might raise us to be as He is, so far as man may. His power can subdue all that dishonours our nature. Those who, while bearing their cross in His steps, are formed after His likeness, shall be transfigured, and appear with Him in His glory.

My body tells me of my humiliation. It draws down my soul, and opens ways to sin. It fails, and suffers, and dies. But death does not end me, or send me forth to live for ever without a body. I may know that I shall rise, leaving behind me all that tells of a fallen state, and live on with a body fashioned after the glorious model of my Lord's. My spirit shall be pure, and shall call my body to no base service. My body shall be no dull weight to be lifted and forced; no vantage-ground for evil, needing to be watched and dreaded and held down by my spirit. Both alike shall be changed and glorified, and shall be immortal companions in happy, holy service. I need not be cast down by my humiliations now; for it all is meant to fashion me, and to form in me, day by day, the character of Christ. When that secret work of God is done in my spirit, I shall be called to the presence of my glorified Saviour. I shall see, as He is, Him Whom now I know by faith. In body and in spirit I shall be glorified together with Him. But am I preparing for this glory, or going on towards the hopeless humiliation of my whole nature?

O Lord Jesus, raise me from the dishonour of sin, and change my whole being by Thy grace, till I appear with soul and body glorified like Thine.

A house eternal, built by God, shall lodge the holy mind,
When once those prison walls have fallen by which 'tis now confined.
We know that when the soul unclothed shall from the body fly,
'Twill animate a purer frame with life that cannot die.

TWENTY-FOURTH FRIDAY AFTER TRINITY.

"No man, having put his hand to the plough, and looking back, is fit for the kingdom of God."—LUKE ix. 62.

SO Christ warns, in plain words, those who have any calling in His kingdom. All have to break up the hard earth of their natures, that the divinely-planted seed may take root downwards, and bear fruit upwards. All have to prepare for God's harvest-time by working for others. He who means not to fail must with single eye look forward; he must go straight on, with firm, steady will and hand and step. He who lets eye and thought wander, will soon turn back in heart, will stop, leave his plough, and go back. How few are steadfast!

I have put my hand to the plough whenever in any way I have professed readiness to follow or to work for Christ. I have looked back whenever I have lost heart, or grown weary, or faltered in my duty; whenever I have yielded to anything that drew my love from Christ, or made my will unsteady. To look back in thought is to lay bare the heart to temptation. If I am half-hearted and irresolute, I can do no work for God, or man, or my own soul, as God would have it done. If I am to be fit for God's trust, and worthy to labour in His kingdom's cause, I must have one foremost aim in life, and force all earthly things to help or to give way to it. Vainly I lay hold of what God puts into my hands, if I stand still, if I let go, if I fail to press straight forward, always breaking fresh ground, and doing my work with my might. Have I, perhaps, not only looked, but gone back? Am I away from my holy work an idler or hinderer in God's field? Is my work shallow, and careless, and uneven, such as it will shame me to give account of when night comes?

Almighty God, Who dost give me my work, and art my guide and strength, keep me steadfast in well-doing, till I have finished all according to Thy good pleasure.

> Go, labour on; 'tis not for nought;
> Thy earthly loss is heavenly gain;
> Men heed thee, love thee, praise thee not:
> The Master praises,—what are men?

Twenty-Fourth Saturday after Trinity.

"The wages of sin is death; but the gift of God is eternal life through Jesus Christ our Lord."—ROM. vi. 23.

SIN is toil under hard task-masters. Man is warned what he works for in this service. He is surely paid in full, though not all at once. He dies from God by degrees, as one power after another is given up to sin, till he is dead even while he lives. At last the soul leaves the body to corruption, and knows its own state of death. Eternal life is God's free gift in Christ. Men work by the power of that life; they do not earn life by working. That life of God is born in man, that it may free him from the hold of sin and death.

My body must die, and pass painfully to what sin has made the end of man's life here. In my soul are the seeds of a worse death; but, as a member of Christ, I have life from God, able to save my soul from dying, that I may live unto God for ever. Evil and good, death and life, strive in me. If I choose to serve sin, I am ruled and formed by my master at his will; what is high, and pure, and of heaven in my nature, as God has made it, is neglected, trampled down, killed; I lose the love of good, and the power to do it; the life of God at last returns to Him Who gave it, and I have perished. If I cherish and obey the power of God within me, living after the guidance of the Spirit, I find holiness grow to be more and more its own reward. Christ is formed in me, and lifts my whole nature towards the freedom of the sinless and undying. Death of the body ceases to alarm: it is the way to fulness of life. The life of Jesus may be manifested in my mortal body now. It will be shown perfectly in that glorified body, which shall share with my glorified spirit life on high for ever.

O God, make strong in me the life Thou hast given me in Christ, that I may never serve sin, or die from Thee, but may claim my freedom as a child of Thine, and an heir of eternal life.

Sweet to reflect how grace divine my sins on Jesus laid;
Sweet to remember that His blood my debt of suffering paid;
Sweet in His righteousness to stand, which saves from second death;
Sweet to experience, day by day, His Spirit's quickening breath.

The Twenty-fourth Sunday after Trinity.

"Somebody hath touched Me: for I perceive that virtue is gone out of Me."—LUKE viii. 46.

CROWDS thronged and pressed on Christ; only one touched, so as to reach the source of Divine virtue. She felt her sore need, and was sure that in Christ she could find healing. The weak woman made her way past all that was between, till she could put forth her hand and touch Him. Through the hem of the Lord's garment the waiting gift was sent out to meet her faith. Christ had drawn her to Him. When she would have gone away, He called her back to own what she had received, and to be made whole indeed.

Christ is the One healer. He waits to put forth the virtue that is in His Divine person. Through His Human Nature His gifts pass. In His sacraments and means of grace He, as it were, lets me touch the hem of His garment, and bring my soul into contact with His Godhead. By faith I come, and touch, and yield myself to be made whole. I may be where Christ is, and hear His words, and mark His works in vain. I may even touch Him in the holiest means of grace, and be unhealed. My touch may be like Judas' kiss, or the touch St. Thomas asked for in unbelief, or the careless crowding of the people. If I would find a blessing, I must come with a sense of want, with lowly faith, and true hope. I must press through all difficulties and discouragements, in spite of my own weakness and my soul's foes. If my faith be true, and lead me to Him, He will not scorn it, though it be not the wisest. When His virtue has gone out to me, I shall know Him better, and He will make me wise. He will give me more than at first I hope for.

O Lord, away from Whom I perish, draw me to Thee, that with a true, lowly, earnest faith I may touch Thee, and that Thy virtue may go forth to heal my soul.

> Reach me out Thy gracious hand,
> While I of Thy grace receive;
> Hoping against hope, I stand,
> Dying, and behold, I live.

TWENTY-FIFTH MONDAY AFTER TRINITY.

*Wilt thou be made whole?"—*JOHN v. 6.

A FOUNTAIN is open, whose healing virtue always flows. Crowds throng where the life-giving waters move. Some have no true clear end in view. They take their sinful state for granted. Some will not stir, unless a stronger will than their own rouse them. Some cling to part of their sickness, and will not be "made whole." Christ works no half cure; nor does He remove the deadliness of sin without removing the sin.

My Saviour knows my case,—how long I have lain in sin, and how miserably. His will and power are sure. He asks me, "Wilt thou be made whole?" He will not save me in spite of my will or without my will. If the love and power present to heal leave my state unchanged, I only am to blame. Do I use prayer and means of grace seeking nothing, hoping for nothing, and so getting nothing? Have I grown to feel as if this always must be so? Am I without earnest watchfulness to gain and put forth grace? Am I unwilling to be made quite "whole," so as to lose zest for some loved sin, or be fit for some heavy task? Do I only want to be made safe from fear of death, not to be freed from the sin that spoils my life? Christ asks about my will, that I may learn my want of will, and that He may make me willing. He sets before me the full healing He gives, that I may seek that, and that He may show His power in me by making me "whole." My will must not only yield to His, but act with it. I must be ready to rise, and go, and do, at His word, in the strength He gives.

O Good Physician, rouse my soul, that I may know my need, and long for health. Grant me the will to receive and obey the grace that is able to make me whole.

> Search all my hidden parts, whate'er impure
>   Thy light discovers there, do Thou destroy;
> The bitterest pain I willingly endure,
>   Such pain is followed by eternal joy.
> Oh! cleanse me from my stains of darkest hue,
> And in Christ's image form my soul anew.

TWENTY-FIFTH TUESDAY AFTER TRINITY.

"I pray not that Thou shouldest take them out of the world, but that Thou shouldest keep them from the evil."—JOHN xvii. 15.

CHRIST has work for His disciples to do in the world, and for the world to do in them. He wills them to stay in the world, that they may witness for Him, and be trained to purity and firmness. They are not free to shun the conflict, or to hide their light. They may not be cowardly, or selfish. They are most safe while they strive in brave, patient faith to fill well the place God gives them, praying to be kept from evil, and cheered by knowing that Christ pleads for them.

I must not weary in my work, or fret to lay down my cross. God knows when I am fit for the crown. I must not hold aloof from the world, or shrink from duties, in fear or sloth. God would not leave me where I am, if it were better for me or for His cause that I should be away. I am not forgotten. I am prayed for and cared for. Christ knows in what sort of world I am, for He has lived in it himself; He knows my weakness, and what help I need. It is not His will that the evil all around should harm me, but that I should be kept safe by the power of God, while I strive to make the evil in the world less. There is no danger if I watch, and join my prayers with those of Christ. I may be as He was—in the world, but not of it; separate from sinners, though living among them; tempted, and growing perfect through trial. I may, while here, carry with me the spirit of a purer world. I may be diligent in the world, without having the world in my heart, or letting the evil which mixes with its work, and cares, and joys, touch me. When I have done my part faithfully in an evil world, God will give me a place in one where no evil comes.

O Lord, keep me from the evil in the world, and enable me to fill my place well, that I may weaken the power of evil, and grow daily more fit for the world where all enjoy the rest of holiness.

If I may nearer draw through lengthened grief and pain,
Then to continue here must be my gain;
Till I am so refined, I can the glory bear
Of that excess of joy I thirst to share.

TWENTY-FIFTH WEDNESDAY AFTER TRINITY.

"To me to live is Christ, and to die is gain."—PHIL. i. 21.

ST. PAUL speaks calm, sober words of sure confidence. His life's aim was to know Christ, to love Him, to follow Him, to work for Him, to grow like Him, to be with Him. In Him he trusted and hoped. More than this; Christ lived in him, ruling his thoughts, and will, and life. So he knew that to die would be gain. It would be to exchange the wearing strain of work for the reward of work well done, the watch and fight with sin for the peace of righteousness; to have in full that which even in part was his best joy; to be with Christ and be like Him, serving Him joyfully and perfectly.

If Christ be not my life, if I do not live by Him and for Him, death is only loss; I go from all I trust in and love; I go out of reach of the calls of grace, and the hopes which even the careless value. If Christ lives in me, becoming more and more a ruling Presence, giving my will and powers their aim, then my life is a holy thing, full of Divine strength and peace. Angels rejoice as Christ's life more plainly shines out in mine. And the promise is full of glory. As the days of trial draw towards their end, as the old nature dies on its cross, the time comes nearer when the Christ being formed in me shall put off all that now hides its brightness, and checks its free activity. I shall die from the state of weakness, and struggling, and sore trial, and sin. I shall leave behind all that is of earth, and proves me fallen. I shall live to know what God is and gives, to have what Christ's death won, to be what He lives to make me. Death and what comes after draw nigh. Does my state now tell me that the end of my life here is to be gain, or the loss of all?

Almighty, Ever-living God, grant me to be so one with Christ in my life of trial and hope, that I may pass through death to the rest and joy which He prepares.

> Bid us with Thee to watch and pray,
> With Thee to die, with Thee to rise,
> With Thee to bear our cross each day,
> With Thee to soar beyond the skies.

TWENTY-FIFTH THURSDAY AFTER TRINITY.
"Rejoice evermore."—1 THESS. v. 16.

SINNERS in a world of care have much trial. They have more cheer. Joy is better and stronger than sorrow. Sin alone is good ground for loss of joy. The penitent can rejoice in the love that calls and restores him. Man ought to rejoice in life's harmless pleasant things. His joy must not be bound up with what passes away, or be such as ends in heaviness. Man has the blessings of grace now, and the hope of glory. He can "rejoice in the Lord alway," if no other joy be left. He must live so as to find joy in God, and that his rejoicing may be for evermore.

I dare not scorn the joys God gives me here, because things above are better. It is ungrateful to refuse them, except for God's sake or my neighbour's. Joys help to form my character as truly as trials. By due use of them I learn thankfulness; I grow stronger to bear my cross when the time comes. Only let my laughter not be that of fools. In all my joy let me rejoice in the Lord, remembering thankfully the Giver. Though sorrowful, I may and should be always rejoicing. Earthly sorrow should bring out more the value of that joy which God gives, and the world cannot take away. Suffering for God and truth is a pledge of added blessedness, and a new call to rejoice. Even sorrow for sin, if it be true, assures of loving-kindness and salvation, in which I am right to rejoice. My religion, if it be real, makes me ever surer that God is Love, and leads me to show love in all my life. So I must grow glad as I go forward, and find ever new cause to rejoice in the Lord with a joy increasing evermore.

O merciful Father, Who dost train Thy children by joy and sorrow, teach me to enjoy thankfully Thy least gifts, and so to rejoice in Thee now that I may rejoice with Thee for ever.

My heart for gladness springs, it cannot more be sad,
For very joy it laughs and sings, sees nought but sunshine glad.
The sun that glads mine eyes in Christ the Lord I love;
I sing for joy of that which lies stored up for me above.

TWENTY-FIFTH FRIDAY AFTER TRINITY.
"Rejoicing in hope; patient in tribulation."—ROM. xii. 12.

HOPE is made up of wish for the good God offers, and trust in God's word. It is a duty and a needful help. It honours God; it braces man to press on heartily through trial. Gloom makes hope's light brighter. As the world proves vain, the heart is drawn towards what stands firm. Joy in things hoped for grows as they become the heart's all. The hopeful can be patient. The patient who wait quietly on God have a right to hope. All are bound to live so as to have a true hope, and to use their hope to help their life.

My soul's foes vex, and the world's cares try me. I do not see the good in store, and my weakness often casts me down. But I dare not doubt God, or slight what He holds before me. Want of hope warns of weak faith, or cold love, or a heart bound to earth, unhumbled, impatient. I distrust God without cause, or I have good cause to distrust myself. Perhaps I only wish for a felon's pardon, not for a son's blessing. If I fail in hope, my work and my witness for God suffer. I need hope, as well as faith and love, to form my character and guide my life. If grace is mine to reach after what faith shows me, I can be more than patient—I can greatly rejoice, though for a season, if need be, I am tried. Tribulation need not dim my joy in that which each day brings nearer. I should put the aim of my hope plainly before mind and heart. I should take all this life's joy as a pledge of God's changeless love, and when trial comes, look forward with glad, patient hope. If I seek what I hope for, in God's way, God will give more than I ask or think.

O God of hope, show my faith the good Thou preparest for Thy children, that I may live so as to have a true hope of gaining it, and be able to rejoice even in the tribulation which trains me for the enjoyment of it.

Though mountains crumble into dust, Thy promise standeth fast,
Who follows Thee in pious trust shall reach the goal at last;
Though strange and winding seem the way, while yet on earth I dwell,
In heaven my heart shall gladly say, "Thou, Lord, dost all things well."

TWENTY-FIFTH SATURDAY AFTER TRINITY.

"The blessing of the Lord, it maketh rich, and He addeth no sorrow with it."—PROV. x. 22.

GOD'S way to all well-being is the one sure safe way. He waits to bless the upright, who work under His eye, in His name, and for His glory. He shows how to gain and keep health, friends, and all life's true cheer. Those only who seek God's blessing on all they do, and seek most the wealth that lasts, are wise for this world. What they get does not shame. They have not sold better things for it. It does not warn of sorrow in store, when their gains are gone, and their sin remains.

If I choose some earthly end as my first aim, God may let me have it. But I surely miss other good, and forsake the way of God's blessing. What is won fails to fill the heart's void; the thought of how I have won it and what it leads to adds sorrow. I can spare any earthly good which God's will denies me. I cannot spare God's blessing. With that, I am rich; wanting that, I am poor. My Maker knows, and tells me, what is my true good, and the way to it. The diligence and high-mindedness that are part of a life lived to please God, are means to success in this life. I have God's blessing, while in all I do, I try in His strength to be what He wishes. That blessing is worth more than all I may have to give up for it. I will not have what I cannot ask Him to bless. I will not spoil God's gifts by adding to them the gains of sin. I will forego earthly good, rather than feel the sorrow of self-reproach and dread of God. Whatever makes me rich now shall be mine, so as not to leave me less rich towards God, but so as to be the pledge of a love that has better things in store.

O Lord, from Whom all true joy comes, bless me with Thy gifts of grace, that I may have Thy blessing on all my earthly store of good, and, while thankfully enjoying the tokens of Thy love, may not lose the true riches.

> Oh! 'tis not in grief to harm me,
> While Thy love is left to me;
> Oh! 'twere not in joy to charm me,
> Were that joy unblessed by Thee.

The Twenty-fifth Sunday after Trinity.

"This He said to prove him: for He himself knew what He would do."—JOHN vi. 6.

CHRIST'S followers were wearied and in want. Christ knew what He could do, and meant to do. In His question to Philip He asked for faith, not bread. He put the whole difficulty of the case, to call out what faith the disciples had, and to make plain His power. Faith was tried with a hard proof, that it might grow sure and strong. He sought to win men to trust Him for the true bread by which their souls might live.

The questions "whence?" and "how?" are often forced on me when I can give no answer. God puts them to me, that I may feel my helplessness, and fall back on Him. I often cannot see my way, or know what to do. God always sees His way, and is never at a loss for means. When things seem to me at their worst, He is ruling them to prepare for what He wills to do. If I am a disciple, specially if my trials come from going after Christ, I need not doubt. He knows how and when best to show that He careth for me. He knows what He will do, when He draws me away where only He can help. When He proves me with hard questions about His truth, or His cause, or my own good, it is enough for me that He knows all. I can obey Him, and wait in faith. He knows why His secret ways are not made plain to me, and why His words tell of more than my thoughts can grasp. He knows how to bring me through trial to surer peace and fuller joy. He knows how to lead me, by daily mercies, to seek from His hands the food my soul needs.

O Lord, Who knowest all things, and for Whom nothing is too hard, give me such calm faith that, when I am proved, I may always be able to wait patiently for what Thou wilt do in Thine own time and way.

> They their Master's love who share
> Ask not how His Spirit moveth;
> This their only, constant care,
> To rest in faith on Him Who loveth.

TWENTY-SIXTH MONDAY AFTER TRINITY.

" We have an altar."—HEB. xiii. 10.

THE sacrifices under the Law spoke of Christ, and of our union with God through Him. The sin-offering atoned for man's unholiness; the trespass-offering for actual sins against God's law. In both the victim died in the sinner's stead, and the blood was presented to restore him to his place. In the burnt-offerings, always being consumed before God, man owned that life, and all its powers were God's. The smoke from the altar of incense, mingling with that of the burnt-offering, imaged the people's prayer and praise joined with the offering of themselves. In the peace-offering man ate before God of what the altar and the priest shared, thus having communion with God. The show-bread overlaid with incense spoke of the rest of God's people, adoring in His presence.

In the service of the Holy Communion which Christ gave to His Church, we have what all these things meant. We show the Lord's death as the atonement offered for our sinfulness and our sins by Him Who was made one with us. We plead the blood which He brought before the heavenly mercy-seat, in token of peace and reconciliation. We eat at God's table of the bread of God. One with Him, we present ourselves, our souls and bodies, a holy sacrifice. The incense of our prayer and praise rises before the mercy-seat, along with our offering of Christ and devotion of ourselves to God's service. In the calm joy of the Holy Presence, we anticipate the time when, like the incense-covered show-bread, we are placed in the inner sanctuary where God is, to be all His own, and be blessed in a life of perfect worship.

Forgive me, O Lord, and take me to Thy favour; let my worship rise to Thee with the offering of myself, and be acceptable; give me glad, thankful union with Thee, and receive me at last to the joy of Thy presence.

Thou standest at the altar, Thou offerest every prayer,
In faith's unclouded vision we see Thee ever there,
And, through Thy blood accepted, with Thee we keep the feast;
Thou art Thyself the Victim, Thou art Thyself the Priest.

TWENTY-SIXTH TUESDAY AFTER TRINITY.

"Abide with us."—LUKE xxiv. 29.

EACH coming of Christ to the soul is in order to stay as an abiding source of added strength and gladness. In the Holy Communion He is present in a way beyond all other ways. He gives Himself, the sum of all good gifts. It is not enough to come with careful preparation, to hail the Lord adoringly, and to receive Him with all the soul's devotion. All is not done. The new power of Divine life that has come must be kept safe in a loving, thankful heart. Faith and gratitude must be deepened and proved by thanksgiving, above all by devotion of the will and life.

Each communion which, after earnest preparation, I receive devoutly, binds me to a new life. I am other than I was before receiving. Christ has again come to feed and cheer my soul. In all His Divine love and power He has been present to make me more one with Himself, and lift me to a higher level of godliness. If I have not had this hope and aim, I have not come aright. Let me think over what I have sought, and faith knows God has given. Let me try to know the mystery of Christ's work, the whole benefits of which He assures to me when He gives me that by which He dwells in me and I in Him. Let me learn to feel my unworthiness of any love or mercy. Let me adore and bless Him Who not only died for me, but bestows the meat indeed and drink indeed, to be a means of everlasting life and a pledge of His everlasting love. Let me thank Him with my lips and from my heart. Let me put forth the new life He brings, by devoting afresh to Him myself, my soul and body, my thoughts, my will, and my love.

Give me grace, O my Saviour, with thankful hope to cherish each new coming of Thy Presence to my soul, that I may ever go forth with fresh strength and gladness, to glorify Thee by a life more like Thine.

> Our needy souls sustain with fresh supplies of love,
> Till all Thy life we gain and all Thy fulness prove,
> And, strengthened by Thy perfect grace,
> Behold, without a veil, Thy face

Twenty-sixth Wednesday after Trinity.

"The husbandman waiteth for the precious fruit of the earth, and hath long patience."—JAMES v. 7.

GOD sows good seed in man's nature, and gives the right blessing in its season. He is patient till the precious fruit ripen for the heavenly garner. Man must work in patience, waiting for the increase. Snows and frosts and dark days have their use, as well as sunshine. The joy of harvest does not come at once, but at the end of long, hard work done in faith and hope. Man must not lose heart, though the soil is hard to labour, and growth is slow, and the time of rest and joy seems far off.

God bears with me, though I try His patience. He asks me to be patient, and trust Him. He knows how to order the course of things, so that all may at last be well. Through my fault the harvest may be delayed, and God's sowing may be made in vain. I must be patient with God, Who has His own right time and means for all things. He may prove me by seeming to withhold His favour. Let me not be hasty to ask, "Lord, how long?" but try to own Divine love working wisely towards its sure end. Let me be patient with men for whom I pray and work, showing the gentle perseverance which God shows in dealing with me. God knows how and when to give the increase. Let me be patient with myself when I find that the roots of evil are not all yet gone, that graces do not grow fast, and that there is small promise of full, ripe fruit. The soil has been much left waste, and I must not grudge the labour my own sin has made needful. Let me go on, strong in heart and will, waiting on God till He gives the fruit of all.

Almighty and merciful Father, bestow upon me such sure faith in Thee, that I may patiently persevere, till in Thine own way and time, I enjoy Thy blessing and aim at rest.

> We sow 'mid perils here, and tears—
> There the glad hand the harvest bears
>   Which here in grief hath sown ;
> Great Three in One, the increase give,
> The gifts of grace by which we live
>   With heavenly glory crown.

TWENTY-SIXTH THURSDAY AFTER TRINITY.

" The harvest truly is plenteous, but the labourers are few; pray ye therefore the Lord of the harvest, that He will send forth labourers."—MATT. ix. 37, 38.

CHRIST has come, and died, and sent the Holy Spirit, that the whole field of man's nature should bear rich fruit for God. God wills to work through means, and give men their part to do. Much of the world is left uncared for. Much of the Church gives poor return. God waits for prayers to show the will of those whom He calls to work for and with Him. Prayer is the first work which He accepts and blesses. God is ready to send forth all, each in his own place, gifted to be true labourers.

Does God indeed wait for my prayers, and thus give me a real part in the gathering in of the spiritual harvest for which He has at such cost prepared? So I am plainly taught. God alone puts it into man's heart to labour for Him, and bestows the gifts needful. God alone gives the increase of any toil. But He commonly works by means of men. Prayer is part of all work to which He calls me. He asks me to ask Him, and so to make myself one in will and aim with His great love. The state of the world, after all Christ has done, cannot but move me. If I have any love for God and man, or care for my own soul, I must care for others. If I wish to please God, I must do my best, that others may be led to live so as to give Him joy. It is vain to pray that others may work, if I hang back myself. Let me say with all my heart, "Here I am, send me." Let me seek that "sending," without which all I do is vain; and labour where He wills, knowing that the work is God's, and the reward from Him.

Almighty God, send me forth gifted to labour well in the place Thou dost choose for me, and earnest to unite myself with Thy work of love by praying that Thy labourers may be increased, and their zeal made more devoted.

<pre>
    The power belongs to Thee alone
      Fit instruments to raise,
    Whose lives may make Thy goodness known,
      And spread their Saviour's praise.
</pre>

Twenty-sixth Friday after Trinity.

"Being made perfect, He became the author of eternal salvation unto all them that obey Him."—Heb. v. 9.

CHRIST learned obedience, and was made perfect by the ceaseless doing and bearing of the Divine will. By the prayer which His whole life was, He drew into Him the power of God, Who was "able to save Him from death." Now in His glory He saves all who will obey Him, as He obeyed His Father. He trains them in the same way of suffering and self-rule. By what they do and bear, He perfects them after His Pattern. He gives, not passing relief from passing trial, but eternal salvation.

If the sinless man Christ Jesus, one Person with the Eternal Son, learned obedience in the school of the cross, I dare not ask why God does not train me without pain. It is not strange that I cannot reach my perfection save through discipline like His. For I am fallen; my will is turned from God's. I need to be saved, not only from evil outside me, but from evil in myself. To Christ I turn in all life's griefs, or when sin wells up in my soul, or when some strong force of sin comes against me. He alone can keep me safe day by day, and bring me safe at last out of reach of harm for ever. He tells me how to be of those whom He saves. As He did not His own man's will, but His Father's, so I must be ready to yield my will to His in all things, and to obey Him in wholehearted faith. I must long to go where He wills, to do and bear what He wills, looking always to Him that I may be kept true to the end. He is more than a guide, more than a sender of strength. He comes to be in me and live over again in me the life He lived for me. He comes to bear and to do in me what His will lays upon me.

O Lord, Who by the way of the cross didst gain Thy perfection and become the full source of grace, save me in Thine own way from all sin, and form me after Thy perfect likeness.

> Blessings more than heart can know are in Jesus stored,
> And upon His Church below ever are outpoured;
> Till her work is finished here she shall be His care,
> Then in heaven shall she appear, and be perfect there.

TWENTY-SIXTH SATURDAY AFTER TRINITY.

"*Jesus Christ the same yesterday, and to-day, and for ever.*"
—HEB. xiii. 8.

CHRIST is God, and changes not. What He was eternally before He took flesh, He showed Himself as man. What He was in His humiliation, He is in His glory. He loves souls as when He gave Himself to die. He hates sin as when He felt its curse and met the tempter. He will be the same on the judgment seat, and for ever. He is able and ready to teach and heal and save the least and worst, as when He "went about doing good." What men in old time found Him tells what all may find Him now. Always He is the same sure resting-place for faith, and hope, and love.

Jesus Christ has made God known for all in all times. The Gospels tell, not what once was for others, but what now is for me. Though I forget Christ, He remembers me. Though I go from Him, His love follows me. Though I doubt Him, He is true still. None ever found Him fail to keep His word, and He will not fail me. He is not more loving when my way is smooth and bright, than when all things seem against me, and my soul is cast down. He asks no less whole-hearted forsaking of sin and self to follow Him, than when He was on His way to Calvary. He offers no less grace and strength to those who will take up the cross. He is as ready as ever to give rest and joy to those who love Him and know His love. He will not draw back from His great promise of reward. He will not be untrue to His holiness shown in His firm warnings against sin, and solemn pleadings with men who will not come to Him for life. I pass my days with Him near me Who died on the cross to save me, and Who will be my Judge. He is always God, and the same always.

O Lord Jesus Christ, reveal Thyself to me, that, sure of Thy unchanging love and holiness, I may live before Thee always as a steadfast disciple.

> Thy truth unchanged hath ever stood;
> Thou savest those that on Thee call;
> To them that seek Thee Thou art good;
> To them that find Thee, all in all.

St. Andrew's Day.

"Master, where dwellest Thou? He saith unto them, Come and see."—JOHN i. 38, 39.

ST. ANDREW was a disciple of the preacher of repentance. When pointed to the "Lamb of God," he followed Him, and asked, "Where dwellest Thou?" He obeyed the call to "come and see." He brought his brother to Christ; he left his father for Christ. He was a faithful disciple while still toiling with his nets. He forsook all when Christ called him to part from earthly ties, and spread the net of God's kingdom. With a like willingness, he followed to death upon the cross.

If I have been warned of sin, and taught my soul's needs, I will be glad to be shown the Lamb of God, Who taketh away the world's sin, of which mine is a part. If I am in earnest, I will at once go after Him Whom I have found, and learn from Himself where and how I can abide with Him, that He may cleanse me till I am pure. I will not neglect my daily tasks, but do them in the spirit and with the hope of one who has found the Messias. What I have proved good for myself I will try to lead others to share and enjoy. I will watch with lowly readiness for each new call of my Lord, Who will give strength to obey, when His right time comes. If I must be without friends, or home, or earthly wealth, He Who calls me to higher work, nearer to Himself, has manifold more good to give me. If I must bear the cross and die on it, He Who made the cross glorious will bring me to glory by its means. By the same grace that draws me to Him, and gives power to work and suffer for Him, I will go after Him to where He dwells now.

O Lamb of God, may I ever abide in heart where Thou dwellest. Give me zeal to bring others to know Thee. Make me do Thy will in my daily life, and yield what is dearest, and bear what is hardest, at Thy word.

As St. Andrew heard Thee, Saviour,
By the lake of Galilee,
May we hear, and help each other
Day by day to follow Thee.

The Conversion of St. Paul.

" Who art Thou, Lord ? . . . Lord, what wilt Thou have me to do ?"—Acts ix. 5, 6.

SAUL was in earnest, and full of zeal. He thought he acted up to his full light. Without knowing it, he resisted the misgivings of his conscience—those "pricks" which he found "hard to kick against." Now the truth has flashed on him ; he only asks to know Him Whom in blind unbelief he had persecuted, and to be shown His will, that he may do it. By the grace of God Saul becomes St. Paul, a preacher of the faith which once he destroyed. He bears persecution for Christ, and is ready to die for Christ's people.

Though, like Saul, I live in all good conscience before God, and am "zealous towards God," I may be a persecutor of Christ. If one so well taught, and wise, and candid as Saul could be blinded by prejudice, and blaspheme the Christ, Whose honour he believed he upheld, it becomes me to be swift to hear, and slow to religious wrath. What I wish to find right may be wrong. What I like to prove false may be God's eternal truth. Those whom I scoff at and torment may be dear to my Lord, and taught by His Spirit. I am apt to cling to my old prejudices, and refuse to give a hearing to unwelcome truth which, though not new, is new to me. Love for truth is apt to corrupt into hatred of those who hold what I think untrue. I must have a faith, and stand fast in it, and stand up boldly for it. But I must beware of kicking against Divine warnings, either in faith or life. I am safe while I look up with true, lowly, earnest longing for light and guidance, such as Saul had when he cried, "Who art Thou, Lord ? What wilt Thou have me to do?"

O Lord, give me Thy light and grace so to know Thee and do Thy will, that my zeal may be wise, and that my knowledge may be used to Thy glory.

> I would not see but in Thy light ;
> I would not walk but by Thy might ;
> Or work a work, or speak a word,
> Or think a thought, without my Lord

The Presentation of Christ, or the Purification of St. Mary the Virgin.

"*Holy to the Lord.*"—LUKE ii. 23.

THE birth of "that Holy Thing," Who was the Son of God, had no stain; but the mother of Jesus obeyed the law, and gave an offering for purification. The world's Redeemer was Himself presented to God, and redeemed with a small sum of money. He Who was one with the Father presented Himself in His human nature as "the Firstborn among many brethren." In Him all who were to be sons and daughters of the Lord God Almighty were accepted and hallowed.

The mother of my Lord sets me an example of lowly obedience to each rule of God's Church. It becomes me to fulfil all righteousness, meekly asking what God has said, not what trouble and cost I can safely spare myself. I grudge not the first and best of what God gives. When I lay it before Him, I own that all I have is His by right; and what good I enjoy is made better with His blessing. I am one with Christ; in union with Him I was presented before God, and dedicated to His service. God accepted me then, and is not willing to cast me off now. He knew all I would be; He knows what I am. In my baptism my part in Christ's offering of Himself was claimed for me. I am bound to go on as Christ did, through all life on earth, yielding my whole self to my Father. I am bound to ask wherewith and in what ways God would have me come before Him, and to obey in faith. I could not dare to present myself to God, except in union with Christ. I can grow more one with Him, and so for His sake be more acceptable.

Almighty Father, grant me with pure will to devote myself always to Thee, and so to live in union with Thy Son Jesus Christ, that I may be made worthy of Thee.

> Rejoice, ye sons of men—your purest praises yield;
> The everlasting Son, see in the flesh revealed!
> The world's Redeemer comes to pay
> His own redemption price to-day.

St. Matthias's Day.

" I will raise Me up a faithful priest, that shall do according to that which is in Mine heart and in My mind."—1 Sam. ii. 35.

JUDAS was an apostle, though a traitor. His office was holy, though his life was false. He fell from the place to which Christ called him, to the place his sin made him fit for. Doubtless souls were brought to Christ by him whose sin parted him from Christ. The work and crown Judas put from him were given to Matthias. The eleven did their best to choose wisely. They left the result with God, Who searcheth hearts. In answer to their prayers He made known His will.

God's gifts are real, though a Judas bear them to me. But I am bound to pray that men may be saved from the sin of touching holy things with unholy hands, and that those who hold Christ's commission may exercise it faithfully. If evil be in high places in the Church, I am not therefore to forsake Christ, or to despair of the Church. My part is to be warned, lest I fall or fail in my lowly place, and to work, as well as pray, that the evil may be overruled for good. Judas fell in spite of his Master's warnings. Christ showed His care for the Church by providing that Matthias should be chosen in his stead. In all that has to do with Christ's kingdom in my own soul and in the world, I may count on His help. He will save me from mistake, and lead me right, if I use the means of judging that I have, and pray with a single aim to find out His will that I may do it. He may, in answer to my prayers, clear all doubt from my mind, or He may seem to withhold a sign. But I need not fear if I try honestly and prayerfully to do the best.

O Lord, Who knowest all hearts, and canst work with what means Thou willest, give me faith in Thy care for Thy Church and for me ; enable me so to use my talent well, that I may be among Thy chosen ones at last.

> Dread Searcher of the hearts,
> Thou Who didst seal by Thy descending Dove
> Thy servant's choice, oh, help us in our parts,
> Else helpless found to learn and teach Thy love.

Annunciation of the Blessed Virgin Mary.

"Behold the handmaid of the Lord; be it unto me according to thy word."—LUKE i. 38.

GOD'S great angel was sent to the lowly village maiden. Out of all Eve's daughters she was foreknown, and chosen, and prepared. Highly favoured was she, from whose body God the Son, by the power of the Holy Ghost, took His body that in man's nature He might save man. Full of grace must she have been whom God gifted for so high a mission. She had loved and done God's will in her low estate. She was God's handmaid, ready to be, and do, and suffer what God willed.

Only one could be blessed as Mary was. In her place of honour, as the mother of Jesus, she was alone. I fail to realise the great mystery of that joy. But her highest blessedness was not in this her own exaltation; rather that God the Son was made man to be her Saviour. Her spiritual union was a loftier thing than even her wondrous human relationship. In such union I may be as the "brother, and sister, and mother" of the Lord. He was born of woman, by the power of the Holy Ghost, that, by the same Spirit, I might be new-born and made one in nature with Him. I may know, indeed, that the Lord is with me, that Christ dwells in me, and I in Him. I may know that I am partaker of the Divine nature, and a child of God, through Him Who took human nature by becoming the Son of Mary. Let me bow, like her, to each message and calling of God. Let me yield myself to the Holy Spirit's influence. Let me be ready to bear whatever reproach or sorrow may pierce through my soul, if I may be a means for working out God's ends of love to myself and the world of sinners.

Grant, O Lord, that by the power of the Holy Ghost I may live in spiritual union with Thy Son Jesus Christ, and with pure heart and will obey Thee always.

> Blest in the message Gabriel brought,
> Blest by the work the Spirit wrought;
> From Whom the great Desire of earth
> Took human flesh and human birth.

St. Mark.

"Speaking the truth in love."—EPH. iv. 15.

AMONG the gifts of the ascended Saviour were apostles, evangelists, pastors, and teachers. Man can know what God says, and can be sure. He can stand firmly on this ground, unmoved by the shifting blasts of man's vain opinions. When God speaks, He claims to be believed. It is ingratitude and insult, to neglect or reject His words. A true faith guides to a true life. The truth of God and the love of God unite for the perfecting of the saints, "till we all come in the unity of the faith, and of the knowledge of the Son of God, unto a perfect man."

God means that I give heed to His words, and hold them fast. I thank God that I am not left to my own guesses, or the changing views of men. I have the safeguard and the inspiration of God's truth. I can receive that, letting its divine power form and rule me. I can learn Christ's own words; I can see in His life and work as man, Him Who shows God. I can learn the ways by which to have His grace in me, and to put it forth. I can abide in Him Who is the truth, and bring forth fruits of holiness by the working of His love. Only under the influence of the full truth which God reveals to faith, can I have right love for God and man. The clearest truth is vain for me, if it be only in my mind, and does not sway my heart and life. Truth is made known that I may be true, and faithfully fulfil the end God sets before me. God's truth is heaven's light, to make my way plain and safe. God's grace enables me to prove the power of truth in a godly, righteous, and sober life.

Almighty God, give me sure faith in the truth of Thy word, and pour Thy grace into my heart, that I may grow in the knowledge of Thee as Thou art made known in Christ, and may be perfected among Thy saints.

> The lion-faced, he told abroad
>   The strength of love, the strength of faith;
> He showed the Almighty Son of God,
>   The man Divine, Who won by death.

St. Philip and St. James's Day.

"*Lord, show us the Father, and it sufficeth us.*"—JOHN xiv. .

ST. PHILIP longed to see God. St. James taught how in daily life to become fit for the vision of the Divine glory. St. Philip did not clearly know Christ as one with the Father; but he was a faithful disciple, ready to be shown truth. He cared not what he had to leave; it sufficed him to be with Christ and hear His words. So he grew towards the perfect knowledge of God. Those who would see the Father, learn from St. James to walk step by step after Christ till they are with Him where He is, in His Father's house.

It is not enough to know of Christ's life and work as man, or to believe Him as a human teacher telling me about God. All is vain, if I know not Himself as God the Son revealing God the Father. I can see God, not apart from Christ, but in Him. God veils Himself from unbelief. My faith grows true and clear as I am "long time with" Jesus, doing the Divine will. I learn from St. James the use of life's trials and temptations in preparing me to see God as He is. It "sufficeth" me now to know that I am being led on towards that which St. Philip holds forth as the goal of man's desires. I shrink not from those things which darken earth, and make me look up for light. I am glad of the purity which well-borne sorrow gives. I pray for the wisdom I so lack, but which God never tires of bestowing. I watch each turning of my way as I follow Christ, remembering the value of common duties and the danger of common faults. I seek to know Christ by the grace gained through union with Him, and the works of holiness in which He trains me. I hope to abide in His love, till in God's presence I receive the crown of life.

Draw me near to Thee, O Lord, and be Thou with me, revealing the Father, that I may grow in the knowledge of God and in holiness, without which none can see Him.

> O Way Divine, through gloom and strife
> Bring us Thy Father's face to see;
> O heavenly Truth, O precious Life,
> Lead us through toil to rest in Thee.

St. Barnabas the Apostle.

"He was a good man, and full of the Holy Ghost and of faith."—ACTS xi. 24.

ST. BARNABAS was the son of consolation, for he was full of the Holy Ghost the Comforter. That Presence made him "a good man," so that he had ground for comfort; he was full of faith, so that no earthly loss or trial could shake his peace. He had proved his faith in heavenly good, and his desire to comfort wanting brethren, by selling his lands and laying the price at the apostles' feet. He was glad when he saw what told of the work of God's grace in others. He urged them so to cleave to the Lord with steadfast will, as to make their consolation everlasting.

Earthly comfort is dearly bought at the cost of the heart's peace. There is more cheer in caring for others' need than for one's own selfish ease. The love which leads me to part with what God asks is new and better consolation. Like St. Barnabas, let me be ready to lay my all at God's feet, using it for Him while it is in my hands, yielding it when and as He wills. I wish not to be soothed in my sin, but to have the good comfort of those who with purpose of heart cleave unto the Lord, and so receive of His goodness, being full of the Holy Ghost and of faith. I pray for sure ground of peace, whether God gives me peace or sees well to try me. I rejoice with the truth's triumphs, and am glad when God's grace blesses men. I do all, by self-denying example, and however the Holy Ghost enables me, to lead others to find and keep man's one true abiding consolation. So I prove and strengthen my own hold on God, and the power of His goodness in me. My own comfort deepens, as I am the means of comforting others.

Fill me, O Lord, with the Holy Ghost and faith, that I may have sure ground of consolation, and may bring others to enjoy the comfort which the work of Thy grace gives.

> The world's a room of sickness, where each heart
> Knows its own anguish and unrest;
> The truest wisdom there, and noblest art,
> Is his who skills of comfort best.

St. John Baptist's Day.

"A prophet? yea, I say unto you, and more than a prophet."
—MATT. xi. 9.

ST. JOHN the Baptist was foretold by God, wonderfully born, filled from the first with the Holy Ghost, borne witness to by Christ. He was, to those willing to receive it, "Elias which was for to come." He warned men of sin, and gave them the baptism of repentance, to make them ready for the Lord and for His baptism of the Holy Ghost and fire. He was no bending reed, shaken by every passing breath of man's opinion; no self-pleaser, seeking his own indulgence. He struck straight to the conscience of each. He spoke out God's will and God's purposes, as the voice of One Who had a right to be heard.

How great was he whom God thus prepared for so high a work, and of whom Christ spoke such words! What a grand calling, to be the link between Moses and Christ, to prepare the way of man's Redeemer! I am greater, if I am but the least in that kingdom of heaven, which St. John said was at hand, but did not enter while on earth. God comes to me in Christ, as He did not to him who baptized Christ, and pointed to Him as the Lamb of God. I need St. John's warnings, as well as the Saviour's loving promises. I am not ready for the precious blood till I have been shown my sin, and taught to long for cleansing. I am not ready to follow Jesus in the way of peace till I have been in the desert with St. John. Alas! the stern voice must sound on. I am apt to rest in my privilege and calling, so as to fail in bringing forth fruits meet for repentance. I must not only be warned, but make my own protest against sin. I must fear none but God, and face any loss rather than be untrue to Him.

O merciful God, may the stern warnings of Thy Word warn me to flee from the wrath to come and to fear sin, so that I may gladly hear the Saviour's promises of grace, and may rejoice in His full salvation.

Lord, give us grace, that we all evil may forsake,
May boldly speak the truth for Thee, the lowest place may take;
So when Thou com'st again Thy realm redeemed to see,
Thy steps shall find 'mid hearts of men a way made straight for
    Thee.

St. Peter's Day.

" Upon this rock I will build My Church ; and the gates of hell shall not prevail against it."—MATT. xvi. 18.

ST. PETER was the foremost of the twelve apostles of the Lamb, whose names are on the twelve foundations of the City of God. Christ is the Chief Corner Stone, holding all together in unity and strength. He is the Rock, on Which the spiritual temple of living stones is built. Other foundation can none lay than that which God laid in the incarnation of His Son. The truth that Jesus is God is the foundation, resting on which all truth is firm. It is no tale or thought of man, but God's own revelation. While the Church builds on this, no art or malice of foes can harm her.

While with the heart I believe that Jesus is God, and with my mouth confess, as St. Peter did, I have good hope in seeking righteousness and salvation. Otherwise, all rests on man's unstable thoughts or likings, not on sure truth learned from God. Let me hold St. Peter's faith with his devotion ; but let me not need falls to make me lowly and trustworthy. If I fail in trial, there is hope while I see God's loving appeal in the Master's eye that turns on me. The Church is Christ's Church so long as she holds and teaches this truth, which St. Peter, on behalf of all the apostles, openly confessed. She may at times seem, like St. Peter, to put away the cross, and so call down the Lord's reproof. She may even in act and word seem as if she knew not her Lord ; but if the faith is in her, His look can call it out to active life. He makes her truer, stronger than before. He gives her back the keys. He calls her to prove her devotion by shepherding His sheep, and feeding the lambs of His flock.

Keep me ever, O Lord Jesus, in the safe fold where Thy sheep are fed and guarded. Give me grace to believe in my heart unto righteousness, and to confess Thee with my mouth unto salvation.

   O Rock of Ages, one Foundation
    On which the living Church doth rest—
   The Church, whose walls are strong salvation,
    Whose gates are praise. Thy name be blest !

St. James the Apostle.

" Ye know not what manner of spirit ye are of."—LUKE ix. 55.

ST. JAMES and his brother wished to call down fire to avenge the wrong done their Master. But the just God knew why judgment fell at Elijah's word. The God of love does not trust His lightnings in the rash hands of men. The religious bitterness of the Samaritans gave no right to call down Heaven's vengeance. St. James mistook the Spirit of His Master, Who came to win men by the kindly warmth of love, not to destroy them with the flame of wrath. He needed still to learn the way to the place of honour near Him Who died to save His foes.

When my faith is reviled, or I am hindered in my Master's work, it is often hard to know whether love for Christ or self-love feels the wrong most. I dishonour Christ if I vent my private feelings in His name, or use in His war unchristian weapons. It is His cause, not mine, that Satan and the world assail. I must show His spirit of long-suffering, and not dare to wish Him to be as ungentle as I am. How should I fare, did He deal with my unfaithfulness as I am tempted to deal with those who will not hear me or follow with me? It were no worse to call down fire from heaven than to assail with that burning fire "set on fire of hell"—a fierce tongue. Let me show my religious power and truth by the Spirit I am of. Let me make known the truth, and enforce it by the quiet strength of God's love in me. God waits patiently; so may I. The Samaritans who refused Christ afterwards welcomed one of the "sons of thunder," who called down on them the Holy Ghost. Where I see least hope there may be the smoking flax, which roughness would quench.

O Lord Jesus, Who dost bear with me, though I am cold and often fail to welcome Thee, give me of Thy Spirit, that I may be always ready to bring near Thy love to my foes, and to pray for those who despitefully use me.

> Take up the lesson, O my heart,
> Thou Lord of meekness, write it there;
> Thine own meek self to me impart
> Thy lofty hope, Thy lowly prayer.

St. Bartholomew the Apostle.

"Greater works than these shall he do; because I go unto My Father."—JOHN xiv. 12.

CHRIST went to the Father, to come again in power. In His lowliness as man He hid Himself, and held His Divine might in restraint. Only a few saw Him, or knew of the virtue that went forth from Him. He wrought more miracles by the hands of the apostles than by His own. Through their preaching He won more believers in His Gospel than had obeyed His own voice. By His power in the Church He overcame the world that had rejected Him. Wherever the Church is now, there is the Almighty working spiritual miracles.

I need not envy those who saw Christ, and heard His voice. He does greater works for souls now than when He was with men as Jesus of Nazareth. All the gifts He gained when He ascended are for my use. The Spirit makes Christ present in power. The Church, of which I am a member, lives with Christ's life, and is strong with His almightiness. Her past triumphs are an earnest of what God's might shall yet enable her to do. And I can, in my own self, do greater works than any done in those who came to Christ's feet for blessing. Greater saintliness is within my reach than was possible before Christ went to the Father. I can cast out spirits of evil from my souL I can conquer habits of sin, so as to rise from the soul's death. I can regain lost powers of seeing, and knowing, and doing good. I can work miracles for God in others' souls, so as to turn many to righteousness. I can do all this; yet not I, but God's grace with me, Christ Himself strengthening me. He, by the Spirit, is one with me. Nothing is too hard for the Lord; so I can do all that is according to His will.

O Lord, Who didst go to Thy Father that Thou mightest come to be in and with Thy Church, give me Thy power to do, and bear, and triumph for Thy glory.

> With watchful love He waits to pour
> His gifts of grace and pardon down,
> That we, for whom the Cross He bore,
> May win the everlasting crown.

St. Matthew the Apostle.

"God, Who commanded the light to shine out of darkness, hath shined in our hearts."—2 Cor. iv. 6.

LEVI, the publican, was called to be St. Matthew, the apostle, evangelist, martyr. He left the sin of his business before he left his business. He was a disciple before he left all. Christ healed his soul's blindness, and showed him the light of the Gospel. So the god of this world could not hide the glory of the true God. St. Matthew rose and followed at the first word. He made a feast, using some of the unrighteous mammon to bring his old comrades under his Master's influence, that they might be Christ's followers, too, and friends in the new life.

The example and the Gospel of St. Matthew call me to follow Christ. He Who is the "Image of God" ever beckons me after Him, pointing to those whose deeds showed their faith, and who have left a record that He Whom they trusted proved true. All I have must yield its throne in my heart. What I love best must be subject to Christ, not His rival. He sees me in my daily work: I must daily arise in it to more heavenly-mindedness, even though I need not arise from it to do special work for God. I must walk and work in the world as a disciple, and be ready to leave anything, or to go to be with Christ at His bidding. The god of this world tries to hide truth from me, or to darken my soul, so that the light may shine on me in vain. I need not grope in darkness, or be deceived by the glare of earth. He Who at first said, "Let there be light," has brought down heaven's light to men. He shines with His own grace in my heart, that I may see Him now by faith, and prepare to behold His glory.

O Lord Jesu Christ, Who art the Image of God, show me the light of Thy truth, and let Thy grace shine in my heart, that I may forsake all with which the god of this world would blind my soul, and may follow Thee.

Praise, Lord, for him whose Gospel Thy royal right declared,
Who, worldly gains forsaking, Thy path of suffering shared;
From all unrighteous mammon, oh! give us hearts set free,
That we, whate'er our calling, may rise and follow Thee.

St. Michael and all Angels.

"Are they not all ministering spirits, sent forth to minister for them who shall be heirs of salvation?"—HEB. i. 14.

ANGELS work God's ends of judgment and of mercy. They kept the way of the tree of life. They made known the Incarnation to Mary, and Joseph, and the shepherds. Angels ministered to Christ after the temptation. One strengthened Him in His agony. Angels bore Lazarus to rest. The angel of the Lord smote Herod. St. Paul argues from the fact that angels are present in the assemblies of the Church. Christ warns none to offend His little ones, because the angels, to whose care they are given, always behold God's face. Angels were present at Christ's resurrection and ascension. He will come to judge the world with the holy angels around Him.

I miss much comfort if I neglect what God tells me of the holy ones whom He sends to care for me. My Father gives me help and cheer through human friends. So He uses those strong pure beings who love to serve me for His sake. Christ did not scorn their aid in His sore trial. I ought to be thankful for it. Though I seem like Lazarus, cast out and forgotten, I am in the thoughts of God's good angels, who never tire of caring for me. Though I seem the least among men, yet if I am one of Christ's weak ones, my angel stands before God. If I fear God, the angel of the Lord campeth round me in time of danger. He is given charge over me, to keep me in all my ways, and lead me on safely. I bless God for human friends. I bless Him also for the love of those pure spirits whom He teaches to find their joy in helping mine. I would not grieve a brother man who loves me, nor the good guardian-angel, to whom, under God, I always owe more than I can tell.

I thank Thee, O God, for the love and care of Thy holy angels. Grant that they may always minister to me, and that I may so serve Thee after their example here that I may at last be borne by them to Thy rest.

> Still may they succour us, still may they fight,
> Lord of angelic hosts, battling for right;
> Till where their anthems they ceaselessly pour,
> We with the angels may bow and adore.

St. Luke the Evangelist.

"Do the work of an evangelist."—2 Tim. iv. 5.

ST. LUKE is believed to have found what healed his own soul, while, as a physician, he ministered to St. Paul's body. In his life he showed the power of the Gospel, as his writings preached it, and told of the spread of Christ's Church. His knowledge of man's body helped him in caring for man's soul. He saw the same God in the workings of grace, Whose wonders he had traced in the not less mysterious workings of nature. He laid his skill and education at Christ's feet, to be hallowed for the highest ends.

Whatever may be my powers, or education, or place in life, I am called to be an evangelist. What I know of Christ I must make known. Of all that I have received I must freely impart. My natural gifts, my store of knowledge, or skill in any art, my powers, gained or improved by toil and practice, must help to the great end for which I am sent into the world. God will guide and help me how to use all for His glory. I can preach the Gospel, not in word only, but in what my life shows me to be. To "do the work of an evangelist" means more than to talk or write. I can prove that the truth is real to me by ways that will offend none, and may win many. I can find God in His Word and in His works, and adore His wisdom in redemption and sanctification, as in creation. I can minister to men's bodies, looking on them as shrines of the Divine Presence, redeemed by Christ to be holy. While bringing God's comfort to sick bodies and wounded souls, I can preach the Gospel of God's love in Christ for sick souls, by showing the love with which it inspires me.

O Lord, in mercy heal my soul, and make me zealous for the well-being of my neighbour. Call me to such devotion in Thy service, that I may bring many to believe Thy Word, and to come in faith for Thy healing.

O true Physician! heal the souls
That sick and wounded lie;
With wholesome medicine of Thy Word,
Oh! heal them lest they die.

St. Simon and St. Jude, Apostles.

"The servant is not greater than his lord."—John xv. 20.

JUDE called himself the servant of Jesus Christ. Simon was full of zeal for the same Lord. Christ called them "not servants," but "friends," for He told them all things; He manifested Himself to them as He did not unto the world. So they met the world's hate calmly. It was the hate of the world, out of which they were chosen, which hated Christ and those who were His. They kept the sayings of Him they loved; they lived to build up the Church, in which He might dwell and be loved, and which might keep His sayings.

In the faith of the apostles I have the "sayings of Christ." His friends, to whom all He did and said was made known in its true meaning, speak for Him to me. They died for what they had seen and heard, and the Holy Ghost taught them. They knew it to be true, and could not but speak it. They handed down "the faith once delivered to them." It has the same worth now as when martyrs bore witness to it. I do not ask what men say now, but what Christ's apostles knew and spoke as God's Word. My place is, as a servant, to hear my Lord's sayings, and keep them; not to ask the world what it thinks He ought to have said. If the world loves me, perhaps it is that I am of the world, and though called, am not chosen out of the world. The world hates Christ and the Father, as it always did. If I am, like St. Simon and St. Jude, a true servant of Jesus Christ, and zealous in His cause, I am sure to feel some of the hate meant for Him. If my Christ and my faith are what the world likes, I need to beware lest my Christ be Antichrist, and my faith false.

O Lord, give me a ready mind and an obedient will, that I may always hear Thy sayings, and live as a faithful member of the Church, which Thou hast chosen out of the world, to keep and teach Thy truth.

> We are brothers and comrades, we stand side by side,
> And our faith and our hope are the same;
> And we think of the Cross on which Jesus has died,
> When we bear the reproach of His name.

All Saints' Day.

"*Compassed about with so great a cloud of witnesses.*"
—HEB. xii. 1.

WE glorify God in all His saints. We think not of one fruitful branch in the true Vine, but of all with their ripe wealth of varied holiness. The just, made perfect, have care for those who are still pilgrims in this tempted life. Witnesses of our conflict, they pray as they did on earth, but with purer prayers, from more unselfish loving hearts. We thank God for them. We praise Him Whose grace has made them saints, and Whose glory is shown in them. We learn what we may become.

All saints are the triumph of the manifold grace of God. Each part of Christ's own holiness shines in His members, whom, one by one, He has trained for each high place of glory. These holy ones have risen to where they are by the same path I tread so painfully, by the strength of the same grace that I may use. I take courage to follow them as they followed Christ. It cheers me to look away from the strife and evil round me, and be in spirit with that part of the Church where love to God, Whose presence is joy, rules the life of all. I am glad to turn away towards those who are so high above me, and yet own me as a fellow-citizen, and look down with a kindliness they learn from God. I press on hopefully, knowing that a welcome awaits me in God's home, where those, once as far off as I, are now safe in glory. I thank God that His love is in His saints, and that they remember, as Christ did, the days of their flesh. I am sure that they feel more and pray more for the Church below than those who still are sinners in this world of care. I pray that I may be helped by their prayers, and, in God's time, pass to their reward.

O Lord, Thou King of Saints! give me Thy grace and the will to use it, that, following those who have gone after Thee to Thy glory, I may praise Thee in this life of trial, and in the endless life of perfect holiness and joy.

O sweet communion! fellowship Divine!
We feebly struggle, they in glory shine;
Yet all are one in Thee, for all are Thine.

All Souls' Day.

"*God is not the God of the dead, but of the living.*"
—MATT. xxii. 32.

THOSE who leave earth do not forget or grow cold. They are not to be forgotten or less loved. The quiet land should seem more dear because they make it more a home. They are nearer to the full reward; but it is one life that quickens us and them, it is the same grace that leads us forward. They still worship the one God, and pray for those God taught them to love on earth. When we pray we draw nigh to Him with Whom they are. We cannot but think of them, and wish for them all good from God, Who knows how best to bless each one.

Friends go away before me; I shall join them soon. Meanwhile I do not let them be out of mind, or less dear. I do not love them only in memory of old days or in hopes of a glad meeting. I think of them and love them now, while God's love makes them more loving and more worthy to be loved. They have not grown selfish in their peaceful waiting. They are nearer to Christ the Head. They are nearer to me than if they had gone to another land on earth. I cannot tell how close they may come at times. I am sure that in some true way I am the better for their love. I thank God for what they were to me, and for what they are now, and for what I hope to find them. I live as if their eyes met mine still. I think much of what God is doing for them, and what they do for God. I desire for them all the unknown blessing that God bestows in Paradise. I pray that God's loving will may be done in them and me till we share the full bliss of heaven.

O Lord, by Whom all souls live, I thank Thee for those whom Thy love has called from the life of trial to the life of rest. I trust them to Thy care. I pray Thee that by Thy grace I may be brought to enjoy with them the endless life of glory.

> God would not have us from them part,
>   But cling to them with tenderest love,
> That they may upward draw our heart
>   To seek the things that are above.

Birthday.

"So teach us to number our days, that we may apply our hearts unto wisdom."—Ps. xc. 12.

THE newly-born begins an endless climb or fall. He is apart from others, yet others influence him and feel his influence. He is gifted by God with powers of spirit, soul, and body,—knit together, and acting on one another, which may be developed, or weakened, or wholly lost. The seeds of good and evil are in him. He can be made partaker of the Divine nature. He can grow like God, or choose to become as those who fell from heaven.

I live, and must live on. For what end have I life's powers and possibilities? I was born that I might be new born into a heavenly household, and be trained for the high employments of God's full-grown children. When I could know God's claim on me, and mine on Him, He gave me grace, by the hands of His chief pastor, to do my part as a Christian; He confirmed my rights as His adopted child, and confirmed me for my duties. While I let His Fatherly hand lead me, that hand is ever over me in blessing. God gives me Christ's Body and Blood to make me one with Him, to strengthen and gladden my soul, and to be the pledge of immortality. How serious my life is! How much I owe, as years pass, to the love of my Maker, Preserver, Redeemer, Sanctifier! How great claims my brethren in Christ have on me! In what direction am I moving? what am I becoming? I am God's child by creation, and also by spiritual adoption. Am I led by the Spirit, so as to be a son of God indeed, with good hope that I shall be at last among the "children of the resurrection"?

Almighty and eternal God, to Whom I owe life and all good, I bless Thee for Thy mercy in time past; I pray Thee that each year I may more perfectly fulfil the end of my being, till I reach the everlasting home.

> Less, less of self each day, and more, my God, of Thee,
> Oh, keep me in the way, however rough it be;
> More moulded to Thy will, Lord, let Thy servant be,
> Higher and higher still, liker and liker Thee.

" Beg of God, by prayer, that He would give you the spirit of obedience and profit, and that He would by His Spirit write the Word in your heart, and that you describe it in your life."

INDEX OF SUBJECTS.

Adoption, 42, 52, 125.
Amendment of Life, 45, 111, 235.
Ascension, 192.
Atonement, 133, 151, 198, 367.
Backsliding, 276, 277, 337, 375.
Baptism, 55, 210, 211, 251, 308.
Beatitudes, 173, etc.

Charity, 104, 105, 224, 225, 226, 227, 228, 237, 271.
Coming of Christ, 9, 13, 30.
Companions, 87.
Commandments, the Ten, 118, etc.
Confirmation, 45, 409.
Conviction of Sin, 109, 234, 245, 253.
Confession of Christ, 68, 314.
Confession of Sin, 110, 254
Cross, Last Words from, 139, etc.

Death, 14, 145.
Departed Friends, 408.
Distrust of Self, 27, 274, 276, 289, 291, 337, 353, 392.
Earnestness, 66, 93, 120, 243, 273, 278, 310, 311, 313, 316, 357, 378.
Example of Christ, 125, 132, 166.
Excuses, 222.

Faith, 133, 163, 229, 244, 258, 270, 292, 300, 315, 324, 370, 371, 380, 384.
Faith, Weak, 214, 361.
Faith, Intelligent, 208, 212, 299.

Faith, Examples of, 49, 79, 80, 82, 133, 342, 363.
Faith, The, 212, 213, 286, 376, 403.
Fasting, 112.
Fear of God, 120, 217, 269, 285.
Forgiveness of Injuries, 185, 365, 401.

Gentleness under Provocation, 171, 401.
God's Care, 30, 76, 77, 229, 244, 259, 319, 320, 341, 359, 360.
God's Love, 85, 216, 232, 236, 320, 321, 345, 348.
God's Wisdom, 90.
God to be Glorified, 61, 67, 181.
Gospel, 286, 287, 340.
Grace, 291, 296, 298, 377.
Growth to Perfection, 53, 242, 264, 288, 325, 366, 368, 402.

Honesty, 78, 127, 221, 347, 363.
Holy Spirit, 202, 203, 204, 266, 267, 276, 279, 409.
Holy Scripture, 16, 17.
Holy Communion, 196, 197, 198, 199, 200, 201, 385, 386.
Holiness, 53, 54, 65, 164, 175, 252, 261, 265, 329, 336, 366, 378.
Hope, 52, 247, 299, 318, 362, 370, 380, 382.
Humility, 70, 137, 290, 291, 333, 334.

Incarnation, 34, 35, 37, 41, 47, 51.

Joy, 351, 381, 382.

INDEX OF SUBJECTS.

Judgment, the Last, 21, 28, 220, 281, 353, 376.
Judgment in this Life, 234, 260, 281, 332, 376.

Knowing and Doing, 54, 74, 75, 117, 169, 215, 268, 301, 335, 397.

Life in Christ, 159, 296, 327.
Love of Christ, 168, 322, 323, 390.
Love of God, 85, 216, 232, 236, 320, 321, 345, 348.
Love to God, 85, 216, 217, 302, 338, 341.
Love to Neighbours, 176, 178, 248, 303, 304, 305, 344, 391.

Mediation of Christ, 191, 193, 194, 195, 206, 367.
Meditation, 46.
Means of Grace, 258, 300, 312, 324, 377, 409.
Meekness, 174.
Ministry, 23, 24, 161, 162.
Mystery, 96, 263.

Obedience, 170, 182, 295.

Parable of the Sower, 98, etc.
Patience, 84, 179, 387.
Peace, 71, 72, 160, 178, 257, 266, 319, 346.
Perseverance, 95, 131, 164, 294.
Praise, 350, 351.
Prayer, 188, 189, 190, 205, 246, 304, 351, 388.
Prayer, the Lord's, 180, etc.
Purity, 53, 56, 67, 124, 177, 265, 271, 309.
Pride, 289, 333.
Presumption, 81, 102, 115, 135.

Religion in Common Life, 58, 59, 66, 73, 78, 83, 346.
Repentance, 11, 22, 31, 107, 109, 135, 235, 399.

Responsibility, 75, 221, 272, 280, 281, 306.
Resurrection, 153, 154, 155, 158, 240, 374.
Resurrection, Spiritual, 156, 157.
Reverence, 26, 181, 285.
Reward, 283, 292, 294, 373.

Sacrifice, 133, 151, 198, 385.
Self-denial, 56, 92, 132, 308, 309.
Self-deceit, 102, 124, 132, 337.
Self-examination, 43, 103, 108, 343.
Shepherd, The Good, 167, 230, 231, 232.
Suffering, 218, 239, 240, 247, 256, 270, 275, 331, 341, 342, 351, 369, 374.
Sorrows of Christ, 105, etc.
Strength in God, 356, 358, 363.
Sympathy, 64, 344, 398.
Sympathy of Christ, 60, 142, 148, 238.

Temptation, 113, 186, 275, 309.
Temptation of Christ, 113, 114, 115, 116.
Thanksgiving, 246, 304, 307, 339, 352.
Time, Value of, 121.
Tongue, Government of, 88, 249, 293.
Trinity, 209.
Truth, 127; 347.

Union with Christ, 199, 206, 223, 308, 369, 372, 373, 376, 380, 389.
Union in Christ, 42, 158, 201, 297, 328, 330, 408, 409.

Watchfulness, 10, 20, 274, 326, 337, 354.
Will of God, 58, 148, 183.
Worldliness, 57, 81, 89, 165, 219, 250, 264, 314, 316, 379.
Worship, 284, 285, 349.

INDEX OF TEXTS.

GENESIS.		PSALMS.		ST. MATTHEW.	
	PAGE		PAGE		PAGE
iii. 4,	102	xcv. 6,	349	i. 23,	35
iii. 9,	103	xcv. 7, 8,	19	ii. 10,	49
xiii. 12,	81	xcvi. 2,	350	ii. 11,	50
		ciii. 13,	345	iii. 3,	22
EXODUS.		civ. 24,	90	iv. 1,	113
xx. 3,	118	cxvi. 12, 13,	339	iv. 4,	114
xx. 4,	119	cxix. 59,	111	iv. 7,	115
xx. 7,	120	cxix. 106,	45	iv. 10,	116
xx. 8,	121	cxxxix. 23,	108	v. 3,	172
xx. 12,	122			v. 4,	173
xx. 13,	123	PROVERBS.		v. 5,	174
xx. 15,	126	vi. 19,	127	v. 6,	175
xx. 17,	128	viii. 17,	85	v. 7,	176
		x. 19,	88	v. 8,	177
1 SAMUEL.		x. 22,	383	v. 9,	178
ii. 35,	394	xiii. 20,	87	v. 10,	179
		xiv. 9,	86	v. 16,	61
2 SAMUEL.				v. 20,	252
xii. 7,	253	ISAIAH.		v. 48,	242
		lv. 6,	31	vi. 9,	181
1 KINGS.				vi. 10,	182, 183
xi. 9,	276	JEREMIAH.		vi. 11,	184
		v. 25,	332	vi. 12,	185
2 KINGS.		xxxii. 40,	269	vi. 13,	186, 187
v. 10,	300			vi. 16,	112
		EZEKIEL.		vi. 21,	318
JOB.		xiii. 10,	27	vi. 33,	317
iii. 17,	32			vi. 34,	319
		DANIEL.		vii. 7,	188
PSALMS.		vi. 10,	363	vii. 11,	259
iv. 6,	348			vii. 14,	310
xix. 12,	343	JOEL.		vii. 21,	268
xxxii. 5,	110	ii. 12,	107	viii. 8,	70
li. 3, 4,	109			viii. 17,	238
lxv. 2,	189	MALACHI.		viii. 24,	76
xc. 12,	409	iii. 16,	43	viii. 26,	77

INDEX OF TEXTS.

St. Matthew.

	PAGE
ix. 37, 38,	388
x. 29,	364
xi. 9,	399
xi. 28,	168
xi. 29,	169
xi. 30,	170
xii. 20,	359
xii. 33,	265
xii. 37,	249
xii. 44,	130
xiii. 30,	84
xiii. 44,	255
xiv. 31,	361
xvi. 18,	400
xviii. 3,	40
xviii. 6,	360
xviii. 9,	313
xviii. 32, 33,	365
xx. 6,	91
xx. 16,	95
xx. 22,	331
xxi. 9,	9
xxii. 11,	353
xxii. 32,	408
xxii. 39,	303
xxiv. 35,	15
xxiv. 44,	20
xxv. 4,	326
xxv. 18,	232
xxv. 21,	280
xxv. 40,	373
xxv. 41,	28
xxvi. 26, 28,	197
xxvi. 38,	147
xxvi. 39,	148
xxvi. 50,	136
xxvii. 46,	142
xxvii. 61,	152

St. Mark.

	PAGE
ii. 5,	342
ii. 17,	312
iv. 34,	96
vii. 34,	293
viii. 4,	258

St. Mark.

	PAGE
ix. 24,	214
x. 21,	264

St. Luke.

	PAGE
i. 38,	395
ii. 7,	36
ii. 14,	47
ii. 19,	46
ii. 20,	48
ii. 21,	44
ii. 23,	393
ii. 49,	58
ii. 51,	59
ii. 52,	60
iii. 21, 22,	55
v. 8,	245
v. 12,	69
vi. 41,	237
vii. 23,	324
vii. 47,	338
viii. 5,	97, 98
viii. 7,	100
viii. 13,	99
viii. 15,	101
viii. 46,	377
ix. 23,	132
ix. 29,	262
ix. 55,	401
ix. 62,	375
x. 27,	302
x. 41, 42,	257
xi. 1,	190
xi. 2,	180
xi. 23,	129
xi. 28,	301
xii. 8,	68
xii. 48,	75
xiii. 24,	311
xiv. 11,	334
xiv. 18,	222
xv. 2,	196
xv. 4, 5,	230
xv. 6,	231
xv. 9,	232
xv. 13,	233

St. Luke.

	PAGE
xv. 14,	234
xv. 18,	235
xv. 20,	236
xvi. 2,	272
xvi. 8,	273
xvi. 13,	316
xvi. 22,	218
xvi. 22, 23,	219
xvi. 25,	220
xvi. 31,	221
xvii. 17,	307
xviii. 11,	289
xviii. 13,	290
xviii. 14,	333
xviii. 31,	106
xix. 26,	281
xix. 41,	146
xxii. 61,	135
xxiii. 28,	138
xxiii. 34,	139
xxiii. 43,	140
xxiii. 46,	145
xxiv. 29,	386
xxiv. 34,	153
xxiv. 39,	154
xxiv. 51,	192

St. John.

	PAGE
i. 14,	37
i. 17,	34
i. 38, 39,	391
ii. 4,	62
ii. 10,	63
ii. 16,	26
iii. 5,	210
iii. 12,	208
iii. 14,	133
iii. 16,	321
iv. 24,	284
v. 6,	378
vi. 6,	384
vi. 56,	199
vii. 17,	215
x. 11,	167
xi. 25, 26,	327

INDEX OF TEXTS.

St. John.

	PAGE
xii. 43,	250
xiii. 6,	134
xiii. 17,	18
xiv. 6,	206
xiv. 8,	397
xiv. 12,	402
xiv. 21,	117
xiv. 26,	202
xiv. 28,	191
xv. 5,	296
xv. 20,	406
xvi. 8,	203
xvi. 24,	195
xvi. 26, 27,	194
xvi. 33,	369
xvii. 15,	379
xviii. 11,	149
xix. 5,	150
xix. 26, 27,	141
xix. 28,	143
xix. 30,	144
xx. 19,	160
xx. 21,	161
xx. 23,	162
xx. 29,	33
xxi. 20,	39

Acts.

ix. 5,	372
ix. 5, 6,	392
x. 34, 35,	207
xi. 24,	398
xvi. 31,	163
xx. 35,	305

Romans.

i. 16,	340
v. 10,	159
vi. 11,	156
vi. 20, 21,	260
vi. 22,	261
vi. 23,	376
viii. 14,	267
viii. 16,	266
viii. 23,	240

Romans.

	PAGE
viii. 26,	205
viii. 28,	341
viii. 32,	320
xii. 1,	56
xii. 2,	57
xii. 9,	65
xii. 11,	66
xii. 12,	382
xii. 15,	64
xii. 18,	71
xii. 21,	72
xiii. 7,	78
xiii. 11,	10
xiii. 12,	11
xiv. 12,	21
xv. 4,	17

1 Corinthians.

iv. 1,	23
vi. 19,	204
vi. 19, 20,	67
ix. 25,	92
ix. 26,	93, 94
x. 12,	274
x. 13,	275
x. 17,	201
x. 24,	227
xi. 26,	198
xi. 27,	200
xii. 4,	279
x ii. 2,	105
xiii. 4,	224, 225
xiii. 4, 5,	226
xiii. 5, 6, 7,	228
xiii. 12,	263
xiii. 13,	104
xv. 1,	286
xv. 10,	291
xv. 22.	155

2 Corinthians.

iv. 6,	403
iv. 7,	24
iv. 17,	247
v. 7,	371

2 Corinthians.

	PAGE
viii. 12,	306
xii. 9,	298
xiii. 14,	209

Galatians.

ii. 20,	322
iii. 6,	82
iii. 24,	287
iii. 26, 27,	251
iv. 5,	42
v. 6,	315
v. 17,	309
v. 24,	308
vi. 2,	344
vi. 7,	241
vi. 9,	131
vi. 14,	314

Ephesians.

iii. 19,	323
iv. 4,	328
iv. 15,	396
iv. 25,	347
v. 1,	125
v. 15,	354
v. 20,	352
vi. 10,	356
vi. 13,	357

Philippians.

i. 6,	368
i. 10, 11,	366
i. 21,	380
ii. 5,	137
ii. 12, 13,	164
iii. 20,	370
iii. 21,	374
iv. 5,	30
iv. 6,	246

Colossians.

i. 18,	297
iii. 1,	157
iii. 17,	83

INDEX OF TEXTS.

1 THESSALONIANS.		HEBREWS.		2 PETER.	
	PAGE		PAGE		PAGE
ii. 12,	329	xi. 25,	80	ii. 15,	165
iv. 11,	346	xii. 1,	407	iii. 11, 12,	29
iv. 14,	158	xii. 11,	239	iii. 18,	325
v. 16,	381	xii. 12, 13,	243		
v. 21,	212	xii. 16,	89		
		xii. 28,	285	1 JOHN.	
1 TIMOTHY.		xiii. 8,	390	ii. 1,	367
ii. 1,	304	xiii. 10,	385	ii. 17,	12
iv. 8,	283	xiii. 16,	248	ii. 28,	13
				iii. 2,	52
2 TIMOTHY.		ST. JAMES.		iii. 3,	53
iii. 16,	16	i. 25,	335	iii. 7,	54
iv. 5,	405	ii. 10,	295	iii. 8,	51
iv. 8,	38	iii. 17,	271	iii. 24,	223
		iv. 7, 8,	358	iv. 18,	217
TITUS.		iv. 17,	74	iv. 19,	216
ii. 12,	73	v. 7,	387		
		v. 13,	351		
HEBREWS.		v. 16,	254	JUDE.	
i. 12,	41			3,	213
i. 14,	404	1 PETER.		5,	211
iv. 14,	193	i. 5,	244		
v. 9,	389	ii. 11,	124		
vi. 1,	288	ii. 15,	171	REVELATION.	
vi. 19, 20,	362	ii. 17,	355	ii. 4,	277
ix. 27,	14	ii. 21,	166	ii. 9,	256
x. 24, 25,	330	ii. 24,	151	ii. 10,	294
xi. 5,	336	iii. 15,	299	iii. 1, 2,	337
xi. 6,	292	iv. 19,	270	iii. 15,	278
xi. 7,	79	v. 7,	229	iii. 20,	25

THE END

M'Farlane & Erskine, Printers, Edinburgh.

www.ingramcontent.com/pod-product-compliance
Lightning Source LLC
Chambersburg PA
CBHW050847300426
44111CB00010B/1156